FREEDOM OF SPEECH IN
EARLY STUART ENGLAND

This book discusses a central chapter in the history of free speech in the Western world. The nature and limits of freedom of speech prompted sophisticated debate in a wide range of areas in the early seventeenth century; it was one of the 'liberties of the subject' fought for by individuals and groups across the political landscape. Discussions of free speech raised serious questions about what it meant to live in a free state, and how far England was from being such a state. Examining a wide range of sources, from rhetorical handbooks to parliamentary speeches and manuscript miscellanies, Dr Colclough demonstrates how freedom of speech was conceived positively in the period *c.* 1603 to 1628, rather than being defined in opposition to acts of censorship. Attending to the importance of context and decorum, this major contribution to **Ideas in Context** recovers a tradition of free speech that has been obscured in studies of the evolution of universal rights.

DAVID COLCLOUGH is Lecturer in English at Queen Mary, University of London.

IDEAS IN CONTEXT

Edited by Quentin Skinner (*General Editor*), Lorraine Daston,
Dorothy Ross, and James Tully

The books in this series will discuss the emergence of intellectual traditions and of related new disciplines. The procedures, aims, and vocabularies that were generated will be set in the context of the alternatives available within the contemporary frameworks of ideas and institutions. Through detailed studies of the evolution of such traditions, and their modification by different audiences, it is hoped that a new picture will form of the development of ideas in their concrete contexts. By this means, artificial distinctions between the history of philosophy, of the various sciences, of society and politics, and of literature may be seen to dissolve.

The series is published with the support of the Exxon Foundation.

A list of books in the series will be found at the end of the volume.

FREEDOM OF SPEECH IN EARLY STUART ENGLAND

DAVID COLCLOUGH

Queen Mary, University of London

CAMBRIDGE
UNIVERSITY PRESS

PUBLISHED BY THE PRESS SYNDICATE OF THE UNIVERSITY OF CAMBRIDGE
The Pitt Building, Trumpington Street, Cambridge, United Kingdom

CAMBRIDGE UNIVERSITY PRESS
The Edinburgh Building, Cambridge, CB2 2RU, UK
40 West 20th Street, New York, NY 10011–4211, USA
477 Williamstown Road, Port Melbourne, VIC 3207, Australia
Ruiz de Alarcón 13, 28014 Madrid, Spain
Dock House, The Waterfront, Cape Town 8001, South Africa

http://www.cambridge.org

First published 2005

Printed in the United Kingdom at the University Press, Cambridge

Typeface Adobe Garamond 11/12.5 pt.   *System* LATEX 2$_\varepsilon$ [TB]

A catalogue record for this book is available from the British Library

Library of Congress Cataloguing in Publication data
Colclough, David, 1971–
Freedom of speech in early Stuart England / David Colclough.
p.   cm. – (Ideas in context)
Includes bibliographical references and index.
ISBN 0 521 84748 6 (bound)
1. Freedom of speech–England–History–17th century.   2. Great Britain–Politics and
government–1603–1625.   I. Title.   II. Series.
KD4110.C65   2005
342.4208′53 – dc22   2004054645

ISBN 0 521 84748 6 hardback

Contents

Illustrations

Acknowledgements

I owe a profound debt of thanks to the institutions and individuals who have supported me during the writing of this book, and I am grateful for the opportunity to acknowledge them here. The project was begun while I held a Junior Research Fellowship at King's College, Cambridge, and I would like to thank the then Provost (Sir Patrick Bateson) and Fellows for electing me, and my colleagues (especially Peter de Bolla and Ian Donaldson) for their interest in my work. After two years at King's I was appointed to a Lectureship at Queen Mary, University of London, and the School of English and Drama has been an extremely congenial environment in which to continue work on this book. The Research Fund of the School has generously provided grants towards the expenses incurred during my research, and I benefited from a semester's sabbatical leave towards the end of the project. This was extended by an award from the Arts and Humanities Research Board's Research Leave Scheme, which came at a crucial stage. I was fortunate to have Fellowships at the Folger Shakespeare Library, Washington, DC, and the Huntington Library, San Marino, during this period. Both were marvellous places in which to work, and I am grateful to their ever-friendly and helpful staff, especially Carol Brobeck at the Folger (who even shepherded me through the thickets of the Internal Revenue Service) and Susan Green, Anne Mar, and Mona Shulman at the Huntington. I have relied more frequently on the resources and goodwill of other research libraries, and would like to thank the staff of the Bodleian Library, Oxford, the British Library and, especially, Cambridge University Library for their assistance over many years.

My debts to individual scholars are legion. I must begin by thanking Quentin Skinner, who from the very inception of this project has been unendingly encouraging and challenging. His enthusiastic commitment to a proper dialogue between intellectual and literary historians is a model to me, and has been enacted in his enormously generous responses to my work (he has read and commented on the entire manuscript in one form or another). Above and beyond this, in his writing and conversation he continues to make me think about why work such as this might be important – and how it might be better. Lorna Hutson has been a close and critical reader of my work and I hope that it has benefited from her attention. Jeremy Maule suggested avenues of inquiry that I would not have thought of, and provided many references on a forest of postcards; it is a source of profound sadness and regret that I cannot thank him properly. David Norbrook first got me thinking about John Hoskyns, and has continued to share his knowledge and critical insights. Markku Peltonen read the whole manuscript, and made many characteristically astute, frank, and productive suggestions. For discussions of manuscript miscellanies at the British Library I am grateful to Maria Reardon. For all sorts of assistance and encouragement I would like to thank my colleagues at Queen Mary, especially Julia Boffey, Richard Bourke, Warren Boutcher, Jerry Brotton, Maria Delgado, Michael Edwards, Markman Ellis, Anne Janowitz, Lisa Jardine, Graham Rees, Chris Reid, Maria Wakely, and David Wootton. Colleagues elsewhere who have offered invaluable advice, information and conversation include Gavin Alexander, Cathy Curtis, Heather James, Susan James, Ludmilla Jordanova, Lauren Kassell, Michèle Le Dœuff, Rebecca Lemon, Joad Raymond, Richard Serjeantson, Bill Sherman, Cathy Shrank, Debora Shuger, and Phil Withington.

Some of the material in this book has been tried out in seminars and conferences in Cambridge, London, Norwich, Oxford, Sheffield, and New York, and I have learnt a great deal from the responses it received. Richard Fisher at Cambridge University Press deserves decoration, let alone thanks, for his assistance and for his superhuman patience during the time it took for this long-promised manuscript finally to arrive at his desk. I would also like to thank my copy-editor, Jean Field, for the matchless efficiency and good cheer with which she dealt with a sometimes unruly manuscript.

As well as those in the community of early modern scholarship whom I have already thanked, I have relied heavily on and tested the limits of my friends. For their good counsel, occasional and timely admonition, and hospitality I am especially grateful to Nick and Heidi Adams, Marcella and Michael Bungay Stanier, Tom Harrison, Catherine Pickstock, and Norman and Johanna Platt. My parents, Linda and John, have been a constant source of support and have never expressed any of the bewilderment I am sure they must have felt at the fact that I was still writing the same book. Finally, it is difficult to express how much I owe to Lucinda Platt. She has read every word in this book (and some that didn't make it) and given it, and me, more attention than I am sure they deserve.

Some of the material here has previously appeared in other versions: part of chapter 1 was published in *Rhetorica* 17:2 (1999): 177–212; part of chapter 3 in Stephen Clucas and Rosalind Davies (eds.), *The Crisis of 1614 and the Addled Parliament: Literary and Historical Perspectives* (Aldershot: Ashgate, 2003), pp. 51–61; and parts of chapter 4 in *Huntington Library Quarterly* 61:3 and 4 (1998): 369–400 and in Lorna Hutson and Erica Sheen (eds.), *Literature, Politics and Law in Renaissance England* (Basingstoke: Palgrave, forthcoming). For permission to reprint, I am grateful to the editors. I am also grateful to the Bodleian Library, University of Oxford, for permission to reproduce the images in chapter 4.

Abbreviations

BL	British Library
Bod.	Bodleian Library, University of Oxford
CSPV	*Calendar of State Papers and Manuscripts . . . Venice*
DNB	*Dictionary of National Biography*
Folger	Folger Shakespeare Library, Washington, DC
HMC Ancaster	*Historical Manuscripts Commission Report on the Manuscripts of the Earl of Ancaster* (London: His Majesty's Stationery Office, 1907)
HMC Downshire	*Report on the Manuscripts of the Marquess of Downshire* (London: His Majesty's Stationery Office, 1924)
HMC Salisbury	*Calendar of the Manuscripts of the Most Honourable the Marquess of Salisbury. K.G.* (London: His Majesty's Stationery Office, 1940)
Huntington	Henry E. Huntington Library, San Marino, CA
LSJ	*A Greek-English Lexicon*, compiled by Henry George Liddell and Robert Scott, revised by Sir Henry Stuart Jones, with the assistance of Roderick McKenzie (Oxford: Clarendon Press, 1968)
OED	*Oxford English Dictionary*
PRO	Public Record Office, London
Rot. Parl.	*Rotuli Parliamentorum ut et Petitiones et Placita in Parliamento*, 6 volumes (London, n.d.)
STC	A. W. Pollard and G. R. Redgrave (eds.), *A Short-Title Catalogue of Books Printed in England, Scotland, & Ireland, And of English Books Printed Abroad 1475–1640*, second edition revised by W. A. Jackson, F. S. Ferguson, and Katherine F. Pantzer, 3 volumes (London: Bibliographical Society, 1976–91)

Parliamentary Proceedings

CD 1621	*Commons Debates in 1621*, ed. by Wallace Notestein, Frances Helen Relf, and Hartley Simpson, 7 volumes (New Haven: Yale University Press, 1935)
CD 1628	*Commons Debates 1628*, volume II: *17 March–19 April 1628*, ed. by Robert C. Johnson and Maija Jansson Cole, assisted by Mary Frear Keeler and William B. Bidwell (New Haven: Yale University Press, 1977)
CD 1629	*Commons Debates for 1629*, ed. by Wallace Notestein and Frances Helen Relf (Minneapolis, 1921)
CJ	*Journal of the House of Commons*
LJ	*Journal of the House of Lords*
PP 1610	*Proceedings in Parliament 1610*, ed. by Elizabeth Read Foster, 2 volumes (New Haven: Yale University Press, 1966)
PP 1614	*Proceedings in Parliament 1614 (House of Commons)*, ed. by Maija Jansson (Philadelphia: American Philosophical Society, 1988)
PP 1625	*Proceedings in Parliament 1625*, ed. by Maija Jansson and William B. Bidwell (New Haven: Yale University Press, 1987)
PP 1626	*Proceedings in Parliament 1626*, volumes II and III: *House of Commons*, ed. by William B. Bidwell and Maija Jansson (New Haven: Yale University Press, 1992)

Note on the text

In quotations from early modern printed books and manuscripts I have
retained original spelling and punctuation, except in the case of long 's',
which has been modernised. Expanded contractions are indicated by under-
lining, thus: 'commo<u>n</u>wealth'. Dates are Old Style, except that the year is
taken to begin on 1 January; where there is any chance of confusion, I have
used the following notation: '5 February 1620/1'.

Introduction

This book argues that freedom of speech was considered to be a significant civic virtue in the early years of the seventeenth century. Its nature and limits were the object of sustained and sophisticated debate in a wide range of areas, and it was one of the 'liberties of the subject' fought for by individuals and groups across the political landscape. More than this, discussions of free speech raised serious questions about what it meant to live in a free state, and how far England was from being such a state.[1] My intention is to show how freedom of speech was conceived positively in the period from *c.* 1603 to 1628. This book thus engages with recent work on censorship and the control of print, on manuscript culture, and on early modern conceptions of liberty.[2] It makes use of the techniques of literary, intellectual, and political history in its attempts to recover some neglected aspects of the political language of early modern England; and it draws on the work of scholars such as David Norbrook and Quentin Skinner in arguing that political, literary, and rhetorical texts and traditions worked together to allow people in this period to take on public identities as citizens.[3] To conceive of free

---

[1] On early modern conceptions of the free state and their relation to ideas of the freedom of the subject, see Quentin Skinner, *Liberty before Liberalism* (Cambridge: Cambridge University Press, 1998), esp. pp. 23–36.

[2] See especially Cyndia Susan Clegg, *Press Censorship in Jacobean England* (Cambridge: Cambridge University Press, 2001); C. S. Clegg, *Press Censorship in Elizabethan England* (Cambridge: Cambridge University Press, 1997); S. Mutchow Towers, *Control of Religious Printing in Early Stuart England* (Woodbridge: The Boydell Press, 2003); Harold Love, *The Culture and Commerce of Texts: Scribal Publication in Seventeenth-Century England* (Amherst: University of Massachusetts Press, 1998); Alastair Bellany, *The Politics of Court Scandal in Early Modern England: News Culture and the Overbury Affair, 1603–1660* (Cambridge: Cambridge University Press, 2002); Andrew McRae, *Literature, Satire, and the Early Stuart State* (Cambridge: Cambridge University Press, 2004); J. H. Hexter (ed.), *Parliament and Liberty from the Reign of Elizabeth to the English Civil War* (Stanford: Stanford University Press, 1992); Glenn Burgess, *Absolute Monarchy and the Stuart Constitution* (New Haven: Yale University Press, 1996); Skinner, *Liberty before Liberalism*.

[3] See Skinner, *Liberty before Liberalism* and 'John Milton and the Politics of Slavery', in Skinner, *Visions of Politics*, three volumes (Cambridge: Cambridge University Press, 2002), volume II: *Renaissance Virtues*, pp. 286–307; David Norbrook, *Writing the English Republic: Poetry, Rhetoric and Politics,*

speech as a prerequisite not only of a free subject, but of a free state, entailed a critique of the existing political system that did not necessarily lead to anti-monarchism, but did require a rethinking of the role and powers of the monarch that was regarded as unacceptable by both James I and Charles I.

There are, moreover, several areas of some importance to free speech debates in the period that I have deliberately not discussed. There is no extended treatment of the place of satire here: this is, in part, because this important genre is the subject of a recent monograph by Andrew McRae.[4] Censorship has been the subject of much recent research, and my desire has been to study what might be seen as the other side of the free speech debate, concentrating on positive conceptions of freedom of speech rather than identifying it only at the moment of its repression.[5] Slander, similarly, is an area whose focus on questions of personal honour and reputation is somewhat distant from the questions that most concern me here.

While I pay some attention here to instances of speech being restrained or punished, I am concerned to move away from examining cases of restriction that we can retrospectively identify as free speech issues to instances of early modern individuals themselves discussing freedom of speech. This book asks what range of meanings was available for seventeenth-century discussions of the subject, and how these framed both a conceptual language and a practice of frank speaking in the period. What did it mean for Thomas Wilson to discuss 'freenesse of speache' in *The Arte of Rhetorique*; or for Thomas Scott to rejoice at the restoration of 'lawfull libertyes, and freedome of speech' in his *Vox Dei* of 1624; or for Sir Henry Poole to announce in 1621 that 'There is nothing so dear to the subject as liberty, no liberty so good as that in parliament, none in parliament greater than the freedom of speech'; or for a compiler of a manuscript miscellany to place a libel against Francis Bacon close to copies of proceedings in Parliament concerned – as his marginal note says – with freedom of speech? What did these people mean when they referred to freedom of speech? How would their readers or auditors have understood them, and what traditions would they have drawn upon in order to do so?

In their discussions of freedom of speech, people in early Stuart England drew upon a number of intellectual traditions. They took what was to hand, and they adapted it to their own circumstances. At the same time, especially

1627–1660 (Cambridge: Cambridge University Press, 1999). See also Markku Peltonen, *Classical Humanism and Republicanism in English Political Thought, 1570–1640* (Cambridge: Cambridge University Press, 1995).

4 See McRae, *Literature, Satire, and the Early Stuart State.*

5 See Clegg, *Press Censorship in Jacobean England* and *Press Censorship in Elizabethan England.*

in the invocation of classical precedents, they attempted to understand, or mould, the situations in which they found themselves by describing them in terms derived from cultures very different from their own. At the heart of early Stuart debates on free speech was the question of how best to advise a prince – the question of counsel. Almost all the authorities on this subject, from the Bible to the humanists of the previous century, agreed that the prince and the commonwealth benefited from a plenitude of advice, and that that advice should always be as frank as possible. But it was also a truism that virtue was not always dominant in either the prince or the counsellor, and that the temptation to flatter instead of admonish was a strong one. Perhaps the prince was quick to anger, or acutely aware of the social distance between himself and his advisers; perhaps the adviser was more concerned with his own interests than with those of his king or country. History abounded with examples of counsellors becoming servile in order to save their own skins or advance their careers, or, most importantly, because their capacity to speak freely was subject to the will of their prince.[6] Moreover, as writers such as Plutarch had shown many centuries ago, the flatterer was not just adept at saying soothing words to his prince: he was aware of the value of some well-chosen false frankness. As I show in the first chapter of this book, apparent freedom of speech might be flattery in disguise, and it was the responsibility of the prince and his other counsellors to distinguish between the two.

The language of counsel provided a framework for understanding government in early modern England: its intricacies seemed to address virtually every problem that might arise in political life. It was a growing and developing language, and one that changed each time it was used to analyse events and situations. When, in the Parliaments of 1624–6, MPs attacked the Duke of Buckingham as a prototypical purveyor of evil counsel and monopoliser of the king's ear, they could invoke biblical injunctions on the importance of many counsellors (often drawn from the Psalms), classical Latin critiques of over-influential advisers, prosecutions of over-mighty subjects (such as Empson and Dudley in the reign of Henry VII), or humanist works on the education of princes and counsellors (such as Erasmus' *Education of a Christian Prince* or Sir Thomas Elyot's *Book named the Governor*). Local and immediate concerns were interpreted with the help of inherited traditions, in the course of which these traditions were themselves modified. The terminology and the argumentative strategies used to describe, practise, and defend freedom of speech were thus at once highly specific to

---

[6] See Skinner, *Liberty before Liberalism*, pp. 36–57.

the ideological and political culture of early Stuart England and part of a continually developing tradition.

My purpose here, then, is to trace the traditions and languages on which early Stuart discussions of freedom of speech relied, and to describe and analyse their subsequent application. Freedom of speech was, I argue, conceived of as a duty and a right. Despite the currency of a highly developed language of rights in the realms of moral and political philosophy from well before the period of discussion, however, the language of rights used in relation to freedom of speech tends to be of the order of basic assertion rather than theoretical complexity. In fact, in many of the arenas of debate that I treat here, terms such as 'liberty', 'freedom', and 'right', whose precise limits and applications were being carefully defined in relation to human action and in the sphere of jurisprudence, are used interchangeably in relation to speech.[7] Debates on freedom of speech were predominantly pragmatic: they were linked to the practices of civic life. The importance of such a pragmatic conception of free speech is something I return to in the Epilogue as part of a reflection on the implications of this study for current thinking on the subject.

One of the defining qualities of freedom of speech in the early seventeenth century was its limitation: it was not conceived as anything like a universal right. Yet the limits that were placed on it were not themselves stable. They could include more or less fixed categories such as social status (a gentleman might be considered to have more right to freedom of speech than an artisan) or institutional affiliation (MPs had a formal right to freedom of speech when Parliament was sitting); but in the absence of any detailed written guarantee of even such limited rights, other arguments and other criteria were brought into play, and even apparently fixed categories could be pliable. In the case of parliamentary freedom of speech, which was the only formally secure version of the right, it could be argued that MPs' rights extended to anything written or said during a session ('in Parliament time'), and some argued that those rights even extended to other citizens writing at such a time: this was the position taken by the authors of the *Admonition to Parliament* in 1572.[8] On the other hand, Tudor and Stuart monarchs regularly attempted to put limits on parliamentary freedom of

---

[7] Exceptions to this statement can be found in some of the parliamentary debates (see chapter 3 below), where the terms have rather precise local meanings. On the history of theories of subjective rights, see Richard Tuck, *Natural Rights Theories: Their Origin and Development* (Cambridge: Cambridge University Press, 1979); Annabel S. Brett, *Liberty, Right, and Nature: Individual Rights in Later Scholastic Thought* (Cambridge: Cambridge University Press, 1997).

[8] See Clegg, *Press Censorship in Elizabethan England*, p. 51; A. N. McLaren, *Political Culture in the Reign of Elizabeth I* (Cambridge: Cambridge University Press, 1999), p. 177.

speech, arguing that some areas of policy were outside its remit and that some instances of what MPs claimed was free speech were in fact licentious or treasonous talk.

In early Stuart discussions of freedom of speech, what seventeenth-century writers called 'decorum' was all important. Consideration of the time at which, the place in which, and the persons to whom one was speaking all played a large part in the way in which claims to the right or obligation to speak out were framed. They could, moreover, affect those claims from the point of view of the speaker or the audience. That is, an individual might claim that his right to free speech was determined by the fact that he was in Parliament or that the extremity of the times required extraordinary outspokenness; or he might argue that his own civic identity varied contextually, with different circumstances (the apparent misgovernment of the realm by a bad counsellor, for example) requiring different kinds of identity as well as action. Depending on where and when they were speaking, early Stuart persons could think of themselves as inhabiting the role of an active counsellor or of a more or less passive subject. This is not to suggest that political identities were so protean as to be entirely unstable or inconsistent, or that political positions were only taken in reaction to local and immediate pressures, with no thought of broader ideological commitments. Rather, different kinds of loyalties and actions might be invoked by specific circumstances while at the same time relying on an established set of beliefs or traditions of thought. As Patrick Collinson puts it, writing of the overlapping political communities of early modern England, 'citizens were concealed within subjects'.[9] Thomas Scott, the puritan pamphleteer, who plays a large part in chapter 2 of this book, argued that although he was nominally a lowly minister of the church who owed loyalty and obedience to his monarch, the times in which he found himself were so dangerous, the threats from Spanish intrigue so clear and present, that he was obliged to enter the public realm and take on the voice of a prophet: 'necessitie', he asserted, 'supplie's the place of an ordinary calling'.[10]

The emphasis on decorum that I have been describing as a key feature of early Stuart discussions of freedom of speech, the importance of adapting to circumstances, and the absolute centrality of persuasiveness as a quality of that speech, are all elements of rhetoric. The suffusion of rhetorical modes of speech and thought throughout early modern culture is familiar to us, and recent work has expanded our knowledge of the ways in which this

---

[9] Patrick Collinson, '*De Republica Anglorum*: Or, History With the Politics Put Back', in *Elizabethan Essays* (London: The Hambledon Press, 1994), pp. 1–29, at p. 19.
[10] [Thomas Scott], *Vox Dei* (n.p., n.d. [1624]), sig. D.

set of skills was taught and used, and of how its categories inflected ways of thinking about and organising the world more generally.[11] Free speech is most often considered now as the very opposite of rhetoric – as a plain and unornamented form of utterance whose characteristics are honesty and bluntness, and which is distinct from speech acts whose primary intention is to persuade or move an audience by the manipulation of linguistic forms. In early Stuart England, however, freedom of speech was consummately rhetorical – most notably in the sense that there was a rhetorical figure of free speech, *parrhesia* (or, in Latin, *licentia*). *Parrhesia* is the subject of my first chapter, and I show there how its meanings shifted and were manipulated from its earliest uses in ancient Greek drama and oratory, through its codification as a rhetorical technique in Roman handbooks, to the digest and translation of those handbooks in the sixteenth and seventeenth centuries. *Parrhesia* begins as the name of a quality of speech belonging to citizens in the Greek polis – speech reflecting their status as free men. In Greek and, later, Roman rhetoric, it describes a kind of frank admonition addressed to one's audience; but it also comes to refer to the apology that is made before such an exclamation. The author of the *Ad Herennium* goes even further, and suggests that self-consciously announced frankness can even be a cloak for flattery; and it is the tension between apology and outspokenness, openness and deception, that is taken up in Renaissance rhetorical treatises. There an awareness of the importance of frank speech to the orator as a civic figure is balanced and, finally, I suggest, overcome, by concerns about the dangers of unseasonable counsel and the difficulty of applying republican virtues to a monarchical context. Freedom of speech remains rhetorically coloured, and the rhetorical tradition of *parrhesia* is an important strand of the theory of counsel.

Parrhesia is not only a rhetorical term, however, and in chapter 2 I explore an area – that of religious culture, specifically preaching and pamphleteering – where the word was made part of a quite different tradition. The counsellor's freedom of speech was a prerequisite for the proper fulfilment of his duty, and both republican and imperial versions of the classical past insisted that frankness was a central virtue of the adviser. The compulsion to speak out thus came from a desire or necessity to be virtuous, as well as from the firmly held belief that ultimately the safety of the realm was more important than either one's own safety or the comfort of the ruler. In

---

[11] See primarily Ann Moss, *Printed Commonplace Books and the Structuring of Renaissance Thought* (Oxford: Clarendon Press, 1996); Quentin Skinner, *Reason and Rhetoric in the Philosophy of Hobbes* (Cambridge: Cambridge University Press, 1996); Peter Mack, *Elizabethan Rhetoric: Theory and Practice* (Cambridge: Cambridge University Press, 2002).

the Christian tradition, which English humanists in the late sixteenth and early seventeenth century attempted ingeniously to wed to their beloved classical exemplars, freedom of speech was an attribute of the true believer when facing persecution. Bearing witness to Christ and to the truth of one's faith, even in the face of death, was an obligation placed upon all Christians. The history of the early church abounded with examples of clerics (usually bishops) taking a firm stand against emperors, asserting the range of their authority and the supremacy of the law of God over the law of the *saeculum*. Early Stuart churchmen thus appealed to the biblical and early Christian tradition of religious *parrhesia* when dealing with what they saw as the encroachment of secular authority on the realm of conscience, and laid claim to the right to admonish monarchs. Hugh Latimer's sermons before King Edward VI were the apogee of this tradition in the sixteenth century, and represented, to some extent, the temporary triumph of religious *parrhesia*: Latimer's sharp counsel, in the mould of St Ambrose, was not just tolerated, but invited.

Under James I and his son Charles I, bishops, and preachers more generally, were more circumspect, and I analyse the deft and decorous means by which a successful court preacher such as John Donne adapted his advice to take account of anxiety about the power of the pulpit in the early seventeenth century. It is, I go on to argue, in the religious pamphlets of figures such as Thomas Scott and John Reynolds that the traditions of Ambrose and the Apostles are most vigorously followed in this period. Scott was not a bishop but an ordinary minister of the Word, and yet the extremity of the times in which he found himself, with the court prey (as he saw it) to the pernicious influences of Spanish popery, led him to take on the mantle of a prophet and the voice of an apostle, and to produce outspoken fictions. These plausible narratives claimed to offer greater truth than the accounts that were being presented to the people by the king and his officials. Scott claimed to speak on behalf of the commonwealth, and to be impelled to do so by his conscience, his duty as a subject, and the operations of the Holy Spirit. His freedom of speech, that is, was specific to the times, and not something that he would claim in times of safety. Blending a committed humanist republican outlook with a militant Protestant belief in the need for international resistance to Roman Catholicism, he established himself as an archetypal unofficial religious counsellor. He was unwarranted by the institutions of government, unprotected by institutional privilege, but, as he saw it, just as obliged to speak frankly to his superiors as was St Paul.

Members of Parliament were not only warranted as counsellors (by the writ of summons that was issued before each session) but afforded a formal right to freedom of speech in their debates. In chapter 3 I examine how this right was used, debated, extended, and criticised during the Parliaments of James I and the first two of Charles I. Parliamentary freedom of speech was a frequent subject of debate during this period, and I argue that rather than being skirmishes over a limited and relatively insignificant privilege or smokescreens for the pursuit of vendettas concerning the power of influential peers, as has sometimes been suggested, these debates were in fact central to many of the most important and far-reaching conflicts in early Stuart politics. MPs claimed freedom of speech in order to treat grave issues of fiscal, religious, and foreign policy; both to advise the king, and to warn him against evil counsellors. James and Charles were concerned to set the limits of parliamentary freedom of speech themselves, however, and the early years of the seventeenth century saw this only recently established right subjected to a multitude of different tests and definitions. Many MPs, drawing on the classical humanist traditions discussed in my first chapter, regarded their right to freedom of speech as of a piece with, and essential to the maintenance of, a whole range of other rights they possessed as MPs or as subjects – roles that overlapped, rather than being mutually exclusive. They claimed that since the ability to speak out for the safety of the realm was essential to their identity as counsellors, its forcible removal by others, or its relinquishment by themselves, would entail their reduction to a servile status. As with many of the debates over the extent of the king's power over his subject's property, when discussing freedom of speech MPs increasingly claimed that it was not any specific threat to their speech on the part of the king that worried them most: it was his very possession of power to control that speech. If they were always subject to the king's definition of what was loyal frankness and what licentious boldness, then they could not act or speak freely; hence they demanded, repeatedly, to be able to set the limits of parliamentary free speech themselves, and to be responsible for the punishment of those who overstepped the boundaries that were agreed by the House of Commons. In the debates on freedom of speech in the early Stuart Parliaments many of the arguments outlined in my discussion of counsel are put to use. Moreover, those debates, far from being purely dependent upon the special character of parliamentary free speech, in fact frequently rely upon the notion that Parliament, Members of Parliament, and parliamentary speech are – or should be – representative of the commonwealth at large.

Parliament was both a very particular locale with its own conventions and privileges and an institution that was taken by many to have a truly representative function. Having examined, in chapter 3, the ways in which

MPs deployed arguments about free speech taken from extra-parliamentary traditions, in my final chapter I analyse some cases of parliamentary debate being followed and engaged with outside the institution. Political information and news of various kinds were collected avidly by people in early Stuart England, and one of the main resources they employed to amass, preserve, and process this material was the manuscript miscellany. One of the most important aspects of the manuscript miscellany for this study is its very miscellaneousness; that is, the degree to which a very broad range of texts is collected in its pages by its compiler and read alongside one another. One might find records of parliamentary proceedings (from manuscript, printed, or oral sources) alongside libellous poems, extracts from printed books, *sententiae*, and sermon notes. The compilers of these miscellanies, I argue, think that the various texts copied are susceptible to the same kind of reading techniques, rather than being divided by generic categorisation or by issues of origin and trustworthiness. For example, a set of libels might address the same subject treated in parliamentary reports, and these in turn will be informed by extracts from printed works. I am especially interested in the way that libels are used in this context: even in the best of recent scholarship, they tend to be read in isolation from the other contents of the miscellany where they appear, and are thus interpreted as local and responsive to the individuals or events to which they refer. If we instead consider the miscellany *in toto*, both libels and parliamentary debates can be seen as part of a wider concern about the counsel that was allowed to reach the king and the range of information that was allowed to reach his people – precisely the kinds of argument, as I have suggested, that are central to the idea of free speech in this period.

By concentrating on the contents of manuscript miscellanies, I wish to suggest not that a culture of political opposition can be identified in the country during the early seventeenth century, but rather that the very desire to collect material on freedom of speech and counsel made individuals into civic beings. Private individuals, in thinking of themselves as citizens and using texts to develop their political language, took on public personae and thus laid claim to the right and obligation to speak, write, and read freely and to participate in the governance of the realm. This is the case even when that participation led to the desire for quietude and non-participation, as in the case of Sir William Drake, whose reading habits have been meticulously reconstructed by Kevin Sharpe.[12] Sharpe is at pains to point out that

---

[12] Kevin Sharpe, *Reading Revolutions: The Politics of Reading in Early Modern England* (New Haven: Yale University Press, 2000).

although Drake read voraciously in political philosophy on the kinds of issue I have been discussing, this did not make him a revolutionary. This is surely true; but it did mean that he was an active critic of the political world, and that – whether he would have liked it or not – made him a citizen. My discussion of manuscript miscellanies in chapter 4 is intended, with the preceding chapter, to contribute to the debate over the relationship between the localities and the political 'centre' of early Stuart England, and I concur with those scholars who have suggested that this relationship was a dynamic and mobile one. This is, at least in part, because MPs themselves were also important figures in their own counties, and tended to spend rather more time performing local civic duties such as administering their estates and acting as Justices of the Peace than they did sitting at Westminster.

Manuscript was still a vital medium in early Stuart England, and as well as avoiding the hurdles of the licensing system that scrutinised printed books, the production of a manuscript miscellany was a way for individuals to organise knowledge and to share texts and opinions with like-minded neighbours and acquaintances. The interest in freedom of speech evinced by many miscellanies is, I suggest, highly significant for our understanding of the way that people in early Stuart England thought about their rights and their political identities.

Throughout this book I argue that the only way we can come to a fuller understanding of early Stuart conceptions of freedom of speech is by attending to, and seeking the origins of, the terms in which such conceptions were couched. As I have suggested, this requires both a concentration on the highly specific forms that vocabularies took during the period under consideration and an awareness of their origins and histories. It is necessary, then, briefly to discuss the chronological choices I have made in writing this study. I have chosen to concentrate on the relatively short period from 1603 to 1628 partly because the early Stuart period has been neglected in previous narratives of the history of free speech. I have been concerned to fill in some of the gaps between the *causes célèbres* of the sixteenth century (such as Peter Wentworth's speech in 1576 or John Stubbs's prosecution in 1579 for writing the *Gaping Gulf*) and the breakdown of censorship and so-called explosion in print at the beginning of the Civil War. My account is not intended to create a still smoother pathway from repression to freedom; rather, I hope to show just how complex and discontinuous the history of a category such as freedom of speech is. I have, accordingly, resisted the temptation to take this story up to the 1640s precisely to avoid suggesting that the debates and conflicts I describe led more or less inevitably to conflict between crown and Parliament. I do believe, as will be clear, that many of the shapes that free-speech debates took in the period from 1603 to 1628 displayed concerns about the liberty of the subject which would be taken up in the final collapse of relations between Charles I and his Parliament; but I want to maintain a sense of the distinctiveness of the years I discuss as well as their connections to earlier and later discussions and events. There is, I hope, room for much more work on freedom of speech in the early Stuart period: this book is intended to raise questions about how such work might be carried out, not to attempt to determine its shape.

CHAPTER I

Parrhesia, *or licentiousness baptised freedom: the rhetoric of free speech*

What is less 'figured' than true freedom?

Quintilian.[1]

THE TEMPORALITY OF RHETORIC

The literate culture of early modern England was permeated by rhetoric. The Renaissance, after all, not only saw what Brian Vickers has described as the 'reintegration' of rhetoric, but also its reformation and dissemination, in Latin and the vernacular, in new editions of the classical texts and newly written works, among a vast proportion of the literate population of Europe.[2] This much has been familiar for some time, although its implications for the study of the period have been variously interpreted. C. S. Lewis, writing in 1954, was well aware of the importance of rhetoric to the mental world of the Elizabethan writer, whom he described as 'growing up from boyhood in a world of "prettie epanorthosis", paronomasia, *isocolon*,

---

[1] Quintilian, *The Orator's Education* [*Institutio oratoria*], ed. and trans. by Donald A. Russell, 5 volumes (Cambridge, MA: Harvard University Press, 2001), volume IV, 9. 2. 27, p. 49: 'Quid enim minus figuratum quam vera libertas?' (p. 48).

[2] See Brian Vickers, *In Defence of Rhetoric* (Oxford: Clarendon Press, 1988; corrected edition, 1997), chapter 5, 'Renaissance Reintegration'. Vickers extrapolates from the enormous number of rhetoric handbooks published between 1400 and 1700 that during this period 'there must have been several million Europeans with a working knowledge of rhetoric' (p. 256). Many of the 'newly written' works of this period were of course more often translations, part-translations, or compilations of ancient texts, frequently feeding off one another; as Vickers stresses, 'the author of a rhetoric textbook is a kind of bricoleur' (p. 269). Elsewhere he quotes Susenbrotus' self-denigrating announcement that 'collector, non author, ego sum' (Brian Vickers, 'Rhetoric and Poetics', in *The Cambridge History of Renaissance Philosophy*, ed. by Charles B. Schmitt, Quentin Skinner, and Eckhard Kessler (Cambridge: Cambridge University Press, 1988), pp. 715–45, at p. 721). See also James J. Murphy, *Renaissance Rhetoric. A Short-Title Catalogue of Works on Rhetorical Theory from the Beginning of Printing to A.D. 1700* (New York: Garland, 1981); John Monfasani, 'Humanism and Rhetoric', in *Renaissance Humanism: Foundations, Forms, and Legacy*, ed. by Albert Rabil, Jr., 3 volumes (Philadelphia: University of Pennsylvania Press, 1988), volume III, *Humanism and the Disciplines*, pp. 171–235; Peter Mack, *Elizabethan Rhetoric: Theory and Practice* (Cambridge: Cambridge University Press, 2002).

and *similiter cadentia*'.[3] For Lewis, though, this forest of figures had the effect of making much of the writing of the time virtually inaccessible to the modern reader: 'rhetoric,' he declared, 'is the greatest barrier between us and our ancestors'.[4] Recent criticism has tended to the opposite extreme: some scholars have begun to see the catalogue of schemes and tropes not as an impediment, but rather as a key which can unlock the complexities of early modern texts.[5] To note the figurative strategies of a text and be able to name them can thus become the beginning and the end of a reading, with the critic performing a task strikingly similar to that of the Elizabethan schoolmaster and exclaiming from time to time, 'Hic est figura'.[6] As Richard Sherry asked in 1550, though, after describing this practice, 'what profit is herein if they go no further?'[7]

Such limited and limiting discussions of rhetoric are most often the result of reading into it an immutability inconsistent with the evidence of both manuals and of figures at work in texts. Of course, when a classical rhetorical handbook is translated or adapted by an early modern writer the implication is that the lessons it contains and the analyses it offers are as applicable and accurate at the time of translation as they were at the time of writing. This direct linking of the conditions of antiquity and the present was at the heart of the humanist enterprise and the idea of the Renaissance.

---

[3] C. S. Lewis, *English Literature in the Sixteenth Century excluding Drama* (Oxford: Clarendon Press, 1954), p. 61. An example of the pervasiveness of the figures in educational settings is given by Vives' plan for 'a table of figures of speech, which can be hung up on the wall so that it will catch the attention of the pupil as he walks past it, and force itself upon his eyes', Juan Luis Vives, *On Education: A Translation of the De tradendis disciplinis*, trans. by Foster Watson (Cambridge: Cambridge University Press, 1913), p. 134, quoted in Vickers, *In Defence*, p. 261.

[4] Lewis, *English Literature in the Sixteenth Century*, p. 61. Lewis goes on to develop the point: 'this change of taste makes an indivisible wall between us and them. Probably all our literary histories, certainly that on which I am engaged, are vitiated by our lack of sympathy on this point.'

[5] This dichotomy sidelines another attitude to rhetoric, particularly evident in the wake of Paul de Man, which considers it as necessarily subversive of 'ideology'. For de Man's reading of rhetoric see the three collections of essays, *Blindness and Insight. Essays in the Rhetoric of Contemporary Criticism* (New York: Oxford University Press, 1971), *Allegories of Reading. Figural Language in Rousseau, Nietzsche, Rilke, and Proust* (New Haven: Yale University Press, 1979), and *The Rhetoric of Romanticism* (New York: Columbia University Press, 1984). For a critique of de Man's conception of rhetoric, see David Norbrook, 'Rhetoric, Ideology and the Elizabethan World Picture', in *Renaissance Rhetoric*, ed. by Peter Mack (Basingstoke: Macmillan, 1994), pp. 140–64, at p. 141; Vickers, *In Defence*, pp. 453–69.

[6] Richard Sherry, *A Treatise of the Schemes and Tropes Gathered out of the Best Grammarians and Orators* (London, 1550), quoted in Vickers, *In Defence*, p. 259.

[7] Ibid. A further problem with such an approach is its excessive concentration on figurative language (*elocutio*) at the expense of the discovery and deployment of arguments (*inventio* and *dispositio*) – a distortion only partly supported by the approaches of early modern handbooks. For a valuable corrective, see Norbrook, 'Rhetoric, Ideology and the Elizabethan World Picture', pp. 140–2. For an argument stressing the importance of *elocutio* as part of the integrated system of rhetoric, see Brian Vickers, 'Rhetorical and Anti-rhetorical Tropes: On Writing the History of *Elocutio*', *Comparative Criticism* 3 (1981): 105–32.

But it is vital to ask precisely what conditions were identified as similar, how far this identification was prescriptive and not descriptive, and what institutional contexts were envisaged for the pedagogical enterprise of which the rhetoric manuals were a part.[8] Moreover, it is important to acknowledge the diversity of treatments offered by early modern handbooks themselves. While the catalogue of schemes and tropes has remained more or less constant from its first classifications, their relative status has altered according to historical conditions. Consequently, as Roland Barthes pointed out, the taxonomic operations of a rhetorical text can serve as an index to its ideological framework; the particular arrangement of schemes and tropes (and the divisions of 'rhetoric' as a whole, the attention paid to the different *genera* and their uses, and so on) at a specific historical moment are highly revealing of a text's political alignments, or, more accurately, are themselves a political index.[9]

Rhetorical figures, then, are not stable categories. They describe elements of speech or writing which are defined as transgressive in relation to an imagined (but never defined) norm, and which are imagined to have specific suasive effects in particular local conditions. The best way of understanding how an individual figure – or a rhetorical theory – works is therefore to investigate the tradition of its definition in the rhetorical archive, the effects which it is variously imagined to have, and the contexts in which its use is deemed appropriate. Perhaps surprisingly, there has so far been very little work done on tracing the understanding of individual figures through the treatises in which they appear and the texts and recorded speeches in which they are deployed.[10]

---

[8] Much valuable work is currently being done in this area: Quentin Skinner, *Reason and Rhetoric in the Philosophy of Hobbes* (Cambridge: Cambridge University Press, 1996) offers an excellent survey of rhetoric teaching in the late sixteenth and early seventeenth centuries which gains much of its strength from returning to the classical texts themselves and reconsidering what were considered to be the powers and the ends of oratory; Warren Boutcher, 'Pilgrimage to Parnassus: Local Intellectual Traditions, Humanist Education and the Cultural Geography of Sixteenth-century England', in *Pedagogy and Power: Rhetorics of Classical Learning*, ed. by Niall Livingstone and Yun Lee Too (Cambridge: Cambridge University Press, 1998), pp. 110–47, situates Roger Ascham's *The Scholemaster* (1570) and John Hoskyns's *Directions for Speech and Style* (c. 1599) in a changing pedagogical enterprise whose aims were closely linked to local conditions.

[9] Roland Barthes, 'The Old Rhetoric: An Aide mémoire', in Barthes, *The Semiotic Challenge*, trans. by Richard Howard (Oxford: Basil Blackwell, 1988), pp. 11–94.

[10] An important exception to this is Quentin Skinner's treatment of *paradiastole* in *Reason and Rhetoric*, chapter 4, 'The Techniques of Redescription', pp. 138–80, and in two articles, 'Moral Ambiguity and the Renaissance Art of Eloquence' (F. W. Bateson Memorial Lecture), *Essays in Criticism* 44:4 (October 1994): 267–92 and 'Thomas Hobbes: Rhetoric and the Construction of Morality', *Proceedings of the British Academy* 76 (1991): 1–61.

The aim of this chapter will be to follow the history of one such rhetorical figure from its use in ancient Greek oratory and its definition in Roman handbooks, through to its appearance in the manuals, texts, and speeches of early modern England. That figure has the Greek name of *parrhesia* or, in Latin, *licentia* – what comes to be known as the figure of frank speech.[11] A predictable degree of surprise that there should be a figure of frank speech at all is exemplified in the quotation which heads this chapter, from Quintilian's *Institutio oratoria* – one of the three most important classical rhetorics for early modern readers, along with the pseudo-Ciceronian *Rhetorica ad Herennium* and Cicero's *De inventione*.[12] It is important to be aware, however, that Quintilian's comment occurs in the midst of his discussion of that figure and its possible uses, during a not entirely successful attempt to disentangle 'genuine' from 'simulated' forms of exclamation.[13] In a twenty-first-century western culture whose discussions of free speech are likely to be predicated on a language of human rights rather than eloquence the classification of this figure is particularly striking, and potentially unnerving. This is partly the effect of extending that language of rights into past conceptions of free speech, and of interpreting such rights as outside considerations of context. The need to regard every speech-act or writing as taking place in an imaginary locus, stable and free from tradition, in order to support this kind of thinking is particularly evident in current discussions of First Amendment law in the United States, as analysed by Stanley Fish.[14] The ways of thinking that it leads to are seriously undermined by a historical consideration of the figure *parrhesia*, which, as I shall show, resists attempts to uncover a teleology of the right of free speech in a recognisable form.[15]

[11] *Parrhesia*, from Greek πᾶς (all) + ῥῆσις (speech). I am indebted in this chapter to Diane Parkin-Speer, 'Freedom of Speech in Sixteenth Century English Rhetorics', *Sixteenth Century Journal* 12:3 (1981): 65–72. My differences with Parkin-Speer's reading of the rhetoric of free speech will be discussed below.

[12] On the importance of these texts to the humanist curriculum in sixteenth-century England, see Skinner, *Reason and Rhetoric*, pp. 23–35. Many other classical treatises were also widely popular, notably Cicero's *De oratore, Topica*, and *De partitione oratoria* (Skinner, *Reason and Rhetoric*, p. 34). See T. W. Baldwin, *William Shakspere's Small Latine and Lesse Greeke*, 2 volumes (Urbana: University of Illinois, 1944), volume I, pp. 1–68.

[13] For a fuller exposition of this passage, see below, pp. 34–5.

[14] See Stanley Fish, *There's No Such Thing as Free Speech, and It's a Good Thing, Too* (Oxford: Oxford University Press, 1994), especially chapters 4, 5, 6, 7, 8, and 9, pp. 60–138.

[15] Although Diane Parkin-Speer notes that 'In sixteenth century England freedom of speech came to mean the right to express the truth as the speaker or writer perceived it', she goes on to state, rather vaguely, that 'The right to speak the truth *naturally* led *eventually* to the modern understanding of this civil right' (my italics) ('Freedom of Speech', p. 65). Partly because of the brevity of her account, she tends to collapse historical differences between Greek, Roman, and English sources, the main distinguishing feature considered being the advent of Christianity.

PARRHESIA IN ANCIENT GREECE: FREEDOM
IN WORD AND DEED

From the very beginning freedom of speech and rhetoric have had a close relationship.[16] Indeed, in ancient Greece the need to codify rules for effective speaking was partly necessitated by the privilege accorded to citizens, as George Kennedy points out:

Technical rhetoric [the rhetoric of the handbooks, usually forensic in origin] came into existence under the conditions of the Greek city-states where all citizens were deemed equal and were expected to be able to speak on their own behalf. In origin it is associated with freedom of speech and with amateurism, first in the law-courts, but also in democratic political assemblies.[17]

Athens in particular was celebrated by its literary citizens as the home of free speech, and this soon became part of its mythology.[18] The political system which allowed full participation for citizens in the proceedings of the assembly (*ekklesia*) developed a terminology of its own, and it is in the literary celebration of these rights that the term *parrhesia* appears for the first time.[19] I will therefore devote a certain amount of space in this section to

[16] I would like to thank Thomas Harrison for invaluable discussions of and suggestions for the material concerning ancient Greece. An essential text for the study of *parrhesia* is Michel Foucault, *Fearless Speech*, ed. by Joseph Pearson (Los Angeles: Semiotext(e), 2001), a transcript of lectures given by Foucault at the University of California at Berkeley in 1983. This material circulated for some years in samizdat form, and I am grateful to James Tully and Quentin Skinner for providing me with a copy of it before its publication.

[17] George A. Kennedy, *Classical Rhetoric and Its Christian and Secular Traditions from Ancient to Modern Times* (London: Croom Helm, 1980), p. 23. On freedom of speech generally in the ancient world, see Arnaldo Momigliano, 'Freedom of Speech in Antiquity', in *Dictionary of the History of Ideas*, 6 volumes, ed. by Philip Wiener (New York: Charles Scribner's Sons, 1973), volume II, pp. 252–63.

[18] On Athenian democracy as characterised by freedom of speech, see sources cited by Robert W. Wallace, 'Private Lives and Public Enemies: Freedom of Thought in Classical Athens', in *Athenian Identity and Civic Ideology*, ed. by Alan L. Boegehold and Adele C. Scafuro (Baltimore: Johns Hopkins University Press, 1994), pp. 127–55; p. 127. See also the discussion of *parrhesia* in S. Sara Monoson, *Plato's Democratic Entanglements: Athenian Politics and the Practice of Philosophy* (Princeton: Princeton University Press, 2000), chapter 2, 'Citizen as *Parrhēsiastēs* (Frank Speaker)', pp. 51–63.

[19] I. F. Stone has shown that there were three words for freedom of speech in ancient Athens, aside from *parrhesia*: *isegoria*, *isologia*, and *eleutherostomia*. Each had a slightly different meaning, with *isologia* and *isegoria* in particular being more directly linked to participation in the assembly. Momigliano, 'Freedom of Speech in Antiquity', suggests that by the middle of the fifth century *isegoria* was 'old fashioned' (p. 259). My concentration in this section on *parrhesia* is dictated by its continued use in oratory and its adoption by Roman and Renaissance rhetoricians. See I. F. Stone, *The Trial of Socrates* (London: Jonathan Cape, 1988), chapter 17, 'The Four Words', pp. 215–24. See further Luigi Spina, *Il cittadino alla tribuna. Diritto e libertà di parola nell'Atene democratica* (Naples: Liguori, 1986). For further instances of the term, see *A Greek-English Lexicon*, compiled by Henry George Liddell and Robert Scott, revised edition with supplement (Oxford: Clarendon Press, 1968), under *parrhesia*.

examining its uses and meanings in ancient Greece, evidence which forms the basis of its later rhetorical codification. This lexical survey will explore the range of attitudes and oratorical performances which the term covers in its original contexts and will help us to understand the manoeuvres of later writers who define or employ the word or the figure in their texts.

Parrhesia is first used as part of the reflection of Athenian civic ideology found in Euripidean tragedy:[20] in the *Hippolytus*, first performed in 428 BCE, the despairing Phaedra imagines life in Athens as the best possible future for her family:

> PHAEDRA:
> I cannot bear that I should be discovered
> a traitor to my husband and my children.
> God grant them rich and glorious life in Athens –
> famous Athens – freedom in word and deed.
>
> (ll. 420–3)[21]

Similarly, in *Ion* (written about 420–410 BCE), Euripides shows the protagonist imagining the best possible outcome of his search for his mother:

> ION:
> I pray my mother is Athenian,
> So that through her I may have rights of speech.
> For when a stranger comes into a city
> Of pure blood, though in name a citizen,
> His mouth remains a slave: he has no right
> Of speech.   (ll. 671–5)[22]

In a rather later text, Plato's *Gorgias* (*c.* 390 BCE), there is an almost offhand reference to the freedom of speech allowed in Athens in the conversation between Polus and Socrates:

---

[20] See Stone, *The Trial of Socrates*, p. 222. For the argument that *parrhesia* is a term developed for specifically literary reasons (including its metrical utility and the semantic possibilities of plays on the word *pan*), see Spina, *Il cittadino alla tribuna*, pp. 30–1. On Euripidean *parrhesia*, see Foucault, *Fearless Speech*, chapter 2, pp. 25–74.

[21] Euripides, *Hippolytus*, trans. by David Grene, in *Euripides I: Four Tragedies* (Chicago: University of Chicago Press, 1955), pp. 157–221, at p. 181. For a suggestive account of the place of rhetoric in Greek tragedy, and on ancient Greek attitudes to rhetoric more generally, see Stephen Halliwell, 'Between Public and Private: Tragedy and Athenian Experience of Rhetoric', in *Greek Tragedy and the Historian*, ed. by Christopher Pelling (Oxford: Clarendon Press, 1997), pp. 121–41.

[22] Euripides, *Ion*, trans. by R. F. Willetts, in *Euripides III: Four Tragedies* (Chicago: University of Chicago Press, 1958), pp. 177–255, at p. 214. Stone, *The Trial of Socrates*, p. 222, notes the herdsman's anxiety in *Bacchae* over whether he can speak freely before Pentheus: see Euripides, *Bacchae*, trans. by William Arrowsmith in *Euripides V: Three Tragedies* (Chicago: University of Chicago Press, 1959), pp. 141–222, at p. 184, ll. 668–73.

SOCRATES: I'm perfectly willing to take back anything you like, but on one condition.

POLUS: What is that?

SOCRATES: That you keep in check the tendency to make long speeches which you showed at the beginning of our conversation.

POLUS: What? Am I not to be allowed to say as much as I choose?

SOCRATES: It would certainly be hard luck, my good sir, if on arriving in Athens, which allows freedom of speech above all other cities in Greece, you found that you alone were denied that privilege.[23]

The fact that Socrates' trial in 399 BCE had become (at least for his followers) a *cause célèbre* of Athenian freedom of speech suggests that this passage could well be intended ironically.[24] In Plato's record of the trial, Socrates presents his frank statement of the truth in opposition to what he calls the 'flowery language' of his accusers and denies their 'accusation' that he is a 'skilful speaker':[25] here frankness is opposed to oratory in general rather than, as in several other texts, a specific abuse of oratory – a natural enough move given Plato's distrust of that 'spurious counterfeit of a branch of the art of government'.[26] The strategy of presenting what the speaker defines as necessary frankness as an antidote to questionably manipulative or devious 'rhetoric' is one that is at the heart of the use of *parrhesia* throughout its history.[27] This does not necessarily mean, however, that *parrhesia* is more

---

[23] Plato, *Gorgias*, trans. by Walter Hamilton (Harmondsworth: Penguin, 1960), pp. 41–2.

[24] See Plato, *The Apology*, in *The Last Days of Socrates*, trans. by Hugh Tredennick (Harmondsworth: Penguin, 1969), pp. 45–76, especially pp. 45–6, 74. See further the impressive unpacking of the possible motives for and implications of the trial in K. J. Dover, 'The Freedom of the Intellectual in Greek Society', in *The Greeks and their Legacy: Collected Papers*, volume II (Oxford: Basil Blackwell, 1988), pp. 135–58. Also Stone, *The Trial of Socrates, passim*; T. C. Brickhouse and N. D. Smith, *Socrates on Trial* (Oxford, 1989); Gregory Vlastos, *Socrates: Ironist and Moral Philosopher* (Cambridge: Cambridge University Press, 1991), pp. 293–7; Robert Parker, *Athenian Religion: A History* (Oxford: Clarendon Press, 1996), chapter 9, 'The Trial of Socrates: And a Religious Crisis?', pp. 199–217; Wallace, 'Private Lives and Public Enemies', *passim*. There is an extended consideration of Plato's attitude to *parrhesia* in Monoson, *Plato's Democratic Entanglements*, chapter 6, 'Philosopher as *Parrhēsiastēs* (Frank Speaker)', pp. 154–80.

[25] Plato, *The Apology*, p. 45.

[26] Plato, *Gorgias*, p. 44. For Plato's distrust of *parrhesia* as an aspect of democracy, see *The Republic*, trans. by H. D. P. Lee (Harmondsworth: Penguin, 1955), 557e, p. 329. Momigliano, 'Freedom of Speech in Antiquity', notes that he approves it when 'granted as a privilege to the wise counsellor (*Laws* 694b; *Laches* 188e)' (p. 260); see also Stone, *The Trial of Socrates*, pp. 227–30. For a provocative attempt to argue that 'Plato's texts defend the idea of parrhesia and appropriate this democratic strategy of civic discourse for philosophy', based on the argument that Plato quibbles with the definition of Athenian freedoms as based on *parrhesia*, see S. Sara Monoson, 'Frank Speech, Democracy, and Philosophy: Plato's Debt to a Democratic Strategy of Civic Discourse', *Athenian Political Thought and the Reconstruction of American Democracy*, ed. by J. P. Euben, J. R. Wallach, and J. Ober (Ithaca: Cornell University Press, 1994), pp. 172–97, at p. 172; the arguments are developed in Monoson, *Plato's Democratic Entanglements*.

[27] For a classic example of this strategy, see Mark Antony's claims for bluntness in his elaborate and manipulative funeral oration in William Shakespeare, *Julius Caesar*, III.ii, ll. 73–264. In the *Rhetoric*,

generally identified with plainness of style, or freedom from the elaborate and copious. Frank speech can be as ornate as the speaker wishes to make it.

As well as being linked with Athenian democracy in particular, free speech is identified in many Greek texts with nobility of station or of spirit. In Sophocles' *Trachiniai* (dated tentatively to around 420 BCE), Deianira's nurse dares to speak out and offer advice to her mistress, thereby momentarily elevating herself to the status of 'the free'.[28] This 'elevation', though, is very fleeting, and it is important to note both that Deianira ascribes it to 'a lucky cast', to chance, and that it serves not to undermine the rigid social hierarchy marked out by the privilege of free speech but rather to reinforce it. The nurse has performed something which is 'worthy of the free', not shown that she is worthy to *be* free, or that such categories are at all mobile.[29]

One of the most striking examples of this belief in the transparency of nobility through free speech and action occurs in Book I of Herodotus' *Histories*, where Herodotus narrates the story of Cyrus' rise to power.[30] Here Cyrus reveals his true identity to Astyges, the grandfather who had tried to have him killed, through his free way of speaking. His innate nobility is evident from what Herodotus' sixteenth-century translator calls 'his bold answeare to Astyges', the freedom of his speech before one whom he ought to respect if he were really a herdman's son.[31] Like the passage from the *Trachiniai*, Herodotus here demonstrates how closely linked were the right to free speech and the need to maintain supposedly natural hierarchies.

Aristotle advises that effectual eloquence depends upon a careful admixture of the exotic and the 'natural':

one should make the language unfamiliar, for people are admirers of what is far off, and what is marvellous is sweet . . . authors should compose without being noticed and should seem to speak not artificially but naturally. (The latter is persuasive, the former the opposite; for [if artifice is obvious] people become resentful, as at someone plotting against them, just as they are at those adulterating wines.)

(Aristotle, *On Rhetoric: A Theory of Civic Discourse*, trans. by George A. Kennedy (New York: Oxford University Press, 1991), 1404b, Book 3, chapter 2, pp. 221–2.)

[28] Sophocles, *The Women of Trachis*, trans. by Michael Jameson, ll. 49–63, in *Sophocles II: Four Tragedies* (Chicago: University of Chicago Press, 1957), pp. 63–119, at pp. 74–5.

[29] Cf. Euripides' *Phoenician Women*, where Polyneices explains to Jocasta that the worst aspect of exile is that 'a man cannot speak out'; Jocasta, horrified, replies, 'but this is slavery, not to speak one's thought'. Euripides, *The Phoenician Women*, trans. by Elizabeth Wyckoff, in *Euripides V: Three Tragedies*, pp. 67–140, at p. 85, ll. 391–2.

[30] Herodotus, *The History*, trans. by David Grene (Chicago: University of Chicago Press, 1987), volume I, pp. 83–93.

[31] *The Famous Hystory of Herodotus*, trans. by B. R. [1584], The Tudor Translations, second series 6 (London: Constable and Co., 1924), p. 76 margin.

Slaves and women were both denied the citizen's right to free expression, and thus full participation in the *polis*; importantly, in the texts I have looked at this denial is represented as a natural lack, the privilege as an inherent quality.[32] For these Greek writers, freedom is defined by and depends upon the enslavement of others – as Gorgias says, oratory 'confers on every one who possesses it not only freedom for himself but the power of ruling his fellow-countrymen'.[33]

The texts I have dealt with so far have offered some examples of the way that freedom of speech was discussed and valued in ancient Greece, and the way in which the term *parrhesia* was specifically associated with the democratic rights of the Athenian citizen. By the fourth century BCE, it seems that the semantic field of the term had widened, and thus in particular contexts it could have a very specific value and polemical weight. *Parrhesia*, as Arnaldo Momigliano argues, gradually became a 'philosopher's virtue', detached from the practice of politics – although its earlier significance never entirely disappears.[34] Increasingly, in late antiquity the term shifts to refer to relations of *philia* rather than to a democratic quality; partly as a result of the increased importance of relations of patronage to the politics of the Greek world.[35] The Epicureans and the Cynics both cultivated *parrhesia* as a prime value of their moral philosophical thought: while writers like Philodemus and Plutarch celebrated frankness as a necessary part of the relationship of a great patron to their client, Diogenes regarded harsh admonition as the obligation of the truth-telling philosopher speaking from the margins of such relations.[36] These three traditions all informed

---

[32] Democritus wrote that *parrhesia* was an inherent quality of *eleutheria*, or liberty (fragment 226D); see Momigliano, 'Freedom of Speech in Antiquity', p. 259.

[33] Plato, *Gorgias*, p. 28.

[34] See Momigliano, 'Freedom of Speech in Antiquity', p. 260; on the detachment of the term from a political context in Athenian funeral orations, see Nicole Loraux, *L'invention d'Athènes. Histoire de l'oration funèbre dans la «cité classique»* (Paris: Mouton, 1981), pp. 178, 212.

[35] This association surely existed earlier, in a less organised fashion; Aristotle writes in the *Nicomachean Ethics* that frankness is to be exercised 'towards brothers and comrades'. See Aristotle, *Ethics*, trans. by J. A. K. Thomson, rev. by Hugh Tredennick (Harmondsworth: Penguin, 1976), 9.2.9, 1165a, 29–30, p. 291. See further Stanley B. Marrow, SJ, '*Parrhesia* and the New Testament', *Catholic Biblical Quarterly* 44:3 (July 1982): 431–46, pp. 433–4; Monoson, 'Frank Speech, Democracy, and Philosophy': p. 175, n. 6.

[36] Philodemus of Gadara (*c*. 110–40 BCE), a student of Zeno of Sidon, wrote a work entitled *Peri parrhesias* which dealt with the importance of frank criticism to Epicurean pedagogy; see Περὶ παρρησίας, *De libertate dicendi*, ed. by A. Olivieri (Leipzig: Teubner, 1914) and further, Clarence E. Glad, 'Frank Speech, Flattery, and Friendship in Philodemus', *Friendship, Flattery, and Frankness of Speech. Studies on Friendship in the New Testament World*, ed. by John T. Fitzgerald (Leiden: E. J. Brill, 1996), pp. 21–59. Some sources are provided in Abraham J. Malherbe, *Moral Exhortation, A Greco-Roman Sourcebook* (Philadelphia: The Westminster Press, 1986), pp. 48–67. On Plutarch

the rhetorical understanding of *parrhesia* to varying degrees, as will be seen from my examination of Roman and Renaissance texts below.[37]

Returning to the more political uses of *parrhesia*, I want now to move on to some instances of free speech in action from fourth-century oratory, as a way of approaching more closely the techniques that would later be classified by rhetoricians as *parrhesia* or *licentia*.[38] By the time that Isocrates and Demosthenes were writing, Athenian democracy was in decline, and it is perhaps this fact which in part explains the number of references to boldness to be found in their writings.[39] Their outspoken references to the dangerous demagogues who win over the populace with devious rhetoric and bare-faced flattery may seem out of place given that Isocrates was himself the target of Plato's attacks on the sophists; but it is precisely this willingness to engage in angry admonition that was regarded by Thucydides as one of the primary qualities of Pericles, the ideal Athenian leader.[40] The self-conscious frankness found in the fourth-century orators, then, could convincingly be seen as an implicit allusion to that period of Athenian supremacy and freedom.

In 355 BCE, at the age of eighty-one, Isocrates published the oration 'On the Peace', urging the surrender of the Athenian maritime empire as

see below pp. 42–3, and also Troels Engberg-Pedersen, 'Plutarch to Prince Philopappus on How to Tell a Flatterer from a Friend', *Friendship, Flattery, and Frankness of Speech*, ed. by John T. Fitzgerald (Leiden: E. J. Brill, 1996), pp. 61–79. According to Diogenes Laertius, when Diogenes of Sinope was asked what was the most beautiful thing in the world, he replied '*parrhesia*' (Diogenes Laertius, *Lives of Eminent Philosophers*, trans. by R. D. Hicks, 2 volumes (London: Heinemann, 1925), volume II, pp. 70–1 (6.69)). On Diogenes and Cynic uses of *parrhesia*, see Marrow, '*Parrhesia* and the New Testament', p. 435; David E. Fredrickson, 'Παρρησία in the Pauline Epistles', *Friendship, Flattery, and Frankness of Speech*, pp. 163–83, at p. 166; William Klassen, 'Παρρησία in the Johannine Corpus', ibid., pp. 227–54, at pp. 229, 233. The Epicurean version of *parrhesia* was later mediated by Horace: see Norman W. DeWitt, 'Parresiastic Poems of Horace', *Classical Philology* 30 (October 1935): 312–19; Agnes Kirsopp Michels, 'Παρρησία and the Satire of Horace', *Classical Philology* 39 (July 1944): 173–7; R. L. Hunter, 'Horace on Friendship and Free Speech', *Hermes* 113 (1985): 480–90.

[37] *Parrhesia* is also a term found in biblical texts, specifically the New Testament; I discuss the religious use of the term in chapter 2 below.

[38] At no stage in any of the surviving Greek works which treat rhetoric is *parrhesia* mentioned as a rhetorical figure; this is unsurprising given that Aristotle, for instance, unlike the Roman writers, does not undertake to catalogue the schemes and tropes.

[39] Demosthenes uses the word *parrhesia* twenty-six times, Isocrates twenty-two; see Momigliano, 'Freedom of Speech in Antiquity', p. 260.

[40] On Plato's targeting of Isocrates, and the latter's responses, see Vickers, *In Defence*, p. 149; Isocrates, *Against the Sophists*, trans. by George Norlin, in Isocrates, *Works*, 3 volumes (London: Heinemann, 1928–9), II. On Pericles see Thucydides, *The Peloponnesian War*, trans. by Thomas Hobbes [1629] (Chicago: University of Chicago Press, 1989), II. 65, pp. 125–6. On Plato's conception of his (and Socrates') mission to reform the citizenry from its love of flattery, see Plato, *Gorgias*, pp. 123–30 (which ends with harsh criticisms of Pericles) and Vickers, *In Defence*, pp. 86–8.

a way of ending the Social War.[41] Peace, writes Isocrates, is 'a theme on which none of the orators has ever made bold to address you'.[42] The whole speech, in its outspoken criticism of Isocrates' audience, is an example of *parrhesia* in action; it also, more significantly, continually draws attention to its own frankness. This explicit announcement of the intention to speak freely characterises uses of *parrhesia*, ensuring that the audience or reader is aware of the speaker's valorisation of his or her words, and is forced to take a position in relation to this valorisation: is this true free speech or simply abuse? Is it appropriate or not? Such questions force the auditor or reader into an area of ethical consideration which immediately validates the notion of free speech even if what is being responded to is not accepted as such.

The basis of Isocrates' criticism of the people of Athens is that they have created a political environment where speakers are expected only to flatter and not to tell the truth.[43] He goes on to announce his concern for his own safety in being so candid, and transfers the accusation of recklessness from his own discourse, which might seem dangerous to himself, to the flattering demagogues whose speeches are dangerous to the state:

I know that it is hazardous to oppose your views and that, although this is a free government, there exists no 'freedom of speech' [παρρησία] except that which is enjoyed in this Assembly by the most reckless orators, who care nothing for your welfare, and in the theatre by the comic poets.[44]

Throughout the rest of the discourse, he draws attention to his frankness and presents it as the only possible antidote to the complacency and ignorance of his audience. He expresses astonishment at the possibility that other orators may be advising the people to imitate 'those who lived at the time of the Persian Wars',

and in the same breath would persuade us to act in a manner contrary to theirs and to commit blunders so gross that I am at a loss what I should do – *whether I should speak the truth as on all other occasions or be silent out of fear of making myself odious to you*. For while it seems to me the better course to discuss your blunders, I observe that you are more resentful towards those who take you to task than

---

[41] Norlin states that 'it is certain . . . that Isocrates did not deliver it, and it is likely that he composed it as a political pamphlet to be circulated among a reading public' (Isocrates, *On the Peace*, in *Works* II, pp. 2–97, at p. 5); the oration is thus in some senses an early instance of the phenomenon of *letteraturizzazione*, or 'the application of rhetoric to written composition' (George A. Kennedy, *A New History of Classical Rhetoric* (Princeton: Princeton University Press, 1994), p. 28).

[42] Isocrates, *On the Peace*, p. 25.   [43] Ibid., p. 9.

[44] Ibid., p. 15. On the frankness and satire of ancient comedy, see Stephen Halliwell, 'Comic Satire and Freedom of Speech in Classical Athens', *Journal of Hellenistic Studies* III (1991): 48–70.

towards those who are the authors of your misfortunes. Nevertheless I should be ashamed if I showed that I am more concerned about my own reputation than about the public safety. It is, therefore, my duty and the duty of all who care about the welfare of the state to choose, *not those discourses which are agreeable to you, but those discourses which are profitable for you to hear* . . . there exists no remedy for souls which are ignorant of the truth and filled with base desires other than the kind of discourse which boldly rebukes the sins which they commit.[45]

Isocrates follows this assertion of his duty with what one might imagine to be the somewhat superfluous explanation that 'I have said these things at the outset because in the rest of my discourse I am going to speak without reserve and with complete frankness.'[46] Further on, he returns to the question of how his strictures are to be interpreted – as therapeutic home truths or as potentially treasonous – and warns that his audience should look beyond shared vocabularies to intention and context:

I want to say a word by way of leading up to this point, fearing that, on account of my many strictures, I may give the impression to some of you of having chosen to denounce our city . . .

But those who admonish and those who denounce cannot avoid using similar words, although their purposes are as opposite as they can be . . .

These, then, are the things which I have to say in defence of my harshness both in the words which I have spoken and those which I am about to speak.[47]

In his lengthy self-justification Isocrates invokes a number of contextual factors to excuse his boldness: the nature of the audience; their potential reaction to a speech of this nature, and the intention of the speaker. Any who attempt to challenge him are, by this argument, making a terrible error of judgement and playing into the hands of the state's enemies. It does, however, rely almost entirely on a degree of trust being established precisely through the mechanism of Isocrates' apparently reckless free speech.

Although Demosthenes' political outlook was far from congruent with that of Isocrates, he has recourse in two orations to strikingly similar uses of *parrhesia* – which at this stage we could tentatively define as consisting of bold speech, and self-conscious reference to and/or apologies for, such boldness. The two most obvious common features of Demosthenes' and Isocrates' *parrhesia* are the condemnation of populist orators, and the tendency of the people to react angrily to those who tell them uncomfortable

---

[45] Isocrates, *On the Peace*, pp. 31–3 (my italics).   [46] Ibid., p. 33.

[47] Ibid., pp. 51–3. A similar distinction is made in the *Panegyricus* (c. 380 BCE), where Isocrates writes that 'a distinction must be made between accusation, when one denounces with intent to injure, and admonition, when one uses like words with intent to benefit; for the same words are not to be interpreted in the same way unless they are spoken in the same spirit' (Isocrates, *Panegyricus*, trans. by George Norlin, in Isocrates, *Works*, volume I, pp. 115–241, at p. 201).

'truths'; at the beginning of the *Third Olynthiac*, Demosthenes requests the audience's indulgence:

> I must ask you to bear with me if I speak frankly [παρρησίας], considering only whether I am speaking the truth, and speaking with the object that things may go better in the future; for you see how the popularity-hunting of some of our orators has led us into this desperate predicament.[48]

A little later he alludes to his likely unpopularity and, again like Isocrates, refers to the inhibitions on freedom of speech in Athens at this time.[49] In the *Third Philippic*, the references to free speech become even more confrontational, with Demosthenes pointing out the inconsistency of current Athenian policy – liberty of speech is allowed universally in everyday circumstances, yet it is no longer a part of the political process, he complains.[50]

Here Demosthenes is almost teasing the audience, daring them to refuse to hear him and admit that they prefer flattery to counsel; his aim, clearly, is to arouse the emotions of the auditors while gaining their sanction for his outspokenness.

Two further speeches concerning Philip which were formerly attributed to Demosthenes contain similar references to the undermining of free speech and the dangers of orators who flatter their hearers, alongside requests for indulgence from the audience. In the speech *On Halonnessus*, the charge is directly against Philip himself for having attempted to stifle free speech in the Assembly.[51] In the *Fourth Philippic* the unknown writer prefaces his criticism of the Athenians' tendency to sell their 'interests at every opportunity' by 'beseeching you not to be offended with me, if I speak the truth boldly [παρρησίας]',[52] and declares in the peroration,

> There you have the truth spoken with all freedom [παρρησίας], simply in good will and for the best – no speech packed by flattery with mischief and deceit, and intended to put money into the speaker's pocket and the control of the State into our enemies' hands.[53]

The Greek texts I have discussed here display many of the key aspects of thinking about *parrhesia* that are later codified in rhetorical works, and they also provide, as I shall show, a point of reference for writers and

---

[48] Demosthenes, *Third Olynthiac*, trans. by J. H. Vince, in Demosthenes, *Works*, 7 volumes (London: Heinemann, 1930), volume 1, pp. 42–63, at p. 45.

[49] Ibid., p. 61: 'For you do not allow liberty of speech [παρρησία] on every subject, and indeed I am surprised that you have allowed it now.'

[50] Demosthenes, *Third Philippic*, in Demosthenes, *Works*, volume 1, pp. 222–65, at p. 227.

[51] [Demosthenes], *On Halonnessus*, in Demosthenes, *Works*, volume 1, pp. 148–73, at p. 151.

[52] [Demosthenes], *Fourth Philippic*, in Demosthenes, *Works*, volume 1, pp. 265–313, at p. 299.

[53] Ibid., p. 313.

speakers appealing to freedom of speech as an ethical and political necessity. The characteristic voice of the free speaker that appears in the orations of Demosthenes and Isocrates is particularly influential: restrictions on free speech in the assemblies led in their works, as we have seen, to a certain nostalgia for a lost time of open debate. Of course, the democracy of Pericles that they allude to wistfully was, at least according to Thucydides, so in name alone;[54] and there is a further apparent double-bind. The kind of frankness undertaken by both Isocrates and Demosthenes is represented by them as necessary only because the people are under the sway of flatterers; it is a means of awakening them from self-indulgent slumbers. Yet this same frankness – the freedom to direct harsh criticism at an audience of one's peers, rather than simply the right to speak – is regarded as a positive quality in and of itself. The clear implication is to some extent a familiar one: that freedom of speech is recognised as such, or becomes an object of comment, only if it transgresses certain rules of decorum, and is thus closely linked to the idea of counsel through admonition. The verbal formulas common to Isocrates, Demosthenes, and the latter's imitator(s) demonstrate, I would argue, a considerable degree of self-consciousness about the use of frank speech as an effective part of an eloquent and persuasive discourse. Without reading back into these texts qualities or intentions specific to a later age of codified rhetoric, one can discover a set of ideas about how to discuss speaking out which show that *parrhesia* is already considered to be an important part of the orator's armaments.[55]

LIBERTY AND LICENCE IN ROMAN RHETORIC

It is in the hugely influential handbooks of ancient Rome that we find the first full codification of rhetoric; its division into three branches and five parts, and the classification and listing of the tropes and schemes.[56]

[54] See Thucydides, *The Peloponnesian War*, volume II. 65, p. 126: 'It was in name a state democratical, but in fact a government of the principal man.'

[55] On the etymological – and hence semantic – links between ornament and armament in rhetorical terminology, see Vickers, *In Defence*, pp. 314–15; Skinner, *Reason and Rhetoric*, pp. 48–9.

[56] Aristotle, *On Rhetoric*, trans. by Kennedy, Book I, chapter 3, pp. 47–51, outlines the three branches of rhetoric, but does not systematically treat the other divisions fundamental to Roman discussions of the subject. On the divisions of rhetoric see particularly Richard A. Lanham, *A Handlist of Rhetorical Terms*, second edition (Berkeley and Los Angeles: University of California Press, 1991), pp. 163–80. Earlier Roman rhetorical works than those which survive are known to have been written by, among others, Cato and Antonius. See Harry Caplan, 'Introduction', in [Cicero], *Ad C. Herennium, de ratione dicendi (Rhetorica ad Herennium)*, trans. Harry Caplan (London: Heinemann, 1954), pp. vi–xxxix, p. vii. References to this text will hereafter be to *Ad Herennium*, with page numbers (and book, chapter, and paragraph divisions where appropriate).

In several treatises we find freedom of speech listed among those figures.[57] The place and function of rhetoric changed considerably in its assimilation to Roman society, with emphasis within the three branches moving from political (or deliberative) oratory to judicial (or forensic) and, among the five parts, attention focusing on invention.[58] These changes in emphasis were, in turn, largely a result of differences in political and legal conditions; as George Kennedy writes,

in Rome . . . the patron–client system was already in existence before the Romans became aware of Greek rhetoric around 200 B.C., and oratory in Rome, in the lawcourts, the senate, and assemblies, was practised chiefly by a relatively small number of professional orators, highly conscious of techniques and of their own roles.[59]

Written codification, and the classification of free speech as a rhetorical figure, were thus concomitant with a decline in opportunities for political oratory, and restrictions on free speech in practice; this became particularly noticeable with the end of the Republic and the beginning of Imperial rule under Augustus.[60] As in Greece, the freedom of one party to speak depended upon the silencing of another, though again the details were significantly different; as George Kennedy puts it,

freedom of expression in Rome was a relative matter. It was not something to which every citizen was entitled, but something he might derive from noble birth or wealth or might achieve by successful public service and personal merit. The freedom of an

---

[57] For a full discussion of the nature of Roman rhetoric, see George A. Kennedy, *The Art of Rhetoric in the Roman World 300 B.C.–A.D. 300* (Princeton: Princeton University Press, 1972); Vickers, *In Defence*, pp. 26–82.

[58] See Vickers, *In Defence*, p. 26.

[59] Kennedy, *Classical Rhetoric and Its Christian and Secular Traditions*, p. 23.

[60] See Kennedy, *A New History of Classical Rhetoric*, who asserts that '*letteraturizzazione* . . . is largely a phenomenon of periods in which opportunities for civic oratory were reduced, often with the loss of freedom of speech that characterized Greek democracies and the Roman republic' (p. 28). Cf. Kennedy, *Classical Rhetoric and Its Christian and Secular Traditions*, pp. 111–12:

At the end of the fourth century in Greece and again at the end of the first century B.C. in Rome, opportunities for significant oral discourse declined. This decline was occasionally the result of systematic efforts by tyrants to prevent freedom of speech, but in larger part it resulted from transference of decision-making from the local level to the centralized bureaucracy of large states like Macedon, Syria, Egypt, and Rome, and from the development of Roman law, which provided equitable solutions to many problems on the basis of formulae and precedent rather than through argument from probability, ethos, and pathos.

Momigliano, 'Freedom of Speech in Antiquity', suggests that, unlike in Athens, in Rome freedom of speech was not directly connected with the more general notion of *libertas* (p. 261).

individual was limited by that of his peers and superiors; when Augustus excelled all men in authority their rights of expression shrank in proportion.[61]

It is, however, in the earliest surviving Latin handbook, the *Rhetorica ad Herennium* (written around 86 BCE), that the first full rhetorical treatment of *parrhesia* occurs, translated into Latin as *licentia*.[62] The *Ad Herennium* was, along with Cicero's *De inventione*, one of the most popular rhetorical texts of antiquity.[63] In fact, it was considered from the time of Jerome actually to be by Cicero, and though this ascription was challenged first by Lorenzo Valla and then Raphael Regius in the fifteenth century, it continued to be associated with and published alongside works by Cicero throughout the sixteenth century.[64] Its consideration of the figures, therefore, including *licentia*, underpins much Renaissance thinking on the subject.

Licentia occurs in Book IV of the *Ad Herennium*, which is devoted to style, or *elocutio*; after discussing various 'vices of composition' (*vitia in compositione*), the author moves on to the task of 'conferring distinction [*dignitas*] upon the style'.[65] *Licentia*, as might be imagined, is included as a figure of thought, and the author defines it thus: 'it is Frankness of Speech when, talking before those to whom we owe reverence or fear, we yet exercise our right to speak out, because we seem justified in reprehending them,

---

[61] Kennedy, *The Art of Rhetoric in the Roman World*, p. 302. As Kennedy points out, Augustus' restrictive effect on freedom of speech was not entirely intentional: he regularly attended and consulted the senate, but

his interest could be felt as intimidation, and through the tribunate he had veto of any action. Thus it proved difficult to attain the kind of responsible reaction he wanted. Sometimes the senate would veer wildly into abject flattery and at other times rather arbitrarily oppose him. Once he ran out of the chamber in anger at opposition and was followed by cries that senators should be allowed to say what they liked about the senate (Suet., *Aug.* 54). Constrained as it was, the senate was the only possible scene of political oratory, for the function of the assemblies became purely formal. (*The Art of Rhetoric in the Roman World*, p. 303)

[62] This translation, with its implicit association of 'liberty' with 'licence' (an association which would be exploited in the Reniassance) could be seen as evincing a basic distrust of the notion of free speech, as argued by Momigliano, 'Freedom of Speech in Antiquity', p. 261. The negative connotations of the term dominate its Renaissance definition as found in Robert Estienne's *Thesaurus Linguae Latinae* of 1573: 'Licentia, licentiae. In verbis semper in malam partem accipitur, scilicet pro temeritate loquendi quae velis. In factis in malum accipitur, nonnunquam in bonum. Est autem licentia, Impunita facultas loquendi, vel agendi quaecunque placent' ([Robert Estienne], *Thesaurus Linguae Latinae*, 3 volumes (Lugduni, 1573), volume III, sig. [C8]).

[63] See Vickers, *In Defence*, p. 28.

[64] For a discussion of the authorship and attribution, see Caplan, 'Introduction', *Ad Herennium*, pp. vii–xiv; on the importance of the text to sixteenth-century English rhetorical education, see Skinner, *Reason and Rhetoric*, pp. 32–3.

[65] *Ad Herennium* IV. xiii, pp. 274–5.

or persons dear to them, for some fault'.[66] Two examples follow, one from a deliberative, and one from a forensic, context.[67] The author goes on to consider the problem that this kind of frankness runs the risk of lessening its effect through its potential offensiveness:

> if Frank Speech of this sort seems too pungent, there will be many means of palliation, for one may immediately thereafter add something of this sort: 'I here appeal to your virtue, I call on your wisdom, I bespeak your old habit,' so that praise may quiet the feelings aroused by the frankness. As a result, the praise frees the hearer from wrath and annoyance, and the frankness deters him from error. This precaution in speaking, as in friendship, if taken at the right place, is especially effective in keeping the hearers from error and in presenting us, the speakers, as friendly both to the hearers and to the truth.[68]

The most important feature to note about this passage is the association between frankness and 'praise' (*laus*) or flattery; they are not, as in the Greek texts, directly opposed to one another, but rather held together as having usefully complementary effects. Before certain audiences, either frankness or 'praise' alone could be unhelpful, one causing 'wrath and annoyance' and the other 'error'; but when combined they prevent either. The emphasis at the end of the passage on the speaker's self-presentation is also significant: here the combination of frankness and praise is shown as useful in the construction of an *ethos*, or an attractive and persuasive character, by the orator.[69]

So far the author's treatment of *licentia* has only hinted at a potentially less frank use of the figure, largely by raising the question of excusing, or palliation. In the following paragraph he explicitly addresses the idea of duplicitous *licentia*; a 'frankness effect', one might call it, that announces itself as crossing the bounds of decorum while in fact presenting the familiar, and that serves to flatter the audience or, again, to improve the *ethos* of the

---

[66] Ibid., IV. xxxvi. 48, p. 349: 'Licentia est cum apud eos quos aut vereri aut metuere debemus tamen aliquid pro iure nostro dicimus, quod eos aut quos ii diligunt aliquo in errato vere reprehendere videamur' (p. 348).

[67] Ibid., IV. xxxvi. 48, pp. 348–51.

[68] Ibid., IV. xxxvii. 49, pp. 350–3:

Eiusmodi licentia si nimium videbitur acrimoniae habere, multis mitigationibus lenietur; nam continuo aliquid huiusmodi licebit inferre: 'Hic ego virtutem vestram quaero, sapientiam desidero, veterem consuetudinem requiro,' ut quod erit commotum licentia id constituatur laude, ut altera res ab iracundia et molestia removeat, altera res ab errato deterreat. Haec res, sicut in amicitia item in dicendo, si loco fit, maxime facit ut et illi qui audient a culpa absint, et nos qui dicimus amici ipsorum et veritatis esse videamur (pp. 350–2).

[69] On the construction of *ethos*, see ibid., I. v. 8, pp. 14–16; more generally, see Skinner, *Reason and Rhetoric*, pp. 128–33. Skinner draws attention to the *Ad Herennium*'s stress on the importance to the process of the use of invective, criticised by Quintilian (pp. 130–1).

speaker. Once again, examples are given from the assembly, or forum, and the law courts:

There is also a certain kind of frankness in speaking which is achieved by a craftier device, when we remonstrate with the hearers as they wish us to remonstrate with them, or when we say 'we fear how the audience may take' something which we know they all will hear with acceptance, 'yet the truth moves us to say it none the less'. I shall add examples of both these kinds. Of the former, as follows: 'Fellow citizens, you are of too simple and gentle a character; you have too much confidence in every one. You think that every one strives to perform what he has promised you. You are mistaken, and now for a long time you have been kept back by false and groundless hope, in your fatuity choosing to seek from others what lay in your power, rather than take it yourselves.' Of the latter kind of Frank Speech the following will be an example: 'I enjoyed a friendship with this person, members of the jury, yet of that friendship – although I fear how you are going to receive what I say, I will yet say it – you have deprived me. Why? Because, in order to win your approval, I have preferred to consider your assailant as an enemy rather than as a friend.'[70]

'Thus', concludes the author laconically, having moved in the space of a few pages from considering free speech as the 'right to speak out' to suggesting how it could be used as 'a craftier device', 'this figure called Frankness of Speech will, as I have shown, be handled in two ways: with pungency, which, if too severe, will be mitigated by praise; and with pretence, discussed above, which does not require mitigation, because it assumes the guise of Frank Speech and is of itself agreeable to the hearer's frame of mind'.[71]

In contrast to this full and revealing discussion of *licentia* in the *Rhetorica ad Herennium*, Cicero's rhetorical works barely mention the figure. In the

---

[70] *Ad Herennium*, IV. xxxvii. 49, pp. 352–3:

Est autem quoddam genus in dicendo licentiae quod astutiore ratione conparatur, cum aut ita obiurgamus eos qui audiunt quomodo ipsi se cupiunt obiurgari, aut id quod scimus facile omnes audituros dicimus nos timere quomodo accipiant, sed tamen veritate commoveri ut nihilosetius dicamus. Horum amborum generum exempla subiciemus; prioris, huiusmodi: 'Nimium, Quirites, animis estis simplicibus et mansuetis; nimium creditis uni cuique. Existimatis unum quemque eniti ut perficiat quae vobis pollicitus sit. Erratis et falsa spe frustra iam diu detinemini stultitia vestra, qui quod erat in vestra potestate ab aliis petere quam ipsi sumere maluistis.' Posterioris licentiae hoc erit exemplum: 'Mihi cum isto, iudices, fuit amicitia, sed ista tamen amicitia, tametsi vereor quomodo accepturi sitis, tamen dicam, vos me privastis. Quid ita? Quia, ut vobis essem probatus, eum qui vos oppugnabat inimicum quam amicum habere malui' (p. 352).

[71] Ibid., IV. xxxvii. 50, pp. 354–5:

Ergo haec exoratio cui licentiae nomen est, sicuti demonstravimus, duplici ratione tractabitur: acrimonia, quae si nimium fuerit aspera, mitigabitur laude; et adsimulatione, de qua posterius diximus, quae non indiget mitigationis, propterea quod imitatur licentiam et sua spontest ad animum auditoris adcommodata (p. 354).

Orator, his last rhetorical text and an attempt to justify his own oratorical style against the *Attici*, *licentia* appears briefly in a long list of the figures of thought (*sententiarum ornamenta*)[72] to be used by the ideal orator: 'he will take the liberty to speak somewhat boldly; he will even fly into a passion and protest violently'.[73] The presence of the figure in this list is significant largely as a part of Cicero's project in the *Orator* to assert the importance to the orator of *movere*, 'to arouse emotion', in contrast to the emphasis placed by the *Attici* on *docere*, 'to instruct'. *Licentia* is thus seen as an important part of such emotional appeals, and the incitement of a violent reaction as an important aspect of the figure rather than a concomitant effect.[74] Such an emphasis on the importance of 'inflaming' the audience can be traced in a number of Cicero's rhetorical works; it is discussed as something which needs to be artfully effected by the orator, but also experienced by him in order to be properly persuasive.[75] This tension between 'art' and 'nature' is crucial to rhetorical theory, but here in the context of figures of thought it sheds light specifically on the place of *licentia / parrhesia* within such theory.

The fullest exposition of his ideas on the arousing of emotions occurs in Cicero's *De oratore*, where he attempts to work out the relationship between the orator's experiencing and projecting of emotions and to avoid as far as possible the accusation that rhetoric is an art of deception (in contrast to the *Ad Herennium*'s discussion of the 'crafty device' of *licentia*). In Book II, Marcus Antonius explains to his listeners that in order to move, the speaker himself must be moved.[76]

He admits that it might be difficult to credit the orator's ability to be moved so frequently and upon the right occasion, or when delivering set-piece speeches, but argues that in delivering moving declamations the speaker will be moved by his own words.[77] This is a potentially dangerous area, since its implication that words could be selected by reason, but

---

[72] Cicero, *Orator*, in *Brutus and Orator* trans. by G. L. Hendrickson and H. M. Hubbell (London: Heinemann, 1939), xxxix. 137, pp. 306–509, pp. 408–9.

[73] Ibid., xl. 138, pp. 412–13: 'ut liberius quid audeat; ut irascatur etiam, ut obiurget aliquando'.

[74] In the *Brutus*, Cicero praises Lucius Philippus for being 'notably free and outspoken in his language' (*libertas in oratione*) (Cicero, *Brutus*, xlvii. 173, pp. 148–9). See also Cicero, *Orator*, xxxvii. 128, p. 403; xxxviii. 132, p. 405.

[75] Cf. Cicero, *Brutus*, xxiii. 93, pp. 84–5, where Cicero explains that Galba's extant writings show nothing of his skill because when he was writing rather than speaking he was not 'fired by a kind of innate emotion, which produced a style of speaking earnest, passionate, and vehement' (*incendebat efficiebatque ut et incitia et gravis et vehemens esset oratio*).

[76] Cicero, *De oratore*, trans. by E. W. Sutton and H. Rackham, 2 volumes (London: Heinemann, 1942), I, II. xlv. 189–90, pp. 333–5.

[77] Ibid., II. xlvi. 191, pp. 334–5: 'ipsa enim natura orationis eius, quae suscipitur ad aliorum animos permovendos, oratorem ipsum magis etiam quam quemquam eorum, qui audiunt, permovet' (p. 334).

then in their delivery cause the right kind of emotions to be aroused in the speaker, leads to further and further regression in the search for authenticity or artifice in the discovery of argument. Antonius responds to the possible objection that in these circumstances a degree of acting might be required by arguing that actors are themselves moved when delivering their lines, since the author was when he wrote them. Artifice and emotion cannot be separated.[78]

By thus introducing the notion of 'inspiration' from the realm of poetry to the realm of oratory, Cicero here, via Marcus Antonius, attempts to overcome ethical critiques of the orator's emotional manipulation of his audience. In this scheme, even when *licentia* is used deliberately and with what the author of the *Ad Herennium* would call 'craftiness' to achieve a certain effect, it avoids deception by itself inspiring feelings in the speaker. This discussion provides the reader with a frame of reference within which to interpret the very brief mention of free speech in Crassus' list of figures of thought in Book III of the *De oratore*, where he recommends it (like the author of the *Ad Herennium*, and as in the *Orator*) alongside anger (*iracundia*) and invective (*obiurgatio*) as 'free use of the voice and even uncontrolled vociferation to amplify the effect'.[79]

Cicero's own use of *licentia* in his early speech *Pro Sexto Roscio Amerino* is typical of the examples we have seen so far, in that his freedom is first mentioned, and excused, in the exordium, as part of his construction of an *ethos* and with a simultaneous criticism of current political conditions. He explains why he, rather than a more eminent orator, is speaking:

even if I were to say freely all that there is to be said, my words will by no means be spread abroad in the same manner and become public property. In the next place, no word of theirs can pass unnoticed, owing to their rank and dignity, nor can any rashness of speech be allowed in their case owing to their age and ripe experience; whereas, if I speak too freely, my words will either be ignored, because I have not yet entered public life, or pardoned owing to my youth, although not only the idea of pardon but even the custom of legal inquiry has now been abolished from the State.[80]

---

[78] Ibid., II. xlvi. 193, pp. 336–8.

[79] Ibid., II, III. liii. 205, pp. 164–5: 'vox quaedam libera atque etiam effrenatior augendi causa' (p. 164).

[80] Cicero, *Pro Sexto Roscio Amerino*, in *Cicero IV: The Speeches*, trans. by John Henry Freese (London: Heinemann, 1930), I. 3, pp. 111–263, pp. 123–5:

si omnia, quae dicenda sunt, libere dixero, nequaquam tamen similiter oratio mea exire atque in volgus emanare poterit; deinde quod ceterorum neque dictum obscurum potest esse propter nobilitatem et amplitudinem neque temere dicto concedi propter aetatem et prudentiam; ego si quid liberius dixero, vel occultatum esse, propterea quod nondum ad rem publicam accessi, vel ignosci adulescentiae poterit; tametsi non modo ignoscendi ratio, verum etiam cognoscendi consuetudo iam de civitate sublata est (p. 124).

A little further on in the speech, Cicero again refers to free speech in the context of an apology, this time in listing the factors that conspire to render his attempt to speak out inevitably inadequate: 'my poor abilities, my youth, and the times in which we live prevent the use of appropriate language, impressiveness, and freedom of speech'.[81]

A more manipulative use of *licentia* occurs in Cicero's celebrated speech *Pro Q. Ligario*, from which Quintilian later derived his examples of the figure. The effect of the speech was held up by Plutarch as proof of Cicero's rhetorical powers: Caesar was 'so extremely affected' by the passages on Pharsalia 'that his whole frame trembled, and he let drop some papers out of his hand'; in sum, he was 'subdued by the force of eloquence', and ended by acquitting Ligarius.[82] The entire speech is, by virtue of attempting to defend what was considered to be an indefensible cause, an instance of outspokenness; but there are also some explicitly frank individual passages. Two of these are discussed by Quintilian in his *Institutio oratoria* (see below);[83] Cicero's strategy in the first of them is implicitly to praise Caesar's clemency in the expectation that this praise will lead to mercy being exercised on this occasion as well as those he invokes. We can observe a similar manoeuvre in two other sections of the speech: the first of these is where Cicero declares that

I will speak without reserve what I feel, Caesar [*Dicam plane, Caesar, quod sentio*]. If, in the greatness of your fortunes, the clemency, in which you purposely, yes, purposely, persist – and I realize what I am saying – had not been equally great, then your triumph would have been overwhelmed in a flood of bitter mourning.[84]

Further on in the oration, he refers directly to his exploitation of Caesar's 'generosity' in allowing his *licentia*, especially towards Quintus Tubero, Ligarius' accuser; here he is also insinuating that Tubero's actions were themselves highly suspect, though he affects to avoid direct accusation (using *paralipsis / occultatio*):

Mark, Caesar, how great a measure of free speech, or rather of effrontery, your generosity accords to us. If Tubero replies that Africa, whither the Senate and the lot had sent him, would have been handed over by his father to you, I shall have

[81] Cicero, *Pro Sexto*, IV. 9, pp. 128–9: 'His de rebus tantis tamque atrocibus neque satis me commode dicere neque satis graviter conqueri neque satis libere vociferari posse intellego. Nam commoditati ingenium, gravitati aetas, libertati tempora sunt impedimento' (p. 128).
[82] Plutarch, *Cicero* 39, quoted by N. H. Watts in the introduction to *Pro Q. Ligario*, in Cicero, *The Speeches*, trans. by N. H. Watts (London: Heinemann, 1931), p. 456.
[83] Cicero, *Pro Q. Ligario*, III. 7, pp. 464–5; IV. 10, pp. 466–7.
[84] Ibid., V. 15, pp. 470–1.

no hesitation, even in your presence, to whose interest it was that he should do so, to censure such a policy in the severest language.[85]

Cicero here both flatters Caesar and asserts his own fearlessness as a speaker, a strategy designed to arouse and exploit emotional responses which may be played off against one another (anger at the speaker's frankness; pride in one's own clemency). In considering Quintilian's treatment of the figure of *licentia* the link in *Pro Q. Ligario* between flattery, manipulation, and the emotions will be developed as Quintilian explores the relations between frankness and exclamation.

Writing at the end of the first century CE, Quintilian in his *Institutio oratoria* initially mentions free speech in terms and a context which are strikingly similar to Cicero's in the *Orator* and *De oratore*. After having explicitly directed the reader to Cicero's treatment of 'figures of thought and speech' and announced that his discussion will be restricted to 'those Figures of Thought which form a departure from simple ways of making a statement', he lists others which 'are valuable features of oratory to the extent that one cannot really conceive of oratory without them'.[86] 'What emotions of the stronger kind', he asks in the course of this list, 'will there be in the absence of free and unbridled speech, anger, reproach, earnest prayers, and curses?'[87] Of these same figures, he goes on to explain that

This is where the movement and action of oratory are to be found; without these things it is dead, and there is no breath, as it were, to animate the corpse . . . Generally, indeed, these procedures are open and direct; they do not falsify themselves, they confess what they are. But they do give scope for Figures, as I said.[88]

Quintilian thus seems anxious to introduce a distinction between natural expression, or qualities of discourse, on the one hand, and figuration, on the other. The former can occur in a speech or text, but, as he points out, 'these things must not only be present, they must be deployed and varied (like the notes of a lyre) so as to charm the hearer with their combined

---

[85] Ibid., VIII. 23, pp. 478–9: 'Vide quid licentiae, Caesar, nobis tua liberalitas det vel potius audaciae' (p. 478).

[86] Quintilian, *The Orator's Education*, 9. 2. 1–2, pp. 34–5.

[87] Ibid., 9. 2. 3, pp. 36–7: 'Qui adfectus erunt vel concitati detracta voce libera et effrenatiore, iracundia, obiurgatione, optatione, execratione?' (pp. 34–6).

[88] Ibid., 9. 2. 4–5, p. 37: 'Motus est in his orationis atque actus, quibus detractis iacet et velut agitante corpus spiritu caret . . . Verum ea plerumque recta sunt, nec se fingunt sed confitentur. Admittunt autem, ut dixi, figuras' (p. 36).

music'.[89] It is this artful deployment – hence, the intention of the orator to achieve a certain effect – that distinguishes a figure from a mere quality.

Later in Book IX of the *Institutio*, Quintilian offers a more complex and extensive discussion of *licentia*, in the context of his remarks on exclamation. Here he expands on the distinction drawn above between nature and artifice:

> The Figures adapted to intensifying emotions consist chiefly in pretence. We pretend that we are angry, happy, frightened, surprised, grieved, indignant, desirous of something, or the like . . . Some people call this Exclamation, and count it among Figures of Speech. When these expressions are sincere, they do not come under our present topic; but if they are feigned and artificially produced they are undoubtedly to be regarded as Figures. The same may be said of Free Speech, which Cornificius calls Licence, and the Greeks *parrhesia*. For what is less 'figured' than true freedom? Yet flattery is often concealed under this cover. When Cicero says in *Pro Ligario*, 'After the war had started, Caesar, indeed when it was largely over, I deliberately, of my own free will, and under no compulsion, joined the forces raised against you', he is not only thinking of the interests of Ligarius; he can give no higher praise to the victor's clemency. On the other hand, in the sentence 'What was our object, Tubero, except to get the power which *he* has?' he succeeds, remarkably, in representing the cause of both sides in the war as good, but in the process courts the favour of the man whose cause had been bad.[90]

This passage is worth quoting at length partly as an example of the way in which Quintilian places himself, and his description of *licentia*, in a rhetorical tradition through both quotation and allusion – as well as the attributed quotations from Cicero's *Pro Q. Ligario*, he quotes from the orations *Pro Milone, Pro Murena, In Catilinam*, and the *Second Philippic*.[91] The other most noteworthy elements of this discussion are the proximity of *licentia* to exclamation, within a section on 'intensifying emotion', and the

---

[89] Ibid.: 'Quae cum adesse debent, tum disponenda atque varianda sunt, ut auditorem, quod in fidibus fieri videmus, omni sono mulceant'.

[90] Ibid., 9. 2. 26–9, pp. 47–9:

Quae vero sunt augendis adfectibus accommodatae figurae constant maxime simulatione. Namque et irasci nos et gaudere et timere et admirari et dolere et indignari et optare quaeque sunt similia his fingimus . . . Quod exclamationem quidam vocant ponuntque inter figuras orationis. Haec quotiens vera sunt, non sunt in ea forma de qua nunc loquimur: adsimulata et arte composita procul dubio schemata sunt existimanda. Quod idem dictum sit de oratione libera, quam Cornificius licentiam vocant, Graeci παρρησίαν. Quid enim minus figuratum quam vera libertas? Sed frequenter sub hac facie latet adulatio. Nam Cicero cum dicit pro Ligario: 'suscepto bello, Caesar, gesto iam etiam ex parte magna, nulla vi coactus consilio ac voluntate mea ad ea arma profectus sum quae erant sumpta contra te', non solum ad utilitatem Ligari respicit, sed magis laudare victoris clementiam non potest. In illa vero sententia: 'quid autem aliud egimus, Tubero, nisi ut quod hic potest nos possemus?' admirabiliter utriusque partis facit bonam causam, sed hoc eum demeretur, cuius mala fuerat (pp. 46–8).

[91] See ibid., 9. 2. 26, pp. 48–9, n. 39.

notion of freedom of speech as potentially a 'cover' for flattery. The latter is the pretext which for Quintilian distinguishes the 'figure' of free speech from 'true freedom' (*vera libertas*); thus in the *Institutio oratoria*, *licentia* is regarded as always necessarily a 'pretence' (*adsimulatione*), in the terms of the *Ad Herennium*; if it is a 'natural' exclamation then it is not a figure and does not come within the realm of rhetoric. This contrasts with both the *Ad Herennium*, which in allowing 'natural' free speech as a figure appears to collapse it into artifice, and with Cicero's vigorous attempts to extend the power of inspiration (*afflatus*) and 'naturalise' the figures of thought *tout court*.

The last Roman writer I want to consider is Tacitus. There is no direct treatment of *licentia* as a rhetorical figure in his works, but his comments on the nature of rhetoric and description of an act of censorship are of great interest in this context.[92] In the early *Dialogus*, Tacitus makes two of his speakers offer very different perspectives on frank speech. The first we are already familiar with; that boldness is 'natural', and consists more in loss of control (albeit deliberate) than in strategy – although the notion that part of the pleasure of rhetoric inheres in boldness is an addition to this outlook as it has been observed thus far. Early in the dialogue Marcus Aper says of oratory that 'Quite the most exquisite delight comes from speaking extempore, in bold fashion and even with a touch of daring.'[93]

Later, however, Maternus wants to question the very idea of oratory presented by the other speakers, arguing vehemently that effective rhetoric is directly linked to violence, social upheaval, and sedition – here a heavy note of irony enters the text. He disparages the days when oratory had a substantial place in the political conduct of the state:

Think again of the incessant public meetings, of the privilege so freely accorded of inveighing against persons of position and influence – yes, and of the glory you gained by being at daggers drawn with them, in the days when so many clever

---

[92] Tacitus' works were, as is well known, of increasing influence both stylistically and politically in early seventeenth-century England. On the uses of Tacitus in late sixteenth- and early seventeenth-century England, see, for example, Peter Burke, 'Tacitism', in *Tacitus*, ed. by T. A. Dorey (London: Routledge & Kegan Paul, 1969); Burke, 'Tacitism, Scepticism, and Reason of State', in *The Cambridge History of Political Thought 1450–1700*, ed. by J. H. Burns with the assistance of Mark Goldie (Cambridge: Cambridge University Press, 1991), pp. 479–98; David Womersley, 'Sir Henry Savile's Translation of Tacitus and the Political Interpretation of Elizabethan Texts', *Review of English Studies* 42:167 (1991): 313–42; J. H. M. Salmon, 'Seneca and Tacitus in Jacobean England', in *The Mental World of the Jacobean Court*, ed. by Linda Levy Peck (Cambridge: Cambridge University Press, 1991), pp. 169–88.

[93] Tacitus, *Dialogus de oratoribus*, in *Agricola, Germania, Dialogus*, trans. by M. Hutton and W. Peterson, revised by R. M. Ogilvie, E. H. Warmington, and M. Winterbottom (London: Heinemann, 1970), 6. 6, pp. 244–5: 'Sed extemporalis audaciae atque ipsius temeritatis vel praecipua iucunditas est.'

speakers could not let even a Scipio alone, or a Sulla, or a Pompeius, and when, taking a leaf out of the book of stage-players, they made public meetings also the opportunity of launching characteristically spiteful tirades against the leading men of the state: how all this must have inflamed the able debater and added fuel to the fire of his eloquence![94]

The slighting reference to the links between rhetoric and drama and the invocation of the 'inflamed' state of the orator seem to glance at the passages of Cicero discussed above. The fact that Maternus is himself a poet makes the irony of his remarks even more apparent.[95] 'Really great and famous oratory', Maternus goes on to complain, 'is a foster-child of licence, which foolish men called liberty, an associate of sedition, and a goad for the unbridled populace';[96] and he develops the link with disregard for social hierarchy, saying that oratory 'owes no allegiance to any' and is 'devoid of discipline'.[97] He goes on to claim that rhetoric is simply unknown in stable societies like Sparta and Crete, whereas 'Rhodes has had some orators, Athens a great many: in both communities all power was in the hand of the populace – that is to say, the untutored democracy, in fact the mob.'[98]

The embittered tone of the conclusion to the *Dialogus*, itself an 'anatomy of the decline of eloquence'[99] (where a place for eloquence is equated with freedom of speech), characterises the lengthy discussion of censorship under Tiberius found in Book IV of the *Annals*.[100] There Tacitus has a long descrip-tion of Cremutius Cordus' prosecution for licentious writing, which quotes the latter's defence of free speech and criticises the consulate's mishandling of the affair.[101] In his speech, Cremutius Cordus himself warns that it is

---

[94] Tacitus, *Dialogus*, 40. 1, pp. 340–3:

   Iam vero contiones adsiduae et datum ius potentissimum quemque vexandi atque ipsa inimicitiarum gloria, cum se plurimi disertorum ne a Publio quidem Scipione aut <L.> Sulla aut Cn. Pompeio abstinerent, et ad incessendos principes viros, ut est natura invidiae, populi quoque ut histriones auribus uterentur, quantum ardorem ingeniis, quas oratoribus faces admovebant!

[95] Earlier in the *Dialogus* Secundus asks Maternus whether he is afraid of criticism by 'court circles' for his play *Cato*, to which the latter replies that he is far from undertaking any self-censorship and that if there are any lacunae in the *Cato*, they will be supplied by his new play, *Thyestes*; see *Dialogus*, 2–3, pp. 232–7. This passage is mentioned by Kennedy, *A New History of Classical Rhetoric*, p. 191.

[96] Tacitus, *Dialogus*, 40. 2, pp. 342–3: 'est magna illa et notabilis eloquentia alumna licentiae, quam stulti libertatem vocabant, comes seditionum, effrenati populi incitmentum'.

[97] Ibid., 40. 2, pp. 342–3.

[98] Ibid., 40. 3, pp. 342–3. For a reading of these passages which also emphasises the irony of Maternus' comments, see Vickers, *In Defence*, pp. 45–7.

[99] Ibid., p. 47.

[100] On the *Dialogus* as part of a wider analysis of the decline of eloquence, see Kennedy, *A New History of Classical Rhetoric*, pp. 190–1. For an account of Roman prosecutions for outspokenness in the periods of Augustus and Tiberius (which relies rather heavily on later, and/or polemical, texts), see Frederick H. Cramer, 'Bookburning and Censorship in Ancient Rome. A Chapter from the History of Freedom of Speech', *Journal of the History of Ideas* 6:2 (April 1945): 157–96.

[101] Tacitus, *Annals*, trans. by John Jackson, 3 volumes (London: Heinemann, 1937), 2, IV. xxxiv–xxxv, pp. 58–63. Kennedy, *A New History of Classical Rhetoric*, notes that, in contrast to Tacitus,

foolish to react angrily to unwelcome texts, 'for things contemned are soon things forgotten: anger is read as a recognition',[102] and then (deploying the figure of *paralipsis*, or *occultatio*) refers in somewhat double-edged terms to the extent of the privilege of free speech among the Greeks: 'I leave untouched the Greeks; with them not liberty only but licence itself went unchastised.'[103] After he concluded his defence, Tacitus records, the condemned author 'left the senate, and closed his life by self-starvation'.[104] It was futile to burn his books, however, Tacitus explains, because 'copies remained, hidden and afterwards published: a fact which moves us the more to deride the folly of those who believe that by an act of despotism in the present there can be extinguished also the memory of a succeeding age. On the contrary', he goes on, 'genius chastised grows in authority'.[105] The undesired effect of the consulate's impolitic actions in banning Cordus' books is here stressed above any intrinsic moral value those actions might have, emphasising the need for the admonished party as well as the outspoken critic to take account of context. Similarly, Tacitus emphasises the authority that accrues to 'genius' purely because of its chastisement rather than its own worth as either criticism or expression. This awareness of the authority that free speech claims through its openness to being punished – or, as some would claim, its hope of being punished – continues to exercise the concerns of writers on rhetoric and free speech into the Renaissance and beyond.

PARRHESIA IN EARLY MODERN ENGLAND: 'THE VNPROFITABLE LIBERTY OF VNTIMELY ADMONITIONS'?

In this section I want to consider how it was that writers in early modern England attempted to translate the figure of *parrhesia* or *licentia* from its Greek and Roman rhetorical origins to the unrecognisably different

'the younger Seneca says (*Consolation to Marcia* 22. 7) that Cremutius Cordus committed suicide before his trial' (p. 188). Jonson inserted this section from the *Annals* virtually word for word in *Sejanus*; see Ben Jonson, *Sejanus, His Fall* [1603], III, ll. 407–60, in Jonson, *Volpone and Other Plays*, ed. by Lorna Hutson (Harmondsworth: Penguin, 1998), pp. 150–2.

102 Tacitus, *Annals*, IV. xxxiv, pp. 60–3.
103 Ibid., IV. xxxv, pp. 62–3: 'Non attingo Graecos, quorum non modo libertas, etiam libido impunita.'
104 Ibid.
105 Ibid: 'Libros per aediles cremandos censuere patres: set manserunt, occultati et editi. Quo magis socordiam eorum inridere libet, qui praesenti potentia credunt extingui posse etiam sequentis aevi memoriam. Nam contra punitis ingeniis gliscit auctoritas.' Writing in 1589, Francis Bacon used this passage in his advice to Elizabeth I on the handling of the Marprelate controversy, *A Wise and Moderate Discourse, concerning Church-affairs* (1641); see Annabel Patterson, *Censorship and Interpretation: The Conditions of Writing and Reading in Early Modern England*, new edition (Madison: University of Wisconsin Press, 1990), p. 18.

conditions in which they were writing. The act of will required to eradicate almost 1,500 years of history and trace a direct link between Cicero's Rome and sixteenth-century England sometimes appears staggering; but it is clear from the curricula of the newly established grammar schools that this extraordinary historical telescoping was at the heart of the humanist enterprise, and therefore of the teaching of rhetoric. Further, the polemical enterprise of vernacular publication itself frequently evinces a complicated desire both to equal (or to surpass) the ancients on their own terms, and to re-establish a domestic tradition, often with alternative connections to Roman origins.[106] The paganism of the ancients seems on the whole to have been easy either to excuse or to ignore. Equally, though, and far from surprisingly, Tudor writers were continually confronted by awkward reminders that they were not in fact living in the heyday of the Republic; these they tried to overcome in a number of ways, and many of the handbooks I will examine display a great uncertainty about how to assimilate a figure seemingly lodged firmly in the conditions of democratic assembly, even if often deployed to criticise the failings of such assemblies.[107] In this context, the works of Quintilian and Tacitus could be particularly attractive because of their handling of the problems of rhetorical and ethical action in a monarchical state, just as the use of Roman republican and Greek democratic writers could have a polemical edge.[108] Richard Mulcaster thus argued that the place of rhetoric in a monarchy was by necessity severely constrained, and that oratory was studied at the expense of logic, which would lead to true wisdom:

We do attribute to much to toungues, which do minde them more then we do matter chiefly in a monarchie: and esteeme it more honorable to speake finely, then to reason wisely.: where wordes be but praised for the time, and wisdom winnes at length. For while the *Athenian*, and *Romaine* popular gouernementes did yeald so much vnto eloquence, as one mans perswasion might make the whole assembly to sway with him, it was no meruell if the thing were in price, which commaunded: if

---

[106] See R. F. Jones, *The Triumph of the English Language: A Survey of Opinions Concerning the Vernacular from the Invention of Printing to the Restoration* (Stanford: Stanford University Press, 1953); Richard Helgerson, *Forms of Nationhood: The Elizabethan Writing of England* (Chicago: University of Chicago Press, 1992).

[107] A similar attempt – largely on the part of the upper classes – to assimilate ancient rhetoric to later conditions, which was disrupted by the use of *parrhesia* (a phenomenon which might have served as a model for some sixteenth- and seventeenth-century churchmen), occurred in the late Roman Empire, as explored by Peter Brown; see Peter Brown, *Power and Persuasion in Late Antiquity: Towards a Christian Empire. The Curti Lectures 1988* (Madison: University of Wisconsin Press, 1992), pp. 30, 42, 106–11. For more on this tradition, see chapter 2 below.

[108] On Quintilian and Tacitus as providing models for the subject in a monarchical state, see Skinner, *Reason and Rhetoric*, pp. 69–70.

wordes were of weight, which did rauish: if force of sentence were in credit, which ruled the fantsie, and bridled the hearer. Then was the toungue imperiall bycause it dealt with the people: now must it obey, bycause it deales with a prince, and be seruaunt vnto learned matter, acknowledging it to be her liege, & mistresse.[109]

More xenophobically, Roger Ascham in *The Scholemaster* and Sir Henry Wotton in a familiar letter both linked rhetoric with the dangers of Italian republicanism.[110] Wotton, writing after the imprisonment of John Hoskyns in 1614, drew attention to the limits of parliamentary privilege in a monarchical state, exasperatedly describing the speeches of the last session as 'better becoming a Senate of Venice, where the treaters are perpetual princes, than where those that speak so irreverently are so soon to return (which they should remember) to the natural capacity of subjects'.[111] Challenging the speeches' claims to 'frankness', he went on to complain about the manipulation of evaluative and moral terms in Parliament; Hoskyns, he wrote,

is in for more wit, and for licentiousness baptised freedom. For I have noted in our House, that a false or faint patriot did cover himself with the shadow of equal moderation, and on the other side, irreverent discourse was called honest liberty; so as upon the whole matter, 'no excesses want precious names'.[112]

We have seen how closely linked discussions of *parrhesia / licentia* are to an idea of the importance of oratory to civil life, and sixteenth-century English rhetoricians considered their texts to be part of an attempt to foster such involvement in the 'commonweal'.[113] Humanist scholars responsible for the establishment of grammar schools and the teaching of classical rhetoric placed a significant emphasis on the Ciceronian ideal of the *vita activa* and on rhetoric as a socially cohesive force.[114] Indeed, as Quentin Skinner has

---

[109] Richard Mulcaster, *Positions Wherein those Primitive Circumstances be Examined, which are necessarie for the training vp of children, either for skill in their booke, or health in their bodie* (London: Thomas Vautrollier for Thomas Chare, 1581), sigs. Hh^v–Hhij. I am grateful to Markku Peltonen for drawing this passage to my attention.

[110] See Roger Ascham, *The Scholemaster* [1570], ed. by John E. B. Mayor (London: George Bell and Sons, 1907), p. 142, quoted in Victoria Kahn, *Machiavellian Rhetoric from the Counter-Reformation to Milton* (Princeton: Princeton University Press, 1994), p. 272, n. 6.

[111] Wotton writing to Sir Edmund Bacon, in Logan Pearsall Smith, *The Life and Letters of Sir Henry Wotton*, 2 volumes (London, 1907), volume II, pp. 36–7. For a full discussion of debates in the 1621 Parliament, see chapter 3 below.

[112] Ibid. For more on Hoskyns, see chapter 4 below.

[113] See Arthur J. Slavin, 'Profitable Studies: Humanists and Government in Early Tudor England', *Viator* I (1970): 307–25.

[114] See Vickers, *In Defence*, pp. 270–6. On the multiple significations of the term 'humanist' in sixteenth-century usage, see Michael Pincombe, 'Some Sixteenth-Century Records of the Words *Humanist* and *Humanitian*', *RES* new series, 44:173 (1993): 1–15.

reminded us, the study of the *ars rhetorica* was indissoluble from the desire to mould the *vir civilis*, as described in Cicero's *De officiis* and Quintilian's *Institutio oratoria*: 'without a mastery of this art, it was argued, no one can hope effectively to discharge the most important duties of nobility or citizenship'.[115] As John Guy writes, the problem facing English humanists was therefore how to imagine the *vir civilis* in the world of 'service, benefits, and the *cursus honorum* prevailing at the royal court. Their objective was to define the role of the active citizen as a "counsellor" of the ruler.'[116] Based exclusively on classical precedents or mediated through the tradition of the *ars praedicandi* teaching (preaching itself providing a strong model of effective oratory), rhetoric was in post-Reformation England regarded once more as an essentially political tool, equipping the educated individual with the intellectual means necessary to participate in counsel and legislation. The acquisition of the institutional means to achieve this aim was, however, another matter. Many of the handbooks attempt, with varying degrees of success, to delineate a sphere where the reader will be able to exercise his civic abilities.[117] This might take the form of scholarly activities in the service of a noble patron, the courtly activities of such an individual, parliamentary life, or participation in local politics. Finding a convincing equivalent to the assembly or forum, though, was more than most English writers could (or dared to) manage, and many of the greatest anxieties surrounding rhetoric and free speech in this period centre on its proper place.[118] Is there a space where deliberative rhetoric can be exercised as it was by Cicero? How similar *are* the conditions of debate, and what, precisely, in these circumstances, is the sixteenth-century orator being trained for? Hobbes famously saw the origins of the Civil War as being partly the result of an intellectually successful assimilation of Greek and Roman conditions precisely through rhetorical training. Here I will examine how successful such assimilation was

---

[115] Skinner, *Reason and Rhetoric*, pp. 66–74, at p. 67.

[116] John Guy, 'The Rhetoric of Counsel in Early Modern England', in *Tudor Political Culture*, ed. by Dale Hoak (Cambridge: Cambridge University Press, 1995), pp. 292–310, at p. 294. See also Guy, 'The Henrician Age', in *The Varieties of British Political Thought, 1500–1800*, edited by J. G. A. Pocock, with the assistance of Gordon J. Schochet and Lois G. Schwoerer (Cambridge: Cambridge University Press, 1993), pp. 13–46; Skinner, *Reason and Rhetoric*, pp. 69–74. For a more extended consideration of the language of counsel in the sixteenth and early seventeenth centuries, see below, pp. 62–76.

[117] For a comparison of two contrasting ideas of the civic place of rhetoric in the sixteenth century, see Boutcher, 'Pilgrimage to Parnassus', pp. 19–46.

[118] For a persuasive account of Milton's *Areopagitica* as participating in this argument over the assimilation of classical (specifically Greek) ideas about participative democracy to early modern England, see David Norbrook, '*Areopagitica*, Censorship, and the Early Modern Public Sphere', in *The Administration of Aesthetics: Censorship, Political Criticism, and the Public Sphere*, ed. by Richard Burt (Minneapolis: University of Minnesota Press, 1994), pp. 3–33.

in the handbooks themselves, specifically in the case of *parrhesia*.[119] I will concentrate on the sixteenth-century handbooks since it is they, and their classical sources, that determine the rhetorical understanding of *parrhesia* in the seventeenth century.

With rhetoric being linked so easily to democratic or republican politics, it seems clear that one problem in translating *parrhesia* to sixteenth-century England might be its potential danger to rigid social stratification. Even in those texts like Philodemus' *Peri parrhesias*, devoted to the exercise of frankness between social unequals, it was deemed essential that both parties should base their delivery and acceptance of frank advice on good faith in the intentions of the counsellor / friend to advise and of the advised willingly to accept such advice. Clearly, the rhetorical explanations of the Roman rhetorics complicate this severely, and surround such relations with even more uncertainty than is already present. I have shown how in some ancient Greek texts free speech is associated with social standing, and used to reinforce existing hierarchies; but it is important to remember that these texts were not simply representing social realities. Rather, they were engaged in acts of representation designed in their turn to reinforce such hierarchies. They thus reveal the extent to which the restriction of free speech is always active and ongoing. Here too the struggle over definitions is apparent: one person's frank counsel is another's sedition, as Demosthenes was well aware. The risks of advocating *parrhesia* to the readers of sixteenth-century rhetoric handbooks should be clear enough: how far should an author appear to advocate the use of bold language before others *as if* the speaker and his audience were grounding their interaction on a previously established set of consensual protocols when the place of duty as against right in giving advice was violently contested, and the institutional place of the counsellor increasingly clearly delimited? Perhaps especially in the realm of secular discourse, it is problematic to advise the pursuit and utterance of unwelcome

---

[119] Hobbes argued that the anti-royalists had been

> so educated, as that in their youth having read the books written by famous men of the ancient Grecian and Roman commonwealths concerning their polity and great actions; in which books the popular government was extolled by that glorious name of liberty, and monarchy disgraced by the name of tyranny; they became thereby in love with their forms of government. And out of these men were chosen the greatest part of the House of Commons, or if they were not the greatest part, yet by advantage of their eloquence, were always able to sway the rest.

> (Thomas Hobbes, *Behemoth: The History of the Causes of the Civil Wars of England*, in *The English Works of Thomas Hobbes of Malmesbury*, ed. by William Molesworth, 11 volumes (London, 1839–45), volume VI, p. 168, cited in Norbrook, 'Rhetoric, Ideology, and the Elizabethan World Picture', p. 161, n. 8.)

'truths', when a speaker is unlikely to have the power to decide what is true and what out of season.

As a result, a text offering a schematic account of the components of a parrhesiastic relationship and a pragmatic description of the figure of *parrhesia* in use could be particularly valuable. It could also improve our understanding of how this figure became a key term and conceptual tool in the process of political negotiation and counsel. Moreover, it offers a counterbalance to the rather stark treatments of some rhetorics and picks up the threads of one alternative tradition of thinking about *parrhesia* which I discussed on pp. 16–25 above.

Such a text, a key contribution to the dispute over how true frankness motivated by *amicitia / philia* can be told apart from either licentiousness or flattery, was Plutarch's essay from the *Moralia* on 'How to Tell a Flatterer from a Friend' ('Quomodo adulator ab amico internoscatur'), translated in 1603 by Philemon Holland.[120] There Plutarch notes that frankness (he uses the term *parrhesia* throughout) is the mark of true friendship, but that it can easily be usurped by the flatterer: just as the flatterer is an expert at imitating all the other signs of friendship,

> in this point also he will not seem to come short, nor leave it behind for want of imitation; but after the fashion of fine and excellent cooks, who use to serve up tart, bitter and sharp sauces together with sweet and pleasant meats, for to divert and take away the satiety and fulness which soon followeth them, these flatterers also use a certain kind of plain and free speech [παρρησίαν]; howbeit, neither sincere and natural is it, nor profitable, but (as we commonly say) from teeth outward, or (as it were) beckoning and winking slightly with the eye under the brows, not touching the quick, but tickling aloft only, to no purpose.[121]

In this essay Plutarch shows himself to be fully aware of the range of rhetorical exercises a flatterer will attempt in order to make his frankness seem authentic, and he attempts throughout to make clear what the crucial

---

[120] See Plutarch, *Moralia*, trans. by Frank Cole Babbitt, 14 volumes (London: Heinemann, 1927), I, 264–395; Plutarch, *The Philosophie, Commonlie called, the Morals*, trans. by Philemon Holland (London: Dent, n.d., ?1911), pp. 36–101. On *amicitia / philia* as necessary conditions for the exercise of *parrhesia* and counsel, see Brown, *Power and Persuasion*, p. 61; Guy, 'The Rhetoric of Counsel', p. 294.

[121] Plutarch, *The Philosophie*, p. 43. Equally, Plutarch writes, frankness can descend into licentiousness even when attempting to offer advice:

> the very comical poets in old time, exhibited and represented to the theatres many grave, austere, and serious remonstrances, and those pertaining to policy and government of state: but there be scurrile speeches intermingled among, for to move laughter, which (as one unsavoury dish among many other good viands) mar all their liberty of speech and the benefit thereof; so it is vain and doth no good at all. (*The Philosophie*, p. 85)

differences are between the two in time, place, and subject. It could be argued that he also somewhat audaciously uses the occasion of the essay to flatter his addressee, Prince Philopappus. The text is not only a reflection on how to identify the true friend, but also an attempt to persuade Philopappus that Plutarch is that true friend. It thus implies that Philopappus is able to recognise the difference between a flatterer and a friend, and that this ability will enable him to select Plutarch. Plutarch therefore ingratiates himself with his addressee precisely by playing on the problems of recognition and negotiation to be found in the discourse of flattery and frankness that his essay apparently untangles.[122] 'How to Tell a Flatterer from a Friend' was highly influential on the 'mirror to princes' literature of the Renaissance in its applicability to both the counsellor and the prince: Holland emphasises in the 'Summary' preceding his translation that the essay 'I assure you is to be well read and marked in these days of all persons, but those especially who are advanced above others in worldly wealth or honourable place.'[123] Erasmus appended a Latin translation of the Greek text, addressed to Henry VIII, to his *Education of a Christian Prince* of 1516, and Sir Thomas Elyot in turn translated it into English at the king's request; it is referred to in Castiglione's *Il Cortegiano* (first published in Italian in 1528 and in Sir Thomas Hoby's English translation as *The Book of the Courtier* in 1561), and in Elyot's *The Book Named The Governor* of 1531.[124]

Perhaps the most rhetorically alert text to draw on Plutarch's essay was Erasmus' *Parabolae*, or 'Parallels' (1514). This is a virtuoso exercise in the art of analogy using examples drawn from Plutarch, Aristotle, and Pliny, including several taken from Plutarch's essay in the *Moralia*. Erasmus describes the *parabola* as 'nothing more than a metaphor writ large',[125] and draws attention to its importance as a rhetorical weapon: 'deprive the orators of their arsenal of metaphor', he writes, 'and all will be thin and

[122] See Engberg-Pedersen, 'Plutarch to Prince Philopappus on How to Tell a Flatterer from a Friend'; for an analogous instance concerning Isocrates, *Epistles* 3, see David Konstan, *Friendship in the Classical World* (Cambridge: Cambridge University Press, 1997), pp. 93–5 and (on Plutarch) pp. 98–105.

[123] Plutarch, *The Philosophie*, p. 37.

[124] See Erasmus, *The Education of a Christian Prince and Panegyric for Archduke Philip of Austria*, trans. by Neil M. Cheshire, Michael J. Heath, and Lisa Jardine, ed. by Lisa Jardine (Cambridge: Cambridge University Press, 1997), pp. xii–xiii; Count Baldassare Castiglione, *The Book of the Courtier*, trans. by Sir Thomas Hoby, ed. by Virginia Cox (London: Dent, 1994), p. 81; Sir Thomas Elyot, *The Book Named the Governor*, ed. by S. E. Lehmberg (London: Dent, 1962), praises and recommends Erasmus' *Education* at pp. 39–40 and refers to Plutarch's essay at pp. 154–5.

[125] Erasmus, *Parallels. Parabolae sive similia*, trans. and annotated by R. A. B. Mynors, in *Collected Works 23: Literary and Educational Writings I: Antibarbari / Parabolae*, ed. by Craig R. Thompson (Toronto: University of Toronto Press, 1978), pp. 122–277, p. 130.

dull'.[126] In his dedicatory epistle to Pieter Gillis, a eulogy of the humanist friendship they enjoy, Erasmus offers an example of the figure which shows how such friendship can be strengthened or tainted by the proper handling of *parrhesia* and flattery:

Hemlock is poisonous to man, and wine neutralises hemlock; but if you put an admixture of wine into your hemlock, you make its venom much more immediate and quite beyond treatment, because the force and energy of the wine carries the effect of the poison more rapidly to the vital centres. Now merely to know such a rare fact in nature is surely both elegant and interesting as information. Suppose then that one were to adapt this by saying that adulation poisons friendship instantly, and that what neutralises that poison is the habit of speaking one's mind, which Greek calls *parrhesia*, outspokenness. Now, if you first contaminate this freedom of speech and put a touch of it into your adulation, so that you are flattering your friend most insidiously while you most give the impression of perfect frankness, the damage is by now incurable.[127]

Sounding rather pleased with himself for this example (drawn from Plutarch, *Moralia* 61b),[128] Erasmus asks Gillis, 'would this not win credit as an ingenious application of the parallel? I think it would.'[129] He goes on to use it, slightly rephrased, in the main text of the *Parabolae*, in the course of a series of parallels concerning the dangers of flattery to friendship and the flatterer's abuse of frankness.[130] The text demands consideration in the context of this survey of rhetorical uses of *parrhesia* in the Renaissance for a number of reasons: as well as showing, as I have mentioned, a full appreciation of both the possibility and the dangers of mixing flattery and frankness, Erasmus places the notion within a rhetorical and a political tradition. The use of Plutarch's essay associates Erasmus' parallel and his series of examples of the power of the flattery-and-frankness cocktail with the self-advertisement of the counsellor as one who gives timely advice with genuine openness. Erasmus himself may have hoped to be appointed tutor to Prince Charles (later the Emperor Charles V), for whom he wrote *The*

---

[126] Erasmus, *Parabolae*, p. 131. Erasmus writes of the text that 'it will not be found out of the way to attach this book to my *Adagia* or, if so preferred, to my *Copia* as a kind of supplement, since it has so much in common with the former and contributes eminently to abundance of style' (p. 134).

[127] Ibid., pp. 131–4.

[128] See ibid., p. 131, n. 72; Plutarch, *Moralia*, pp. 326–7; Plutarch, *The Philosophie*, pp. 67–8.

[129] Erasmus, *Parabolae*, p. 134.

[130] See ibid., p. 146:

If a man takes neat wine, which is normally valuable against hemlock poisoning, and mixes it with the hemlock, he makes the poison invincible, because the heat of the wine carries the force of the poison straight to the heart. Similarly the toady, who knows that freedom to speak out is a specific against flattery, mixes freedom and flattery together, and so makes his flattery more dangerous.

See further pp. 146–7 for other parallels using the example of the 'toady'.

Education of a Christian Prince four years after the *Parabolae* appeared.[131] Placing himself in the tradition of counsel in a text devoted to the provision of rhetorical armaments, Erasmus hopes to ensure that the humanist reader will draw lessons for his conduct of eloquence and friendship from the work, lessons which can in turn be applied in counselling princes. It is becoming clear that *parrhesia* is, by the sixteenth century, a key figure and even a guiding concept for the conduct of political life through negotiation and dialogue – and can thus be used polemically to urge for those values to be necessary components of politics. The complex of ideas and attitudes embedded in Plutarch's discussion of flattery and in the more sceptical Roman treatments of *parrhesia* is found in many later works, one of the most notable of which is William Cavendish's *Discourse against Flatterie*, written when he was under the tutelage of Thomas Hobbes.[132] Cavendish uses the analogy of sweetened poison to describe flattery or 'disguising dissimulation, with the pretence of libertie, and freedome in speech', and warns strongly against the tendency of flatterers to 'make the world beleeue . . . that they be the only men that giue good and honest aduice, and discreet cautions'.[133] Flatterers, he goes on to lament, often triumph over the most honest advisers by this tactic, analysed in such detail by Plutarch:

they will colour their *Flattery* with the shew of *Friendship*, vsurping the offices, behauiour, nay euen carrying the name & counterfet of amity so artificially, in taking vpon them the highest part of friendship, wh^ch is free reprehension, that the shadow is hard to be distinguished from the substance.[134]

The tendency to disguise flattery as freedom of speech is the most dangerous vice, says Cavendish towards the end of his treatise, echoing the *Ad Herennium* and Quintilian's *Institutio*, and giving an example from Tacitus:

Tacitus also recites an example, though somwhat more grosse, that may bee referred to this sort of *Flatterers*. When the Emperour *Tiberius* was in the *Senate*, one rose vp, and said, it was fit that euery man should speake freely, and in matters belonging to the Common-wealth, no man ought to hold his peace: *Tiberius* and all the *Senate* were in expectation what so bold a preamble would produce, and then with the Prouerbe, *Parturiunt montes, nascetur ridiculus mus*, saith he, *Caesar*, there is a fault wee all blame you for, though none dare take the hardnes to tell you of it, you spend your self too much in caring for vs, wearing your body both day and night

[131] See Erasmus, *The Education of a Christian Prince*, ed. by Jardine, p. x.
[132] [William Cavendish, second Earl of Devonshire], *A Discourse against Flatterie*, in *Horae Subseciuae, Observations and Discourses* (London, 1620).
[133] Ibid., sigs. Ff3^v, Ff5^r.   [134] Ibid., sigs. Hh8^v–Ii^r. On the success of flatterers, see sig. Ff6^v.

in labours for the *Republike*, not valuing your owne safety and health, in regard of our happinesse and prosperity. This kinde of *Flattery* that goes in the habit of franknesse and libertie of speech, is very obscure.[135]

Writers on *parrhesia* in the sixteenth century offer two major responses to the fears concerning flattery and the dangers of outspokenness that I have discussed above. These could be summarised as a concentration on either content or style – matter or manner, as the rhetoricians might have put it. That is, the writer either follows his ancient sources in defining *parrhesia* as boldness of speech and suggests where or why it might occur, or he diverges from them and defines it as being a figure of excusing, essentially an apology for speaking out, rather than the act of speaking out itself – the *Ad Herennium*'s methods of palliation (see above, p. 29). The latter is much easier to define as a rhetorical figure, figures of words and sentences always being more susceptible to intelligible explanation than the figures of thought: a writer can fairly easily suggest an example or typical formulation. The treatment of the figure may still be lent a positive or negative tone, but it is always inevitably less dangerous than what we could call the 'traditional' definition of *parrhesia*. This requires the writer to justify speaking out, to suggest motives for it and, if possible, to give examples of where it might take place. It is particularly troublesome given that, perhaps in response to criticisms of rhetoric's openness to being used for deception, hardly any early modern authors explicitly admit the potential for flattery into their treatment of *parrhesia*. The possibility of using either form of *parrhesia* in a 'politic' fashion is certainly written into several texts, as I shall argue below – but it remains implicit in the majority of cases, usually being suggested by examples rather than in the main text.[136] They thus both avoid arriving at and suggest the possibility of a position which could be interpreted as endorsing outspokenness to one's social superiors, and could slip into the crimes of uttering seditious words or of *scandalum magnatum*. I will now survey a range of English rhetorics in the late sixteenth century, considering their discussions of *parrhesia* in the light of these straitened circumstances.[137]

---

[135] Ibid., sigs. Kk6ʳ–Kk6ᵛ; cf. sigs. Kk6ᵛ–Kk7ʳ.

[136] The only explicit description of *parrhesia*'s potential for flattery or duplicity that I have found in a rhetorical text of this period is in a Continental work (though one printed in England), Susenbrotus' *Epitome troporum ac schematvm et grammaticorum & rhetorum* (London: Gerard Dewes, 1562), sig. Eiiᵛ. More material on *parrhesia* that would have been available to English readers was collected in Lycosthenes, *Apothegmata* (Paris, 1560), pp. 588–613. I am grateful to Peter Mack for this reference. Vossius, in his *Oratorium institutionum* (1616), wonders whether *parrhesia* is a figure properly so called at all; I am indebted to Richard Serjeantson for drawing my attention to this text.

[137] There are two technical characteristics of the early modern reception of classical rhetoric which deserve some consideration in terms of their treatment of *parrhesia*. Firstly, emphasis in English (as

The first major English treatise on rhetoric which adopted a recognisably Ciceronian approach to the subject was also the first to mention *parrhesia*: Thomas Wilson's *The Arte of Rhetorique* (1553) (compiled largely from Quintilian in its first two books, and turning to Cicero for its third book, on 'Elocution').[138] 'Freenesse of speeche' comes in the section of this third book devoted to 'exornation of sentences'; Wilson places its uses firmly in the context of counsel and admonition and, like Demosthenes, he also regards it as an antidote to flattery:

> [margin: *Libera vox*] Freenesse of speeche, is when we speake boldely, & without feare, euen to the proudest of them, whatsoeuer we please, or haue list to speake. Diogenes herein did excel, and feared no man when he sawe iust cause to say his mynde. This worlde wanteth suche as he was, and hath ouer many suche as neuer honest man was, that is to say, flatterers, fawners, and southers of mennes sayinges.[139]

The implicit play on words in the last sentence here maintains the contrast between the flattering 'soother of men's sayings' and the bold 'sooth sayer' who, like Diogenes, is not afraid to say whatever he 'list[s] to speake'. The choice of Diogenes as an exemplum of free speech, and the phrasing of Wilson's definition, suggest that *libera vox* here has more to do with the assertion of the duty to speak the 'truth' whatever the circumstances than it does with context-dependent counsel; or, indeed, with flattery and deception.[140] This is potentially a dangerous position to take, as I have argued above, since its stress on the ethical duty to speak the truth could

---

well as many Continental) handbooks was increasingly placed on *elocutio* as the most important of the five parts: lengthy and elaborate catalogues of schemes and tropes were *de rigueur* (see Vickers, *In Defence*, pp. 282–3). We have seen how frequently *licentia* appears in Roman treatises in the context of emotional appeal, and here too sixteenth-century texts display a significant shift, giving even greater prominence to *movere*, at the expense of *docere* and *delectare*, than their Roman sources (see Vickers, *In Defence*, pp. 276–81). One might, then, expect these treatises to display some considerable interest in a figure such as *parrhesia*, repeatedly described as having an inflaming effect on the passions of an audience.

[138] See G. H. Mair, 'Introduction', in Thomas Wilson, *The Arte of Rhetorique*, ed. by G. H. Mair (Oxford: Clarendon Press, 1909), pp. xix–xx; hereafter Wilson, *The Arte of Rhetorique* [1560]. Wilson's work was preceded by Leonard Cox, *The Arte or Crafte of Rhetoryke* (London, ?1530), a translation of Apthonius' *Progymnasmata*, and Sherry, *A Treatise of Schemes and Tropes*. On Wilson, see further Albert J. Schmidt, 'Thomas Wilson and the Tudor Commonwealth: An Essay in Civic Humanism', *Huntington Library Quarterly* 23 (1959–60): 49–60; Mark E. Wildermuth, 'The Rhetoric of Wilson's *Arte*: Reclaiming the Classical Heritage for English Protestants', *Philosophy and Rhetoric* 22:1 (1989): 43–58.

[139] Thomas Wilson, *The Arte of Rhetorique* (London: Richard Grafton, 1553; facsimile Gainesville, FL: Scholars' Facsimiles and Reprints, 1962), sig. Ddii^v.

[140] Wilson's stories about Diogenes, Cicero, and the ancients were taken from Nicholas Udall's translation of Erasmus' *Apothegmes* (1542); see Mair, 'Introduction', Wilson, *The Arte of Rhetorique*, p. xxvi.

be difficult to sustain alongside social propriety or decorum. It is, however, congruent with Wilson's emphasis on his own boldness both in publishing the book at all and in his defence of it before a Roman court, in the *Prologue* to the 1560 edition. Wilson begins by describing the 'boldnesse' of those 'that seeke without feare to sett foorth their knowledge: & suffer their doinges to be sene, they care not of whom'.[141] He then describes his arrest in Rome as a heretic (on the charge of being the author of *The Arte of Rhetorique* and *The Rule of Reason*), and his conduct before his judges: 'I tooke such courage, and was so bolde, that the Iudges then did much maruaile at my stoutnesse.'[142] *The Arte of Rhetorique* was published the year after Mary's accession to the throne, and soon afterwards Wilson fled England; it was during his religious exile that this arrest took place. The passage on *parrhesia* should thus be considered, at least in part, in the context of religious and political change in England: the duty to speak the truth is an imperative of conscience which could have drastically different results for a Protestant such as Wilson at the time the book was written (in the reign of Edward VI), published (1553), or reissued (1560).[143]

Another perspective could be taken on Wilson's definition, however, where 'speaking truth' might be read as 'individual expression'. It is worth remembering that Diogenes acquired a certain popularity precisely because of his tendency to 'say his minde', and that frank speech is perhaps for Wilson (and his readers) so immediately recognisable as admirable that it becomes a guarantor of a virtuous reputation – and can be manipulated as such.[144] Here there is a similarity to the position taken in the orations by Isocrates and Demosthenes discussed above (pp. 21–5); and it is significant that Wilson would go on to translate the latter's *Olynthiacs* and *Philippics*. In that translation, published in 1570, Wilson deals explicitly – and forcefully – with the problem of cultural difference facing the humanist admirer of Greek oratory, arguing in his 'Preface to the Reader' that 'neuer did glasse so truely represent a mans face, as Demosthenes doth shewe the worlde to vs, and as it was then, so is it now, and will be so still, tyll the consummation and ende of all things shall be'.[145] Wilson goes on to stress

---

[141] Wilson, *The Arte of Rhetorique* [1560], sig. Aiiii.   [142] Ibid., sig. Av.

[143] On Wilson's *Arte* as part of a wider attempt to reclaim pagan rhetoric for the *ars praedicandi*, see Wildermuth, 'The Rhetoric of Wilson's *Arte*'.

[144] The reference to Diogenes aside, Wilson's phrasing is very similar to that of the *Ad Herennium*, while his placing of the figure directly before 'stomacke griefe', or *iracundia*, then *deprecatio*, and *conciliatio*, shows a debt to Cicero's *De oratore* and *Orator*.

[145] Demosthenes, *The Three Orations of Demosthenes chiefe Orator among the Grecians, in fauour of the Olynthians, a people in Thracia, now called Romania: with those his fower Orations titled expressely & by name against Philip of Macedonie: most needefull to be redde in these daungerous dayes, all of*

the importance of his translation to the crucial concerns of the ethical and political life: Demosthenes' style and message remain pertinent, he argues, since

The Deuill neuer ceaseth from the beginning of the worlde to make diuision betwixt Countrie and Countrie, to stirre ciuill warre, to emboulden the commons agaynst their superiors, to put euill thoughts into Counsellors heades, and to make people ambicious and couetous, and to corrupt the hearts euen of the uery messengers and preachers of Gods word, continuing his practyse styll in all places wyth all men.[146]

The translations of the *Third Olynthiac* and the third and fourth *Philippics* share the concern of the *Arte of Rhetorique*'s passage on *parrhesia* with free speech as a vital component of counsel, itself necessary to the maintenance of the state, and with the dangers of flattery. Marginal comments to the *Third Philippic* note that 'Bolde speach vpon good cause deserues fauor' and that 'Free speaking forbidden, bringeth daunger to the state', while the margin of the *Fourth Philippic* outlines 'Thre chiefe poynts fit for Counsellors, 1. to be bolde, 2. plaine, and 3. faythfull.'[147] While the brief discussion of *parrhesia* in the *Arte of Rhetorique* touches on the figure's most important aspects in its classical definition (particularly in what we could call the 'anti-flattery' tradition), the translations of Demosthenes display the figure in operation and make an even stronger case for the contexts in which it could operate: those where the citizen is compelled to offer bold counsel to the prince. Demosthenes' style and his concerns are seen as equally necessary for and applicable to fifth-century Athens or the dangerous years around 1570 in Wilson's declaration that he was

> *them that loue their Countries libertie, and desire to take warning for their better auayle, by example of others,* trans. by Thomas Wilson (London: Henrie Denham, 1570; facsimile Amsterdam: Theatrum Orbis Terrarum, 1968), sig. **j. In his dedication to Sir William Cecil, Wilson explains that he was inspired to the task of translating Demosthenes by the example of John Cheke, who had taught him at Padua (sigs. [*]–*j[v]).

146 Ibid. At sigs. *iv[v] and Ai Wilson favourably compares Demosthenes to Cicero for his 'playne familiar maner of writing and speakyng' (sig. *iv[v]).

147 Demosthenes, *The Three Orations*, sigs. Kiii[v]–Kiv, Piiii[v]. In the 'Argument' which prefaces the *Third Olynthiac* Wilson explains Demosthenes' intentions thus:

> with the people he blameth the Orators and Counsellors, that seekes onely to serue the peoples humor, and so to marre all thereby in the ende . . . [he shows] howe daungerous persons in the common weale are those wicked Counsellors and licencious people that will follow their own fansie, and haue their owne will in all thinges. (sig. Eii[v])

> One striking instance of the kind of linguistic updating that accompanies Wilson's belief in Demosthenes' continuing relevance is his translation in the *Third Olynthiac* of 'δῆμος' ('the people') as 'the Commons' (sig. Fiii).

caried streightways (I trust by Gods good motion) to make certaine of [his translations] to be acquainted so nigh as I coulde with our Englishe tongue, aswell for the aptnesse of the matter, and needefull knowledge now at this time to be had: as also for the right notable, and most excellent handling of the same.[148]

The only English rhetoric other than Wilson's which treats *parrhesia* solely as boldness of speech is Abraham Fraunce's Ramist handbook *The Arcadian Rhetorike* (1588).[149] Like Wilson, Fraunce places *parrhesia* among figures of sentences, of which he writes that they 'are more forcible & apt to persuade than those of words, which be rather pleasant and fit to delight. Generallie, as in tropes there is a kinde of delicacie, so in these of sentences, appeareth force and maiestie.'[150] There appears to be a suggestion here that Fraunce would link figures of words with 'pleasing' and thus more with flattery and apology, where some of his fellow rhetoricians would choose to place *parrhesia*. Choosing to consider it a figure of sentences, however, Fraunce, like Quintilian, considers it as a variety of exclamation:[151] 'Licence also & libertie of speech seemeth to be a certaine exclamation; when in the presence of those to whome otherwise we owe dutie and reuerence, wee speake boldly and confidently.'[152] 'For examples', he continues, 'let these suffice till I call to minde better', and lists relevant passages from the set of key classical and recent vernacular texts which are his reference points throughout the work: the *Iliad*; the *Aeneid*; Sidney's 'Old' *Arcadia*; Tasso's *Gerusalemme Liberata*; Sallust, and Boscàn.[153] Of these examples, the two most interesting are those taken from Virgil and Sidney; here, unlike Wilson, Fraunce allows a certain potential for dissimulation in *parrhesia*. His chosen passage from the *Aeneid* is taken from Book II, where Aeneas recounts the story of the fall of Troy to Dido: the Greek traitor Sinon tells Priam that the Trojan horse is a religious offering and that if it is taken within the city's walls 'Asia would even advance in mighty war to the walls of Pelops, and such would be the doom awaiting

---

[148] Demosthenes, *The Three Orations*, sig. [*]ᵛ.

[149] Following Omer Talon's *Rhetoricae Libri Duo* (Paris, 1545) – translated by Dudley Fenner in *The Artes of Logike and Rhetorike* (1584), on whom see below pp. 52–3 – Fraunce allows rhetoric only two parts in comparison to the Ciceronian five: 'Eloqution and Pronuntiation', or *elocutio* and *actio*. See Abraham Fraunce, *The Arcadian Rhetorike* (London: Thomas Orwin, 1588; facsimile Menston: Scolar Press, 1969), sig. A2.

[150] Fraunce, *The Arcadian Rhetorike*, sigs. E4ᵛ–[E5].

[151] Fraunce lists the following 'diuers affections' that may be aroused by exclamation: 'wonder and admiration' (*The Arcadian Rhetorike*, sig. [E5]); 'despaire' (sig. [E5]ᵛ); 'wishing' (sig. [E7]); 'indignation' (sig. [E7]ᵛ); 'derision' (sig. [E8]ᵛ); 'protestation or obtestation' (sig. F); 'griefe and miserie' (sig. Fᵛ); 'pitie and commiseration' (sig. F2), and 'cursing' (sig. F2ᵛ).

[152] Ibid., sig. [F4]ᵛ.

[153] For the full references to examples of *parrhesia* taken from these works, see Abraham Fraunce, *The Arcadian Rhetorike*, ed. by Ethel Seaton (Oxford: Basil Blackwell, 1950), p. 134.

our offspring.'[154] Of the four passages from Sinon's tale, three are quite obviously exclamatory, or describe exclamations,[155] while the fourth is more closely linked to other instances of *parrhesia* we have encountered: there Sinon declares to Priam that 'whatever befalls, I will tell thee all truly'.[156] The key terms *liber-* or *licent-* that are found in Roman discussions of the figure do not appear here, and Fraunce seems to be concentrating on the importance to *parrhesia* of its self-announcement. The most telling feature of this example, though, is that it is part of a discourse not just intended to persuade, but to deceive Sinon's Trojan audience. 'Frankness' is shown in the context of one of the most celebrated acts of deception in literature, and thus removed, when read in this larger context, from the realm of exclamation in which Fraunce initially places it.[157] While Sinon's words serve as adequate examples of exclamation if they are read out of context – or rather, in the new context given them by Fraunce – when their origin is recalled they are revealed to be not simply exclamations performed in order to deceive, but part of an entirely duplicitous narrative.

While not so shocking as the Virgilian example, Gynecia's confession in the fifth and last Act of the 'Old' *Arcadia* shows a similarly troubled idea of the connections between frankness and truth, though here the speaker's intention is truthful.[158] Gynecia's speech is certainly an exclamation, proceeding from guilt and emotional turmoil, uttered before an important person (Euarchus the judge), and its effect is to arouse the emotions of her audience: Sidney describes 'the whole people concurring in a lamentable cry', when she concludes – 'so much had Gynecia's words and behaviour stirred their hearts to a doleful compassion'.[159] This more recognisable moment of 'natural' *parrhesia* is soon to be retrospectively questioned, however, when the supposedly dead Basilius revives, revealing that

[154] Virgil, *Aeneid*, trans. by H. R. Fairclough, 2 volumes (London: Heinemann, 1935), volume I, Book II, ll. 57–198, pp. 298–309; ll. 192–4, pp. 306–7:

> sin manibus vestris vestram ascendisset in urbem,
> ultro Asiam magno Pelopea ad moenia bello
> venturam, et nostros ea fata manere nepotes.
> (p. 306)

[155] Ibid., Book II, ll. 94–6, pp. 300–1.

[156] Ibid., Book II, ll. 77–8, pp. 298–9:

> Cuncta equidem tibi, rex, fuerit quodcumque, fatebor vera. (p. 298)

[157] For evidence of Sinon's currency in the sixteenth century as an example of the dangerous powers of rhetoric, see William Shakespeare, *The Rape of Lucrece* [1594], ed. by John Roe (Cambridge: Cambridge University Press, 1992), ll. 1500–68, pp. 214–17.

[158] Fraunce's example is found in Sir Philip Sidney, *The Old Arcadia*, ed. by Katherine Duncan-Jones (Oxford: Oxford University Press, 1985), p. 330.

[159] Ibid., p. 331.

the drink he had received was neither (as Gynecia first imagined) a love potion nor (as it was after thought) a deadly poison, but a drink made by notable art, and as it was thought not without natural magic, to procure for thirty hours such a deadly sleep as should oppress all show of life.[160]

The 'truth' of an exclamation or an instance of free speech is often, as we have seen, difficult to assess, so Fraunce might be forgiven for selecting such a passage as this to exemplify *parrhesia* – especially if we bear in mind his caveat that they only serve 'till I call to minde better'. But the instability of both in relation to the kind of admonitory frankness that Fraunce focuses on in his definition tends to emphasise the deceptive and uncontrollable aspects of *parrhesia* rather than its place in effective civic discourse. The figure we find in *The Arcadian Rhetorike* is more likely to lead the reader to distrust frankness that draws attention to itself than to aspire to it – unless their motives are highly questionable.

Fraunce's description of *parrhesia* as a kind of exclamation is supported, as I have shown, by Quintilian. However, a likely contemporary source for his Ramist discussion is Dudley Fenner's *The Artes of Logike and Rhetorike* (1584), itself a translation of the *Rhetoricae libri duo* by Ramus' friend and associate Omer Talon (Audomarus Talaeus).[161] Fenner, a godly minister, takes his examples from Scripture and in his section on *parrhesia* selects texts which emphasise the calling of the evangelists to bear witness to the truth.[162] In the process of listing the variety of emotions which can be aroused by exclamation, Fenner writes that 'sometimes here is vsed a certaine liberty of speech, wherein is a kinde of secrete crying out: As, pet.3. Act saith: *Ye men of Israel heare these words.* And Paul. 1. Cor. 11. *Would to God you could suffer a little my foolishnes, and indeede ye suffer me.*'[163] Fenner's examples maintain the idea of *parrhesia* as bold speech, but he concentrates less on the apostles' compulsion to speak in the face of danger than on the potential effect on their audience. In this way he plays down both the status of religious free speech as a public challenge to secular power (a subject I will address in

---

[160] Ibid., p. 359.

[161] The phrasing of the two works is occasionally strikingly similar: Fenner writes of a figure of a sentence that 'it hath in it a certain manly maiestie, which farre surpasseth the softe delicacy of the former figures'; cf. Fraunce, *Arcadian Rhetorike*, sig. [E5], quoted p. 50 above. See Dudley Fenner, *The Artes of Logike and Rhetorike, plainlie set foorth in the Englishe tounge, easie to be learned and practised: together with examples for the practise of the same, for Methode in the gouernment of the familie, prescribed in the word of God: And for the whole in the resolution or opening of certaine parts of Scripture, according to the same* (Middleburg, 1584); facsimile in *Four Tudor Books on Education*, intro. by Robert D. Pepper (Gainesville, FL: Scholars' Facsimiles and Reprints, 1966), sigs. [D4]–[D4]ᵛ.

[162] Fenner was removed from Peterhouse, Cambridge, before taking his degree, probably because of his involvement with the 'puritan' group surrounding Thomas Cartwright; see Pepper, 'Introduction', in Fenner, *The Artes of Logike and Rhetorike*, p. xix. On *parrhesia* and the evangelical tradition, see further below, chapter 2.

[163] Fenner, *The Artes of Logike and Rhetorike*, sig. [D4]ᵛ.

chapter 3) by describing it as a 'secrete crying out' and ignores the element of apology highlighted by some of his contemporaries.

Henry Peacham's *The Garden of Eloquence* stands between the two approaches to *parrhesia* which I have described as operating in the sixteenth century, combining the notion of boldness with that of apology.[164] The book was first published in 1577 and then heavily revised and expanded in 1593, and the weight accorded by Peacham to each aspect of *parrhesia* also alters significantly between the two editions. The 1577 edition is dedicated to John Elmer, Bishop of London, and in his dedicatory epistle Peacham describes his classically based and celebratory theory of rhetoric.[165] Its conclusion explains his understanding of rhetoric's place in civil society and articulates his desire to equip the subjects of the realm with its tools. In outlining his ambitions for the book he asks Elmer to accept 'my wel meaning, which is (as farre as my small ability is able to extend) to profyte this my country, and especially the studious youth of this Realme, and such as haue not the vnderstanding of the Latyne tounge'.[166]

Peacham situates his definition of *parrhesia* among the 'second order' of 'Shemates Rhetoricall' – those, he explains, which 'are such as doe make the Oration not onelye pleasante and plausible, but also very sharpe and vehement'.[167] The definition itself continues this blending of pleasantness and vehemence, as Peacham carefully balances the need to break social decorum when the situation demands it against the need to maintain it by taking into account the crucial aspects of rhetorical decorum: time, person, and place. *Parrhesia*, for Peacham in the 1577 *Garden of Eloquence*, involves knowing exactly how much 'sharpness' is required by a given situation and ensuring that the measure is not exceeded:

Parrhesia, when speaking before them whome we ought to reuerence and feare, & hauing somthing to say, which either toucheth themselues, or their friends, do desire them to pardon our boldness, shewing that it were great pittie, y^t for lack of admonition, vices should be maintained, & vertues oppressed. Now in this figure, great warinesse must be vsed, least to much boldnesse bringeth offence. And therefore the time, the place, and chiefly the persons, ought wel to be considered of; which rule wise men haue always vsed, and fooles abused.[168]

---

[164] Peacham refers to and uses examples from the *Ad Herennium*, Cicero's rhetorical works, and Quintilian, deriving much of this material (along with some definitions) from Susenbrotus; for a full discussion of his use of sources, see William G. Crane, Introduction, in Henry Peacham, *The Garden of Eloquence* (London: H. Jackson, 1593; facsimile, Gainesville, FL: Scholars' Facsimiles and Reprints, 1954), pp. 9–23, hereafter Peacham, *The Garden* (1593).

[165] Henry Peacham, *The Garden of Eloquence* (London: H. Jackson, 1577; facsimile, Menston: Scolar Press, 1971), sigs. Aii–Aiii; hereafter Peacham, *The Garden* (1577).

[166] Peacham, *The Garden* (1577), sigs. Aiii–Aiii^v.   [167] Ibid., sig. Kiiii.

[168] Ibid., sigs. Mii^v–Miii.

Peacham goes on to give a series of examples, the first from Cicero's speech against Antony; in his exposition he stresses the importance of Cicero's apologies to the Senate, but also emphasises the moral imperative that underlies them:

In the beginning hee vseth a defence or a mitigation, saying, that he doeth speake with great perill, and feare how his wordes will be taken, but not withstanding, he promyseth, that which he will say, shall be for the maintenance and dignitie of the Senate, wherby he doth obtayne their fauour, and their good willes to hear him. Afterward he prayeth them, not to reiecte hys wordes, before he hath declared the whole, howsoeuer they seeme at the fyrst. And fynally, that they would take without offence whatsoeuer he should vtter, promysing that it should be all for their commoditie and aduancement, and spoken euen of good will . . . For before he opened the wound, he would laye to a medycine, and prepare the mynds of the Senate to here willingly, what he had to say. Likewyse, when we alledge that wee ought not to kepe in the truth for feare of men, but boldlye expresse the veritie without respect of persons.[169]

Peacham goes on to offer scriptural examples that suggest an alternative, religious, impetus for speaking freely and that link the political oratory of which the Ciceronian passage was a part with the godly appeal to a higher authority. Peacham's first example, Job 32:21–2, had in fact been used in Parliament the previous year as one of Peter Wentworth's biblical authorities for his famous motion on liberty of speech.[170] Irritated by what he saw as Elizabeth's repression of 'godly' preachers and her failure to take action against Mary Queen of Scots, Wentworth had made a claim for freedom of speech in Parliament as one instance where God and the law were superior to the monarch. After arguing for the necessity of free speech as an essential component of parliamentary deliberation ('without it it is a scorne and mockery to call it a parliament house'), Wentworth explicitly rejected the claims of decorum to restrict his speech, in a classic piece of parrhesiastic justification:

Now to the impediments thereof to which by God's grace and the little expedience [*sic*] I have I will utter plainly and faithfully. I will use the words of Eliha, 'Behold, I am as the new wine which hath noe vent and bursteth the new vessells in

---

[169] Ibid., sigs. Miii–Miii^v.

[170] For Wentworth's speech see *Proceedings in the Parliaments of Elizabeth I*, ed. by T. E. Hartley, 3 volumes (Leicester: Leicester University Press, 1981–95), volume I: *1558–1581*, pp. 45–434; J. E. Neale, *Elizabeth I and her Parliaments*, 2 volumes (London: Jonathan Cape, 1953–7), volume I: *1559–1581*, pp. 318–32. Neale's sources are Inner Temple Petyt MS 538/17; BL Stowe MS 302; *State Papers Domestic Elizabethan* 107/30 and *CJ* I, 104. See further chapter 3 below; Mack, *Elizabethan Rhetoric*, pp. 1–2, 241–3; A. N. McLaren, *Political Culture in the Reign of Elizabeth I: Queen and Commonwealth 1558–1585* (Cambridge: Cambridge University Press, 1999), pp. 26–7.

sunder'; therefore I will speake that I may have a vent, I will open my lipps and make answer, I will regard noe manner of person, noe man wyll I spare, for yf I should goe aboute to please men I know not how soone my maker wyll take me away.[171]

Although the passage from the Book of Job is an obvious biblical locus for *parrhesia*, in the year after such a *cause célèbre* it would still have immediate connotations, at least for those readers involved in or aware of parliamentary events. The other most pressing issues for godly (and even not-so-godly) English citizens in the previous year had been the linked questions of how far Elizabeth was prepared to support the open revolt of the States General of the Low Countries, and how open she was to the increasingly energetic courtship of the Duke of Anjou.[172] In this context Peacham's suggestions for putting *parrhesia* into action could easily drift into dangerous waters, and his second example, Galatians 1:10, does nothing to mitigate the effect: 'Preach I mans doctryne, or Gods, or goe I about to please men, for if I should, I were not ye seruant of Christ.'[173] The final example returns to the medical imagery Peacham deployed earlier, reinforcing the image of the orator as the physician of the body politic: 'if my bitter words greue you, remember I pray you, that sore diseases cannot be cured with easy medicynes'.[174]

By 1593 England was at war with Spain, and Peacham dedicated the revised edition of *The Garden of Eloquence* to a minister of state rather than a churchman, apologising to Sir John Puckering, Lord Keeper of the Great Seal, lest it seemed 'a matter importunate, to interrupt your Lordships graue, deep, and weightie considerations, sitting as you do at the sterne of the commonwelth in these daies of danger'.[175] Peacham appears increasingly aware of rhetoric's openness to criticism and sounds a defensive note throughout the epistle, although even in the course of this defence he maintains the large claims for oratory advanced in the 1577 edition, asserting

---

[171] *Proceedings in the Parliaments of Elizabeth I*, volume 1, p. 426.

[172] On the events of these years see Wallace T. MacCaffrey, *Queen Elizabeth and the Making of Policy, 1572–1588* (Princeton: Princeton Unversity Press, 1981), pp. 217–66; MacCaffrey, *Elizabeth I* (London: Edward Arnold, 1993), pp. 188–217; Neale, *Elizabeth I and her Parliaments*, volume 1, pp. 313–69.

[173] Peacham, *The Garden* (1577), sig. Miii^v.

[174] Ibid. This example is taken from Peacham's main source, Susenbrotus' *Epitome*; however, it is worth noting that in his definition of *parrhesia* Peacham works far more independently of Susenbrotus (and his other sources) than is often the case in *The Garden*. Susenbrotus stresses *parrhesia*'s usefulness in winning authority and draws on Quintilian's description of its usefulness for flattery; Peacham, as we have seen, ignores these aspects of the figure – and the examples that he adds serve to emphasise his own interpretation of it. See Susenbrotus, *Epitome troporum ac schematvm*, sig. Eii^v.

[175] Peacham, *The Garden* (1593), sig. ABii.

that as well as being beautifying, figures are 'as martiall instruments both of defence & inuasion'.[176] 'And being so', he asks,

what may be more necessary or more profitable for vs, then to hold those weapons alwaies readie in our hands, wherewith we may defend our selues, inuade our enemies, reuenge our wrongs, ayd the weake, deliuer the simple from dangers, conserue true religion, & confute idolatry? for look what the sword may do in war, this vertue may performe in peace.[177]

A strong sense of alertness to the dangers of rhetorical abuse is perhaps evident in the new category of 'Figvres of Permission', in which Peacham now places *parrhesia*. These are 'such formes of speech as do after a sort commit the cause in hand, or matter in controuersie to the consideration and iudgements of others, as either of the iudges or the aduersaries, and the formes do serue most specially to confirmation'.[178] This categorical change thus places far less emphasis on the moral self-assertion of the orator, tending instead towards the evasion of such a position. The definition of the figure, while remaining close to that of 1577, also places noticeably greater weight on the importance of apology and of humility before one's audience:

Parrhesia, is a forme of speech by which the Orator speaking before those whom he feareth, or ought to reuerence, & hauing somewhat to say that may either touch themselues, or those whom they fauour, preuenteth the displeasure and offence that might be taken, as by crauing pardon afore hand, and by shewing the necessitie of free speech in that behalfe, or by some other like formes of humble submission and modest insinuation.[179]

The rephrasing of 'desiring' with 'crauing' pardon is surely significant, as is especially the addition of the whole phrase 'by some other like formes of humble submission and modest insinuation'. Peacham's *parrhesia* is decidedly less outspoken than it was sixteen years earlier. In his examples he omits the medical allusions and the last example entirely, and while retaining the other three adds that Cicero claimed to speak not simply with 'good will' (a phrase shared by both versions), but with 'entire affection'. These changes may, of course, be attributed to stylistic preference, but this seems insufficient. Peacham's anxiety appears in the subsequent section on 'the vse of this Figure', which briefly asserts an aggressive and strong function for *parrhesia*, but does not quite fit with the description he has just given:

---

[176] Ibid., sig. [ABiv].   [177] Ibid.   [178] Ibid., sigs. Qiii^v–[Qiv].   [179] Ibid., sig. R.

This figure serueth to insinuate, admonish, and reprehend, and may fitly be called the Herald or Ambassador of speech, which is the onely forme that boldly deliuereth to great dignitaries and most high degrees of man, the message of iustice and equitie, sparing neither magistrates that peruert lawes, nor Princes that do abuse their kingdomes.[180]

Immediately it has been proffered, however, this attractively 'sharp' picture is retracted by the necessary 'caution' on the use of *parrhesia* (these, given for most of the figures, were additions in the 1593 text). This caution reinforces the attention to decorum advised in 1577; but, more than this, it seems an attempt to restrict the use of the figure as far as possible without explicitly singling out a named group. The final distinction between the extraordinary ministry of the prophets and the changed circumstances of latter-day preachers and orators indicates the changes in Peacham's hopes for Protestant oratory, leaving it a perceptibly depleted armoury and remit: 'this figure,' warns Peacham,

doth best beseeme a man of wisedome and grauitie, who is best able to moderate the forme of his speech, and to restrain it from that rude boldnesse which doth more hurt then good, from whence there oft springeth a malice in the hearer against the speaker: a contempt of his doctrine, and sometimes a punishment of his person, for now and then a rude *Vae vobis* doth cause a *Coram nobis*. As for the Prophets they were extraordinary men, and therefore their examples in this respect are not to be imitated.[181]

This shows a distinct shift from the 'style' to the 'content' of *parrhesia* in two editions of the same work. With George Puttenham's celebrated *Arte of English Poesie* (1589), we begin to find *parrhesia* treated exclusively in the second of the ways I have outlined above: as a figure of excusing for speaking boldly rather than the act of speaking boldly itself. It thus becomes increasingly difficult to distinguish *parrhesia* from the figure of *diorthosis* or *praecedens correctio*, and to establish how far frankness is integral to the figure and how far it is subsidiary to the act of self-excusing. This shift in emphasis, as I have argued, reflects an increasing sense of anxiety about the place of *parrhesia* in an ordered society, and Puttenham in particular is constantly aware of the possibility that rhetoric, being by definition a breach of linguistic decorum, can easily be considered at the same time as

---

[180] Heralds and ambassadors were traditionally privileged with freedom of speech, on the 'don't shoot the messenger' principle: their status as so privileged is important to classical as well as early modern discussions, notably in Herodotus' *History*.

[181] Peacham, *The Garden* (1593), sig. Rii. On the extraordinary warrant of the prophets, see further chapter 2 below.

a breach of *social* decorum. He frequently attempts to defend it from such charges, stressing at the opening of the third book, 'Of Ornament' that the poet should

delight and allure as well the mynde as the eare of the hearers with a certain noueltie and strange maner of conueyance, disguising it no little from the ordinary and accustomed: neuerthelesse making it nothing the more vnseemely or misbecomming, but rather decenter and more agreable to any ciuill eare and vnderstanding.[182]

Part of Puttenham's defence is explicitly to divorce eloquence from political contexts, emphasising that his discussion concerns the poet or 'maker' and not the civic orator, as he explains when addressing the issue of rhetoric as linguistic abuse:

As figures be the instruments of ornament in euery language, so be they also in a sorte abuses or rather trespasses in speach, because they passe the ordinary limits of common utterance, and be occupied of purpose to deceiue the eare and also the minde, drawing it from plainnesse and simplicitie to a certaine doublenesse, whereby our talke is the more guilefull & abusing . . . which thing made the graue iudges *Areopagites* (as I finde written) to forbid all manner of figuratiue speaches to be vsed before them in their consistorie of Iustice, as meere illusions to the minde, and wresters of vpright iudgement . . . This no doubt is true and was by them grauely considered: but in this case because our maker or Poet is appointed not for a iudge, but rather for a pleader, and that of pleasant & louely causes and nothing perillous . . . they are not in truth to be accompted vices but for vertues in the poetical science very commendable.[183]

However, this distinction is not always rigidly maintained: the very figure of the 'maker' which Puttenham delineates is far from being divorced from the political world of the court in particular and many of his examples are drawn from legal and political contexts.[184] His description of the origin of poetry and oratory also yokes the two firmly to political life: 'the Poet', Puttenham writes, 'is of all other the most auncient Oratour, as he that by good & pleasant perswasions first reduced the wilde and beastly people into publicke societies and ciuilitie of life, insinuating vnto them, under fictions with sweete and coloured speeches, many wholesome lessons and doctrines'.[185] It

---

[182] [George Puttenham], *The Arte of English Poesie* (London: Richard Field, 1589; facsimile, Amsterdam: Theatrvm Orbis Terrarvm, 1971), sig. Qiii^v.

[183] Ibid., sigs. Sii^v–Siii.

[184] See, for example, Puttenham's examples of 'Sarcasmus, or the Bitter Taunt', 'Asteismus, or the Merry Scoffe', and 'Hiperbole, or the Ouer Reacher' (*The Arte of English Poesie*, sigs. Y^v–Yii^v).

[185] Puttenham, *The Arte of English Poesie*, sig. Yiv. Cf. Cicero, *De inventione*, trans. by H. M. Hubbell (Cambridge, MA: Harvard University Press, 1949), I. 2. 2–3, pp. 4–7; Cicero, *De oratore*, I. 8. 31–3,

is in this context that we should consider Puttenham's version of *parrhesia*, which he classifies under the heading of 'Figures sententious, otherwise called Rhetoricall.'[186] This is how he defines the figure:

The fine and subtill perswader when his intent is to sting his aduersary, or els to declare his mind in broad and liberal speeches, which might breede offence or scandall, he will seeme to bespeake pardon before hand, [in margin: *Parisia*, or the Licentious] wherby his licentiousnes may be the better borne withall, as he that said:

> If my speech hap t'offend you any way,
> Thinke it their fault, that force me so to say.[187]

Puttenham's treatment of *parrhesia* immediately considers it as part of persuasion, and recalls the *Ad Herennium*'s discussion of the means whereby strong emotion aroused by frankness may be palliated, relying on the power of frankness to 'sting' an adversary. It is important that the orator is recommended only to '*seeme* to bespeake pardon' (my italics), and that in the example given, the speaker ensures that any offence caused is attributable to his adversaries and not to his intentions: bold or licentious speech (here conflated) must be seen to be produced under pressure from others and not to emerge from a persuasive 'intent' or a desire to 'declare'. This ensures that the audience believes that the decision to adjust the boundaries of decorum for the purposes of the current discourse and to licence licentiousness has been taken by the speaker's adversaries and not by him.

The expanded 1599 edition of Angel Day's epistolary manual *The English Secretary* treats *parrhesia* in its list of 'Tropes, Figures, and Schemes', placing it like Puttenham in the section concerned with 'schemes rhetoricall'.[188] Day's understanding of *parrhesia*, though, is considerably less complex than Puttenham's, and the differences between it and *diorthosis* have been elided completely. The only remaining trace of boldness is in the slightly uncomfortable formulation of Day's definition, where he mistranslates both the meaning of the term *parrhesia* and its function as a figure:

---

pp. 22–5; Quintilian, *The Orator's Education*, 2. 16. 9, pp. 372–5; Peacham, *The Garden* (1577), sig. Aiii.

[186] Puttenham explains that figures rhetorical are 'those other figures which may execute both offices, and all at once to beautifie and geue sence and sententiousnes to the whole language at large' (*The Arte of English Poesie*, sig. Yiv).

[187] Ibid., sigs. Cc–Cc[v].

[188] See Angel Day, *The English Secretary, or Methode of writing of Epistles and Letters: with a declaration of such Tropes, Figures, and Schemes, as either vsually or for ornament sake are therin required. Also the parts and office of a Secretarie, Deuided into two bookes* (London, 1599), sigs. [Kk4][v]–[Mm4][v].

Parresia, or libertie to speake, when by winning of curtesie to our speech we seek to auoid any offence thereof, as thus. *Pardon if I be tedious, the circumstance of the cause requireth it. If my speech seeme vehement, the matter occasioning the same is vrgent. If what I write seeme offensiue to you, you haue to mislike the ill disposition of such as inforce it, and not with me to be agreeued.*[189]

The shift from boldness to apology is shown by the replacement of what might be the expected formulation of 'liberty *of speech*' by 'libertie *to* speake': this weakening of the figure is also apparent in the epistle which deploys it, found in chapter 5, on 'letters inuectiue'.[190] The letter is described as 'an answere purgatorie of the sonne touching matters inuectiue of the former epistle [from his father]', and makes it clear how much Day thinks *parrhesia's* function is to calm rather than to excite emotions:

albeit there is no reason whie, in the measure of all your actions, [in margin: *Insinuatio*] I shoulde or ought to deeme, that you doe, or enterprise anie thing vnaduisedlie: yet for so much as the secret sting of malice is such, as is able to penetrate the wisest, and that where much is feared, the least matter inducing thereunto is made occasion to question of [in margin: *Paresia*], I doe in as lowlie manner as I maie, beseech that but with indifferencie you will see howe and in what sort I am wronged, and giuing credite to what hereby in mine owne defence alledged, you will censure the rest, as to the respect of your fatherlie pietie appertaineth.[191]

The absence of boldness from Day's account of *parrhesia* is an extreme example of the tendency in sixteenth-century translations of the figure to reduce its potency, turning a figure based on (at least the appearance of) the deliberate breaking of decorum into one designed to shore up such decorum.

My excavation of the history of *parrhesia* in this chapter has shown how the figure constructs strategic and artificial but also 'natural' ideas of free speech and provides a vocabulary within which the possibilities for and the place of frank speaking can be understood. The pervasiveness of rhetorical education in sixteenth-century England means that a great many Englishmen would have been aware of the figure and that their conception of free speech would thus have been rhetorically coloured. Those aware of the figure and prepared to deploy it would have been to a great extent convinced of a certain polemical idea of the function of oratory in society, most evident perhaps in the 1577 edition of Peacham's *Garden of Eloquence*. Throughout its history, *parrhesia* is discussed in the context of counselling

[189] Ibid., sig. Ll3ᵛ.   [190] Ibid., sigs. Dd3ᵛ–[Ff4]; the letter is found on sigs. Ee–Ee3ᵛ.
[191] Ibid., sig. Eeᵛ.

and admonishing one's peers and superiors, whether purely to criticise them for what the speaker considers to be irresponsible behaviour, or to flatter them by suggesting that what is presented as frankness is in fact familiar to them. We have seen how disturbing the attempt to translate contexts of counsel from ancient Greece and Rome to early modern England can be, especially evident in the comments by Roger Ascham and Sir Henry Wotton which claim that what is described as 'liberty' is in fact 'licentiousness'. In the following section I will explore the language and practice of counsel in more detail, and this history of *parrhesia* will be seen to be crucial to, if not explicitly mentioned by, many of the texts I discuss there.

I want to end this section with a text that is in many ways exemplary of the attitudes explored in the next: Francis Bacon's *De sapientia veterum*, or *Wisedome of the Ancients* (1609). This was Bacon's attempt to discover in ancient texts (fables in this case) lessons to reform the present state of knowledge, and was one of his most popular works.[192] The first chapter is entitled 'Cassandra, siue Parresia', and in it Bacon sternly stresses the need to consider decorum when offering counsel, lest, as in the case of Cassandra, the free speech of truth sounds to those who matter (in the words of Aeschylus' Clytaemnestra) like 'speech incomprehensible, barbarian, wild as the swallow's song' and works to destruction rather than edification.[193] The example Bacon gives from Cicero as his conclusion points out, like Wotton and in similarly emphatic terms, the dangers dependent on thinking that one is in another time, another country. I quote from Sir Arthur Gorges's 1619 translation of the text:

This Fable seemes to intimate the vnprofitable liberty of vntimely admonitions and counselles. For they that are so ouerweened with the sharpnesse and dexteritie of their owne wit and capacitie, as that they disdaine to submit themselues to the documents of *Apollo*, the God of Harmonie, whereby to learne and obserue the method and measure of affaires, the grace and grauitie of discourse, the differences between the more iudicious and more vulgar eares, and the due times when to speake and when to be silent; Bee they neuer so sensible and pregnant, and their iudgements neuer so profound and profitable, yet in all their endeuours either of perswasion or perforce, they auaile nothing, neither are they of any moment to aduantage or mannage matters, but do rather hasten on the ruine of all those that they adhere or deuote themselues vnto. And then at last when calamatie hath

---

[192] *De sapientia veterum* was translated into English and Italian; on its popularity see Francis Bacon, *Works*, ed. by James Spedding, Robert Leslie Ellis, and Douglas Denon Heath, 14 volumes (London: Longman, 1857–74), volume XII, p. 406.

[193] Aeschylus, *Agamemnon*, trans. by Richmond Lattimore, in *Aeschylus I: Oresteia* (Chicago: University of Chicago Press, 1953), p. 67; the Chorus, in contrast, tell Clytaemnestra that 'what she has spoken is for you, and clear enough' (ibid.).

made men feele the euent of neglect, then shall they too late be reuerenced as deep foreseing and faithfull prophets. Whereof a notable instance is eminently set forth in *Marcus Cato Vticensis*, who as from a watchtower discouered afar off, and as an Oracle long foretold, the approaching ruine of his Countrey, and the plotted tyranny houering ouer the State, both in the first conspiracie, and as it was prosecuted in the ciuill contention between *Cesar* and *Pompey*, and did no good the while, but rather harmed the commonwealth, and hastned on his countreys bane, which *M. Cicero* wisely obserued, and writing to a familiar friend doth in these terms excellently describe, *Cato optimè sentit, sed nocet interdum Reipublicae: loquitur enim tanquam in Republicâ Platonis, non tanquam in faece Romulis. Cato* (saith he) iudgeth profoundly, but in the meane time damnifies the State, for he speakes as in the commonwealth of *Plato*, and not as in the dregs of *Romulus*.[194]

With typical slipperiness (David Wootton has called Bacon 'your flexible friend'),[195] Bacon shows in this text that ancient works could be translated to the present (that is his book's function) and yet draws attention to the potential threat of inappropriate and untranslatable advice. While Thomas Wilson was convinced of the applicability of Greek democratic writings to Elizabethan England, and saw decorum as subsidiary to the call of duty, Bacon regarded decorum as a duty and harmony as undermined by ill-timed frankness. Counsel, for Bacon, should be pragmatic rather than idealistic, and free speech used strategically with 'alleviation' or 'pretence'.

FLATTERERS AND FRIENDS: *PARRHESIA* AND THE TRADITION OF COUNSEL

In the final section of this chapter I move away from the rhetorical treatises in which *parrhesia* was defined and, increasingly, restricted, to a brief consideration of the ways in which the strategies and opportunities for counsel with which it was associated were discussed in the sixteenth and seventeenth centuries. Belief in counsel as a central and indispensable component of the political process was the foundation of early modern discussions of and demands for freedom of speech, and even when works on counsel do not refer directly to *parrhesia*, they concern themselves with the central questions that I have discussed throughout this chapter.[196] How can an

---

[194] Francis Bacon, *The Wisedome of the Ancients*, trans. by Sir Arthur Gorges (London: John Bill, 1619), sigs. A^v–A2^v; cf. Francis Bacon, *De sapientia veterum* (London, 1609), sigs. B–B2.

[195] David Wootton, 'Francis Bacon: Your Flexible Friend', in *The World of the Favourite*, ed. by J. H. Elliott and L. W. B. Brockliss (New Haven: Yale University Press, 1999), pp. 184–204.

[196] On counsel, see the works by John Guy cited in note 116 above. Other useful critical discussions include Glenn Burgess, 'The Impact on Political Thought: Rhetorics for Troubled Times', in *The Impact of the English Civil War*, ed. by John Morrill (London: Collins & Brown, 1991), pp. 67–83; F. W. Conrad, '"A Preservative Against Tyranny": Sir Thomas Elyot and the Rhetoric of Counsel',

adviser speak the truth to power without risking his neck? How far can frank advice be palliated without becoming flattery? Should the philosopher (often regarded as the archetypal source of good counsel) take part in public life at all, given the dangers of trying to navigate between the Scylla and Charybdis of compromise and punishment?

These questions were addressed in England from at least the late fourteenth century, in texts ranging from vernacular poems to Latin treatises.[197] Most of the English (and continental) texts of the early modern period rely upon the same set of classical sources: Cicero's *De officiis* and *De amicitia*; Aristotle's *Politics* and *Ethics*; the pseudo-Aristotelian *Secreta secretorum* (supposedly a letter from Aristotle to Alexander the Great) and, increasingly, Isocrates' *To Nicocles* and several essays from Plutarch's *Moralia* – primarily the essay 'How to Tell a Flatterer from a Friend', discussed above, but also those on 'Learning is Necessary to the Prince', 'With Princes One Ought Especially to Discuss Philosophically' and 'How to Profit by One's Enemies'.[198] Liberty of speech is considered to be essential in virtually all early modern treatments of counsel: if the prince does not actively encourage frankness then his or her counsel will be worthless, and he or she will become the object of flattery framed as counsel, rather than of constructive advice. Lipsius, in his *Six Bookes of Politics or Civil Doctrine*, placed liberty of speech second only to piety in his list of five precepts for counsellors; and while discussing the other side of the counselling relationship in his chapter

in *Reformation, Humanism, and 'Revolution'. Papers Presented at the Folger Institute Seminar 'Political Thought in the Henrician Age, 1500–1550'*, ed. by Gordon J. Schochet with Patricia E. Tatspaugh and Carol Brobeck (Washington: Folger Institute, 1990), pp. 191–206; Conrad, 'The Problem of Counsel Reconsidered: The Case of Sir Thomas Elyot', in *Political Thought and the Tudor Commonwealth. Deep Structure, Discourse and Disguise*, ed. by Paul A. Fideler and T. F. Mayer (London: Routledge, 1992), pp. 75–107; Linda Levy Peck, 'Kingship, Counsel and Law in Early Stuart Britain', in Pocock, *The Varieties of British Political Thought*, pp. 80–115; J. G. A. Pocock, *The Machiavellian Moment. Florentine Political Thought and the Atlantic Republican Tradition* (Princeton: Princeton University Press, 1975), pp. 338–48. Especially useful on the Elizabethan conception of counsel is A. N. McLaren, *Political Culture in the Reign of Elizabeth I: Queen and Commonwealth 1558–1585* (Cambridge: Cambridge University Press, 1999).

[197] On the medieval tradition of counsel, see Judith Ferster, *Fictions of Advice: The Literature and Politics of Counsel in Late Medieval England* (Philadelphia: University of Pennsylvania Press, 1996). For examples, see *Mum and the Sothsegger*, ed. by M. Day and R. Steele, Early English Text Society o.s., no. 199 (London: Oxford University Press, 1936); John Gower, *Vox Clamantis* and *Confessio Amantis*, in *The Complete Works of John Gower*, ed. by G. C. Macaulay, 4 volumes (Oxford: Clarendon Press, 1899–1902), volume III; Sir John Fortescue, *On the Laws and Governance of England*, ed. by Shelley Lockwood (Cambridge: Cambridge University Press, 1997), esp. pp. 114–18 and Appendix B, 'Example of how Good Council Helps and Advantages and of what Follows from the Contrary'; Arthur B. Ferguson, *The Articulate Citizen and the English Renaissance* (Durham, NC: Duke University Press, 1965), pp. 75–6.

[198] See Guy, 'The Rhetoric of Counsel', p. 294, n. 4; Ferguson, *The Articulate Citizen*, pp. 24–5 (on the *Secreta Secretorum* and its translations).

on 'How a prince ought to behaue him selfe in hearing counsel' advised him
to 'loue those that are free of speech, and Hate flatterers which are hurt-
full'.[199] At the beginning of his hugely influential *To Nicocles*, explaining
his motives in writing the text, Isocrates noted that while the education of
private individuals included 'freedom of speech [*parrhesia*] and the privilege
which is openly granted to friends to rebuke and enemies to attack each
others faults' kings are deprived of this privilege. In contrast, he writes, they
'live all their lives, from the time when they are placed in authority, without
admonition; for the great majority of people do not come into contact with
them, and those who are of their society consort with them to gain their
favour'.[200] Consequently, those in authority should be conscious of their
susceptibility to flattery and should learn to trust those who, like Isocrates,
offer plain advice: 'Regard as your most faithful friends', he warns, 'not
those who praise everything you say or do, but those who criticize your
mistakes . . . Distinguish between those who artfully flatter and those who
loyally serve you, that the base may not fare better than the good.'[201]

The counsellor was variously imagined as being the prince's inferior
governor, to be entrusted with the administration of provinces of the realm
or with the management of policy, or as a philosopher or sage who would
proffer more general advice on the moral conduct of government.[202] He

---

[199] Justus Lipsius, *Sixe Bookes of Politics or Civil Doctrine*, trans. by William Jones (London, 1594), sigs.
[Giv]–[Giv]ᵛ; sig. Hiiᵛ.

[200] Isocrates, *To Nicocles*, trans. by George Norlin, in Isocrates, *Works*, 3 volumes (London: Heinemann,
1929), I, pp. 40–71: 41, 43. Much of Isocrates' argument in this work anticipates Plutarch's 'How to
Tell a Flatterer from a Friend'. Sir Thomas Elyot translated both of these texts, the Plutarch from
Erasmus' Latin translation and Isocrates in his *The Doctrinal of Princes* (1533), for which see *Four
Political Treatises by Sir Thomas Elyot* (Gainesville, FL: Scholars' Facsimiles and Reprints, 1967),
pp. 1–39. The passage from Isocrates was incorporated wholesale by Castiglione into Book 4 of *The
Book of the Courtier*, where he goes on to trace a direct progression from the failure of courtiers to
be faithful friends to the prince's banishment of counsel from his method of governance and his
descent into licentiousness; see Count Baldassare Castiglione, *The Book of the Courtier*, trans. by
Sir Thomas Hoby, ed. by Virginia Cox (London: Dent, 1994), p. 296.

[201] Isocrates, *To Nicocles*, pp. 55–7.

[202] On the counsellor as an 'inferior governor' or 'magistrate', with a reference to Aristotle's image of
the prince's extra sense and limbs (note 203 below), see Elyot, *The Book named The Governor*, p. 13.
On the counsellor as 'sage', with examples of kings famed for their love of sages and dire warnings
that all the evils of the commonwealth derive from the absence of sages' counsel, see Anthony of
Guevara, *The Diall of Princes*, trans. by Thomas North (London, 1557), sigs. piiᵛ–piiiᵛ; [qiiii]–[qvi]ᵛ;
[Vv]ᵛ–Xiᵛ. The figures of the ruler and the sage were held up as exemplary types, particularly with
reference to Aristotle and Alexander the Great, as in the *Secreta Secretorum* tradition. See M. A.
Manzalaoui, '"Noght in the Registre of Venus": Gower's English Mirror for Princes', in *Medieval
Studies for J. A. W. Bennett*, ed. by P. L. Heyworth (Oxford: Clarendon Press, 1981), pp. 159–83.
A popular antitype of this relationship was to be found in the figures of Plato and Dionysius of
Syracuse, as used by Hythloday in the 'dialogue of counsel' which comprises Book 1 of *Utopia*; see
Thomas More, *Utopia*, ed. by George M. Logan and Robert M. Adams (Cambridge: Cambridge
University Press, 1989), p. 29. On More see further below.

was, in Aristotle's famous formulation, the extra eyes, ears, hands, and feet of the prince whose task in ruling the entire realm would otherwise be near to impossible.[203] The friendly admonition that he was obliged to supply should, it was argued, appeal to the reason rather than (like flattery) to the passions; indeed, the contrast between these appeals to the two different parts of the prince's soul was regarded as one of the tell-tale signs in distinguishing flattery from counsel.[204] However, treatises on counsel had to consider not only the needs of the prince but those of the counsellor. When they reflected on the integrity of the adviser, the classical debate between the relative merits of the active and contemplative life (or *otium* and *negotium*) was repeatedly played out. In the course of their opposition of these competing values, many early modern texts resorted to complex literary techniques in order to find a way out of the apparent double bind of remaining wedded to the truth but separated from the arena in which it could be uttered, or taking a place at the council table and finding one's advice ignored or punished.

Thomas Starkey, in his *Dialogue between Pole and Lupset* (*c.* 1529–32) enacts this dilemma in dialogue form as Lupset attempts to persuade Pole to leave country life in Bisham and assist in counselling Henry VIII.[205] Although Pole remains unconvinced even at the end of the dialogue that he should offer his counsel to the king rather than wait in scholarly retirement to be asked,[206] Starkey has meanwhile found a different solution to the dilemma of counsel by using the text indirectly to offer his own suggestions for reform. Lupset provokes and responds to the extreme views of the supposedly silent and exiled Pole, and Starkey – the invisible puppet-master – mediates and publishes them. Despite the latter's choice of seclusion and

---

[203] See Aristotle, *The Politics*, ed. by Stephen Everson (Cambridge: Cambridge University Press, 1988), 1287[b], p. 79.

[204] See especially Plutarch, 'How to Tell a Flatterer from a Friend', pp. 327–9; Conrad, '"A Preservative Against Tyranny"'. On admonition and friendship, see Cicero, *De officiis*, trans. by Walter Miller (London: Heinemann, 1913), p. 61; Cicero, *De amicitia*, in *De senectute, De amicitia, De divinatione*, trans. by W. A. Falconer (London: Heinemann, 1923), xiii. 44, pp. 154–7; Francis Bacon, 'Of Frendship', in *The Essayes or Counsels, Civill and Morall*, ed. by Michael Kiernan (Oxford: Clarendon Press, 1985), pp. 80–7, at p. 85. In the *Arte of English Poesie*, George Puttenham wrote that the end of a humanist education is to serve a prince and 'truly to Counsel & admonish, gravely not grevously, sincerely not sourly' (George Puttenham, *The Arte of English Poesie*, ed. by Gladys Willcock and Alice Walker (Cambridge: Cambridge University Press, 1970), p. 295; quoted in Skinner, *Reason and Rhetoric*, p. 70).

[205] Thomas Starkey, *A Dialogue between Pole and Lupset*, ed. by T. F. Mayer, Camden Society, fourth series no. 37 (London: Royal Historical Society, 1989). On Starkey see further T. F. Mayer, *Thomas Starkey and the Commonweal: Humanist Politics and Religion in the Reign of Henry VIII* (Cambridge: Cambridge University Press, 1989).

[206] See Starkey, *Dialogue*, pp. 142–3.

study, he is far from adopting the Petrarchan position of investing all power in the *Pater patriae*.[207] While Lupset thinks optimistically that simply having a good prince solves all the problems of the commonwealth,[208] Pole turns the idea on its head and emphasises the dangers if the prince is *not* good: 'frely to speke betwyx you & me', he confides, this would occasion 'a grete destructyon to our cuntrey wych hath byn perceyvyd by our fore fatherys days & at dyverse & many tymys, & schold be also now yf we had not a nobul & wyse prynce, wych is ever content to submyt hymselfe to the ordur of hys conseyl'.[209] Thus it is that a debate between a moderate reformer who favours the life of *negotium* (Lupset) and an extreme exponent of conciliarism and opponent of the royal supremacy who favours the life of *otium* (Pole)[210] is transformed into an opportunity for the extremist to air his views without taking the plunge into the murky waters of public life. It is also an opportunity for the author to express potentially unwelcome views in an indirect fashion, protecting his own counsel and his own position of relative independence. What defuses the extremism of Pole's (or rather, the *Dialogue's*) suggestions is not, as John Guy seems to think, the fact that the work was not printed until 1871, but rather Starkey's careful framing of his (or his character's) outspokenness with the debate over the wisdom of counselling.[211] Further, this framing could serve two purposes: on the one hand, to cast the *Dialogue* in the shape of a purely hypothetical encounter, with the views of neither character able to be attributed to Starkey, and on the other, to challenge the reader to turn a deaf ear to the strident voices of Pole and Lupset and find himself a latter-day Dionysius of Syracuse, rejecting in his pride the wisdom of counsel.

Perhaps the most celebrated contribution to the *otium / negotium* debate is to be found in an earlier text: Book One of Sir Thomas More's *Utopia* (1516), frequently referred to as the 'dialogue of counsel'. Quentin Skinner has shown convincingly how the discussion between the figures of Hythloday and More deploys with extreme care the vocabulary and imagery of the opposed positions – Platonist, or pro-*otium*, and Ciceronian, or

---

[207] See Quentin Skinner, 'Sir Thomas More's *Utopia* and the Language of Renaissance Humanism', in *The Languages of Political Theory in Early-modern Europe*, ed. by Anthony Pagden (Cambridge: Cambridge University Press, 1987), pp. 123–57, at p. 126.

[208] Starkey, *Dialogue*, p. 132.   [209] Ibid., p. 70.

[210] See Guy, 'The Rhetoric of Counsel', pp. 300–1.

[211] Guy rather oddly states that '*had the Dialogue been printed*, it would have propounded the most systematic programme for limited monarchy before the Nineteen Propositions of 1642' ('The Rhetoric of Counsel', p. 300; my italics). It seems to me that if it is true that this is what the *Dialogue* propounds, it propounds it whether in print or manuscript.

pro-*negotium*, respectively – adopted by the characters.[212] Once again, the debate focuses on the problem of how far a philosopher would be able frankly to speak the truth if he were to become a counsellor. Peter Giles and More join together to persuade Hythloday that this would be the best course of action for a man of his wisdom, while Hythloday rejects the blandishments of both his interlocutors. He argues first of all that the prince's official counsellors and favourites surround him or her with a wall of flattery, 'envy everyone else and admire only themselves', and that as a result any challenge to received ideas is immediately rejected.[213] The independent counsellor might be allowed to speak, but his advice is not actually listened to.

When More refuses to be convinced by this line of argument, citing Hythloday's 'friend', Plato, back at him in an attempt to persuade him,[214] Hythloday moves his argument on to the difficulty of influencing princes who are prejudiced against the kind of advice one might offer. It is less that philosophers are reluctant to offer counsel, he says; rather, princes are reluctant to listen to – or even unable to hear – them because of the way they have been educated. Many philosophers have given counsel, Hythloday points out,

in published books, if the rulers were only willing to take their good advice. But doubtless Plato was right in foreseeing that unless kings become philosophical themselves, the advice of real philosophers would never influence them, immersed as they are and infected with false values from boyhood on.[215]

It is not just the peril of being ignored that Hythloday fears as the result of offering unseasonable counsel to such ill-educated rulers, however, and he points out that he might be 'banished forthwith' for his troubles.[216] He asks his interlocutors to imagine him in a council where all the other

---

[212] See Skinner, 'Sir Thomas More's *Utopia*', pp. 131–3. For a comparison of Hythloday with the Stranger in Plato's *Statesman* and the Old Athenian of his *Laws*, see George M. Logan, introduction to More, *Utopia*, p. xx. For a rather different reading of the traditions in which More situates *Utopia*, see Eric Nelson, 'Greek Nonsense in More's *Utopia*', *Historical Journal* 44 (2001): 889–918; see further Eric Nelson, *The Greek Tradition in Republican Thought* (Cambridge: Cambridge University Press, 2004), chapter 1.

[213] More, *Utopia*, p. 14.

[214] Ibid., p. 28: 'Your friend Plato thinks that commonwealths will be happy only when philosophers become kings or kings become philosophers. No wonder we are so far from happiness when philosophers do not condescend even to assist kings with their counsels.'

[215] Ibid., p. 28. Hythloday notes that, as 'More' is presumably aware, 'Plato certainly had this experience with Dionysius of Syracuse' (pp. 28–9).

[216] Ibid., p. 29. On the important function of the fool at Cardinal Morton's table for this discussion of counsel, see David Wootton, 'Introduction' to Thomas More, *Utopia with Erasmus' The Sileni of Alcibiades*, ed. and trans. by David Wootton (Indianapolis: Hackett, 1999), pp. 1–34, at pp. 27–31.

counsellors are recommending policies designed to fill the king's treasury (policies taken from Aristotle's explanation in the *Politics* of how tyrannies are maintained).[217] 'Suppose I were to get up again and declare that all these counsels are both dishonourable and ruinous to the king?' Hythloday asks, 'don't you suppose . . . they would "turn deaf ears" to me?'[218] At this point More almost loses patience with his interlocutor: 'Stone deaf, indeed . . .', he retorts, would be the ears turned to Hythloday's counsel, 'and no wonder!'[219] More has no time for Hythloday's distaste for time-serving, which he instead considers as decorum, or adaptation to context.[220] To be effective, he explains, a counsellor must understand the particular conditions in which a discussion is taking place and pragmatically fashion the form and substance of his advice in accordance with them.[221] More's argument here is similar to Bacon's position in his 'Cassandra, siue Parresia', where he criticises those who fail to recognise 'the due times when to speake and when to be silent'.[222] In this formulation, the imperative upon Cassandra to speak and not be understood, of which Hythloday also complains, is not so much a curse for her as it is for her audience. We can begin to discern a positive recasting of the opposition evident in discussions of *parrhesia* between, on the one hand, fearless outspokenness (which could be seen as a version of the Platonic position taken by Hythloday) and, on the other, flattering adaptation to circumstance. In *Utopia*, 'More' depicts adaptation to circumstance as part of the virtuous active life, and as a foundation of effective counsel, rather than as deceptive and part of the pursuit of self-advancement. For him, and increasingly for early modern works on counsel, effectual persuasion does not necessarily imply duplicity.

The 'dialogue of counsel' in Book One of *Utopia* has often been interpreted in the light of More's own position at the time of its composition: he was already considering whether to accept a post on Henry VIII's council, and had accepted it by August 1517 at the latest.[223] Critics have therefore found it easy to read the debate as a dramatisation of the choices facing him at this point.[224] However, whether one thinks that More the author is expressing his own ideas in the figure of 'More' (as Quentin Skinner

---

[217] More, *Utopia*, pp. 31–3; p. 33, n. 63.   [218] Ibid., pp. 33, 35.   [219] Ibid., p. 35.

[220] Cicero, *Orator*, trans. by H. M. Hubbell, in *Brutus and Orator*, trans. by G. L. Hendrickson and H. M. Hubbell (London: Heinemann, 1962), xx. 70–xxiii. 75, pp. 356–61.

[221] More, *Utopia*, pp. 35–6.

[222] Bacon, *The Wisedome of the Ancients*, sig. A2 (cf. Bacon, *De sapientia veterum*, sig. B ͮ).

[223] See Logan, introduction to More, *Utopia*, p. xix; Jerry Mermel, 'Preparations for a Politic Life: Sir Thomas More's Entry into the King's Service', *The Journal of Medieval and Renaissance Studies* 7 (1977): 53–66; John Guy, *The Public Career of Sir Thomas More* (Brighton: Harvester Press, 1980), pp. 6–7; Skinner, 'Sir Thomas More's *Utopia*', p. 134.

[224] See Logan, introduction to More, *Utopia*, p. xix.

does), or that he is depicting the temptation offered by Hythloday's *otium* (as J. H. Hexter does), such uses of the correspondence between biography and text seem unnecessarily to restrict the questions posed by what is, after all, a highly complex, and carefully constructed, text.[225] We should remember especially that *Utopia*, as it appeared in its earliest editions, did not consist only of the detailed arguments of Book One and Hythloday's description of the island in Book Two. What we now consider the main text was surrounded by a mass of additional material, or 'paratext', all of which is intended to affect the reader's interpretation of the work.[226] It is clear that More – along with Peter Giles and Erasmus, who saw the book through the press – paid much closer attention to the potential of the book as a physical artefact than many of his modern readers have done.[227]

There are several features sometimes overlooked (or only mentioned in passing) which may shed additional light on the book's contribution to the debate on counsel. One of *Utopia's* most striking aspects is the way in which More and his associates foreground the environment in which the book was written. It was surrounded from the very first edition by letters of commendation from More's friends and acquaintances, letters intended to publicise the degree to which humanist intellectuals were excitedly discussing the work.[228] These have the effect of at once introducing the book to the world in its public, printed form, and yet allowing it to retain the air of a private work, a text for circulation among friends. Accompanying the commendatory epistles and poems, *Utopia* offered its early readers a handy map of the island, the Utopian alphabet and a quatrain in the Utopian language,[229] all of which make the text look very like a travel narrative and direct the reader's attention to the second half of its title ('and of the new island of Utopia') rather than the first ('concerning the best state of a

---

[225] See Skinner, 'Sir Thomas More's *Utopia*', p. 135; J. H. Hexter, 'Introduction part I', to Thomas More, *Utopia*, ed. by Edward Surtz, SJ and J. H. Hexter, in *The Complete Works of St Thomas More*, 14 volumes (New Haven: Yale University Press, 1960–97), volume IV, pp. xv–cxxiv, at pp. lxxxiv, xci.

[226] See Gérard Genette, *Paratexts: Thresholds of Interpretation*, trans. by Jane E. Lewin (Cambridge: Cambridge University Press, 1997). Logan and Adams note the book's exceptional quantity of 'ancillary material' (More, *Utopia*, p. 114, n. 4). On the paratext (and especially the place of the adage) see also Wootton, 'Introduction' to More, *Utopia*, pp. 6–13.

[227] On the part of Giles and Erasmus in the production of *Utopia*, see More, *Utopia*, pp. xxx; 114, n. 4.

[228] See ibid., pp. 112–32, for letters from More to Giles, Erasmus to Froben, Guillaume Budé to Thomas Lupset, Giles to Jerome Busleyden, Busleyden to More, Beatus Rhenanus to Willibald Pirckheimer, and Jean Desmarez to Giles, and for poems by Gerard Geldenhouwer and Cornelius de Schrijver, all of which were appended to one of the first four editions of the book (Louvain, 1516; Paris, 1517; Basle 1517 and 1518).

[229] See ibid., pp. 122–3.

commonwealth').[230] In a further complication of the book's generic situation (and hence of the reader's approach to it), the text is surrounded
throughout by marginal annotations, added by Giles, Erasmus, or both
together.[231] These notes – sometimes summaries of points made in the
text, sometimes notes of differences between Utopian customs and those
in Europe, sometimes identifications of *sententiae* – might begin to give the
work the appearance of a learned treatise. However, many of them draw
attention to More's effective use of rhetorical figures, and might hint that
the book is rather to be read as a virtuoso exercise in a certain kind of style.
How do these conflicting – or, at the very least, confusing – generic signals
relate to the work's engagement with questions of counsel in Book One?
One might profitably regard them as attempting to engage the reader's critical attention at every turn, always turning away from simple resolutions
to the problems posed towards yet more problems – just as Hythloday
attempts to win his dispute with More in Book One by appealing to an
'empirical' example of which More has no knowledge, and which in truth he
will never see: his own experiences in Utopia. There, a very text-dependent
argument is only settled by referring to another, but this time more recent,
text – the text we are about to read. This provocation of the reader through
the regular shifting of position, tone, and genre is reminiscent of More's
recommendation in the counsel debate of context-specific forms of advice.
In writing *Utopia* he does not wish primarily to pursue the redress of a
specific grievance so much as to provoke frank debate among his readers
and, in the space of a travel narrative by an 'expert in nonsense',[232] to find a
place where the abolition of private property can be entertained as a subject
for discussion away (if not very far) from the game of reference-spotting
indulged in Book One. Paying attention to the rest of More's title, we should
remember that the work is intended to be 'no less beneficial than entertaining' and in true Horatian fashion to instruct us even by delighting –
even as should harmonious and timely counsel.[233] More's own end, as a

---

[230] The full title, in its original Latin, is *De optimo reipublicae statu deque nova insula Utopia libellus vere
aureus, nec minus salutaris quam festivus, clarissimi disertissimique viri THOMAE MORI inclytae
civitatis Londinensis civis & Vicecomitis*. For the argument that we should follow the priorities
apparently announced here, see Skinner, 'Sir Thomas More's *Utopia*', p. 123. For an argument that
directs us to consider the phrase *nec minus salutaris quam festivus* as crucial, and which is a direct
response to Skinner's interpretation, see Carlo Ginzburg, *No Island is an Island: Four Glances at
English Literature in a World Perspective* (New York: Columbia University Press, 2000), pp. 1–3 and
chapter 1 *passim*.

[231] See More, *Utopia*, pp. xxx, 125, n. 26.

[232] 'Hythlodaeus' is one of More's playful Greek compounds, meaning 'expert in nonsense'.

[233] See Horace, *Ars poetica*, trans. by H. Rushton Fairclough (London: Heinemann, 1942), ll. 333–46,
pp. 478–9; Geldenhouwer writes in his verses 'On Utopia' that 'If pleasure you seek, good reader,
it's here; / If profit, no book is more suited to teach' (More, *Utopia*, p. 129).

frank and resolute counsellor martyred by his inability to serve the times rather than his conscience, serves as a grim postscript to the 'extremely amusing and potentially profitable' counsels of Utopia.[234]

The many-layered texts of Starkey and More addressed themselves to the concerns of would-be counsellors and had such individuals as their intended readers. Other works that treated the same issues, though still imagining that they would be read by counsellors, addressed themselves explicitly to princes. This was the case with Erasmus' *Education of a Christian Prince*,[235] Sir Thomas Elyot's *The Governor* (1531), which was presented to Henry VIII as the 'first fruits' of its author's labours,[236] and Machiavelli's *The Prince*. Machiavelli's treatment of the problem of counsel is notable by virtue of its concentration on the prince's perspective and, especially, its refusal to take a middle road between recommending liberty of speech and calling for its restriction, instead oscillating between apparently contradictory positions. Flattery is the primary and unavoidable danger for the prince according to chapter 23 of Machiavelli's work, but excessive frankness is almost as dangerous. It is only the wisdom of the prince that can maintain the state, he argues, because it is only this wisdom that counters the natural viciousness of his subjects (a sentiment almost directly opposed to the ideas expressed in Elyot's *Governor*): 'men always prove mischievous [*tristi*],' Machiavelli declares, 'unlesse upon some necessity they be forc'd to become good [*buoni*]'.[237]

The humanist treatments of counsel written in the early sixteenth century, with their programmatic and idealistic discussions of the responsibilities of the counsellor, as well as the sceptical mirror image of those ideas outlined in Machiavelli's *Prince*, provided ways of thinking about government and models for political action for people living in Jacobean and Caroline England. Even the most pragmatic discussions of the counsellor's role produced in that period drew on humanist sources and maintained their emphasis on the importance of free speech to the proper fulfilment of that role. The anonymous treatise (by one A.D.B.) *The Covrt of the Most Illvstrious and Most Magnificent James, the First* (1619) is dedicated to the Duke of Buckingham and presented as a defence of the life of the courtier against the 'perverse petulancie' and 'odious aspersions' of poets (who are

[234] The somewhat faint praise of Guillaume Budé, in his letter to Lupset; see More, *Utopia*, p. 116.

[235] For comparisons with More's *Utopia*, see Erasmus, *The Education*, p. viii.

[236] Elyot, *The Governor*, pp. xiii; 6–7. On Elyot and counsel, see McLaren, *Political Culture in the Reign of Elizabeth I*, pp. 70–4.

[237] *Nicholas Machiavel's Prince*, trans. by E[dward]. D[acres]. (London, 1640), p. 195. On Dacres, and early modern English translations and uses of Machiavelli, see Felix Raab, *The English Face of Machiavelli. A Changing Interpretation 1500–1700* (London: Routledge and Kegan Paul, 1964), *passim* and (on Dacres) pp. 96–100; Kahn, *Machiavellian Rhetoric*, pp. 85–235, esp. pp. 124–31.

accused of being motivated by envy).[238] Even as the author admits that courts are full of deception and princes easily provoked, he argues that the courtier must learn to speak freely to his prince and only remain silent when it is an honest course of action:

[margin: Of libertie of speech] Now as touching Liberty, and Freedome in speaking, which Princes (for the most part) doe take very distastefully, I must herein also admonish the Courtier, because indeed they are but few, which freely and faithfully doe aduise, admonish, and aduertise Princes; Thou therefore whosoeuer thou be, which wilt shew thyself not to be a counterfeit, false-hearted, or fained, but rather a faithfull seruant to thy Prince, follow not so fast, seeke not so much the glittering splendour of fickle Fortune, & thine owne priuate commoditie, as the Truth, which by no meanes should be concealed, but honestly reuealed, whensoeuer it may redound, and be conducible to the commoditie, and honest vtilitie of thy KING, and his Common-wealth; therefore thou being wise, wisely forebeare to speake, vntill fit time and occasion, be happily offred vnto thee. Heare what *Salomon* sayes to thee. *Mors & vita in manu Linguae. Life and Death are in the power of the Tongue.* Wherefore, be thou neither a futile, or vnprofitable babler, by vnseemely *Loquacitie*, Neither contrariwise, let thy *Taciturnitie* or secrecie, be vnhonest, but iust and ingenuous.[239]

A.D.B. even advises his courtier-counsellor to accept punishment or death rather than abandon the truth, following the example of Socrates, although his formulation sounds suspiciously ironic:

tis better, and much more commendable, to suffer death it selfe, then either to oppresse or suppresse Truth or good councell. And questionlesse a good Prince, doth much more highly estimate, and valew a faithfull Counsellor, though dead, then a false-hearted flatterer and dissembler, though aliue.[240]

The picture of a king regretfully executing an honest counsellor and holding his memory dear (who else will be causing the counsellor's death?) rather undermines A.D.B.'s apparent idealism here. Even if this text is taken as a flattering defence of courts in general and of James's in particular, it is striking that its author considers the best way of offering such a defence to be a recitation of the humanist rules of good counsel and liberty of speech.

Staying close to A.D.B.'s treatment of the court and praise of dead but honest counsellors, I will conclude this chapter by considering once again

---

[238] A.D.B., *The Covrt of the Most Illvstrious and Most Magnificent James, the First; King of Great-Britaine, France, and Ireland, &c.* (London, 1619), sig. ♠3ᵛ. On this text see also Markku Peltonen, *Classical Humanism and Republicanism in English Political Thought, 1570–1640* (Cambridge: Cambridge University Press, 1995), pp. 136–9.

[239] A.D.B., *The Covrt*, sig. E2ᵛ.

[240] Ibid., sig. E3ʳ. See further E3ᵛ–E4ʳ. At E4ʳ the author advises the counsellor to offer advice even when he is ignorant of the matter in hand, making sure to preface his advice with an apology.

the case of Francis Bacon. As in his treatment of frank speech in *The Wisedome of the Ancients*, in his *Essayes* Bacon is concerned to combine a belief in the necessity of frankness with a Machiavellian awareness of the importance of adaptability to circumstances. His emphasis on decorum goes well beyond the suggestions made to Hythloday by More in the *Utopia* about how to make one's counsel acceptable, and makes Bacon look like a rather more convincing man for all seasons than the martyred More.

Francis Bacon's *Essayes or Counsels, Civill and Morall* (the new title given to the 1625 edition) are, as one would expect from their title, frequently concerned with questions of giving and taking advice. Each of the three major editions that appeared in Bacon's lifetime (and the one presentation manuscript) can be seen as an attempt to advertise the author's skills as a counsellor to influential patrons, whether it be the Earl of Essex, Queen Elizabeth, Prince Henry, the Duke of Buckingham, or James I.[241] Further, throughout his turbulent career, Bacon was continually at pains not just to establish himself as a counsellor to the monarch and others, but to demonstrate to all who would listen the vital importance of counsel, as he understood it, to the practice of politics in and out of Parliament and the court.[242] As MP, holder of a range of increasingly important government posts, and member of the Privy Council, Bacon both evinced and declared his commitment to the life of *negotium*,[243] and – especially in his advice to James and his speeches in the king's Parliaments – he returned again and again to the centrality to that life of negotiation and frank counsel.[244] As Markku Peltonen has pointed out, these features of Bacon's thought, among others, should make us alive to the republican qualities of his politics

---

[241] See Bacon, *The Essayes*, pp. xix–xxx, esp. p. xxvi. Kiernan discusses the presentation manuscript for Prince Henry (British Library MS Harley 5106) at pp. xxi–xxiv, lxxi–lxxvii. See also *Francis Bacon: A Critical Edition of the Major Works*, ed. by Brian Vickers (Oxford: Oxford University Press, 1996), p. 713; Lisa Jardine and Alan Stewart, *Hostage to Fortune. The Troubled Life of Francis Bacon* (London: Victor Gollancz, 1998), pp. 187–8, 333–4 (on the cancelled dedication of the 1612 volume to Prince Henry), 499. The 1625 edition of the *Essays* was published shortly after the death of James I on 27 March.

[242] See Markku Peltonen, 'Bacon's Political Philosophy', in *The Cambridge Companion to Bacon*, ed. by Markku Peltonen (Cambridge: Cambridge University Press, 1996), pp. 283–310, esp. pp. 284, 298–9. For celebrations of the role of counsel see also Francis Bacon, *The History of the Reign of King Henry VII*, ed. by Brian Vickers (Cambridge: Cambridge University Press, 1998), p. 201; Bacon, 'Of the True Greatness of Kingdoms and Estates', in *Critical Edition*, ed. by Vickers, pp. 397–403; p. 397.

[243] For Bacon's commitment to *negotium*, see Peltonen, 'Bacon's Political Philosophy', p. 298.

[244] Bacon was appointed Solicitor-General in 1607, Attorney-General in 1613, Lord Keeper of the Great Seal in 1617, and Lord Chancellor in 1618. See, for example, Bacon's undated (1614?) 'Advice to the King', in Bacon, *Works*, volume XI, p. 371 and his 'Memorial of some Points which may be Touched in his Majesty's Speech to both Houses' (1614), in *Works*, volume XII, pp. 24–30, at p. 26. For more on Bacon in Parliament, see below, chapter 3.

and make us wary of identifying him primarily as a place-seeking royalist or a time-serving scientist on the look-out for research funding.[245]

Bacon's most extended discussion of counsel was the essay 'Of Counsell', which first appeared in the 1612 edition of the *Essayes* – a revision that Bacon originally planned to dedicate to Prince Henry, but which appeared in print not long after the prince's death. The 1625 volume, dedicated to King James's closest counsellor and favourite, the Duke of Buckingham, also appeared at a time of royal mourning, shortly after the king's death on 27 March. By that time Buckingham was already a trusted companion of the new King Charles, while Bacon was living in ill health at his house at Gorhambury, banished from the court after his trial in 1621.[246] This new edition could be read as part of Bacon's ongoing attempt at self-rehabilitation: the book itself in both 1612 and 1625 is certainly a digest of the lessons he had learnt (not to mention the texts he had read) as a *bonus civis* over the course of several decades.[247] In several respects, Bacon's advice is close to that offered by Machiavelli:[248] he concentrates on the problems facing the counselled prince, rather than the counsellor (in contrast to his approach in 'Cassandra, siue Parresia'), and he addresses the perceived 'inconvenience' of weakening one's authority by reliance on counsel, while also discussing the problems of self-interest and flattery on the part of one's advisers.[249]

I have shown how Bacon attempts to solve some of these problems in my discussion of 'Cassandra, siue Parresia'; it became clear there how important he thought the balancing act between frankness and respect. While 'Cassandra' warns against being too baldly frank, 'Of Counsell' offers strategies for extracting frank advice from decorum-bound advisers. Bacon spends a considerable portion of the essay adducing proofs (largely scriptural) of the importance of counsel and its contribution to, rather than diminution of, the king's glory. He also supplies a fable, that of Jupiter and Metis, to establish the conjugal nature of 'the Incorporation, and

[245] Peltonen, 'Bacon's Political Philosophy', *passim*.

[246] For Bacon's fall, see the account by Spedding in *Works*, volume XIV, pp. 209–80; Jardine and Stewart, *Hostage to Fortune*, pp. 444–69.

[247] 'To the Earl of Essex' (July 1600), in *Works*, volume IX, pp. 190–1.

[248] On Bacon and Machiavelli, see Peltonen, *Classical Humanism and Republicanism*, chapter 4; Lisa Jardine, *Francis Bacon: Discovery and the Art of Discourse* (Cambridge: Cambridge University Press, 1974), p. 167; F. J. Levy, 'Francis Bacon and the Style of Politics', *English Literary Renaissance* 16:1 (Winter 1986): 101–22. For a reading of Bacon in the intellectual context of specifically Venetian Tacitism, see Richard Tuck, *Philosophy and Government, 1572–1651* (Cambridge: Cambridge University Press, 1993), pp. 108–12.

[249] Bacon complained of the futility of counsel based on self-interest in a speech concerning Scottish naturalisation in Parliament in February 1606/7; see *Works*, volume X, p. 308. Bacon refers to Demosthenes, and to Parmenio's counselling of Alexander.

inseparable Conjunction of *Counsel* with *Kings*'.[250] Both these defend the
notion of counsel from the charge of automatically lowering the king's
standing in the eyes of his subjects.[251] Another danger is, as we know,
that of flattery masquerading as counsel, and Bacon recommends several preventative measures. Firstly, he suggests, the prince should be careful to choose his counsellors well, so that they are 'faithful, and sincere,
and plain, and direct'; secondly, he should bear in mind that counsellors, being generally competitive, will keep a watch over one another; and
thirdly, he should make sure that his counsellors are more concerned with
his 'business' than his 'person': 'for then he is like to Advise him, and
not to Feede his Humour'.[252] One of Bacon's key recommendations for
the prince seeking good and plain counsel, though, is one which reflects
back upon his own text in a way that has become familiar through this
survey: 'it was truly said', he announces in characteristically sententious
vein, '*Optimi Consiliarii mortui; Books* will speake plaine, when *Counsellors* Blanch. Therefore it is good to be conversant in them; Specially the
Bookes of such, as Themselves have been Actors upon the Stage.'[253] Alive,
but speaking in the pages of a book, and – by the time of the 1625 edition –
in exile, Bacon identifies himself here with the dead voices of those 'actors
upon the stage' of public life: a classically proleptic move for an author
constantly caught between his own age and an imagined future.[254] Like
Erasmus, he suggests that indirect counsel (preferably, in this case, from
another age) may be the safest and most frank that a prince can hope for –
if he knows how to apply it. And it seems clear that Bacon intends his
essay to supply the framework for such application. But he by no means
wishes counsel to become a historical curiosity: the Commission of Union
set up in 1604 is used as an example of a 'Grave and Orderly Assembly',
and praised for the freedom of speech that characterised its proceedings.[255]
Frankness is, for Bacon, still ideally a primary distinguishing feature of

[250] See Bacon, 'Of Counsell', p. 64. Cf. Bacon, 'Metis, or Counsel', in *The Wisedome of the Ancients*,
sigs. [G10]ᵛ–[G11]ᵛ (*De sapientia veterum*, sigs. G2–G2ᵛ).

[251] Bacon asserts that 'the Majesty of Kings, is rather exalted, then diminished, when they are in the
Chaire of Counsell' ('Of Counsell', pp. 65–6).

[252] Ibid., p. 66.   [253] Ibid., p. 67.

[254] See David Colclough, '"Non canimus surdis, respondent omnia sylvae": Francis Bacon and the
Transmission of Knowledge', in *Textures of Renaissance Knowledge*, ed. by Philippa Berry and
Margaret Tudeau-Clayton (Manchester: Manchester University Press, 2003), pp. 81–97.

[255] Bacon, 'Of Counsell', p. 67; the Commission was a favourite example for Bacon, who served on it;
he wrote that 'there was never in any consultation greater plainness and liberty of speech . . . and
all other points of free and friendly interlocution and conference, without cavillations, advantages,
or overtakings' ('The Most Humble Certificate or Return of the Commissioners of England and
Scotland, authorised to treat of an Union for the Weal of both Realms, 2 Jac. I. Prepared, but
Altered' (1604), in *Works*, volume x, pp. 242–5; at p. 244).

successful counsel. The essay ends, indeed, with a pointed recommendation for present practice and the pursuit of frankness: 'a *King*, when he presides in *Counsell*, let him beware how he Opens his owne Inclination too much, in that which he propoundeth: For else *Counsellours* will but take the Winde of him; And in stead of giving Free Counsell, sing him a Song of *Placebo*'.[256]

This last recommendation draws attention to the presence in Bacon's essay, alongside his assertion of the importance of frank counsel, of dissimulation as a necessary part of the prince's self-presentation.[257] The fable of Jupiter and Metis, for instance, is used to show the importance of seeming always in control of one's policy, even when it has been produced by a host of counsellors.[258] This predictable but nonetheless notable focus on the self-presentation of the prince should lead us to think once more about the anticipated function of Bacon's essay. Its combination of terse *sententiae*, classical fable, historical example and local application serve to lend it both a general and a specific authority, and as well as re-advertising Bacon's own qualifications as a counsellor, it could be seen as an attempt to convince an unconvinced king of the benefits of frank counsel. This was a lesson as pertinent to Charles as he faced his first Parliament as it was to James while he was considering whether to call his second. Bacon's *Essayes*, moreover, dramatise the problem, common to discussions of *parrhesia* and of counsel, of where the adviser is speaking from. In 1612 Bacon was on his way to becoming Attorney General, and had proved a staunch defender of the king's prerogative in Parliament; by 1625 he was in disgrace and had to offer his counsel from beyond the margins of the court. In both contexts he was obliged uncomfortably to weigh the interests of the commonwealth against his own and those of the prince, and he did not appear able to regard them as identical. Could a parrhesiastic counsellor in early Stuart England imitate the orators of democratic Athens? Even if he could, such civic frankness could always be interpreted as flattering someone in the audience, as *parrhesia* had from its earliest rhetorical manifestations. In the following chapter I will examine another standpoint from which free speech was claimed and delivered in the early seventeenth century: that of the godly counsellor, or divinely warranted prophet.

---

[256] Bacon, 'Of Counsell', p. 68.
[257] Bacon here echoes the advice of Machiavelli's *The Prince*, Guicciardini's *Ricordi*, and Lipsius, *Sixe Bookes*, sigs. [Piv]ᵛ–Qᵛ; see further Bacon, 'Of Simulation and Dissimulation', in *The Essayes*, pp. 20–3; *Critical Edition*, ed. by Vickers, note, p. 723; Peltonen, 'Bacon's Political Philosophy', pp. 296–7.
[258] Bacon, 'Of Counsell', p. 64.

CHAPTER 2

Freedom of speech and religion

In the previous chapter I set out the ways in which a classical rhetorical tradition (that of *parrhesia*) provided justifications for, and formulas of, outspokenness for early modern persons. *Parrhesia* was shown to signify both the act of speaking frankly and the complex framing apologies for such an act. I then argued for the centrality of the idea of counsel to our understanding of early Stuart notions of free speech: counsel was obliged to be at once frank and decorous, and the techniques associated with *parrhesia* could be crucial to its proper exercise. While the examples and the contexts that I have discussed so far have been both secular and religious, or have included elements of both (as in the cases of Wilson, Peacham, and Wentworth in chapter 1), it is now important to turn to more exclusively religious justifications and uses of free speech. This entails a departure from the Christian humanist discussions which place emphasis primarily on the speaker as an active citizen whose honest and frank speech contributes to the safety of the realm and articulates his part in a just commonwealth; a position reliant on the reinterpretation of classical republican texts. Instead, in this chapter I will begin by focusing on a different tradition of frank speech to which many speakers and writers in the late sixteenth and early seventeenth centuries appealed; one that drew for its examples on the Bible and the history of the early church. Yet it will become clear throughout this chapter that this tradition is far from separable from the classical humanist one which has occupied me so far, and I shall conclude with a discussion of the ways in which they are deployed in tandem to great persuasive and polemical effect in the works of the pamphleteer Thomas Scott.

The most important source for the individual Christian's conceptualisation and practice of frank speech was, as for all else in his or her life, Scripture. The Old Testament provided examples of outspoken and honest counsellors such as Nathan, as well as exhortations to speak frankly to kings and to shun flattery.[1] The New Testament not only contained, in the persons of Christ, the Apostles, and figures like Stephen, the first martyr, outstanding exemplars of plain and bold speaking (simplicity and frankness being a vital pairing for religious discussions of freedom of speech); it also frequently used the term *parrhesia* to describe these acts of boldness or openness.[2] It has been argued that the New Testament use of *parrhesia* is entirely distinct from that found in ancient Greek political works and in the Hellenistic and rhetorical texts I discussed in chapter 1 above.[3] It certainly seems that when the monks and bishops of the early church used the term to describe their frank admonitions to figures in authority, or had it applied to them, they were drawing more on the pagan history of Epicurean and Plutarchan *parrhesia* than they were on the term's biblical uses, as I shall discuss further below.[4] But Stanley B. Marrow admits, even in the course of arguing that 'the New Testament use of *parrhesia* and its verb reflects none of the meanings current in the Gentile world', that 'of course, the term itself does retain the basic meaning of saying everything freely and openly'.[5] Given this fact, it is hard to see how the meaning 'openness towards God' simply trumps the meaning 'frank speech' (what Marrow calls 'mere freedom of speech')[6] when *parrhesia* is used in the New Testament. It is much more likely that these meanings are sometimes superimposed upon each other, and sometimes kept quite separate. David Konstan regards the shift in the term's meaning in Scripture as a 'modulation' rather than a wholly different development, while David E. Fredrickson, S. C. Winter, and William Klassen have shown how *parrhesia* sustains a range of different meanings in different books of the New Testament, ranging from the bold speech of St Paul to his accusers to the open relationship of the individual

---

[1] See, for example, II Samuel 7, 12 and I Kings 1 (Nathan); Job 32:18–22; Proverbs 12:18; 12:22; 16:13; 20:19; 25:13; Psalm 101.

[2] For Stephen's martyrdom, see Acts 7; the headline to verses 18–44 in the King James Version reads 'Stephen speaketh boldly.' On martyrdom and free speech see further below, and John R. Knott, *Discourses of Martyrdom in English Literature, 1563–1694* (Cambridge: Cambridge University Press, 1993); G. W. H. Lampe, 'Martyrdom and Inspiration', in *Suffering and Martyrdom in the New Testament: Studies presented to G. M. Styler by the Cambridge New Testament Seminar*, ed. by William Horbury and Brian McNeil (Cambridge: Cambridge University Press, 1981), pp. 118–35.

[3] See Stanley B. Marrow, SJ, '*Parrhesia* and the New Testament', *Catholic Biblical Quarterly* 44:3 (July 1982): 431–46; Alan C. Mitchell, 'Holding on to Confidence: Παρρησία in Hebrews', in John T. Fitzgerald (ed.), *Friendship, Flattery, and Frankness of Speech in the New Testament World* (Leiden: E. J. Brill, 1996), pp. 203–26.

[4] See Peter Brown, *Power and Persuasion in Late Antiquity: Towards a Christian Empire. The Curti Lectures 1988* (Madison: University of Wisconsin Press, 1992).

[5] Marrow, '*Parrhesia* and the New Testament', p. 439.   [6] Ibid., p. 444.

believer with God in the Johannine corpus.[7] The nature of the speaker's audience makes a large difference to the way in which the term is used. If it is a divine audience (God addressed in prayer), then *parrhesia* does seem to mean something quite a long way from what either Demosthenes, Diogenes, or Plutarch would have meant by it. If, however, the audience is human (a congregation of believers; a group of converts-to-be; or an accusing court), the Greek and Hellenistic meaning of persuasive outspokenness informed by *philia* (and, in the New Testament, *caritas*), comes to the fore. In almost every case, and especially where Apostolic speech is concerned, *parrhesia* is an obligation laid on the speaker by the operation of the Holy Spirit.

I will turn now to some examples of the various ways in which *parrhesia* is used in the New Testament, beginning with those that are farthest from its meanings as discussed in chapter 1. When John describes Jesus's speech and actions he uses *parrhesia* as a marker of plainness and openness, contrasting it with concealment and with speaking in parables. In John 7:4, Jesus's brethren, still doubting him, exhort him to go into Judaea and show his works openly, saying 'For there is no man that doeth any thing in secret, and he himself seeketh to be known openly [παρρησία]. If thou do these things, shew thyself to the world.'[8] The Vulgate translates this use of *parrhesia* as *in palam* (openly in the presence of), depriving it of any association with boldness or frankness. There are very similar uses of *parrhesia* in John 10:24 and 11:54, while in chapter 16 *parrhesia* becomes a plainness of speech that is opposed to parables. Both occurrences of the word are, once again, translated by the Vulgate as *palam* (John 16:25, 16:29). Finally, when Jesus is answering the high priest's accusations after being arrested in Gethsemane, he states that 'I spake openly to the world [παρρησία]; I ever taught in the synagogue, and in the temple, whither the Jews always resort; and in secret have I said nothing' (John 18:20). The only occasion in John's Gospel when *parrhesia* is not translated by the Vulgate as *palam* is in chapter 11. Jesus tries to tell the disciples of Lazarus's death metaphorically, saying that Lazarus is sleeping and that he will go to wake him, but the disciples misunderstand and get stuck on the literal sense. Jesus corrects himself: 'Then said Jesus unto them plainly [παρρησία], Lazarus is dead'

---

[7] David Konstan, 'Friendship, Frankness and Flattery', in Fitzgerald, *Friendship, Flattery, and Frankness of Speech*, pp. 7–19, at p. 15; David E. Fredrickson, 'Παρρησία in the Pauline Epistles', in Fitzgerald, *Friendship, Flattery, and Frankness of Speech*, pp. 163–83; S. C. Winter, 'Παρρησία in Acts', in Fitzgerald, *Friendship, Flattery, and Frankness of Speech*, pp. 185–202; William Klassen, 'Παρρησία in the Johannine Corpus', in Fitzgerald, *Friendship, Flattery, and Frankness of Speech*, pp. 227–54.

[8] All biblical quotations are from the King James Version, unless specified otherwise.

(John 11:14). Here the Vulgate translates 'Tunc ergo Iesus dixit eis manifeste.' All these uses of *parrhesia* emphasise clarity, openness, and plainness: the term is used by John as part of his determination to show that Christianity was not a dangerous underground movement.

A very different set of uses of *parrhesia* can be found in Corinthians and Acts; these are books concerned not with the narrative of Christ's life and actions, as is John's Gospel, but rather with the persuasive acts and speeches of the apostles. In both books, *parrhesia* tends to be translated by the Vulgate not as *palam* but as *fiducia* (confidence, boldness, courage) or *constantia* (steadfastness, firmness, constancy), and by the King James translators not as 'plainly' or 'openly' but as 'boldly' or 'freely'.[9] At II Corinthians 7:4, for example, Paul writes that 'Great is my boldness of speech [παρρησία] toward you, great is my glorying of you' (Vulgate translates as *multa mihi fiducia*). In Acts 2:29, Peter, addressing the crowd who have come to hear the Apostles speaking in tongues, makes use of *parrhesia* in the most classically familiar sense found in the Bible, asking for permission to speak frankly: 'Men and brethren, let me freely speak [παρρησίας] unto you of the patriarch David.' Here the Vulgate translates *parrhesia*, in the only instance that I have found, as *liceat audenter dicere* – a translation much closer to the discourse of *licentia* in the Roman texts discussed earlier than to the language of constancy or boldness. The other occurrences of *parrhesia* in Acts all apply to the bold preaching of the Word by the Apostles, and it is in these scenes, as well as in the bold speech of Paul in his epistles, that many early modern churchmen and religious writers found inspiration for their own boldness of speech. In Acts chapter 4, Peter and John are interrogated by the high priest and his fellows, and astonish them with their 'boldness' (παρρησία; the Vulgate translates as *constantiam*);[10] later the Apostles pray, asking God 'And now, Lord, behold their threatenings, and grant unto thy servants, that with all boldness [παρρησίας] they may speak thy word' (the Vulgate translates as *cum omnia fiducia loqui*).[11] The prayer is answered: 'And when they had prayed, the place was shaken where they were assembled together; and they were all filled with the Holy Ghost, and they spake the word of God with boldness [παρρησίας]' (again the Vulgate translates as *et loquebantur*

---

[9] The translation of *parrhesia* as *fiducia, fidentia,* or *constantia* in Latin versions of the Bible, as opposed to the use of *libertas* or *licentia* in works of the republic and early empire, is noted by Konstan, 'Friendship, Frankness and Flattery', p. 15. See also H. Jaeger, SJ, 'Παρρησία et fiducia', *Studia Patristica* I, Texte und Untersuchungen 63, ed. by K. Aland and F. L. Cross (Berlin: Akademie, 1957), pp. 221–39.

[10] Acts 4:13.   [11] Acts 4:29.

verbum Dei cum fiducia).[12] *Parrhesia* is used in chapters 13 and 14 to describe the outspokenness of Paul and Barnabas towards the Jews at Antioch and towards the people of Iconium, and Apollos' speech in the synagogue at Ephesus in chapter 18.[13] It is once again used to describe Paul's bold speech in chapters 26 and 28, in the former when the Apostle is speaking before Agrippa and in the latter with reference to his preaching in Rome.[14] The first example is a classic example of the freedom of speech that should be exercised by individual believers before those in authority – the kind of scene that would be imitated by bishops in the early church, as well as during the Reformation in England.

Because frank speakers in the New Testament are inspired by the Holy Spirit to testify to their faith to all, *parrhesia* comes to be a quality of boldness and courage rather than either a liberty to be claimed and fought for or a rhetorical figure. It becomes, that is, a Christian virtue, and the boldness of the Apostles – and of Paul in particular – was a model for those who saw themselves as in a direct line of descent from them. While in the Hellenistic world *parrhesia* became a private virtue, to be exercised between friends, this also included the duty to counsel and admonish those in a superior position to the speaker (as we have seen in the case of Plutarch's essay 'How to Tell a Flatterer from a Friend'). Similarly, *parrhesia* as a Christian virtue was something to be exercised among friends or brethren and in one's relationship with God through prayer, but also defined the proper relationship of the individual Christian to those in power. This relationship should consist, Scripture made clear, in the bold and truthful witnessing of the word of God without fear, whatever the circumstances. There was no place here for considerations of decorum, although such concerns would certainly become important as biblical *parrhesia* was put to use in new contexts.

Some centuries after the practice and theory of *parrhesia* became entangled in knotty disputes about the difference between flattery and frankness and the dangers of being misled by false friends in Plutarch's essay, and after its place in Christian life had been cemented in the New Testament

---

[12] Acts 4:31.

[13] Acts 13:46 ('Then Paul and Barnabas waxed bold [παρρησιάσαμενοί]', Vulgate translating as *constanter*); 14:3 ('Long time therefore abode they speaking boldly [παρρησιαζόμενοι] in the Lord', Vulgate *fiducialiter*); 18:26 ('And he began to speak boldly [παρρησιάζεσθαι] in the synagogue', Vulgate *fiducialiter*).

[14] Acts 26:26 ('For the king knoweth of these things, before whom also I speak freely [παρρησιαζόμενος], Vulgate *constanter*); Acts 28:31 ('Preaching the kingdom of God, and teaching those things which concern the Lord Jesus Christ, with all confidence [παρρησίας], no man forbidding him', Vulgate *cum omni fiducia*).

(whose composition roughly coincides with Plutarch's life), it shifted from being an element of friendship to being an attribute of the philosopher. In the fourth and fifth centuries CE, rather than being a civic virtue *parrhesia* belonged to the philosopher, precisely because he was regarded as being outside of the corruption of the *civitas* and politically uncompromised. The tradition drawn on here was that of the frank speech of Plato to Dionysus or, at a pinch, of Diogenes to Alexander. Standing outside the system, the philosopher could be expected to bring ingenuous candour to the court.[15] As Peter Brown has shown, this role was one that also, vitally, came to be adopted by monks and bishops in their relations with the emperor in the early church – even to the exclusion of the frank-speaking philosopher.[16] As Brown writes, 'no ecclesiastical history of the age [the first half of the fifth century] was complete without a vivid scene of confrontation that emphasised the successful *parrhésia* of monks and bishops in their dealings with the emperor'.[17] Monastic and episcopal *parrhesia* relied for its effectiveness on three key elements: the speakers' assertion of their authority over the emperor in divine matters, their awareness of the rules and limits of outspokenness, and the emperor's willingness to listen. When the hermit Macedonius, leading the monks of Syria, spoke boldly to Theodosius in March 387, the emperor had already decided that he could benefit from accepting the admonition – in part because he wanted to legitimise the monks' violence against pagan temples.[18] This willingness to hear frank criticism did not mean that its force was necessarily weakened: as I argue throughout this book, freedom of speech should not be defined solely by its moments of restriction. It is, in fact, always hovering on the borders between liberty and licence (where licence is understood as excessive liberty or abuse of freedom).[19] Just as in relations defined by *philia*, the true friend should be willing to accept harsh but well-meant criticism, so the emperor allowed that he should sometimes accept (and perhaps benefit from) such boldness. In both cases, the danger is, as we have seen in chapter 1, that apparent boldness is disguised flattery; this is no less true in the religious context than in the secular contexts that I have discussed so far.

---

[15] On this development in the history of *parrhesia*, see Brown, *Power and Persuasion*, pp. 61–9.

[16] See ibid., pp. 106–35; on the exclusion of philosophers from the right to *parrhesia*, see pp. 115–17.

[17] Ibid., p. 135.

[18] Ibid., pp. 106–7. Bishop Flavian had brought the monks to intercede with Imperial commissioners who had entered Antioch after statues of the emperor and empress had been pulled down and dragged through the streets.

[19] See *OED* under 'licence', sense 3b. This is the sense in which the word is habitually used throughout this book.

Perhaps the most celebrated instances of *parrhesia* between a churchman and an emperor in the early church, which had a considerable influence on early modern religious free speech, were the encounters between Ambrose of Milan and the Emperors Theodosius and Valentinian. Patrick Collinson has shown just how important Ambrose was as an example to figures in the Elizabethan church, noting Bishop John Jewel's enlisting of Ambrose as an honorary member of the Church of England in his *Apologia Ecclesiae Anglicanae* (1562). Jewel, glancing at what he sees as Roman Catholic servility, argues that in the Church of England ministers are frank to their princes, not flatterers, and that as such they are the natural heirs of Nathan, St John the Baptist, and St Ambrose.[20] In doing so, he also asserts the independence and integrity of the church, in a move that would be crucial to many outspoken religious writers of the following century: 'We say to the prince as St Ambrose sometime said to the Emperor Valentinian: . . . "Trouble not yourself, my lord, to think that you have any princely power over those things that pertain to God".'[21] Ambrose was especially useful to men such as Jewel and Grindal and their successors because he offered, in a form (the epistle) that was a favourite of early modern writers, examples of outspoken counsel to princes; furthermore, within the epistles were descriptions of other imitable acts or familiar scenes: Ambrose preaching to Theodosius; Ambrose acting as an ambassador between Valentinian and Maximus; Ambrose excluded from the court.[22] In addition to the general appeal of his frankness, Ambrose's usefulness to early modern churchmen consisted, as Collinson has pointed out, in three affirmations regularly made by the saint, all of which emphasised the separation of temporal and spiritual power and the primacy of the latter over the former. These were that bishops are to be judges of emperors and not vice versa, that palaces belong to the emperor and churches to bishops, and that the emperor is within the church and not above it.[23]

Ambrose's encounters with Theodosius and Valentinian display, in a number of ways, the blending of biblical and classical *parrhesia* that I have been describing. His determination to bear witness to the word of God and

[20] Patrick Collinson, 'If Constantine, then also Theodosius: St Ambrose and the Integrity of the Elizabethan *Ecclesia Anglicana*', *Journal of Ecclesiastical History* 30:2 (April 1979): 205–29, at p. 205.

[21] *The Works of John Jewel*, ed. by J. Ayre (Cambridge, 1850), IV, p. 898, cited in Patrick Collinson, *The Religion of Protestants: The Church in English Society 1559–1625* (Oxford: Clarendon Press, 1982), p. 10.

[22] See St Ambrose, Letters 41, 21, 24, 51, all in S. L. Greenslade (trans. and ed.), *Early Latin Theology: Selections from Tertullian, Cyprian, Ambrose and Jerome*, The Library of Christian Classics no. 5 (London, SCM Press, 1956), pp. 240–50, 203–8, 220–5, 253–8.

[23] Collinson, 'If Constantine, then also Theodosius', p. 206.

to proclaim the truth no matter what the circumstances are based firmly in the Apostolic and prophetic traditions, while several of the rhetorical techniques deployed in his letters bear a close relation to those treated in Latin discussions of *licentia*. Letter 40, for example (along with Letter 41, the most significant example of Ambrose's frankness) begins with a classic parrhesiastic apology to Theodosius for what is to follow, which manages at the same time to challenge the emperor to listen:

My Lord Emperor, although I am constantly harassed by well-nigh unceasing cares, I have never been in such a fret of anxiety as now, when I see how careful I must be not to expose myself to a charge of high treason. I beg you to listen patiently to what I have to say. If I am not fit to have your ear, then I am not fit to make the offering for you or to have your prayers and petitions entrusted to me. You want me to be heard when I pray for you. Will you not hear me yourself? You have heard me pleading for others. Will you not hear me pleading for myself? Are you not alarmed at your own decision? If you judge me unfit to hear you, you make me unfit to be heard for you.[24]

Already Ambrose is determined to show that his office as bishop, and therefore as the emperor's spiritual guide and ambassador to God, give him not just the right but the obligation to speak out and to be listened to. He goes on to make it quite clear that the relationship of the religious counsellor to his prince places demands on both, and he marshals biblical citations for support:

An emperor ought not to deny freedom of speech, and a bishop ought not to conceal his opinions. Nothing so much commends an emperor to the love of his people as the encouragement of liberty in those who are subject to him by the obligation of public service. Indeed the love of liberty or of slavery is what distinguishes good emperors from bad, while in a bishop there is nothing so perilous before God or so disgraceful before men as not to speak his thoughts freely. For it is written: 'I spake of thy testimonies before kings, and was not ashamed.'[25]

The compulsion to speak out, writes Ambrose, comes from two distinct directions: first, his love for the emperor, and second, his fear of God. This combination is one that would be used to justify frank speaking long after Ambrose, and is used regularly in the early modern period. John Stubbs,

---

[24] Ambrose, Letter 40, in *Early Latin Theology*, p. 229. The letter's (rather unedifying) context is that in the summer of 388 CE the Christians of Callinicum had, with the encouragement of their bishop, set fire to a synagogue; Theodosius ordered that the bishop should rebuild the synagogue. When Ambrose heard of this he wrote Letter 40, arguing that a bishop could not possibly be asked to rebuild the synagogue and asking for an interview with the emperor; see *Early Latin Theology*, p. 226.

[25] Ambrose, Letter 40, in *Early Latin Theology*, p. 229; the quotation is from Psalms 119:46. Ambrose goes on to quote from Ezekiel 3:17, 20, and 21.

for instance, in his *Gaping Gulf* (1579), uses similar terms to justify speaking out against Elizabeth's proposed marriage to the Duc d'Anjou, taking the opportunity to also warn against the evils of flattery:

And seeing the very place of a prince doth bring him some disadvantage through our old Adam, who when he is lift up will hardly yield to the poor advice of them that speak truth in a bare simplicity, the same Lord fill your royal heart with such a tractable and easy sweetness of a yielding nature that you readily and humbly may hearken to all good counsels sent you from God and such as fear God and love your Majesty. Yea, that you may know that it makes most for your safety to encourage and make much of plain, honest speakers and to put out of heart all flatterers. For true, plain men are the best spies of a prince; they watch when you sleep and will ring a timely alarum in your ear before the danger approach; flatterers never watch but when you wake and that they may be seen; they will lull you in security till the sin and punishment thereof be heard at the doors. The Lord deliver you from them even as ravens and dogs.[26]

Ambrose, though, enlists the example of St Paul, and makes it quite clear to Theodosius that in speaking out he is not exceeding the bounds of his office as bishop.[27] He carefully points out that his office as bishop means that he serves two masters – Theodosius and God – but that his obligation to God is greater than that to the emperor. Thus the bishop's 'province' in fact requires him to take actions that could be construed as meddling in 'the affairs of others' rather than precluding it, but these actions are not in fact the 'intrusions' that they may seem: they are the bishop's duty. Throughout this passage Ambrose maintains that his dual service does not, despite appearances, cause a conflict of interest: if the emperor sees things correctly, then he will see that his best interests are at the heart of the bishop's admonitions. Ambrose is, in effect, showing Theodosius that the only alternative to harsh reproof would be sinful flattery, as the end of the passage makes clear. This, along with the argument that the bishop is impelled to speak by the Holy Spirit, is developed in the next section of the letter: 'we speak not as we will, but as we are bidden', writes Ambrose, referring again to his divine rather than his temporal master's bidding – and he goes on to quote Matthew 10:19 and 20: 'When ye shall stand before kings and governors, take no thought what ye shall speak, for it shall be given you in that hour what ye shall speak. For it is not ye that speak, but the Spirit of the Father that speaketh in you.'[28]

---

[26] *John Stubbs's Gaping Gulf with Letters and Other Relevant Documents*, ed. by Lloyd E. Berry (Folger Shakespeare Library: University Press of Virginia, 1968), pp. 30–1.
[27] Ambrose, Letter 40, in *Early Latin Theology*, p. 229; the quotation is from II Timothy 4:2.
[28] Ambrose, Letter 40, in *Early Latin Theology*, p. 229.

Ambrose's letter to Theodosius was a masterpiece of parrhesiastic admonition and justification; but it was not successful: the emperor refused the bishop's request for an interview. In Letter 41, written to his sister, Ambrose recounted the sermon he preached before the emperor in the basilica. The sermon put in even starker terms the obligation to speak frankly in spiritual matters:

In the book of the prophet it is written: 'Take to yourself the rod of an almond tree.' [Jer. 1:11] We have to consider why the Lord said this to the prophet. It was not written without purpose, since in the Pentateuch also we read that the almond rod of Aaron the priest blossomed after it had been long laid up. The rod appears to signify that prophecy or priestly authority ought to be forthright, commending not what is pleasant, but what is advantageous.

The prophet is bidden to take an almond rod because the fruit of this tree has a bitter rind and a hard shell, but is sweet inside. Like it, the prophet also offers hard and bitter things and does not shrink from declaring what is painful.[29]

Backing up his (now public) words with very public actions, Ambrose goes on to describe how even when Theodosius admitted his error, the bishop refused to celebrate mass until the emperor promised that the entire investigation into the burning of the synagogue at Callinicum would be stopped.[30]

Rather as Quintilian offered to early modern rhetoricians, orators, and writers an example of how a technique or a value (eloquence) associated primarily with republicanism could operate successfully in a monarchy, Ambrose gave early modern bishops and churchmen an example of their duty to speak the truth frankly and effectively to a monarch who was also head of the church.[31] It was, as Collinson has argued, difficult for Tudor and Stuart bishops to follow Ambrose's lead when the monarch was the maker and unmaker of bishops;[32] but the general timidity of Elizabethan preachers and the relatively restricted conditions under which they operated contrast with the culture of outspoken preaching under Henry VIII and, especially, his son Edward VI. At the beginning of Edward's reign the treason laws were relaxed and censorship lapsed; this has been linked by Diarmaid MacCulloch with a general encouragement of freedom of religious discussion.[33] Evangelical preaching, with its emphasis on plainness

---

[29] Ambrose, Letter 41, in *Early Latin Theology*, p. 240.   [30] Ibid., pp. 249–50.

[31] See Collinson, *The Religion of Protestants*, pp. 3, 26.

[32] See Collinson, 'If Constantine, then also Theodosius', pp. 210–11.

[33] See Diarmaid MacCulloch, *Tudor Church Militant: Edward VI and the Protestant Reformation* (Harmondsworth: Penguin, 1999), p. 133; for a contrasting account, which emphasises the conflict between Cranmer and Somerset over religious liberty, and the reaction against the 'outburst of preaching and pamphleteering' that followed the government's leniency, see David Loades, *Politics, Censorship, and the English Reformation* (London: Pinter, 1991), pp. 102–3.

and honesty and its reliance on the apostolic tradition, was a vital part of the Reformation, as was the education and advising of princes. Liberty, meanwhile, was a key term for Calvin and his followers – in relation to speech as well as spiritual freedom – and they patrolled its boundaries diligently, careful of its potential for slippage into libertinism.[34] Reformed texts on dogmatics treated freedom of speech as a Christian virtue, prompted by the examples of *parrhesia* in the New Testament discussed above: in his comments on the ninth commandment, Zacharias Ursinus wrote that 'vnder the name of *truth* we comprise liberty of speech, which is a vertu wherby, as much as the time, place, & necessity requireth, we professe the truth freely, & boldly, & are not withdrawne through the fear of danger'.[35]

Patrick Collinson has argued convincingly for Archbishop Edmund Grindal as Ambrose's Elizabethan incarnation;[36] if we were to seek an Ambrose of the previous generation then surely the most obvious candidate would be Hugh Latimer. Latimer's determination to bear witness to the truth even under the 'fear of danger' culminated in his martyrdom in 1555, but it had begun in the reign of Henry VIII, to whom he frequently offered sharp counsel.[37] In 1530 he wrote an outspoken letter to the king, criticising recent proclamations prohibiting the publication of books in English 'containing or tending to any matter of the Scriptures'; he also sent Henry a New Year's Gift of a New Testament with Hebrews 13:4 marked ('the Lord will judge fornicators and adulterers').[38] It was during the reign of Edward VI, however, that Latimer achieved his apotheosis, as a licensed preacher of vehemently admonitory sermons. As with Macedonius' free speech towards Theodosius (see above, p. 82), much of the effectiveness of Latimer's frankness with Edward lay in the fact that it was licensed

---

[34] See MacCulloch, *Tudor Church Militant*, pp. 127ff.

[35] Zacharias Ursinus, *The Summe of Christian Religion*, trans. by Henry Parrie (Oxford, 1587), sig. Rrrᵛ; see Diane Parkin-Speer, 'Freedom of Speech in Sixteenth Century English Rhetorics', *Sixteenth Century Journal* 12:3 (1981): 65–72; p. 69.

[36] Collinson, 'If Constantine, then also Theodosius', pp. 216–21; Collinson discusses Grindal's (heavily annotated) copy of Ambrose at pp. 218–19. See also Patrick Collinson, *Archbishop Grindal, 1519–1583: The Struggle for a Reformed Church* (London: Cape, 1979), pp. 243–4, 266 and *The Religion of Protestants*, pp. 29–30.

[37] Latimer was the first Protestant preacher to address the royal court, giving a sermon at Windsor in Lent 1530; his support of the royal supremacy and divorce, articulated in sermons preached at Cambridge in 1529, gave him a way in, and he was, along with his fellow evangelical Nicholas Shaxton, a client of Anne Boleyn. See Peter E. McCullough, *Sermons at Court: Politics and Religion in Elizabethan and Jacobean Preaching* (Cambridge: Cambridge University Press, 1998), p. 56.

[38] For Latimer's letter to Henry VIII, see Hugh Latimer, *Sermons and Remains*, ed. by George Elwes Corrie, 2 volumes (Cambridge: Cambridge University Press, 1844–5), volume I: *Sermons*, pp. v–vi; on his New Year's Gift, see Susan Brigden, *New Worlds, Lost Worlds: The Reign of the Tudors 1485–1603* (Harmondsworth: Penguin, 2000), p. 64.

(indeed, invited) by the king.[39] In a Lenten sermon preached before Edward at Westminster in 1550 (a key year in Edward's move towards independent religious initiatives),[40] Latimer made use of one of the same biblical examples of frank speech that had been used by Ambrose in his Letter 40, Matthew 10:19, 20 (see p. 85 above).[41]

Latimer's position as a licensed frank speaker, justified both by his king's faith in him and by his obligation to preach the word of God, allowed (or even obliged) him not only to criticise counsel that might be being offered to Edward (marry to make the realm stronger; indulge your pleasures), but to act as a counsellor himself and proffer what he regarded as truly godly counsel. He anticipated that this would be criticised, and highlighted the boldness of his speech by spending time responding in advance to his critics and comparing himself to the prophets Jonah and Elijah. Jonah, Latimer reminds his audience, was a plain and frank speaker when he addressed the people of Nineveh – his 'sermon' ('yet forty days and Nineveh shall be overthrown') was 'a nipping sermon, a pinching sermon, a biting sermon'.[42] Yet the Ninevites followed Jonah's warning and did not – as Latimer argues an Edwardian auditory would have – attack its lack of decorum.[43]

The problem with the category of decorum – a problem glanced at already in chapter 1, and one which I will discuss further in relation to parliamentary free speech – is that unless the speaker is allowed to decide what is appropriate to the time, the place, and the persons, and is not made subject to others' definitions of what is decorous, then it can be used to curtail free speech.[44] However sinful the people of Nineveh might have been, Latimer argues, they were at least good listeners: they knew when to bow to the authority of a plain-speaking prophet, and how to recognise it. The people of Edwardian England, by contrast, might well have rejected him, and would, moreover, have been likely to reject the words of the prophet Elijah (I Kings 18:18) as seditious.[45]

In these sermons Latimer uses his none-too-subtle irony not only to discredit his critics, but powerfully to assert his identity with the biblical prophets whom he saw as his predecessors and who justified his own outspokenness. The implicit argument (were Elijah or Jonah alive today they would be criticised for sedition or for speaking out of season; I am criticised

---

[39] On Edward's fondness for evangelical sermons and encouragement of preaching at court, see MacCulloch, *Tudor Church Militant*, pp. 23–5.

[40] See ibid., pp. 35–6.

[41] Latimer, 'A Most Faithful Sermon Preached Before the King's Most Excellent Majesty and his Most Honourable Council, in his Court at Westminster, by the Reverend Father Master Hugh Latimer, [in Lent] *Anno Domini*, 1550', in *Sermons*, pp. 239–81, at p. 268.

[42] Jonah 3:4.   [43] Latimer, *Sermons*, pp. 240–1.   [44] Ibid., p. 241.   [45] Ibid., p. 250.

for speaking out of season, therefore I am the inheritor of their function, a latter-day prophet) is rhetorically and polemically a strong one, despite its reliance on analogy, because it uses and develops the Reformation topos of the Protestant preacher (or church) as one that recovers, or forges, a direct link between the nascent church of Scripture and the church militant of the present. Analogy thus becomes typology (Jonah is the type of Latimer) and the church, as well as the frank speech of its ministers, can become truly apostolic once more.

Latimer's sermons before Edward VI are packed with frank correction of the king, and with self-conscious references to these admonitions: Latimer is frequently concerned to draw attention to his obligation to speak out, as though he needs to establish this as an essential part of the preacher's task as much as he needs to ensure that the lessons he teaches are learnt. God's sword – his Word – is the only means available to the preacher to correct a king's actions, and it must be used without fear, he argues.[46] Preaching to the court, Latimer contrasts the flattery that is endemic there with his own frankness;[47] yet his assaults on the dangers of attending too delicately to others' definitions of what is decorous do not preclude him from displaying a fine sensitivity to the kind of strategies recommended by More in his dialogue with Hythloday at the beginning of *Utopia*.[48] However much Latimer was aware of their utility when advising a prince of his duty, though, his own discourse rarely makes use of these strategies.

The Epistle to the Reader that preceded the 1549 edition of the second sermon preached before Edward celebrated Latimer's outspokenness in telling terms, and prayed for more like him: 'we lack a few more Latimers; a few more such preachers. Such plain Pasquyls we pray God provide for us, as will keep nothing back.' Not only was Latimer a Pasquil, the writer of the Epistle went on to say; he was (in a comparison Latimer would surely have appreciated) a second Elijah.[49] The combination of plainness (in the figure of Pasquil) and prophecy is a cornerstone of much Reformation writing on religious freedom of speech, and was developed and

---

[46] See Latimer, 'The First Sermon Preached before King Edward, March 8, 1549', in Latimer, *Sermons*, pp. 84–103, at p. 86:

> The king correcteth transgressors with the temporal sword; yea, and the preacher also, if he be an offender. But the preacher cannot correct the king, if he be a transgressor of Gods word, with the temporal sword, but he must correct and reprove him with the spiritual sword; fearing no man; setting God only before his eyes, under whom he is a minister, to supplant and root up all vice and mischief by God's word.

[47] See, for example, Latimer, *Sermons*, pp. 124–5, 292–3.

[48] Latimer, 'The Seventh Sermon of M. Latimer Preached Before King Edward, April Nineteenth, [1549]' [Good Friday], in Latimer, *Sermons*, pp. 216–38, at pp. 231–2.

[49] Ibid., pp. 110–11.

complicated in the ensuing century or so. Latimer was a learned man, renowned for his studiousness both before and after his conversion by Bilney (he was made fellow of Clare Hall when still an undergraduate at Cambridge), but he repeatedly stressed his humble origins and made much of the homeliness of his preaching style.[50] The plain-speaking ploughman was an enormously popular figure for the delivery of religious satire and social critique, from Langland's fourteenth-century *Piers Plowman* through the pseudo-Chaucerian *Ploughman's Tale* to Spenser's *Shepheardes Calender*, and into the seventeenth century with the work of William Browne and George Wither – and Spenser notably praised the Ambrose of the 1560s, Archbishop Grindal, in the July eclogue of his poem.[51] In the representation of him offered in the Epistle to the Reader of his 1549 sermon, and in his sermons themselves, Latimer fuses several identities that allow him to lay claim to a right to free speech before the source of temporal power: he is the plain-spoken son of a yeoman; he is himself a shepherd, insofar as he is a pastor, and therefore plain of speech (his speech, he implies, is naturally unsophisticated); he has suffered for his speech and actions and so can be relied upon to tell the truth in the face of danger; his office as a court preacher obliges him to speak frankly to the king; he is a latter-day prophet whose speech is inspired by the Holy Ghost.

If Latimer's claim to the right to speak frankly and assertion of the frankness of his speech (his rejection of that flattery that imitates frankness) relied in part on his having experienced danger and persecution (he was imprisoned at the end of Henry VIII's reign), then his martyrdom was, especially in the narrative constructed by John Foxe, the ultimate validation of that claim. His *parrhesia* was thus confirmed by two directly opposing conditions: on the one hand, the liberty allowed him by Edward VI, acting as

---

[50] See, for example, Latimer, 'The First Sermon Preached before King Edward, March 8, 1549', in Latimer, *Sermons*, pp. 84–103, at p. 101.

[51] Mid sixteenth-century 'ploughman' works include *A Godly Dyalogue & Disputacion Betwene Pyers Plowman and a Popish Preest* (c. 1550) and *I Playne Piers Which Can not Flatter* (1550?). See Andrew N. Wawn, 'Chaucer, *The Plowman's Tale* and Reformation Propaganda: The Testimonies of Thomas Godfray and *I Playne Piers*', *Bulletin of the John Rylands University Library* 56 (1973–4): 174–92 and 'The Genesis of *The Plowman's Tale*', *Yearbook of English Studies* 2 (1972): 21–40; John N. King, *English Reformation Literature: The Tudor Origins of the Protestant Tradition* (Princeton: Princeton University Press, 1982), pp. 259ff and 'Spenser's *Shepheardes Calender* and Protestant Pastoral Satire', in *Renaissance Genres: Essays on Theory, History, and Interpretation*, ed. by Barbara Kiefer Lewalski (Cambridge, MA: Harvard University Press, 1986), pp. 369–98; Annabel Patterson, *Pastoral and Ideology. Virgil to Valéry* (Oxford: Clarendon Press, 1988), p. 143; Michelle O'Callaghan, *The 'Shepheards Nation': Jacobean Spenserians and Early Stuart Political Culture, 1612–1625* (Oxford: Clarendon Press, 2000), p. 103; David Norbrook, *Poetry and Politics in the English Renaissance*, revised edition (Oxford: Oxford University Press, 2002), chapter 3; Edmund Spenser, 'The Shepheardes Calender', in Spenser, *The Shorter Poems*, ed. by Richard A. McCabe (Harmondsworth: Penguin, 1999), pp. 95–106.

a king open to admonition in the tradition of Theodosius; on the other, the liberty absolutely denied him under Mary I. In a tradition that reached back to the Bible's narratives of the persecution of Stephen the protomartyr and of St Paul, and that was developed in Eusebius' history of the early church, the martyr was the definitive religious parrhesiast; this notion was central to Foxe's recounting of the sufferings of the 'true' church, and to the narratives (written by themselves or others) of later martyrs, such as Henry Barrow, William Prynne, John Lilburne, John Bunyan, and George Fox.[52] The martyr's speech was inspired by the Holy Spirit – as confirmed by texts such as Matthew 10:19–20 and Luke 12:11–12, both used frequently by early modern writers on the subject – and thus had an additionally divine and prophetic status.[53] Indeed, as G. W. H. Lampe argues, in this tradition the martyr's testimony of the true word of God becomes more important than his or her suffering in the imitation of Christ: 'it is the witness before hostile authorities that is the essence of "martyrdom", and the role of the Spirit is not primarily to bring consolation and strength in physical suffering, but to inspire confessors to proclaim the Lordship of Christ with uninhibited freedom (*parrhesia*)'.[54] This understanding lent enormous weight to the textual records left by martyrs of their examinations or 'dying speeches' – again, Foxe's *Acts and Monuments* is witness to this, but should not overshadow later sophisticated uses on the part of such testimonies of the relationship between speech and writing or print.[55] While it was the martyr's actual suffering and death that lent their words their final authority, we can see in the claims of frank speakers like Latimer to be ready to suffer for their outspokenness a pre-emptive claiming of such authority. When a religious parrhesiast – and we could include here John Stubbs, Peter Wentworth, and Sir Philip Sidney in his letter to Queen Elizabeth – told a royal addressee that he placed himself at the mercy of his auditor, this was not only used to intensify the weight of the advice proffered and to guarantee its sincerity (if I am ready to suffer for telling you this, then it is truly outspoken), but was also a kind of proleptic martyrdom of the speaker or writer, whereby the free speech in question was as if spoken by one already suffering for it. Whether

---

[52] On the continuity of this tradition, see Knott, *Discourses of Martyrdom*, pp. 7–9.

[53] On Matthew 10:19–20, see pp. 85, 88 above; on Luke 12:11–12 (which is very close to the passage from Matthew's Gospel), see Knott, *Discourses of Martyrdom*, p. 26.

[54] Lampe, 'Martyrdom and Inspiration', pp. 122–3. Lampe contrasts this tradition with a 'Christocentric' one in which 'it is the actual suffering and death of the Christian disciple that is of primary importance rather than his verbal testimony' (p. 120).

[55] For a brilliant analysis of such phenomena in the late seventeenth century, see Martin Dzelzainis, '*Parrhesia*, Print and Martyrdom in Restoration England', forthcoming in *Martyrs and Martyrdom: Early-Modern Perspectives*, ed. by P. S. Scott. I am grateful to Dr Dzelzainis for providing me with a typescript of his essay.

proleptic or actual, however, the martyr's speech required validation from a larger community in order to attain the status of true religious *parrhesia*. Just as frank speech to a superior could be redescribed as flattery, so a martyr's speech could easily be deemed heresy or treason: the triumphant statements made under examination and at the pyre by Foxe's Protestant heroes were regarded as recalcitrant refusals to acknowledge error by their Marian persecutors, and the prayers or speeches made by Roman Catholic martyrs under Elizabeth were signs of ongoing treasonous intent to their Protestant detractors. Suffering alone could not guarantee that one's words would be treated as truthful and divinely inspired. In James's reign, after the introduction of the Oath of Allegiance in 1606, considerable controversy arose over the question of whether a Roman Catholic who refused to take the Oath and suffered as a consequence could truly be considered a martyr – a controversy entered most notably by John Donne in his *Pseudo-Martyr* of 1610.[56] Once again we confront the suggestion that free speech needs to be recognised as such by a community that has criteria for its definition and use in order to function properly, be that community an oppressed or a dominant one, and that it is vital to recognise how it is being interpreted, and for whose ends, at the time of its utterance (or publication) and after.

During the Reformation, especially in the evangelically optimistic years of Edward VI's reign, models of religious *parrhesia* drawn from the Bible and from early Christian writers like Ambrose guided preachers, polemicists, and poets in their discussions and uses of free speech, especially when considering the difficulty of admonishing their social superiors. For Latimer and many others, preaching was a golden opportunity publicly to perform frank speech and to outline its justification. After what Foxe and others regarded as the period of Marian captivity of the Protestant church, there was, however, no glorious return to the open conditions of the late 1540s and early 1550s. Elizabeth did not invite the kind of sharp counsel from the pulpit that her brother Edward had relished, and however overstated her 'tuning' of the pulpits has been in historical accounts of the period, her assertion of her supremacy over and within the Church and concerning the matters that might come within its purview meant that in many cases pulpits and preachers developed a discreet self-tuning mechanism.[57] The office of

---

[56] On *Pseudo-Martyr* as a clear endorsement of James's position in the Oath of Allegiance controversy, see Johann P. Sommerville, 'John Donne the Controversialist: The Poet as Political Thinker', in *John Donne's Professional Lives*, ed. by David Colclough (Cambridge: D. S. Brewer, 2003), pp. 73–96. On the controversy more broadly, and with especial reference to the Continental context, see Sommerville, 'Jacobean Political Thought and the Controversy Over the Oath of Allegiance', unpublished PhD thesis, University of Cambridge, 1981.

[57] See Collinson, 'If Constantine, then also Theodosius', p. 215.

bishop was far from exalted for much of Elizabeth's reign, while both flattery and frankness from the pulpit could enrage the queen. As Patrick Collinson has argued, aside from in the Lenten sermons, whose occasion positively demanded mortification, preaching was a far less popular form for the expression of religious *parrhesia* under Elizabeth than were letters or written orations – and these were the kinds of text used by Archbishop Grindal in his skirmishes with the monarch over the relationship between queen and church and the use of religious images.[58] In the next section of this chapter I will move on to consider how, even with the accession of James I – whose table William Barlow compared to Constantine's court – preachers balanced precariously on a tightrope between frankness and flattery and were subject to intense royal scrutiny. I will then look at the forms of accommodation reached by one preacher, John Donne, who served under both James and Charles I, before I conclude the chapter by considering the pamphlets of Thomas Scott as the home of religious *parrhesia* in the later years of James's reign.

FLATTERY AND FRANKNESS IN JACOBEAN AND CAROLINE SERMONS

In 1622, as conflict between Protestant and Catholic forces spread across continental Europe and negotiations for the Spanish Match continued apparently unabated, many English preachers used their sermons to spread outspoken anti-Catholic, anti-peace propaganda. To James I, who was trying to live up to his motto of *Beati pacifici* and avoid becoming embroiled in a costly war – or, as his opponents saw it, was leaving his son-in-law and daughter to fend for themselves and failing in his obligations to the broader Protestant population of Europe – such discussion of royal policy was simply unacceptable.[59] In August 1622, James issued through the Archbishops of Canterbury and York a set of 'Directions to Preachers' that responded to the perceived turmoil in the pulpits. Preachers were required to confine themselves to issues covered by the Thirty-Nine Articles and Book of Homilies; Sunday afternoons were to be reserved for catechising, not preaching; no-one under the degree of bishop or dean was to preach

[58] Ibid., pp. 216–21. I am not suggesting that there were no sermons preached under Elizabeth that were critical of the monarch or of specific policies – the negotiations for the queen's marriage in 1579 in particular provoked a series of outspoken sermons, for example. See McCullough, *Sermons at Court*, p. 67. On godly counsel under Elizabeth, see further A. N. McLaren, *Political Culture in the Reign of Elizabeth I: Queen and Commonwealth 1558–1585* (Cambridge: Cambridge University Press, 1999).

[59] On the events of this period and popular responses to them, see further pp. 223–47 below.

on predestination; no preacher of any rank was to 'meddle with matters of state', and there was to be no more 'undecent rayling speeches against the persons of either Papists or Puritanes'.[60] James was clearly – and characteristically – alarmed by the vituperative nature of much of the current discussion, not simply by its anti-Catholic bias (hence the proscription of railing against puritans as well as papists, and the stress on *ad hominem* attacks). His desire for a reunified Christendom and fostering of irenicism entailed a deep suspicion of controversy, as can be seen in his rather hapless attempt to enter the textual battle over the Oath of Allegiance, *Triplici nodo, triplex cuneus, or An Apologie for the Oath of Allegiance* (1607), a work whose argumentative failings and unsuccessful pose of anonymous authorship were assiduously picked apart by Cardinal Bellarmine.[61] The 'Directions to Preachers' proved predictably controversial themselves: along with the suspension of the laws against recusants (enacted two days before the 'Directions' were issued), they led some to suspect the king's 'constancie in the true reformed religion', as John Chamberlain put it.[62] As a result Archbishop Abbot wrote to the clergy explaining and justifying the 'Directions', while the Dean of St Paul's, John Donne, was employed to deliver a sermon on them at the public preaching place at Paul's Cross.[63] Donne's sermon has often been considered an awkward performance, Chamberlain beginning

---

[60] For the text of the 'Directions', see *Documentary Annals of the Reformed Church of England*, ed. by Edward Cardwell (1839), volume II, pp. 146–51. On anti-Catholic sermons in the early 1620s and on the 'Directions' and their success or otherwise, see Thomas Cogswell, *The Blessed Revolution: English Politics and the Coming of War, 1621–1624* (Cambridge: Cambridge University Press, 1989); Louis B. Wright, 'Propaganda against James I's "Appeasement" of Spain', *Huntington Library Quarterly* 6:2 (February 1943): 149–72 (though beware that Wright conflates two different Thomas Scotts); Kenneth Fincham and Peter Lake, 'The Ecclesiastical Policy of King James I', *Journal of British Studies* 24 (1985): 9–207; Cyndia Susan Clegg, *Press Censorship in Jacobean England* (Cambridge: Cambridge University Press, 2001), pp. 167–9. On anti-Catholic writing more generally in early Stuart England, see especially Peter Lake, 'Anti-popery: The Structure of a Prejudice', in *Conflict in Early Stuart England*, ed. by Richard Cust and Ann Hughes (Harlow: Longman, 1989), pp. 72–106; Anthony Milton, *Catholic and Reformed: The Roman and Protestant Churches in English Protestant Thought, 1600–1640* (Cambridge: Cambridge University Press, 1995); Arthur F. Marotti (ed.), *Catholicism and Anti-Catholicism in Early Modern English Texts* (Basingstoke: Macmillan, 1999).

[61] Bellarmine's reply to James was *Responsio ad Librum inscriptum Triplici Nodo Triplex Cuneus* (1608), published under the name of Matthaeus Tortus (one of the Cardinal's almoners). On the Oath, see Sommerville, 'Jacobean Political Thought and the Controversy over the Oath of Allegiance'. On James's irenicism and desires for international ecumenical agreement, see W. B. Patterson, *King James VI and I and the Reunion of Christendom* (Cambridge: Cambridge University Press, 1997).

[62] John Chamberlain to Dudley Carleton, 25 September 1622, in *The Letters of John Chamberlain*, ed. by N. E. McClure, 2 volumes (Philadelphia: American Philosophical Association, 1939), volume II, p. 451.

[63] For Abbot's letter, see David Cressy and Lori Anne Ferrell (eds.), *Religion and Society in Early Modern England* (London: Routledge, 1996), pp. 137–9; Donne's sermon can be found in John Donne, *Sermons*, ed. by George Potter and Evelyn M. Simpson, 10 volumes (Berkeley: University of California Press, 1953–61), volume IV, pp. 178–209.

a long tradition of criticism when he wrote that the Dean 'gave no great satisfaction, or as some say spake as yf himself were not so well satisfied'.[64] Readers' opinions of the sermon tend to be divided on the basis of their own image of Donne, as absolutist apologist for James or as conscience-stricken servant of a demanding king put in an impossible position; but recent work by scholars such as Jeanne Shami and Mary Morrissey has urged us to pay more careful attention to the ways in which Donne balances his conflicting obligations to maintain the dignity of the pulpit and the supremacy of the king.[65] Donne certainly faced a difficult task: his sermon could easily have been heard as supporting the restriction of religious *parrhesia*, and as endorsing what Ambrose would have seen as a very unhealthy juris-dictional trumping of the basilica by the palace. Yet Donne's argument is far from servile: he maintains the need for the preacher to be 'instant, in season, out of season' while reminding his audience that the Bible war-rants the kind of order mentioned by his text (Judges 5:20, 'They fought from heaven; the stars in their courses fought against Sisera') and imposed by the 'Directions'. It is not James's intention to restrict debate, Donne argues; rather, he wishes to ensure that debate is based on sure foundations and is conducted about essential and not indifferent matters.[66] Typically, Donne emphasises the importance of *mediocritas*, of finding a middle way between extremes; thus he stresses that in the 'Directions' there is 'no abat-ing of Sermons, but a direction of the Preacher to preach usefully, and to *edification*', and he goes on to say that 'those Preachers which must save your soules, are not ignorant, unlearned, extemporall men; but they are not over curious men neither'. The preacher should be a 'middle starre' like the North star which is steadfast and provides guidance while being

[64] Chamberlain, *Letters*, volume II, p. 451.

[65] For a range of opinions on the sermon, see Millar MacLure, *The Paul's Cross Sermons, 1534–1642* (Toronto: University of Toronto Press, 1958), p. 105; R. C. Bald, *John Donne. A Life* (Oxford: Clarendon Press, 1970), pp. 433–5; John Carey, *John Donne: Life, Mind and Art*, new edition (London: Faber and Faber, 1990), p. 102; P. M. Oliver, *Donne's Religious Writing: A Discourse of Feigned Devotion* (London: Longman, 1997), pp. 253–60. The works by Shami and Morrissey are Jeanne Shami, ' "The Stars in their Order Fought Against Sisera": John Donne and the Pulpit Crisis of 1622', *John Donne Journal* 14 (1995): 1–58; Mary Morrissey, 'John Donne as a Conventional Paul's Cross Preacher', in *John Donne's Professional Lives*, ed. by Colclough, pp. 159–78; Morrissey, 'Rhetoric, Religion and Politics in the St Paul's Cross Sermons, 1603–1625', unpublished PhD thesis, University of Cambridge, 1998, chapter 1.

[66] The texts to which James redirects his ministers in the 'Directions' (the Catechisms, the Thirty-Nine Articles, and the Homilies), says Donne, provide more than enough material for controversy and debate; Donne, *Sermons*, volume IV, pp. 202–8. Peace, Donne explains, does not consist in an 'indifferencie to contrary Opinions in fundamentall doctrines, not to shuffle religions together', but in a 'peace with persons, an abstinence from contumelies, and revilings' (*Sermons*, volume IV, p. 196).

'none of the greatest magnitude; but yet . . . none of the least neither'.[67] Order is what Donne celebrates and endorses in his sermon at Paul's Cross, and he associates order with decorous debate and discretion on the part of ministers as well as with the proper observation of the hierarchy of the established church, whereby James is its lawful head: it is, Donne remarks, the head and not the body of the church which speaks and which directs its members.[68]

Donne's sermon may have sounded strained to some of his auditors; to the king it was 'a piece of such perfection, as could admit neither addition nor diminution'.[69] He ordered it to be printed at once. It certainly accorded with the general drift of court sermons in the reigns of both James and Charles, which continued an Elizabethan strategy of using flattery and panegyric to counsel the monarch. The almost formal gesture towards the importance of maintaining decorum that Latimer used to frame his direct admonitions was left behind as preachers at court became increasingly wary of alienating their royal auditors. Elizabeth's displeasure could be extremely discouraging, to say the least, but an equally great danger was that she would be alienated from the message being delivered by reform-minded ministers and driven closer to Rome.[70] Similarly, James I's championing of religious moderation and hatred of faction meant that preachers across the doctrinal and ecclesiological spectrum knew that success was likely to come from their able use of the language of consensus and conformity – not from their prophetic outspokenness.[71] This was combined at the beginning of James's reign with a sense of uncertainty about the new monarch's possible plans for the church: continuity was preferable to innovation, and this was most

---

[67] Ibid., p. 209.

[68] Ibid., p. 199. On the importance of 'discretion' to Donne's preaching, see Jeanne Shami, 'Donne on Discretion', *English Literary History* 47:1 (1980): 48–66.

[69] James's 'own word' as recorded in a congratulatory letter to Donne from the Earl of Carlisle, quoted in Bald, *John Donne. A Life*, p. 435.

[70] See McCullough, *Sermons at Court*, pp. 78–9. See also the tract recently attributed to Francis Bacon, which argues that authors of libels ('part of them being devines by profession') should remember that 'we are forbidden in anywise {Ecclesiastes, c. 10, v. 20} to slander [persons of excellent calling]'; Francis Bacon (?), 'An Aduertisement Towching Seditious Wrytings', transcribed in Brother Kenneth Cardwell, 'An Overlooked Tract by Francis Bacon', *Huntington Library Quarterly* 65: 3 and 4 (2002): 421–33, at p. 432.

[71] On the language of conformity, see Lori Anne Ferrell, *Government by Polemic: James I, the King's Preachers, and the Rhetorics of Conformity, 1603–1625* (Stanford: Stanford University Press, 1998). On the use of a consensual lexicon to generate or disguise conflict, see Peter Lake, 'The Moderate and Irenic Case for Religious War: Joseph Hall's *Via Media* in Context', in *Political Culture and Cultural Politics in Early Modern England*, ed. by Susan D. Amussen and Mark Kishlansky (Manchester: Manchester University Press, 1995), pp. 55–83; see also Lake, 'Lancelot Andrewes, John Buckeridge, and Avant-Garde Conformity at the Court of James I', in *The Mental World of the Jacobean Court*, ed. by Linda Levy Peck (Cambridge: Cambridge University Press, 1991), pp. 111–33.

likely to be fostered by gently flattering counsel.[72] James's enthusiasm for decorous religious debate was reflected in his choice of an eclectic range of court preachers and appointment of royal chaplains: the struggle for control of the language of conformity between orthodox Calvinists and proto-Arminians was often played out in the chapel at Whitehall.[73] Furthermore, evangelical Calvinist works continued to be printed in large numbers and to be licensed until the late 1630s.[74] There are, of course, still many examples of sermons delivered before the crisis of 1622 that eschewed the delicacy of decorum, of which Richard Eedes's sermon in August 1603 is a good instance. Eedes, the Dean of Worcester, argued that royal chaplains were there to make monarchs into good kings and good Christians, and that to do so they needed to speak 'in the stile of a commander'.[75] Prince Henry, meanwhile, displayed considerable enthusiasm for admonitory preaching on the Latimer model with his patronage of evangelical divines such as Hugh Broughton and Daniel Price.[76] However, in a context where panegyric was increasingly used as the best means of correction, preaching to the king lost much of its connection with the biblical and Ambrosian models of *parrhesia* discussed above. Instead there is a parallel with the rhetorical use of *parrhesia* where, as I showed in chapter 1, the apology for frankness replaces frankness itself. This process reached its zenith under Charles I, who lacked his father's relish for theological debate and enthusiasm for hearing all the sides of an argument and, by the time he became king, had come to reject his brother's enthusiasm for international Protestantism and frank counsel.[77]

In February 1628/9, almost seven years after he preached for James I at Paul's Cross, and at the very end of the period covered by this book, John Donne gave a sermon at Whitehall on the text 'So speak ye, and so do, as they that shall be judged by the law of liberty' (James 2:12).[78]

---

[72] McCullough, *Sermons at Court*, pp. 102–6.   [73] Ibid., pp. 112–16.

[74] See S. Mutchow Towers, *Control of Religious Printing in Early Stuart England* (Woodbridge: The Boydell Press, 2003).

[75] Richard Eedes, 'The Dutie of a King', in *Six Learned and Godly Sermons*, quoted by McCullough, *Sermons at Court*, p. 105. A later collection of Eedes's sermons, *Three Sermons preached by . . . Doctor Eedes* (London, 1627), was edited by the Shropshire minister Robert Horn, on whom see pp. 219–38 below.

[76] See McCullough, *Sermons at Court*, pp. 185–90.

[77] On the continuity between the religious households of the two Princes of Wales, and especially on Charles's patronage of Henry's 'collegiate community' of anti-Spanish, militant Protestant preachers, see McCullough, *Sermons at Court*, pp. 194–209.

[78] Donne, *Sermons*, volume VIII, pp. 335–54. Paul Harland argues that it is unlikely that Charles was present at the delivery of this sermon, since he usually attended chapel only on Sundays and Tuesdays, and is not mentioned in the sermon's title: Paul Harland, 'Donne's Political Intervention in the Parliament of 1629', *John Donne Journal* 11:1 and 2 ('1992'; actually 1995): 21–37, at p. 34, n. 18. The sermon was delivered on the first Friday in Lent.

The text determines the questions with which Donne will be concerned: when and how to speak and act, and how far the 'law of liberty' either sanctions, demands, or restricts speech and action. First he asks to whom this imperative applies. Citing Athanasius, Origen, Jerome, Epiphanius, and Oecumenicus, Donne explains that the book of James, along with six other Epistles, is peculiarly universal; it encompasses 'all Rules, all Canons of holy Conversation', and it is directed to 'all the Christian world'.[79] Moreover (and this is the point he emphasises), it is 'circular'; that is to say, the reader cannot discern the particulars, the beginning and end, because the book gives 'All rules, for All actions, to All persons, at All times, and in All places'.[80] Following standard preaching practice, Donne begins by establishing the universal applicability of the text he has chosen; he then needs to go on specifically to apply it to his auditors or it will lose its efficacy. In an ingenious piece of argumentation, he contends that although one cannot actually *find* the beginning or the end of a circle, one knows that they are both the same: since the last point (heaven) is a kingdom and a court, surely James's first point in his Epistle is also intended to be a kingdom, and a court.[81] Thus 'the Holy Ghost, in proposing these duties in his general *Ye*, does principally intend, ye that live in Court'.[82]

In his *divisio*, Donne explains that what is most important about his text is not its injunctions – 'speak ye . . . do' – but its qualifications: '*so* speak ye, and *so* do' (my italics). Similarly, it is not the judgement offered by the text that is most significant, but its regulating of judgement; not the liberty that it offers, but its restriction of liberty:

the Court is always under judgement enough. Every discontented person that hath miss'd his preferment, though he have not merited it; every drunkard that is over-heat, though not with his own wine; every conjecturing person, that is not within the distance to know the ends, or the ways of great Actions, will Judge the highest Counsels, and execution of those Counsels. The Court is under judgement enough, and they take liberty enough; and therefore here is a law to regulate our liberty, *A law of liberty: So speak ye, and, &c.*[83]

At the very opening, then, Donne suggests that this sermon on a text apparently encouraging speech and action conditioned by 'liberty' will in fact deal with the ways in which speech could be more discreet, and might suggest that judgement is something that should be passed on our words before we speak rather than being *what* we speak.

---

[79] Donne, *Sermons*, volume VIII, p. 335.   [80] Ibid., p. 335.
[81] Ibid., pp. 335–6.   [82] Ibid., p. 336.   [83] Ibid., p. 337.

The sermon will be divided into two parts, Donne explains: the first will treat the twofold obligation of the text ('so speak ye and so do') and the second the reason (he adds a 'because': '*Quia judicandi*, Because you are all to be judged'). With respect to speaking, Donne uses an analogy to remind his congregation that the chapter from which his text is taken is concerned with the proper relationship of faith and works, and of the importance of *mediocritas*:

> As our *Nullifidians*, Men that put all upon works, and no faith; and our *Solifidians*, Men that put all upon faith and no works, are both in the wrong; So there is a danger in *multi-loquio*, and another in *nulli-loquio*: He that speaks over-freely to me, may be a Man of dangerous conversation; And the silent and reserv'd Man, that makes no play, but observes, and says nothing, may be more dangerous then he.[84]

Well-weighed speech is vitally important because it both frames action and creates communities: 'speech is the Glue, the Cyment, the soul of Conversation, and of Religion too'.[85] There are three groups to whom we are obliged to speak, and Donne considers them in turn: God, kings, and men.[86] Speaking to God, by means of prayer, is necessary because it glorifies God and gives thanks for what we have received. Furthermore, in turning our devotion into words we imitate the action of God in the incarnation and in Scripture. Speaking to kings, like speaking to God, requires mediation: as kings speak to God by means of prayer, so men must speak to kings by way of counsellors.[87] Such counsellors act as stand-ins for the individual who has no royal access.[88] As well as being obliged to speak to the king in a 'humble and reserved' manner, they are all the time under the injunction 'so speak ye . . . as they that shall be judged'. Here Donne introduces as an exemplar the figure of Esther who, as Jeanne Shami has pointed out, serves in many of his sermons as a type of discreet speech and action.[89] Donne succinctly outlines the bind in which the would-be counsellor is placed: obliged to speak with decorum, he is also obliged to speak as one that will be judged by God as well as by the king. Having dealt with the obligations

---

[84] Ibid., p. 337; cf. James 2:14–26.
[85] Donne, *Sermons*, volume VIII, p. 338.   [86] Ibid., pp. 338–9.
[87] Ibid., pp. 338–40. Harland, 'Donne's Political Intervention': p. 26, suggests that the mediators referred to are members of Parliament, but this seems to me excessively to narrow Donne's meaning here, which must at least also include preachers.
[88] See above, p. 64, n. 202.
[89] Jeanne Shami, 'Kings and Desperate Men: John Donne Preaches at Court', *John Donne Journal* 6:1 (1987): 9–23, at p. 16; Shami, 'Donne's Protestant Casuistry: Cases of Conscience in the *Sermons*', *Studies in Philology* 80 (1983): 53–66, at pp. 62–4: 'Donne uses Esther as an example whose discreet choice under perplexing and doubtful circumstances can be imitated by all' (p. 62).

of inferiors to their superiors, Donne moves on to treat the other side of the coin: the obligation to speak to 'men of condition inferior to your selves' is an obligation not to disregard social hierarchy, but to maintain it by being accessible, or 'affable'.[90]

However praiseworthy speech is, and however much it seems to promise access to one's interlocutor – 'the soul of a man is incorporate in his words; As he speaks, we think he thinks' – Donne warns that unless it is regulated it may in fact create a barrier: 'truly the most inaccessible Man that is, is the over-liberal, and profuse promiser: He is therefore the most inaccessible, because he is absent, when I am come to him, and when I do speak to him'.[91] Thus speech, to one's superiors and to one's inferiors, is necessary and laudable, but it must be regulated. Having dealt with the obligations put upon us by his text, Donne goes on in the second half of his sermon to discuss its reference to this regulation – the 'law of liberty' that will judge us.

The most pressing aspect of this *Judicium* is the responsibility to judge oneself according to one's conscience, and to act on this judgement immediately and constantly: 'onely our own conscience rectified, is a competent judge'.[92] In asserting the supremacy of conscience, Donne makes a potentially contentious point for the first time, implying that the law of conscience is a higher law than the law of the land. Such a suggestion was, of course, liable to the saving clauses that the 'rectification' of conscience would take place under the influence of the established church and state, and that the law of the land was identical to what the law of conscience would dictate. However, neither of these is articulated, and to afford the point as much emphasis as Donne does here when preaching at court might seem to be treading a delicate path between decorous exegesis and outspokenness.[93] Having elevated the law of conscience to its supreme position, Donne goes on to make the potentially equally uncomfortable argument that because God proceeds in judgement by way of a law, there is no escaping his judgement and no excuse for sin, wherever and whoever you are. Judgement according to the law, he asserts, is neither arbitrary nor obscure,

---

[90] Donne, *Sermons*, volume VIII, p. 340. Donne is here referring to James 2:2–6.

[91] Ibid., p. 341. Harland, 'Donne's Political Intervention', argues convincingly that in advising accessibility, Donne is 'encouraging the nobility to undertake that which was expected of a king during the sitting of Parliament' – that is, access to the king's person, one of the traditional privileges requested by the Speaker each session along with freedom of speech and freedom from imprisonment (p. 27). He is also, surely, glancing at the importance of royal affability more generally, at a time when 'reserved majesty' seemed to be Charles's preferred style.

[92] Donne, *Sermons*, volume VIII, pp. 343–4.

[93] On Donne's setting of the Divine Law above temporal law or the king, see Shami, 'Kings and Desperate Men', p. 13 and 'Donne's Protestant Casuistry', p. 63.

and it is thus the responsibility of the individual soul to have faith in God's just action. The 'law of liberty' is the Gospel, and Donne explains that the 'liberty' it offers is threefold. Firstly, God is at liberty to publish his Gospel to whomever he pleases, though this means that every Christian will be judged strictly according to it; secondly, it gives the Christian liberty from the state of the natural man for it makes it easier for him to follow God's law; thirdly, it gives the Christian liberty from the state of the Jews since, Donne argues, while 'the Jews were as School-boys, always spelling, and putting together Types and Figures . . . The Christian is come from school to the University . . . to apprehend and apply Christ himself.'[94] The liberty offered by the Gospel is not, however, the kind of liberty that would release us from judgement on our sins: precisely because of the clarity and liberty offered by the Gospel, the responsibility of the Christian to act according to it and his punishment for failing to do so will be greater than that of either the natural man or the Jew.[95] Emulating the circularity he attributes to his text, Donne ends the sermon by returning to its starting points. He asserts vehemently that the law of liberty, the Gospel, is applicable to all, but that this also means that everyone is accountable to it. There is no escape from its obligations, and 'no man can plead ignorance of a Law'.[96] The Christian must be a Christian everywhere, not simply where it is most convenient – and this includes the court.[97] Judgement, like the text and the seven other catholic, canonical, circular epistles, is universally applicable, and Donne has impressed upon his auditors the responsibility to act and speak in the full knowledge and anticipation of this judgement. He characteristically avoids apostrophes to individual sins or sinners which, as well as causing the preacher some trouble if uttered at court, relieve the majority of consciences from the effort of self-examination. Instead, by combining attention to the universality of his message with the need to apply it to the individual, he offers counsel which cannot be easily deflected. In this Caroline sermon, Donne finds a way of avoiding either silencing himself through excessive diplomacy or being silenced for excessive volubility; he asserts the primacy of the law of conscience and the universality of God's judgement, but he discreetly avoids mentioning specific courtly sins or offering royal home truths.

Donne preached this sermon on responsible speech and affability just over a fortnight before Charles I dissolved the last Parliament that would sit

---

[94] Donne, *Sermons*, volume VIII, pp. 349–51.
[95] Ibid., pp. 351–2.   [96] Ibid., p. 354.
[97] Cf. James 2:10: 'For whosoever shall keep the whole law, and yet offend in one point, he is guilty of all.'

for eleven years. The king had no taste for harsh admonition, and was moving increasingly towards the patronage of anti-Calvinists who were far from identifying with the tradition of plain-speaking Reformation Calvinism: in 1628 William Laud, John Howson, and Richard Montagu were all promoted to bishoprics.[98] Preachers like Donne had to find ways of balancing correction with decorum if they were to offer counsel at all.[99] As the royal tide of opinion under James turned increasingly against the 'hotter' sort of Protestant preaching, religious *parrhesia* in the biblical and Ambrosian tradition – *parrhesia* addressed to the monarch – was taken up by writers without the warrant of episcopal office, and in forms that would reach a wider audience than a provincial sermon. The most striking and sustained campaign of frank counsel addressed to the king and country in James's reign was that carried out by the pamphleteer Thomas Scott, and it is to Scott's works that I will now turn, in the final section of this chapter.

FREEDOM OF SPEECH AND THE RELIGIOUS PAMPHLET IN THE 1620S: THE CASE OF THOMAS SCOTT

Thomas Scott's pamphlets of the 1620s blend ideas that derive from an array of ways of thinking about freedom of speech in Jacobean England, many of which are treated in other chapters of this book. Scott was committed to a classical humanist position that elevated the values of active citizenship and stressed the need for a warlike populace whose nobility came from virtue, not birth alone; he praised Parliament as the best origin of counsel and policy.[100] While Peter Lake has made a strong case for Scott's importance as an example of widely held international Protestant views and as the propagator of an ideologically sophisticated puritan position, Markku Peltonen has warned us not to emphasise the 'puritan' origins of Scott's thought at the expense of its dependence on the humanist republican tradition.[101] In this discussion I am especially interested in the ways in which Scott's polemical pamphlets use arguments drawn from the religious tradition of

---

[98] Laud was appointed Bishop of London, Howson to Durham, and Montagu to Chichester. For the effect on religious printing, see Towers, *Control of Religious Printing*, chapters 5 and 6.

[99] An indication of the conditions under which preachers like Donne were operating is given by the fact that in April 1627 a sermon of Donne's was examined by Laud and the king after having given offence; Donne was forgiven after having been interviewed by them both. See Bald, *John Donne. A Life*, pp. 491–5.

[100] On Scott's classical humanism, see Markku Peltonen, *Classical Humanism and Republicanism in English Political Thought, 1570–1640* (Cambridge: Cambridge University Press, 1995), chapter 5.

[101] P. G. Lake, 'Constitutional Consensus and Puritan Opposition in the 1620s: Thomas Scott and the Spanish Match', *The Historical Journal* 25:4 (1982): 805–25; Peltonen, *Classical Humanism and Republicanism*, pp. 232–3.

free speech in order to claim a right to counsel not available to him from his position as a mere minister, and combine with this the assertion of rights and obligations pertaining to a citizen. Scott's humanism may be classical and republican, then, but it is at the same time distinctively and assertively Christian (specifically, Protestant). It would be impossible – and foolhardy – to attempt to separate out these two discourses as if they were useful resources that Scott drew on for argumentative effect: together his pamphlets make a strong argument that the values he promulgates hold together naturally. The Bible and the history of the church combine perfectly, for Scott, with the humanist values of public interest, liberty, and the resistance of tyranny.

In a relatively brief publishing career of six years, Thomas Scott published twenty or more pamphlets, all concerned with what he saw as the absolutely crucial political pressure points of the 1620s: the deviousness of Spanish practices, especially of the Ambassador Gondomar; the threat of popery; the need for a vocal and unrestricted Parliament; the virtue of the Low Countries;[102] the need for citizens to be active and to put public above private interest; the need for local and national government to be properly continuous.[103] But above all he argued for the necessity of truth-telling, of free speech, offered to the highest in the land – and the lowest as well; whoever was able to read, in fact – by the responsible and honest citizen, of whom he offered himself as a shining example. It was not only his ideological position that drew on a long and complex history: Scott's chosen form of publication, the pamphlet, was also, in the shorter history of printing, one that offered a tradition of outspokenness (especially in the religious sphere) and of critical engagement in public debate. In Joad Raymond's words, the

---

[102] See especially [Thomas Scott], *The Belgicke Pismire: Stinging the Slothfull Sleeper, and awaking the Diligent to Fast, watch, Pray; and worke out their owne Temporall and Eternall Salvation with Fear and Trembling* (London, 1622); *The Belgicke Souldier: Dedicated to the Parliament. Or, Warre was a Blessing* (Dort, 1624); *Symmachia: or, a True-Loves Knot. Tyed, betwixt Great Britaine and the Vnited Prouinces* (n.p., n.d. [1624]).

[103] *Vox Populi or Newes from Spayne* was published in 1620; *Sir Walter Rawleighs Ghost* was published in 1626, the year of Scott's assassination by an English soldier (reputedly deranged) named John Lambert. Scott was murdered on 18 June 1626; see *A Briefe and True Relation of the Murther of Mr. Thomas Scott Preacher of Gods Word and Batchelor of Divinite. Committed by John Lambert Souldier of the Garrison of Utricke, the 18. of Iune. 1626. With his Examination, Confession, and Execution* (London, 1628). For a list of Scott's pamphlets, see *STC*. On the biographical and bibliographical confusions surrounding Scott (including his confusion by some historians with another Thomas Scott, also the author of a work entitled *Vox Dei*), see S. L. Adams, 'The Protestant Cause: Religious Alliance with the West European Calvinist Communities as a Political Issue in England, 1585–1630', unpublished DPhil thesis, University of Oxford, 1973; Adams, 'Captain Thomas Gainsford, the "Vox spiritus" and the Vox populi', *Bulletin of the Institute of Historical Research* 49 (1976): 141–4.

pamphlet became, over the course of the seventeenth century, 'part of the everyday practice of politics, the primary means of creating public opinion'.[104] The Marprelate tracts of 1588–9 showed how the pamphlet form could be used polemically to express and to justify frank speech on matters of religious policy, as well as, perhaps even more importantly, demonstrating how complex literary devices could be combined with brevity and plainness.[105] Mockery of scholarship was the stock-in-trade of the pamphlet, with authors relishing the disproportion between the modest size of their publications and their claims to truth, as well as undermining the pretensions of their bombastic opponents: More's apparatus in *Utopia* is a classic example, and the technique was used deftly by Donne in his anonymous anti-Jesuit pamphlet of 1611, *Ignatius his Conclave*.[106] Scott does not exploit the format of his pamphlets as the Marprelate authors and printers had done, and his works are less obviously in the tradition of vituperative ecclesiastical satire.[107] But his works are rhetorically sophisticated, and in more than one of them he exploits the resources of fiction, and especially of prosopopoeia, for his own purposes – to make his argument more vivid, and to avoid (he hoped; or says he hoped) accusations of giving blunt and impertinent advice.[108]

Scott's first pamphlet, and his most celebrated, was *Vox Populi or Newes from Spayne*, which was written while Scott was living in Scotland, in 1619.[109] Its publication, anonymously, in 1620, was timed to coincide with Gondomar's arrival in England for his second term of office as Spanish

---

[104] Joad Raymond, *Pamphlets and Pamphleteering in Early Modern Britain* (Cambridge: Cambridge University Press, 2003), p. 26. Raymond's exemplary study also provides a useful definition of the pamphlet (chapter 1) and a discussion of the relation between pamphlets and news (chapter 4).

[105] On the Marprelate controversy, see Raymond, *Pamphlets and Pamphleteering*, chapter 2; Leland H. Carlson, *Martin Marprelate, Gentleman: Master Job Throckmorton Laid Open in his Colours* (San Marino: Huntington Library, 1981); Patrick Collinson, 'Ecclesiastical Vitriol: Religious Satire in the 1590s and the Invention of Puritanism', in *The Reign of Elizabeth I*, ed. by John Guy (Cambridge: Cambridge University Press, 1995), pp. 150–70; Cyndia Susan Clegg, *Press Censorship in Elizabethan England* (Cambridge: Cambridge University Press, 1997), chapter 8. See also Peter Milward, *Religious Controversies of the Elizabethan Age: A Survey of Printed Sources* (Lincoln: University of Nebraska Press, 1977), pp. 86–93.

[106] John Donne, *Ignatius His Conclave*, ed. by T. S. Healy, SJ (Oxford: Clarendon Press, 1969), esp. pp. 57 and n., p. 132.

[107] On this tradition, see Collinson, 'Ecclesiastical Vitriol'.

[108] Bacon (?), 'An Aduertisement' (written in the mid-1590s), emphasises these features of libels, noting that they are 'artificially vttered, now in persons of Complaynauntes, and by & by in the language of Censors, and accordingly interlaced sometymes with exclamations of greifes' (Cardwell, 'An Overlooked Tract', p. 431).

[109] Scott studied at St Andrews and then at Peterhouse, Cambridge, where he proceeded BD in 1620. See Peltonen, *Classical Humanism and Republicanism*, p. 231. On the importance of his Scottish background to his republican thought, see Peltonen, ibid., p. 233.

Ambassador, and its anti-papist sentiments proved popular enough to warrant seven editions in the year of its first issue.[110] The pamphlet is presented as a word-by-word record of Gondomar's report to the Spanish Council on his return home in 1618, outlining the seeds of dissent he has so far been able to sow, the intelligence that he has gathered, and his general thoughts on the (supposedly weak) state of England under James I. Whether or not contemporary readers believed the pamphlet's claims to veracity, it infuriated Gondomar.[111] Scott had offended not only the Spanish Ambassador, but his own king too in criticising the royal policy of appeasement (and probably embarrassing him before a supposedly friendly foreign diplomat), and the authorities sought the source of the scandal. Despite the lack of an author's name or a place of printing on the title page, the printer of *Vox Populi* was soon discovered, and he in turn gave up Scott, who fled to Holland.[112] The furore over the book did nothing to abate its popularity, and it continued to circulate in manuscript, either transcribed informally or supplied at a cost by scriveners.[113] It seems likely that Gondomar's displeasure over Scott's work was one of the factors behind James's issuing, on 24 December 1620, a proclamation 'against excess of Lavish and Licentious Speech of matters of State'.[114]

In several of his works, beginning with *Vox Populi* and including its sequel, *The Second Part of Vox Populi* (1624); *A Speech Made in the Lower House of Parliament, Anno 1621. By Sir Edward Cicill, Colonel* (1621); *Newes*

---

[110] Wright, 'Propaganda against James I's "Appeasement" of Spain', p. 152; Margot Heinemann, *Puritanism and Theatre: Thomas Middleton and Opposition Drama under the Early Stuarts* (Cambridge: Cambridge University Press, 1980), p. 156; Clegg, *Press Censorship in Jacobean England*, p. 173. *Vox Populi* was translated into French as *Voix du peuple* in 1621; see Wright, 'Propaganda against James I's "Appeasement" of Spain', p. 160.

[111] See *CSPV, 1619–1621*, no. 644, pp. 489–91 (letter to the Doge and Senate of Venice from Girolamo Lando, the Venetian Ambassador in England, 4 December 1620): 'a book by the hand of an unknown author entitled *Vox populi* is circulating in certain quarters, severly castigates the Spanish ambassador here, who therefore foams with wrath in every direction and it is said that he has sent it to the king to make complaint. This has transpired and given rise to much comment' (p. 491); *The Autobiography and Correspondence of Sir Simonds D'Ewes, Bart., During the Reigns of James I and Charles I*, ed. by James O. Halliwell (London, 1845), vol. I, pp. 158–9.

[112] See John Chamberlain to Dudley Carleton, 3 February 1621, in *The Letters of John Chamberlain*, vol. II, p. 339 (Chamberlain writes that the printer obtained his own release by naming Scott); Lake, 'Constitutional Consensus', p. 813 (noting that Scott later claimed, in an act of prophetic self-identification, that he had been forewarned in a dream of the danger to him; see [Thomas Scott], *Vox Regis* (London, 1624), sigs. Aii–Aii^v). On the hunt for Scott, see also *The Autobiography and Correspondence of Sir Simonds D'Ewes*, I, pp. 158–9.

[113] See chapter 4 below, p. 224; Harold Love, *The Culture and Commerce of Texts: Scribal Publication in Seventeenth-Century England* (Amherst: University of Massachusetts Press, 1998), pp. 75, 96–7; Clegg, *Press Censorship in Jacobean England*, pp. 186–7.

[114] On this proclamation and its successor of 26 July 1621, see chapter 4 below, p. 214.

from Parnassus (1622); *A Tongue-Combat* (1623); *Robert Earle of Essex his Ghost* (1624), and *Sir Walter Rawleigh's Ghost* (1626), Scott made use of the techniques of the dramatist. He put into the mouths of characters – either contemporary figures like Gondomar (the two parts of *Vox Populi*), those from recent history (*Robert Earle of Essex*; *Sir Walter Rawleigh's Ghost* (which describes an encounter between the patriotic spook and, once again, Gondomar)), fictional individuals (*A Tongue-Combat*) or even personified nations (*Newes from Parnassus*) – plausible arguments; statements consistent with qualities that Scott identifies as essential to their ideological positions and virtues or vices. There is no attempt at complex character development in Scott's pamphlets, of course: these are polemical works, and he is concerned to persuade his readers as quickly and forcefully as possible, not to perplex them with the ambiguities of motivation. It was the construction of probable events and speeches that Scott saw as a potentially devastating persuasive tool. By making fictions, he argued, he was in fact revealing the truth, since otherwise the people would be hoodwinked by the crafty dissembling of individuals like Gondomar: the speeches made by the Ambassador in *Vox Populi* are what we would surely hear if only we had access to the diabolical behind-the-scenes machinations of the Spanish state. Scott knew his readers' prejudices (or, to be less disparaging, political opinions) all too well, and he played on them skilfully in reporting what he was convinced would be the reality behind the Anglo-Spanish accommodation. Lacing flattery with alarmism, for instance, Scott has Duke Medina del rio Secco put it to Gondomar that the English are surely a tough and warlike people who will resist any attempts at conquest and mass conversion (just look at what happened to the Armada in 1588, he warns); certainly this used to be the case, agrees the Ambassador, but now the citizens have become enslaved to their own comfort: 'for the persons generally their bodies by long disuse of arms were disabled and their minds effeminated by peace and luxury'.[115] If Scott's readers shared his beliefs in the manly virtue of England as a nation, in the wisdom of their king, in the dangers to which a long period of peace could lead (all commonplaces of the humanist republican discourse that flourished in early seventeenth-century England), then they were also likely to believe that Spain remained a threat – as Peter Lake puts it, 'the secular equivalent of the papacy' – and that what they were reading was exactly what Gondomar and his superiors were likely to be saying amongst themselves.[116] Thus Scott's argument – implicit in

[115] [Thomas Scott], *Vox Populi or Newes from Spayne* (n.p., 1620), sig. B2$^\mathrm{v}$.

[116] Lake, 'Constitutional Consensus', p. 813. For an account of Gondomar's part in the negotiations over the Spanish Match that goes some way to supporting Scott's analysis see Glyn Redworth, *The*

Vox Populi, and made explicit in the later *Vox Regis* (1624), which gives an account of the earlier work's composition – was that his prosopopoeias were the truth of the matter, while official statements and declarations, while 'factual' in some sense were more truly fictive, and it was likely to be approved by his (many) sympathetic readers.

Scott also believed that in writing factitious narratives he was working within a venerable and effective tradition of counsel. Replying to his critics in *Vox Regis*, he argued that far from breaking decorum by treating matters of policy at all and, further, by writing in a manner unbefitting to a minister of the Word, he was keeping to the decorum of frank advice-giving: 'sometimes', he reminded his attackers, 'Kings are content in plays and masks to be admonished of divers things.'[117] James I was not the most obvious example of such a king – the dramatic counterpart of *Vox Populi*, Middleton's *A Game at Chesse* (1624), was closed down at his orders after an unprecedented run of nine successive days – but Scott was, as usual, offering counsel under the shadow of description; it would be good, he is implying, were *this* king to be content to be admonished in plays and masques.[118] If *Vox Populi* gave its readers a taste of what Gondomar and his colleagues 'must' have been saying amongst themselves, two other pamphlets by Scott allowed heroic figures from recent history to offer their thoughts from beyond the grave on current affairs – thoughts that tend to take the form of an extended *O tempora, o mores* lament. In *Robert Earle of Essex his Ghost* (1624), the (in Scott's opinion wrongly) disgraced Elizabethan favourite expresses his alarm 'that such a prudent, learned and religious Prince [as James], should be so farre misled, by (some) false hearted Counsellors at home, and fawning Forraine Embassadours from the enemies of God and his Gospell professed in *England*, to the detriment of the Kingdome'.[119] There is general concern in heaven, says Essex, at the news that James is planning to match his son with a Spanish bride.[120] Scott's reasons for employing this

---

Prince and the Infanta: The Cultural Politics of the Spanish Match (New Haven: Yale University Press, 2003). On Gondomar's part in the failure of the 1621 Parliament, see the Ambassador's letters to the Infanta Isabella printed in Brennan Pursell, 'War or Peace? Jacobean Politics and the Parliament of 1621', in *Parliament, Politics and Elections 1604–1648*, ed. by Chris R. Kyle, Camden fifth series no. 17 (Cambridge: Cambridge University Press, 2001), pp. 149–78.

[117] [Thomas Scott], *Vox Regis* (London, 1624), sig. E[v].
[118] Thomas Middleton, *A Game at Chess*, ed. by J. W. Harper (London: Ernest Benn, 1966); on Middleton's play, see Heinemann, *Puritanism and Theatre*, chapter 10; Jerzy Limon, *Dangerous Matter: English Drama and Politics 1623/4* (Cambridge: Cambridge University Press, 1986), chapter 4; Clegg, *Press Censorship in Jacobean England*, pp. 187–8.
[119] [Thomas Scott], *Robert Earle of Essex his Ghost, Sent from Elizian: To the Nobilitie, Gentry, and Commvnalitie of England* ('Paradise', 1624), sig. A2[v].
[120] Ibid., sig. B3[v].

supernatural spokesman are clear: he once again avoids speaking with his own voice, thus gaining authority for his text from the reputation of an ambiguous hero figure; he plays on the tendency among godly opponents of James's pacific policy to nostalgia for the preceding reign,[121] and he makes an implicit argument for the importance of the honest counsellor who is prepared to suffer in order to rescue the monarch from evil counsel. Essex does not declare that he will not touch on secrets of state, but rather that he will only do so insofar as any honest patriot should, giving a warrant to his Jacobean successors (among them Thomas Scott, of course, as well as the nobility addressed by the pamphlet) to do the same: 'I list neither to meddle with the *Arcana imperij*, of your King and State, further then shall beseeme a zealous Patriot, that tendreth still, and wisheth the welfare and flourishing State of his once deare and natiue Country.'[122] Essex's counsel is clear and unambiguous: beware of making treaties with Spain and remain allied with the Netherlands.[123] He speaks from a deep knowledge of the 'cruell Plots, as were practised in my time on Earth, by the King and State of *Spaine*, against the Queene and State of *England*'.[124] Scott's last pamphlet, *Sir Walter Rawleigh's Ghost*, uses a similar technique to describe a different scene. Here, rather than the nobility and commons of England being called upon by a departed paragon, the ghost of Sir Walter Ralegh appears to Gondomar as he is out by the Prado one day.[125] Confronting his nemesis (Gondomar confesses to having engineered Ralegh's execution), the Elizabethan hero and (as Scott would have it) Jacobean fall-guy outlines his knowledge of all the evil Spanish practices with which Gondomar has been involved.[126] Not only does the audience once again gain an insight into the obscure but troubling intrigues of the Spanish state; Scott also offers a fantasy of revenge upon, and plain-speaking to, the master of dissimulation. At the opening of *Sir Walter Rawleigh's Ghost* Scott once again confronts the question of fact versus fiction, as he had in the reply to the critics of *Vox Populi* that he offered in *Vox Regis*. The sheer number of pamphlets and the amount of news that is circulating, says Scott, has made such material all too susceptible to accusations of deception by suspicious readers. Yet his entirely fictitious dialogue between a dead Ralegh and an English-speaking Gondomar is, he insists, truthful:

---

[121] For an extended example of such critical nostalgia, see Fulke Greville, 'A Dedication to Sir Philip Sidney', in *The Prose Works of Fulke Greville, Lord Brooke*, ed. by John Gouws (Oxford: Oxford University Press, 1986).

[122] [Scott], *Robert Earle of Essex his Ghost*, sig. B2.

[123] Ibid., sigs. B2^v–B3^v, B4^v.   [124] Ibid., sig. D.

[125] [Thomas Scott], *Sir Walter Rawleigh's Ghost, or Englands Forewarner* (Utrecht, 1626), sig. B2^v.

[126] Ibid., sigs. B4^v (Gondomar's confession), D, and beyond (Ralegh's accusations).

Although the liberty of these times (wherein your *Currants, Gazettas, Pasquils,* and the like, swarme too abundantly) hath made all Newes (how serious or substantiall soeuer) lyable to the iealous imputation of falsehood, yet this relation I assure you (although in some circumstances it may leane too neare the florish of inuention, yet for the pith or marrow thereof, it is as iustly allayed and knit to truth, as the light is to the day, or night to darknesse.[127]

Scott's strategy of voicing counsel straight from heaven was one that was used by another author, his self-confessed imitator John Reynolds. In his *Vox Coeli*, Reynolds 'reported' on the proceedings of a consultation held in heaven between various deceased members of the English royal family: Henry VIII, Edward VI, Mary I, Elizabeth I, Prince Henry, and Queen Anne. Reynolds addresses the pamphlet to Parliament, of which he, like Scott, had a high opinion, and declares that he was impelled to write it – '(in point of integrity and duty) I hold my selfe bound to bring the truth neerer to your vnderstanding' – at a time 'about some three yeares since' (i.e. 1621) in order to bring about 'the discouery of our apparant and imminent dangers'.[128] Reynolds explains that the book was not published immediately because conditions were extremely unsympathetic to its tone of frank counsel; first, he was discouraged 'because the Seas of our Kings affection to *Spaine* went so lofty, and the windes were so tempestuous, that it could not possibly be permitted to passe the Pikes of the Presse'. Then he saw other faithful counsellors punished:

When albeit my zeale and fidelity againe and againe infused new audacity and courage to my resolutions, to see it salute the light, yet it was impossible for me or it, to be made so happy, because I saw *Allureds* honest letter, *Scots* loyall *Vox Popoli*, D. *Whiting*, D. *Everard*, & *Claytons* zealous Sermons, and others, suppress'd and silenced, as also *Wards* faithfull picture, which yet was so innocent, as it onely breathed forth his fidelity to *England* in silent Rhetorique, and dumbe eloquence.[129]

---

[127] Ibid., sig. A2. Scott's printer has omitted the closing bracket in this passage.
[128] S.R.N.I. [John Reynolds], *Vox Coeli, or Newes from Heaven* ('Elisium', 1624), sigs. A3 (dedication), A3ᵛ, A4.
[129] [Reynolds], *Vox Coeli*, sig. A4ᵛ. On Alured's letter, see chapter 4 below, pp. 212, 220; on Everard's preaching, see Clegg, *Press Censorship in Jacobean England*, pp. 168–9. For a similar complaint, see [Thomas Scott], *Boanerges. Or The Humble Supplication of the Ministers of Scotland, to the High Court of Parliament* (Edinburgh, 1624), sigs. D–Dᵛ. Cf. [Reynolds], *Vox Coeli*, sigs. Kᵛ–K2, where Queen Elizabeth laments that '[Gondomar] hath now brought matters to this passe, that no cinsere aduise, honest Letter, Religious Sermon, or true picture can point at the King of *Spaine*, but they are called in; and their Authors imprisoned (instead of rewarded) though neuer so honest and loyal Subiects'; Henry VIII replies that his daughter is underestimating the commitment of the citizens of England to speaking the truth: 'mee thinkes that this is no subtill policie of *Gondomar*; for the more he striues to suppresse the truth, the more it will flourish and preuaile; For (for the good of England) if one penne, or tongue be commanded to silence, they will occasion and set tenne at libertie to write and speake; as Grasse or Cammomell, which the more it is depressed, the thicker it

But it was impossible to remain silent, writes Reynolds. Like Scott and Wentworth and many others, he suggests that to fail to speak out would not only have been detrimental to the interests of his country: it was physically as well as morally impossible: 'being as well in heart as in tongue an Englishman, and therefore knowing by Grace, what I owe by Nature to my naturall Prince and Country (like Cressus his dumbe Sonne) I would not, I could not bee silent thereat, but must expose this Consultation of *Vox Coeli* to the light and sight of the world'.[130] Reynolds's argument, as his dedication suggests, is concerned as much with the liberty and power of Parliament as it is with the king's policies. The book is a sustained critique of the Spanish Match, and as a document from 1621, it records the fears and anxieties that surrounded the Commons' attempts to give advice on that subject.[131] Queen Mary's match with Philip II was made without any consultation with Parliament, it is pointed out, and we must pray that this is not allowed to happen again; Prince Henry argues that 'If the voice of the Parliament be free, and not enforced, I make no doubt but that the Pope, the King of *Spaine, Gondomar,* and all our Recusants will come short of their hopes for the match.'[132] Perhaps the most audacious part of Reynolds's work, though, is its use of divine authority to back up its argument: Queen Mary is challenged to produce scriptural texts that would support the Spanish Match, but is unable to do so; in response to her counter-challenge, the remaining royals cite a barrage of passages against marrying with foreigners.[133] So far, so reasonably orthodox; but then when the massed monarchs and princes (apart from Mary) agree in their opposition to the match, another character adds his vote: God.[134]

Scott's and Reynolds's voices from heaven identify the authors and the characters they ventriloquise as part of a militant Protestant tradition whose members define themselves by their opposition to Spain and their determination to speak out, whatever the danger, against Spanish and Catholic imperial ambitions. The dangers were real: while Scott made a timely escape and benefited from the support of powerful patrons, Reynolds was

---

will spread and grow'. On Reynolds, see Jerry H. Bryant, 'John Reynolds of Exeter and his Canon', *The Library,* fifth series, 15 (1960): 105–17 and 'John Reynolds of Exeter and his Canon: A Footnote', *The Library,* fifth series, 18 (1963): 299–303; Norbrook, *Poetry and Politics in the English Renaissance,* p. 203.

[130] [Reynolds], *Vox Coeli,* sig. ¶3ᵛ.

[131] On the 1621 Parliament see below, chapter 3, pp. 165–85.   [132] [Reynolds], *Vox Coeli,* sig. I2.

[133] Ibid., sig. L2ᵛ. Henry VIII offers Genesis 24 and 26; Edward VI, Exodus 34, Judges 17; Elizabeth I, Joshua 23 and 2 Chronicles 21; Prince Henry, 1 Kings 11, 16; Queen Anne, Ezra 9, Nehemiah 13.

[134] [Reynolds], *Vox Coeli,* sigs. L4ᵛ–M. The text ends with two letters from Mary, one to Gondomar and one to the English Catholics (sigs. Mᵛ–M4ᵛ). Reynolds had also published his anti-Spanish arguments in *Votivae Angliae* (Utrecht, 1624).

imprisoned for his authorship of the two pamphlets issued in 1624, and his printer was summoned to appear before High Commission.[135] Both writers speak to (and, they claim, from) a wider oppositional community whose interests (those of the country at large) can be served by an active and free Parliament allowed to consult with the king on matters of foreign and religious policy. Their fictions consist, the authors insist, of probable truths that are obscured by the politic fictions of their opponents. Their use of imaginary dialogues, though, however much they are supported by claims of divine authority, might look quite distant from the examples of religious plain-speaking and of biblically based *parrhesia* with which I began this chapter. But Scott's statements are by no means always mediated through other voices; and even when they are, they frequently use a lexicon and develop an ethos for the speaker that are rooted in that tradition and, as I have suggested, blend it with that of classical humanist thought. They frequently spend as much time justifying their outspokenness, and thus providing an ideological framework for free speech, as they do in making their anti-Spanish arguments. *Vox Regis* is an excellent example of this. It contains, as has been seen above, a sustained defence of Scott's actions in publishing *Vox Populi*. It also offers a series of arguments for the necessity of free speech and for the impossibility of silence in the troubled times of the 1620s. Scott's first argument is that his writings are part of the process by which the monarch and his people communicate, which is vital to a healthy commonwealth: 'There is nothing of more moment for the happinesses of a Kingdome, then that the Prince and the People should know each other. For where this is not, there can be no confidence, but iealousie takes place on both sides, and all actions are subiect to double, and so to doubtfull interpretation.'[136] James has himself offered encouragement to Scott's enterprise, by publishing his writings as 'Works', indicating that words and works should be closely linked, and that writing is a pragmatic act which should result in action.[137] The combined points, that communication between the king and his people is essential, and that an activist stance is not only virtuous but fostered by the king, are essential to Scott. In the peroration of his address to the reader, he builds up an ideal picture of open debate and of a public sphere in which honest citizens make the people's private thoughts and discussions public and engage in acts of persuasion with an active and critical readership:

[135] For Scott's support by Dudley Carleton (then Ambassador to the United Provinces), who asked Bishop Harsnet of Norwich to make his case to Archbishop Abbot, see Lake, 'Constitutional Consensus', p. 813; on Reynolds, see Clegg, *Press Censorship in Jacobean England*, pp. 170–5, 185.
[136] [Scott], *Vox Regis*, sig. [∴]. [137] Ibid., sig. [∴]2ᵛ.

This is my shield, this buckler I hold out against all foole fires and feares of other mens idle assention; Vnder this shelter I make my neere approaches, hoping to conquer or come off safe, God leading me on & being my Captaine, the King calling me and giuing encouragement, thou Reader standing indifferent till thou hast read & heard what I say for God, for the King, for thee, for my selfe, who am Gods vnworthy Seruant, the Kings vnworthy Subiect, thy vnworthy Friend. *T. S.*[138]

Such an ideal state is under threat from flatterers and those who would protect the king from his friends, however. These dangerous individuals and evil counsellors want to separate off questions such as the prince's marriage from open discussion, and assert the need to maintain the limits of the private: the marriage of the prince is a private matter, they would argue, and Scott should in turn remember that he is a private person, with no public office to warrant his speech.[139] It is this argument that most angers Scott, who wishes to establish a public sphere of debate and opinion in which the status of both the soon-to-be-betrothed prince and the honest citizen is that of a public person: there may indeed be occasions and places in which they are obliged or able to act and speak as private individuals, but on issues of national importance they cannot retain this status. As Scott puts it, responding to the criticism that he had '*meddled with the marriage of the Prince, which concernes not the subiect*', 'the Prince is to be considered as a publike and priuate person: As a priuate person, he may chuse for his priuate affection, and match where he list; prouided, he neglect not the publike part, which is the principall, but elects with the loue and liking of his people'.[140] If the prince must acknowledge that he acts as a public

---

[138] Ibid., sig. [∴]3. At sig. Aii Scott explains that *Vox Populi* was so named 'as containing the common-peoples priuate and retired discourses' (at sig. F3 he calls it 'the vulgar voice and opinion of the people delivered by my Pen'); at sigs. C^v–C2 he explains further that

the Commons are they, where the disorders of a State, & the mischiefes approaching, are first felt, and soonest discerned. As Kings are for these, so Kings from these may gather the best and most certaine intelligence of their Domestick affaires: which hath made some Princes to disguise themselues, and come amongst these, to heare how all things stood: and made me disguise my selfe, to let his Maiestie heare and see by the Market-folke (who euer talke freely and feelingly of their owne affaires) how the Market went.

See Lake, 'Constitutional Consensus', p. 824 on Scott's desire to 'create an open arena in which policy should be formulated and discussed "in public"'.

[139] [Scott], *Vox Regis*, sig. B3. On the dangers of cabinet councils, to the use of which this line of argument would tend according to Scott, see also Thomas Scott, *The High-Waies of God and the King* (London, 1623), sig. I3^v.

[140] [Scott], *Vox Regis*, sig. B3^v. Scott qualifies this in saying that the prince does not have to please every subject in his choice of a bride, since the consent of Parliament ('the *State representatiue*') includes 'the consent of euerie Subiect' (sig. B3^v). On this passage, see Lake, 'Constitutional Consensus', p. 815. On Parliament and representation, see chapter 3 below, p. 195.

person in choosing his bride, then Scott's critics must acknowledge that in time of crisis individual citizens are obliged to do the same:

The ninth Obiection is, *That I wanted a lawfull vocation to warrant this Worke of mine: and that I follow extraordinarie examples, which are no safe nor sufficient presidents.* To the first I answer, That euerie mans vocation bindes him, to preuent euill, and to doe good . . . And for such as say, That the examples which either are or may be brought to countenance this course of mine, are extraordinarie, and therefore not safe to follow: I answer, That therefore they are to be followed, because they are extraordinarie: For such examples fit extraordinarie times and occasions best.[141]

The examples that Scott, as a minister of the Word of God, is most concerned to adduce in his cause, are biblical ones: he cites the outspokenness of the Apostles to Christ in Mark 4:38 ('Master, carest thou not that we perish?'), of David to God in Psalm 44 ('Wherefore hidest thou thy face, and forgettest our affliction and our oppression?'), and he compares himself to David in Psalm 39 and Jeremiah in Jeremiah 20:9, trying to remain silent 'while the wicked is before me' but having to speak.[142] Pressing home his point with a series of anaphoric questions, beginning 'when I saw' (for instance, 'when I saw iniquitie to abound') and closing with the question 'was it not then a time to speak? Was there not a cause?', Scott invokes Esther as an example of fearless speech, as Donne had in his sermons:[143]

When I saw the poore Commons silently groning vnderneath these pressures, and no man either willing, or daring to make them known to him, whom it most concerned, and who only had power to remedy these mischiefes. Yea, when I heard a generall despaire close vp the hearts of all men, that they should neuer see Parliament againe (which Court was the onely absolute, certaine, and speedie discouerer and remoouer of all such mightie enormities; and in defect whereof, these had presumptuously shot vp, & ouerspred the Church and State in a short time) I could not chuse (the zeale of God, the loue of my Countrey, dutie to my King and his Children, and indignation to behold the enemies of all these triumphing, presenting theselues to my consideration, as to a man distracted with sorrow and astonishment) but a length breake silence, with the resolution of *Hester, If I perish, I perish. For was there not a time to speake? Was there not a cause?*[144]

---

[141] [Scott], *Vox Regis*, sigs. B3ᵛ–B4.

[142] Ibid., sigs. C4ᵛ–D, D–Dᵛ; Psalm 39:1 (this example is also used in [Thomas Scott], *Digitvs Dei* (n.p., n.d. [1623]), sigs. Eᵛ–E2).

[143] See p. 99 above. Scott also uses the example of Esther in *Englands Ioy, for svppressing the Papists, and banishing the* Priests and Iesuites (n.p., 1624), sig. A2ᵛ; he cites the book for Haman as an example of private interest masquerading as public good in *Vox Dei* (n.p., n.d. [1624]), sig. C4.

[144] [Scott], *Vox Regis*, sigs. C4–C4ᵛ.

Scott laments that despite the Bible's warrant, the frankness he is compelled to utter is nowadays considered treason, while flattery is welcomed and makes the powerful even less able to bear the truth.[145] But even if outspokenness may be condemned by some as a sign of excess in the passions, Scott writes that it is a necessary and irresistible force that provokes it:

And vndoubtedly whatsoeuer cold blood may moderately thinke, or stoicall Atheists (who haue quenched the spirit in themselues) resolue and doe, whilst they iudge it frenzie or distemperature in other men (as *Festus* iudged of *Paul*) to haue liuing affections: yet assuredly when God fills the heart, the mouth must run ouer. *I beleeued, therefore I spake*, saith the *Psalmist*. [marg. Ps. 116:10] . . . Truth will haue vent, or breake the Vessell that contains it: for God fills it, to haue it vttered, and not bottelled or barrelled vp in silence.[146]

He goes on to cite the 'wine in new bottles' text (Job 32:19) used by Peter Wentworth in 1576, explaining that he had waited to see whether his elders and superiors would speak out before doing so himself. Seeing the king surrounded, as princes often are, by bad counsellors (he uses the popular example of Rehoboam), Scott is obliged to speak by circumstance, by the failure of others, and by his vocation.[147] His task, and that of preachers and ministers generally, must be to use whatever means they can to alert the king to the truth, and in a passage that stands clearly in the tradition of *parrhesia* based in the Bible and the history of the early church, Scott describes the preacher as a prophet. In prophesying, he argues, past and present actions and their divine punishments are effectively compared, and

would to God this kind of prophecying were more vsed, and better beleeued, that Preachers might be more respected, or at least at libertie to be taught by God, without limitation of man, and to say what God hath done lately, as well as what God hath done long since: But we haue no such custome, no such freedome, nor the present Churches of God.[148]

Much of the latter half of *Vox Regis* is taken up with Scott's explanation of how he only spoke out (in *Vox Populi*) when all legitimate channels of counsel had apparently failed; he acknowledges that he could not use an 'ordinarie course', but at the same time as admitting that his actions require explanation, he makes a strong case for his right to have performed them. His authority comes first from God, is bolstered by James's example, and

---

[145] Ibid., sig. D; cf. sigs. D2–D2ᵛ: '*Truth* hath euer almost beene called *Treason* at Court [marg: Amos 7.11, 12].' On courtly flattery see further sigs. D2ᵛ–D4ᵛ.
[146] Ibid., sig. Dᵛ.   [147] Ibid., sig. Fᵛ.
[148] Ibid., sig. F2. For further examples of parallels between biblical events and current affairs, see [Scott], *Englands Ioy, passim.*

then is reinforced by later developments: the calling of the 1621 Parliament and James's recognition of his subjects' grievances was one instance; its failure (at the hands of evil counsellors, Scott hints) was yet another, and the developments of 1623–4 with the calling of another Parliament and the breaking off of treaties with Spain are a final validation of what Scott has been saying all along.

Scott's short pamphlet appears to be simply an act of self-justification for having apparently broken the bounds of decorum with *Vox Populi*. But it does much more. Announcing its author as a latter-day prophet, it celebrates and makes a case for the importance of Parliament as a source of counsel and a representative body; it attacks the flatterers and evil counsellors who infect the court; in justifying the arguments made in *Vox Populi* it reiterates them and shows how the years since its publication have proven them to be accurate, and in its discussion of the events of 1623–4 the pamphlet disseminates information as well as opinion about Parliament, policy, and counsel into the commonwealth, quoting from James's speeches and Parliament's responses.[149] As in all his pamphlet output, Scott develops an authorial identity that fuses the roles of prophet and citizen: his obligation and his right to speak freely derive from injunctions placed upon all Christians by God and from duties owned by all members of the commonwealth to serve its best interests above their own. In a godly commonwealth prophets are always needed, Scott suggests – not only to point out the parallels between the present and the biblical past, but to act and speak as the successors to Nathan, Esther, St Paul. The pamphlet concludes with a series of apostrophes to Scott's enemies and then to the king, but at the very end he returns to his main theme and simply supplies a list of biblical quotations that sanction free speech to the powerful, whatever the danger.[150]

Scott's argument that prophetic speech is required from ministers when the 'ordinarie course' of criticism fails and when we are in 'extraordinarie times' was one that he reiterated in other pamphlets.[151] The same justification for outspoken speech, for unlicensed counsel, was used by writers and

---

[149] [Scott], *Vox Regis*, sigs. G^v–G2; on this strategy see Cogswell, *The Blessed Revolution*, pp. 293–4.
[150] Ibid., sigs. I4^v–K^v.
[151] For a fabular version of this justification, see the 'Apologue for an Epilogue' at the end of [Scott], *The Belgicke Pismire* (sig. O2^v):

> The *Lyon* slept securely, whilst the *Hunters* were pitching *Toyles* around him. A *Pismire* perceived the danger, and stung the *Lyon* to wake him, with *Tandem resurges*: He furiously start vp, and would wreake his anger on the presumptuous *Pismire*, that durst be so bold and busie to disturbe his rest. To whom the *Pismire* cryed, *My Lord, first looke about you. He* did so, and spyed the Snares of the Hunters; escaped, and gave the *Pismire* thanks, saying;
> Quos perdere vult *Iupiter*, hos dementat
> Quos tueri vult, suscitat.

collectors of verse libels in the early seventeenth century, or was implicit in their works, but Scott's was a determinedly and primarily religious vision.[152] It should come as no surprise to find him comparing himself with Ambrose in his confrontation with Theodosius – nor that he should deftly articulate his expectations of a good hearing by praising not the bishop, but the emperor:

> That Historie betwixt *Theodosius* the Emperour and *Ambrose* Bishop of *Millan*, makes more for the vertue of the Emperour, then for the valour of the Bishop. It is no great matter to say what the Bishop did, since he for so doing may be censured to be *satis audax*, but what the Emperour did and said of the Bishop, when his anger was over, is to the purpose. For as Sozoman records. *Theodosius dixit se solum Ambrosium dignum Episcopi nomine nosse. Theodosius* said he knewe one *Ambrose* onely worthy the name of a Bishop. And this was for speaking truth, and discharging his conscience, though herein he plainly condemned an action of the Emperours, and doubtlesse crost his present desires.[153]

Just as Ambrose had argued to Theodosius that far from exceeding the bounds of his office in admonishing the emperor he was in fact fulfilling his duty as best he could, Scott returns regularly to the argument that there is no hard and fast distinction between public and private persons: the distinction lies rather in the interests that they serve. Thus they may pretend that they are acting for public reasons when in fact they are serving private interests, and this concern for *otium* can be either healthy (yet inferior to public action) or positively sinful (as in the case of Haman's persecution of Mordechai).[154] Private persons are thus likely to be pressed into public action, just as in the Bible prophets often act and speak when priests are either absent, heretical, or silent: 'at all tymes, in defect of ordinary pastors, God hath raysed up prophets to teach his people, and to publish his judgements openly and playnely, though with the perill of their owne liues'.[155] Hence, as Scott states twice in the space of a few pages in *Vox Dei*, 'necessitie supplie's the place of an ordinary calling'; it 'warrants the vndertaking of any action for the avoiding of a certaine mischiefe, either

---

[152] See further below, chapter 4.   [153] [Scott], *Digitvs Dei*, sig. E2.

[154] [Scott], *Vox Dei*, sigs. A[v], C2–C4; cf. [Scott], *Symmachia*, sigs. Biiij[v]–Cij. Praise of public action as virtuous is a common theme in Scott's works: his enthusiasm for the pismire, or ant, is based on its industriousness and communality (it is, he writes, both 'ciuill and social': [Scott], *The Belgicke Pismire*, sig. D[v]), and in an assize sermon preached at Thetford in 1620 he urges his audience (including the Judges), 'let none among you be seene idely to sit at home, whilst these things are doing in the full Country, as if it did not concerne you: but ride, runne, and deale seriously herein, as for your liues and liberties which depend heereupon' (Scott, *The High-Waies of God and the King*, sig. L4). See further the excellent discussion of Scott's use of this humanist topos in Peltonen, *Classical Humanism and Republicanism*, pp. 237–46.

[155] [Scott], *Vox Dei*, sig. B4[v].

to the state where wee liue, or the true religion which wee professe'.[156] These actions might well seem destructive in themselves to those who would prefer calm, safety, and peace – but inaction would only result in the commonwealth becoming a land of slaves. Much better, like Samson, to pull down the temple and perish in the act:

> The Church is in distresse, & in hazard to receiue a blow by this meanes: Hee is no living parte of the Church, that suffers any part to fall, whilest his hand can vpholde it. I had rather pull the house with *Sampson* ouer my head, then grynde in a mill, like an idolatrous and blynde beast, all my life, to the rejoycing of vncircumcised *Philistims* . . . when religion is at the stake, the *Preist*, who (is a man of peace) maye excite to the warre, nay, must blow the trumpet, & must sound the *Alarum.*[157]

Scott's call to arms was, I have argued, as much about fostering a critical and politically informed public as it was about the specific policy issues that alarmed him. This is not to reduce the importance of the latter to a pretext for any kind of discussion: for Scott the need for a vocal and engaged godly citizenry was inextricable from the threats that faced England on the fronts of Spanish intrigue or courtly dissimulation. It was only by encouraging a fondness for otiose calm, and for the pursuit of private interests, that Spain could gain a foothold or a naturally warlike and vigilant people could become enslaved – to their own passions or to a Catholic imperium. Constant vigilance was necessary, and Scott put himself forward as the emblem of the humble, yet faithful and brave, watchman: a figure for his countrymen to emulate as they recognised the importance of debate in the country and of communication between king and people in Parliament and on the page.[158] The kind of order and discretion that Donne had recommended to the clergy in 1622 could, argued Scott, all too often be a smokescreen for flattery, and the freedom of speech that a true follower of Christ would always offer to his prince was precisely the kind of speech that broke boundaries and disrupted order: it burst from its author like wine from new bottles, and it came from the Holy Spirit.[159]

---

[156] Ibid., sig. D; cf. sig. E3. In an extended use of the body politic analogy, Scott suggests that healthy organs should take over the function of those that are damaged, and goes on to give examples of extraordinary prophets (sigs. D–D2, D3–E3).

[157] Ibid., sigs. D2ᵛ–D3.

[158] See especially [Scott], *Digitvs Dei*, sigs. F–Fᵛ; [Scott], *Vox Regis*, sigs. F2ᵛ–F3.

[159] See [Scott], *The Belgick Souldier*, sigs. Bᵛ–B2:

> and so it followes in all the enormous proceedings of irreligious peace, tyrannous governments, wanton passions, unreformed Common-wealths, iealous Princes, the papacy Inquisition, persecution of Saints, and the abuses of ambitious officers, all their deformities are covered with the mantle of order, and innocent soules betrayed to the voice of authoritie with this affrighting: how dare you be disobedient to Princes? raise hurli-burlies and innouation, or seem refractary to the statutes of

Scott was an unwilling martyr, as his consistent use of anonymity and his flight to Utrecht demonstrate: he knew that he was more effectual if his voice could be heard than if he were a silenced figurehead.[160] But he was a martyr none the less and, just as he had lamented the loss of Essex and Ralegh, so two years after his death John Russell added the name of Scott to the list of past examples of honest and heroic counsel in his poem *The Spy*.[161] By 1628 the optimism with which Scott had ended his *Vox Dei* was a dim memory: Russell placed the rise of the anti-Calvinist faction in the Church of England next in line to the Spanish conspiracies that had exercised his forebear.[162] Taking as his motto the Juvenalian *Possibile est Satyras non scribere?*, Russell explains that conditions are such that he is forced to write in verse – even Scott's vituperative prose would not be suited to the current age.[163]

Scott and Reynolds, and Russell after them, as well as many other ministers, maintained in the face of what they saw as increasing encroachment upon the liberties of the people and the security of the commonwealth a commitment to biblically warranted *parrhesia*.[164] Rejecting the restrictions of decorum, they did not instead blandly assert the importance of and right to free speech: they participated in a debate that their works also intended to foster over when and for whom truly free speech was appropriate.[165]

---

government? is it not wisedome to prevent turbulent warre, and keepe mischiefe in awe by pleasing the Princes, though with flattery and absurd soothing their impious and fearefull enormities?

[160] Scott's anonymity (which was in any case transparent) also served importantly to support his self-representation in his works as the voice of a larger community whose importance lay in his representative nature rather than his identity as an author.

[161] I. R. [John Russell], *The Spy. Discovering the Danger of the Arminian Heresie and Spanish Trecherie* (Strasburg, 1628), sig. A^v:

> is there not
> Vnslaughter'd, or vnpoyson'd left one Scot
> Dares tell the blindfold state it headlong reeles
> To *Spanish* thraldome vpon *spanish* wheeles?

[162] In the manner of Donne's *Ignatius his Conclave*, Russell describes a conclave in hell which reveals that Arminius was sent as a missionary from hell to establish popery by the back door while seeming to be a Protestant; see I.R., *The Spy*, sigs. B3^v–B4.

[163] Ibid., sig. A. The epigram adapts that to Juvenal's *Satire I* 'difficile est saturam non scribere'; the poem's opening apostrophe echoes the tone of the same source ('Semper ego auditor tantum?'). See *Juvenal and Persius*, trans. By G. G. Ramsay, rev. edition (London: Heinemann, 1940), p. 2. On Russell, see Andrew McRae, *Literature, Satire and the Early Stuart State* (Cambridge: Cambridge University Press, 2004), pp. 104–5.

[164] For another example of a minister working in this tradition, see my discussion of Thomas Bywater in chapter 4 below, pp. 224–33.

[165] With reference to decorum, Reynolds wrote in *Votivae Angliae* 'and because it is a difficult poynt to satisfie our selues and the tyme together; yet notwithstanding) [sic] I hope that your Majestie will pardon this boldness and affection of myne': S. R. N. I. [John Reynolds], *Votivae Angliae* (Utrecht, 1624), sig. Eii.

Like Ambrose, they attempted to seize the moment and make the best use of their resources in order to encourage those they addressed – from the king to their fellow citizens – to listen and learn, and they made use of the burgeoning market place of print in doing so. Scott married the tradition of religious *parrhesia* to that of classical humanism in his series of works on the crisis of the 1620s and throughout them, in returning again and again to the necessity of frank counsel and open communication between the king and his subjects, he celebrated the place of Parliament.[166] It is to this institution and its complex negotiations over the right to freedom of speech that I turn in the next chapter.

---

[166] On Scott's insistence on the importance of Parliament, see Peltonen, *Classical Humanism and Republicanism*, pp. 238–9, 258, 264; Lake, 'Constitutional Consensus', pp. 823–4.

CHAPTER 3

Freedom of speech in early Stuart Parliaments

There is nothing so dear to the subject as liberty, no liberty so good as that in parliament, none in parliament greater than the freedom of speech.

Sir Henry Poole[1]

FREEDOM OF SPEECH AND PARLIAMENTARY HISTORY

Of all the spaces where freedom of speech was discussed in early Stuart England, only in Parliament was it requested and granted as a formal right. This has led some historians to argue – erroneously, I shall suggest – that conceptions of free speech in the period originate in, or are determined by, the history and traditions of Parliament in general and the House of Commons in particular.[2] In fact, the relationship between parliamentary custom and extra-parliamentary arguments and habits of thought concerning freedom of speech are considerably more complicated than has sometimes been acknowledged. In chapter 1 I showed how the idea of good counsel as necessarily including a duty as well as a right to speak frankly built upon classical descriptions of the *vir civilis* and humanist adaptations of that figure in discussions of the primacy of the *vita activa* to the good life, and I suggested how the obligations and tensions attendant upon the idea of counsel were felt particularly acutely in early Stuart Parliaments. Were MPs most properly thought of as counsellors?[3] Many clearly thought so much of the time, but at various times both James I and Charles I

---

[1] 12 February 1621: *CD 1621*, II: *The Anonymous Journal 'X'*, p. 56.
[2] Studies which take this position, implicitly or explicitly, include J. E. Neale, 'The Commons' Privilege of Free Speech in Parliament', in *Tudor Studies presented . . . to Albert Frederick Pollard*, ed. by R. W. Seton-Watson (London: Longmans, Green & Co., 1924), pp. 257–86; Harold Hulme, 'The Winning of Freedom of Speech by the House of Commons', *The American Historical Review* 61:4 (July 1956): 825–53; J. H. Hexter, introduction to *Parliament and Liberty from the Reign of Elizabeth to the English Civil War*, ed. by Hexter (Stanford: Stanford University Press, 1992), pp. 1–19.
[3] On this question in Elizabethan Parliaments, see A. N. McLaren, *Political Culture in the Reign of Elizabeth I* (Cambridge: Cambridge University Press, 1999), chapter 6.

(as well as members of both Houses) would argue either that they were not first and foremost called to counsel the monarch or that they were failing to counsel well. Parliamentary precedents and other texts and traditions could be appealed to from either position. I will argue in this chapter that while questions of the historical privileges and the proper function of Parliament were often dominant in debates about freedom of speech, these debates also drew on the kinds of arguments that I have outlined in the previous chapters.

Any treatment of parliamentary freedom of speech in this period must confront vigorous debate about the function of the institution not just among seventeenth-century actors but also among its historians. Questions in the historiography of Parliament especially at issue here include those of whether Parliament was primarily a place of political conflict or one of business and administration, of the nature of the relations between Parliament and the localities, and of whether there was a growth in parliamentary 'opposition' to the crown. These are among the *loci classici* of the confrontation between what have been described as 'Whig' and 'revisionist' – and 'post-revisionist' – historical narratives about the early seventeenth century. The early Stuart Parliaments have been the focus of this debate in large part because of historians' desire to establish how far their proceedings contributed to the causes of the Civil War.[4] Earlier narratives which saw the drift towards military engagement in 1642 as a consequence of an increase in parliamentary power, a growth of opposition in the House of Commons, and a growing stress on the liberties of the subject were challenged by G. R. Elton's work on Tudor Parliaments and Conrad Russell's on the early Stuart period.[5] Elton argued that Parliament's primary function was to pass legislation, and that its proceedings were more often characterised

---

[4] Among the considerable body of literature on this issue, some of the most important contributions are Lawrence Stone, *The Causes of the English Revolution* (London: Routledge & Kegan Paul, 1972); Conrad Russell (ed.), *The Origins of the English Civil War* (Basingstoke: Macmillan, 1973); Howard Tomlinson, 'The Causes of the War: a Historiographical Survey', in Howard Tomlinson (ed.), *Before the English Civil War: Essays on Early Stuart Politics and Government* (London: Macmillan, 1983); John Morrill, Brian Manning, and David Underdown, 'What Was the English Revolution?', *History Today* 34 (March 1984): 11–25; Conrad Russell, *The Causes of the English Civil War* (Oxford: Clarendon Press, 1990); Ann Hughes, *The Causes of the English Civil War* (Basingstoke: Macmillan, 1991); John Morrill, *Revolt in the Provinces: The People of England and the Tragedies of War*, second edition (Harlow: Longman, 1999). See further Kevin Sharpe, 'Re-writing the History of Parliament in Seventeenth-century England', in K. Sharpe, *Remapping Early Modern England* (Cambridge: Cambridge University Press, 2000), pp. 269–93.

[5] For the 'Whig' position, see especially Wallace Notestein, 'The Winning of the Initiative by the House of Commons', *Proceedings of the British Academy* 11 (1924–5): 125–75 and *The House of Commons 1604–1610* (New Haven: Yale University Press, 1971).

by harmony than by conflict.[6] Russell built on this work and suggested that much writing on early Stuart Parliaments had been vitiated by the exercise of hindsight: because historians knew that the Civil War was coming, they assumed that their subjects did as well.[7] Emphasising that Parliament was not government, that Parliaments were temporary events, that MPs were divided in their loyalties rather than opposed to the monarch and that Parliament was not where the major political events of the period took place, he also redirected attention to the day-to-day business of Westminster.[8] This 'revisionist turn', supported by the work of several other historians, drew attention to the dangers of writing grand narratives of the progress of freedom.[9] However, it also ran the risk of throwing the baby of real political debate out with the bathwater of methodological slackness. A healthy scepticism about the presence of revolutionary ideologies in early Stuart Parliaments led to an under-emphasis on any form of ideological conflict; the rejection of the notion that post-Civil War ideas of freedom were present in the debates of the 1610s and 1620s may have deprived the ideas of freedom that were being propounded in those decades of the attention they demand.[10]

The attempt to locate the origins of recognisably modern notions of freedom in early Stuart Parliaments is central to these debates. Accounts of the period that located in the Form of Apology and Satisfaction of 1604, the Commons' Protestation of 1621, and the Petition of Right of 1628 a series of landmarks in a constitutional revolution whose telos was either the Bill of Rights of 1689 or even the American Bill of Rights of 1791 have been rightly taken to task for proceeding anachronistically.[11] The danger

---

[6] See G. R. Elton, *The Parliament of England 1559–1581* (Cambridge: Cambridge University Press, 1986) and *Studies in Tudor and Stuart Politics and Government: Papers and Reviews 1946–1972*, volume II: *Parliament and Political Thought* (Cambridge: Cambridge University Press, 1974).

[7] See Conrad Russell, 'Parliamentary History in Perspective, 1604–1629', in Conrad Russell, *Unrevolutionary England, 1603–1642* (London: Hambledon Press, 1990), pp. 31–57.

[8] See Russell, 'Parliamentary History in Perspective, 1604–1629'; Russell, 'The Nature of a Parliament in Early Stuart England' in Russell, *Unrevolutionary England, 1603–1642*, 1–29, and *Parliaments and English Politics 1621–1629* (Oxford: Clarendon Press, 1979).

[9] Other important works from a revisionist perspective include *Faction and Parliament: Essays on Early Stuart History*, ed. by Kevin Sharpe (Oxford: Clarendon Press, 1978); Sheila Lambert, 'Procedure in the House of Commons in the Early Stuart Period', *English Historical Review* 95 (1980): 753–81.

[10] For the reaction against revisionism, especially in relation to political conflict and ideology, see Richard Cust and Ann Hughes (eds.), *Conflict in Early Stuart England: Studies in Religion and Politics, 1603–1642* (London: Longman, 1989); J. P. Sommerville, *Royalists and Patriots: Politics and Ideology in England 1603–1640* (London: Longman, 1999).

[11] On the Form of Apology and Satisfaction, see especially G. R. Elton, 'A High Road to Civil War?', in Elton, *Studies in Tudor and Stuart Politics and Government: Papers and Reviews 1946–1972*,

of treating an event or a text as an 'anticipation' of later events or texts is relevant here, as it is in discussions of the Civil War and its origins.[12] It is especially severe when dealing with the terms in which arguments were conducted in the period under consideration. The first volume in a series devoted to 'The Making of Modern Freedom' is entitled *Parliament and Liberty from the Reign of Elizabeth to the English Civil War*, but as John Morrill has pointed out, the slippage between 'freedom' (especially 'modern freedom') and 'liberty' is significant and, indeed, worrying, and we must be wary when using vocabulary with such a weight of baggage.[13] Morrill chooses to hear a 'death knell' for the volume's project in Derek Hirst's quotation and gloss of a note made by Edward Hyde, the future Earl of Clarendon, in his commonplace book: 'though the name of liberty be pleasant to all kinds of people, yet all men do not understand the same thing by it'.[14] Hirst comments, 'what had, not long before, been an adulatory and vague consensus about liberty had now [by 1646/7] been both defined and fragmented; in a sense one chapter in the history of freedom came, if not to an end, then to an intermission in these years [1640–1660], while a whole series of other chapters, or in some cases the prologues to them, began'.[15] Leaving aside the slightly odd use of a statement made in 1646–7 as 'emblematic' of the developments in the years from 1640 to 1660, there are other problems here, both with Hirst's comment and with Morrill's use of it. Hirst's description of the 'adulatory and vague consensus about liberty' that prevailed in the years before 1640 does not, I will suggest, fit the picture that we receive from looking closely at the early Stuart Parliaments (or at the other arenas of discussion treated in this book). Morrill, on the other hand, while justly admonishing his colleagues for playing fast-and-loose with seventeenth-century and modern connotations of the words 'liberty' and 'freedom', perhaps does not allow as much space as he might to the idea that 'modern freedom' may still be 'made' even if it is by a series of

---

volume II, pp. 164–182 and the further discussion in this chapter, below, pp. 142–5; 152–65. A trenchant recent critique of Elton's argument is offered by Theodore K. Rabb, *Jacobean Gentleman: Sir Edwin Sandys, 1561–1629* (Princeton: Princeton University Press, 1998), pp. 102–8.

[12] On the dangers of such anachronistic readings of texts and events, see Quentin Skinner, 'Interpretation, Rationality and Truth' and 'Meaning and Understanding in the History of Ideas', both in Quentin Skinner, *Visions of Politics*, three volumes (Cambridge: Cambridge University Press, 2002), volume I: *Regarding Method*, pp. 27–56 and 57–89, at pp. 50–1 and 60–1.

[13] See Hexter, *Parliament and Liberty* and the review by John Morrill, 'Taking Liberties with the Seventeenth Century', *Parliamentary History* 15:3 (1996): 379–91.

[14] Edward Hyde, *Commonplace Book*, 1646–7, quoted in Derek M. Hirst, 'Freedom, Revolution, and Beyond', in Hexter, *Parliament and Liberty*, pp. 252–74, at p. 252.

[15] Hirst, 'Freedom, Revolution, and Beyond', pp. 252–3.

negotiations, debates, and conflicts rather than a smooth process of tree-like growth. That a number of chapters in the history of freedom may be opening and closing all at once does not mean that any attempt to trace their relation to modern incarnations of the idea are doomed. Instead it means that we need to work out the relation between these various chapters and, most importantly, pay attention to the various different registers in which they are written (which is, after all, Morrill's argument elsewhere in his review).

I have spent some time on what might seem like a minor scuffle over terminology because I believe, as Morrill does, that an understanding of historical vocabularies is vital to the recovery of past modes of thought. In this book I attempt to show what people in the early seventeenth century meant when they spoke about, or laid claim to, freedom of speech. One of the results, I hope, is that we can see that what they were referring to was very different from anything we might recognise as freedom of speech today. Another result, though, should be that we can see how our own notions of freedom of speech are formed by the debates in which these people were involved, the choices that they made, and the linguistic changes that they provoked. Throughout this chapter I will describe debates in Parliament that frequently return to questions of the definition of key terms. This tendency frequently annoyed James I, although he also joined in fervently with wrangles over the true meaning and import of words and phrases. In the proclamation explaining the dissolution of Parliament in 1621, he wrote that some members of the Commons had picked apart 'words and syllables' of his letters and claimed privileges 'in ambiguous and generall words'.[16] For James, these members had not just resorted to pedantry; they had done so inconsistently, subjecting his statements to a rigorous close reading attuned to connotations while using language loosely themselves. This kind of accusation is sometimes also levelled by historians of the period, who find in the Commons' attention to definition at best a stalling tactic and at worst the signs of an attachment to bombastic rhetoric and nit-picking. Dispute over the import of words is a key part of rhetorical argument, however, and parliamentary rhetoric deserves to be taken seriously rather than dismissed as so much padding.[17] Moreover, my contention here is that

[16] 'A Proclamation declaring his Majesties pleasure concerning the dissolving of the present Convention of Parliament', Westminster, 6 January 1622, in James F. Larkin and Paul L. Hughes (eds.), *Stuart Royal Proclamations*, volume 1: *Royal Proclamations of King James I 1603–1625* (Oxford: Clarendon Press, 1973), pp. 527–34, at pp. 531, 533.

[17] For an excellent recent treatment of parliamentary rhetoric in the Elizabethan period, see Peter Mack, *Elizabethan Rhetoric: Theory and Practice* (Cambridge: Cambridge University Press, 2002), especially pp. 1–2 and chapter 7. Mack discusses freedom of speech at pp. 239–45.

political discourse is not a prelude to or commentary on political action: it *is* political action.[18] When MPs discussed whether their liberties could properly be described as deriving from the grace of the monarch, or when they chose to express their fears that they might be reduced to the condition of slaves, they were participating in the formation of their political world. It is a basic tenet of many current discussions of freedom of speech that words are not distinct from deeds: this perception was also present (though of course in a different form) in the early seventeenth century, and needs to be more widely recognised. Historians of rhetoric and literary scholars have acknowledged this for some time, and in this respect they can inform the work of parliamentary historians.[19]

In this chapter I will return frequently to instances of the contested definition of words. These contests are often the beginnings of debates about free speech, and are the means by which such debates are subsequently conducted. Did a member speak loyally or licentiously? Were his words plain or seditious? Was he transported by zeal or flattering his superiors? There are no final answers to these questions, and it is not my intention to adjudicate in the contests I describe, but to observe the ways in which they proceed and to make explicit the broader claims which often lie behind them. Many of the cases and debates I consider focus on a relatively narrow set of concerns, and in different sessions of Parliament over the 25-year period from the accession of James I to the presentation of the Petition of Right in 1628, discussions of free speech rest again and again on the issues of, for example, whether the king is being misinformed about proceedings in the Commons, whether the liberties of Parliament have been infringed, or exactly how the Commons should or can take action against one of their number. Although this can make the debates seem static, I will argue both that there is a good deal of variation in the ways in which these subjects are treated and that by focusing on such variations we can learn

---

[18] For a fuller discussion of the notion of political languages, and of the relationship between political discourse and action, see the essays collected in Skinner, *Visions of Politics*, volume I: *Regarding Method*, especially chapters 1, 8, and 9.

[19] This association is rendered visible in the depiction of Rhetoric personified as a lady with a sword, or in the image of the Hercules Gallicus, whose tongue is linked to the ears of a group of men by chains; see Wayne A. Rebhorn, *The Emperor of Men's Minds: Literature and the Renaissance Discourse of Rhetoric* (Ithaca: Cornell University Press, 1995), pp. 66–79; Quentin Skinner, *Reason and Rhetoric in the Philosophy of Hobbes* (Cambridge: Cambridge University Press, 1996), pp. 92–3. The Hercules Gallicus emblem appears most famously in Andrea Alciati, *Emblemata* (Padua, 1621), p. 751, reproduced in Rebhorn, *The Emperor of Men's Minds*, p. 69; it is used by Hobbes as a metaphor for the 'Civill Lawes' that bind men to the individual or assembly to whom they have given 'the Soveraigne Power' (Thomas Hobbes, *Leviathan*, ed. by Richard Tuck, rev. edition (Cambridge: Cambridge University Press, 1996), p. 147).

much about the different conceptions of parliamentary freedom of speech available at the time. There are many ways in which the debates of 1614 are significantly different from those of 1621; and many aspects of those debates are specific to the conditions of the early seventeenth century. Nonetheless, they also depend upon and develop from events in the Parliaments of the late sixteenth century. I thus hope to balance due attention to the local context of each session I discuss with an awareness of its place in a broader picture.[20]

One of the most forceful criticisms levelled at nineteenth- and early twentieth-century accounts of early modern Parliaments by the revisionists was that they had equated Parliament with the House of Commons.[21] Parliament, they reminded scholars, was described by its seventeenth-century members as a trinity comprising the monarch, the House of Lords, and the House of Commons.[22] The Upper House has frequently been neglected, and the nature of Parliament as a bicameral institution sidelined. Observing the degree of negotiation and collaboration between the two Houses makes it hard to sustain an idea of the Commons as isolated and consistently opposed to Lords, the Court, or the monarch; and it is important to take account of the client–patron relationships that often obtained between MPs and peers.[23] This is not, however, to underestimate the degree of conflict that sometimes broke out between the two Houses. It is important to establish, if possible, whether an MP was taking a particular position in a debate because he had been encouraged to do so by a noble patron (as John Hoskyns was rumoured to have done in 1614)[24] – but it is also as well to bear in mind that patronage is not the same as ventriloquism.[25] Nonetheless I concern myself here exclusively with the proceedings of the House of Commons. This is because of the particular nature of the Speaker's request for freedom of speech and because of the recurrence and significance of the debates about freedom of speech that took place in the House in the period from 1603 to 1628. There is no comparable set of events in the House of

---

[20] For fuller narrative accounts of the Parliaments of this period, in varying degrees of detail, see S. R. Gardiner, *History of England from the Accession of James I to the Outbreak of the Civil War*, 10 volumes (London: Longmans, Green, & Co., 1884), volumes I–VI; Thomas L. Moir, *The Addled Parliament of 1614* (Oxford: Clarendon Press, 1958); Notestein, *The House of Commons 1604–1610*; Robert Zaller, *The Parliament of 1621: A Study in Constitutional Conflict* (Berkeley and Los Angeles: University of California Press, 1971); Robert E. Ruigh, *The Parliament of 1624: Politics and Foreign Policy* (Cambridge, MA: Harvard University Press, 1971); Russell, *Parliaments and English Politics*; David L. Smith, *The Stuart Parliaments 1603–1689* (London: Arnold, 1999).

[21] See D. L. Smith, *The Stuart Parliaments*, pp. 87–92.

[22] Ibid., pp. 81–6.   [23] Ibid., pp. 87–9.   [24] See below, pp. 162–4.

[25] D. L. Smith, *The Stuart Parliaments*, pp. 87–8.

Lords – although there are some significant moments there (among them the exclusion of the Earls of Arundel and Bristol by Charles I in 1626).[26]

The final aspect of the revisionist critique that I want to consider here concerns the use of parliamentary sources. It is often difficult to reconstruct members' speeches from the fragmentary records of the Clerk as recorded in the *Commons Journal*, and the work of the Yale Center for Parliamentary History in publishing private diaries of the early Stuart Parliaments has vastly expanded the amount of material easily available to historians about the proceedings in both Houses.[27] However, it has been suggested by some historians that a concentration on particular sources above others can have a seriously distorting effect on the image of Parliament that is generated. Parliamentary diaries can sometimes give vivid accounts of a debate and thus prove especially appealing to a scholar interested in conflict; they may record speeches that were never in fact delivered, or tidy up and expand a speech after its delivery.[28] They are likely to be partial, both because of the practical difficulty of taking full notes in the House and because of the diarist's possible biases – even if his bias is merely towards short and pithy contributions – and they may have an agenda dictated by the interests of a patron in the Lords or outside Parliament altogether.[29] Extreme caution is therefore necessary when using these documents to reconstruct the events and speeches of a given Parliament.[30]

These warnings are valuable, but they do not mean that diaries should be passed over in favour of the 'official' record in the *Commons Journal*.[31] The

[26] On Arundel and Bristol, see Russell, *Parliaments and English Politics*, pp. 285, 302–22; Kevin Sharpe, 'The Earl of Arundel, His Circle and the Opposition to the Duke of Buckingham, 1618–1628', in *Faction and Parliament*, ed. by Sharpe, pp. 209–44.

[27] On the *Commons Journal*, see J. E. Neale, 'Commons Journals of the Tudor Period', *Transactions of the Royal Historical Society* 4:3 (1920): 136–70; *CD 1621*, I, 101–12; *CD 1629*, xi–xiv.

[28] On the dangers of casually using parliamentary diaries, and these issues in particular, see John Morrill, 'Reconstructing the History of Early Stuart Parliaments', *Archives*, 21.91 (1994): 67–72 and 'Paying One's D'Ewes', *Parliamentary History*, 14.2 (1995): 179–86, and the debate between Morrill and Maija Jansson: Maija Jansson, 'Dues Paid', *Parliamentary History*, 15.2 (1996): 215–20; John Morrill, 'Getting Over D'Ewes', *Parliamentary History*, 15.2 (1996): 221–30. See further Chris R. Kyle, 'Introduction' to *Parliament, Politics and Elections 1604–1648*, ed. by Chris R. Kyle, Camden fifth series, no. 17 (Cambridge: Cambridge University Press, 2001), pp. 1–12.

[29] On diarists as supplying information about proceedings in the Commons for patrons, see Elton, *The Parliament of England*, pp. 13–14.

[30] See Morrill, 'Reconstructing the History of Early Stuart Parliaments', p. 71 for a set of guidelines for the use of parliamentary sources. Morrill is especially concerned with the effect of quoting diaries as though they provided an accurate record of what was actually said in the House of Commons. Russell has reminded us that, nonetheless, 'the striking thing about the Parliamentary diaries is not the extent to which they say different things, but the extent to which they say the same things' (*Parliaments and English Politics*, p. xvii).

[31] Morrill makes this point in his fourth guideline; 'Reconstructing the History of Early Stuart Parliaments', p. 71.

Journal tends to omit extended descriptions of debates and disagreements, and is much more concerned with the business of the reading and passing of bills. As David Smith has argued, it may thus give an impression of consensus and of the dominance of such business that is just as misleading as anything inferred from the exclusive use of diaries.[32] I have tried in my treatment of the sources to take these minatory suggestions seriously, and to tread carefully when employing and quoting from the private diaries. However, I have felt that sometimes they are less directly applicable to discussion of the debates on freedom of speech than they would be to other kinds of enquiry. I am not attempting to construct a full picture of the business and nature of Parliament in the period under discussion, but quite deliberately focusing on one aspect of that business in order to see how it fits into a broader context of debate. I am especially interested in what Morrill calls 'the heated atmosphere of the Houses at their most tense', into which a reading of the diaries draws one, without wishing to suggest that this atmosphere is representative of much more than what MPs had to say about freedom of speech at such moments.[33] And I am keen to read the debates, wherever possible, with close attention to their use of specific terms. This means that I will often quote from sources directly and gloss the quotations on the assumption that this was what a particular MP said. When I do this, I try to check several sources against each other and resist choosing the most colourful if it is not supported by others.[34] While I am most interested in the kinds of arguments about freedom of speech that actually took place in Parliament, I would not wish to exclude from my consideration the kinds of arguments that MPs thought they heard, or even that they thought *should* take place. These are all important in order to gain as full an understanding as possible of the subject.

The Commons' own actions against those whom they deemed to have slipped from liberty into licentiousness – both MPs and, strikingly in the early seventeenth century, non-members – are an important part of the ongoing debates about the definition of terms and the extent of parliamentary power. When Peter Wentworth delivered his celebrated speech in 1576, he was only about halfway through his defence of liberty and assault on flattery when he was stopped and secluded from the House – by his fellow members.[35] In very different circumstances, in June 1626, Mr More

---

[32] See D. L. Smith, *The Stuart Parliaments*, pp. 12–13.
[33] Morrill, 'Reconstructing the History of Early Stuart Parliaments', p. 71.
[34] Cf. Kyle, 'Introduction' to *Parliament, Politics and Elections*, pp. 4–5.
[35] This is according to the manuscript copies of the speech. See *Proceedings in the Parliaments of Elizabeth I*, ed. by T. E. Hartley, 3 volumes (Leicester: Leicester University Press, 1981–95), vol. 1,

was interrupted for apparently raising the spectre of tyranny in a speech that invoked the threat of 'new counsels' that had been hovering over the Parliament's proceedings. The accounts we have of the little he said before he was stopped agree that he made a comparison between the susceptibility of the French to tyranny and slavishness and the strength and resistance of England and the English. Whitelocke's diary records the speech as follows: 'It is an impossible thing for this kingdom to be brought to that which new counsels have brought other kingdoms to if God should send us a tyrant, as, God be thanked, we have a pious and a good king now.'[36] The Chancellor of the Exchequer, interrupting More, said that talk of tyrants was not appropriate in the House, and other members agreed. Apparent threats or accusations of tyranny couched in a conditional clause were always dangerous, and so it proved here. More was censured by the House and sent to the Tower; he resumed his place four days later, on 7 June. In contrast to Wentworth's case, there is no fair copy of More's speech extant. Another point of difference is that More was dealt with solely by the Commons, while Wentworth had been examined by the Council.

One of the most interesting aspects of More's case is the degree of discussion that took place in the House about what exactly it was that he had said: it was moved that his words should be reported to the House outside of the Committee of the Whole that was in session when they were spoken,[37] and this provoked a debate about the content of his speech. Sir John Finch said '*I think* his words were: we were born free and must be free if the King will keep his kingdom' (my italics);[38] Mr Browne 'did not remember the words so employed,' but did remember a comment about Louis XI that no-one else seemed to,[39] while Mr Herris and Mr Herbert offered their own versions of the speech.[40] This all points to the difficulty that members could encounter in recalling exactly what had been said in the middle of a debate when it was suddenly deemed necessary to go over it again, and adds colour to Morrill's warnings about the way in which different members might hear – and record – different versions of the same words. It also shows how important it was to the House to make sure that

pp. 425–34. Hartley's copy-text is Inner Temple Petyt MS 538/17. J. E. Neale, in his account of this occasion, writes that 'Speaker, Privy Councillors, and others listened to the speech with growing uneasiness', implying that the chief concern was on the part of those with links to the Court and relegating all MPs not in this group to the status of 'others': J. E. Neale, *Elizabeth I and her Parliaments*, volume II: *1559–1681* (London: Jonathan Cape, 1953), pp. 318–32, quotation at p. 325. It is by no means clear that this was the case. For a reading of this speech and its context, see Mack, *Elizabethan Rhetoric*, pp. 1–2, 241–2.

[36] 3 June 1626; *PP 1626*, 3, 353. Compare the accounts of Grosvenor (p. 357) and Lowther (p. 361).
[37] By Mr Wandesford: *PP 1626*, 3, 353, 357.   [38] Ibid., 353.
[39] Ibid., 357.   [40] Ibid., 358.

they agreed about what had been said when it was deemed offensive, so that it could be put on record and dealt with in the most appropriate fashion. In this instance it was

ordered that Mr Herbert should report to the House that Mr More spoke these words: 'That we were born free and must be free if the King would keep his kingdom'; or words to that effect, and that he distrusted upon supposition what a tyrant might do or not do in this kingdom, adding as thanks be to God we have none occasion of that fear having a just and pious King.[41]

Agreement at an early stage (in this case while the Committee was still sitting) about the words used was vital if the House was to be able to proceed without further, time-consuming disputes. It was also important should the case come to the attention of the king: the House could show that they were proceeding clearly and that they were acting, so to speak, with one voice. This could be an issue if the king were informed unofficially of proceedings in the House – and the dangers of 'misinformation' caused a considerable degree of discussion and alarm under both James and Charles.

If MPs' desire to police the limits of one another's speech was almost as important a part of the Commons' understanding of free speech as the claims for liberty and privilege made in the House, then another very significant aspect of that understanding was the concern about discussion of the Commons' proceedings outside the House. Several cases demonstrate this concern, the earliest in James's reign probably being that of the publication of a book on the Union of England and Scotland by John Thornborough, Bishop of Bristol.[42] There were other attempts to control the speech of non-members, even when it did not concern the proceedings of Parliament. Freedom of speech in the early Stuart Parliaments, then, was not only a matter of licensing outspokenness and securing liberty: it also entailed assertions of power within and outside of the House of Commons. It covered the question of the spread of (mis)information, and it raised the issue of the limits of parliamentary jurisdiction. These knotty questions of the limits of liberty and the degree of special licence due to individuals claiming a certain warrant are ones that I have considered in my discussions of rhetoric, counsel, and the religious culture of frank speech in previous chapters. In order to move closer to an understanding of the way

---

[41] Grosvenor, ibid., 358; this agrees with Whitelocke's account except that the latter has 'discoursed upon what a tyrant might do' in place of 'distrusted upon supposition what a tyrant might do' (353).

[42] This case was raised on 26 May 1604: *CJ*, 1, 226, 230.

that they functioned in Parliament, I will now return to the starting point of this chapter: the formal request for and grant of freedom of speech in the Speaker's oration at the opening of each session.

THE SPEAKER'S REQUEST FOR PRIVILEGES: THE FORMAL BASIS OF PARLIAMENTARY FREEDOM OF SPEECH

In the legend of parliamentary freedom of speech, the *fons et origo* is Sir Thomas More's formal request for the privilege in his petition to the king as Speaker of the Lower House in 1523: the first recorded instance of such a request.[43] After the traditional preamble, More's innovatory petition asked that

it may therefore like your most aboundant grace, our most benigne and godly kinge, to give to all your comons here assembled your most gracious licens and pardon, freely, without doubte of your dreadfull displeasure, every man to discharge his consciens, and boldlye, in every thinge incident among [us], to declare his advise; and whatsoever happen any man to say, [that] it may like your noble maiestye, of your inestimable goodnes, to take all in goode parte, interpreting every mans wordes, howe unconingly soever they be couched, to proceed yeat of good zeale towardes the profit of your realme and honor of your royall person.[44]

We do not know whether these were the actual words used by More: the speech only survives in a version recorded by More's son-in-law William Roper in his life of the saint. The first such request to be recorded in the *Lords' Journals* only appeared in 1542.[45] Although Roper thought More's speech worthy of note, it is not altogether clear that it was regarded as such by his fellow parliamentarians. On all the evidence we have, however,

---

[43] In this section I rely extensively on J. S. Roskell, *The Commons and their Speakers in English Parliaments 1376–1523* (Manchester: Manchester University Press, 1965), chapter 2, and on Neale, 'The Commons' Privilege of Free Speech in Parliament'.

[44] William Roper, *The Lyfe of Sir Thomas More, Knighte*, ed. by E. V. Hitchcock, Early English Text Society, original series 197 (London: Oxford University Press, 1935), p. 16.

[45] 'Hodie Communes presentabant Regie Majestati *Thomam Moyle*, singulorum suffragiis electum Prolocutorem suum . . . Supplicavit Regie Majestati "Ut in dicendis sententiis quivis libere et impune eloqui posset quid animi haberet et quid consilii"' (*LJ*, I, 167). See Neale, 'The Commons' Privilege of Free Speech in Parliament', p. 267; Roskell, *The Commons and their Speakers*, p. 42. It must be borne in mind that the records of Parliament before this time are limited, and that the *Commons Journal* only appears in 1547; however, the Parliament Rolls for the medieval period do contain reasonably full records of the Speaker's protestation without the request for freedom of speech; for examples see Roskell, *The Commons and their Speakers*, p. 32, n. 1; Neale, 'The Commons' Privilege of Free Speech in Parliament', pp. 260–4. The first protestation to be officially recorded was made in the first Parliament of Richard II in October 1377 by Sir Peter de la Mare (Roskell, *The Commons and their Speakers*, pp. 32–3).

it certainly stands out, and it may have failed to make the records precisely because of its unusual nature.[46] The Speaker's protestation had previously consisted of two main requests: the first was to be excused from personal responsibility for anything he might say to the king or the Lords. In other words, he was only the mouthpiece of the Commons and not acting in his own right. The second was that he should be able to amend or correct his statements should he have unintentionally misrepresented the Commons in any way.[47] There also seems to have been a clause in some protestations asking for forgiveness in advance for anything he said that displeased the king, on the assumption that it was unintentional.[48] Together these elements offered two branches of protection: one to the Speaker, in order to spare the messenger from being shot; and the other to the Commons, in order to prevent them from being wilfully or accidentally misrepresented.[49]

Clearly missing from this version of the Speaker's protestation as it seems routinely to have been made from at least 1377 to 1523 is any request for a right to speak frankly in the Commons. Asking forgiveness in advance for unintentional offence caused to the king is, on the face of it, a long way from asking that the king allow 'every man to discharge his consciens, and boldlye, in every thinge incident among [us],' in the words of More's protestation. The appearance of this request, and its combination with one that the king should interpret their speeches, 'howe unconingly soever they be couched', favourably (using the rule of interpreting *in mitior sensu*), is therefore a truly significant change. The fact that earlier protestations requested forgiveness suggests that the Commons knew they were likely to offend in their speech,[50] but it does not explicitly refer to outspokenness as something that might be routinely expected from them, let alone something that could be considered part of their duties or rights. And even More's protestation still does not refer to freedom of speech as a parliamentary liberty, or as being part of the Commons' traditions. In 1455 Thomas Young had claimed compensation for his imprisonment in the Tower four years earlier by appealing to the fact that

---

[46] See Elton, *The Parliament of England*, p. 331.

[47] Roskell, *The Commons and their Speakers*, pp. 33–6.

[48] Neale, 'The Commons' Privilege of Free Speech in Parliament', p. 260; Roskell, *The Commons and their Speakers*, pp. 34–6, gives examples.

[49] In this respect the protection offered to the Speaker is similar to that customarily afforded to ambassadors.

[50] For this point, see Roskell, *The Commons and their Speakers*, pp. 39, 50. Roskell writes that 'although there is no clear categorical indication that the Commons in the pre-Tudor period enjoyed free speech *de jure*, certainly there were times when they seem to have practised it *de facto*' (p. 50).

the Commons, 'by the olde liberte and fredom of the Comyns of this Lande' whom they represented, were entitled to have 'theire fredom to speke and sey in the Hous of their assemble as to theym is thought convenyent or resonable withoute eny maner chalenge, charge, or punycion therefore to be leyde to them in any wyse'.[51]

However, as J. S. Roskell points out, this claim was Young's, not the Commons': they may have implicitly supported it by forwarding his petition to the Lords, but there is no record of any official statement making a similar claim.[52] When, then, did freedom of speech properly become a privilege or liberty of Parliament? The answer is that we do not know. By the early years of Elizabeth's reign the request as framed by More had become a standard part of the Speaker's protestation, and Simonds D'Ewes recorded Sir Thomas Gargrave's request in 1559 as follows:

lastly [Sir Thomas Gargrave] came, *according to the usual form*, first, to desire liberty of access for the House of Commons to the Queen's Majesty's presence upon all urgent and necessary occasions. Secondly, that if in anything himself should mistake or misreport or overslip that which should be committed unto him to declare, that it might without prejudice to the House be better declared, and that his unwilling miscarriage therein might be pardoned. Thirdly, that they might have liberty and freedom of speech in whatsoever they treated of or had occasion to propound and debate in the House. The fourth and last, that all the members of the House, with their servants and necessary attendants, might be exempted from all manner of arrests and suits during the continuance of the Parliament, and the usual space both before the beginning and after the ending thereof, as in former times hath always been accustomed.[53]

In 1563 Thomas Williams made the same four requests, which the *Commons Journal* referred to as 'the accustomed petitions'.[54] Williams referred to the granting of freedom of speech in particular as being 'according to the *old antient* Order.'[55] Yet all four requests were not consistently made by

---

[51] Roskell, *The Commons and their Speakers*, p. 41. Young's claim can be found in *Rot. Parl.* volume v, p. 337a.

[52] Roskell, *The Commons and their Speakers*, p. 41; see also Neale, 'The Commons' Privilege of Free Speech in Parliament', pp. 264–5.

[53] 28 January 1559: Sir Simonds D'Ewes, *The Journals of all the Parliaments during the Reign of Queen Elizabeth, both of the House of Lords and House of Commons* (London, 1682), pp. 16–17, quoted in Geoffrey Elton (ed.), *The Tudor Constitution: Documents and Commentary*, second edition (Cambridge: Cambridge University Press, 1982), p. 269 (my italics).

[54] *CJ*, 1, 62; *Proceedings in the Parliaments of Elizabeth I*, ed. by Hartley 1, 77–8, quoted in Elton, *The Parliament of England*, p. 332.

[55] My italics: D'Ewes, *The Journals of all the Parliaments during the Reign of Queen Elizabeth*, p. 66a, quoted in Neale, 'The Commons' Privilege of Free Speech in Parliament', p. 268. This request reads in full 'that the Assembly of the Lower House, may have frank and free Liberties to speak their Minds, without any Controulment, Blame, Grudge, Menaces or Displeasure, according to the old antient Order' (ibid.)

Speakers even by this period.[56] G. R. Elton summarises the situation thus: 'it looks as though Gargrave's four points had become reasonably standardized as the subject matter of the Speaker [*sic*] petition, but that some Speakers did not mention them at all and no one knew of a particular order or phrasing that had become obligatory. As yet there was no common form'.[57] At the same time, Stephen Gardiner could refer in 1547 to Parliament as a place 'where was freedom of speech without danger'.[58] And, significantly, freedom of speech appears as one of the four requests made by the Speaker in Sir Thomas Smith's description of Parliament in his *De Republica Anglorum* of 1565: 'that they might franckely and freely saye their mindes in disputing of such matters as may come in question, and that without offence of his Majestie'.[59]

In a way that is characteristic of the nature of Parliament, it appears that by Elizabeth's reign freedom of speech existed both as a respected custom of the Commons, exercised *de facto* and requisite to the pursuit of their business and, increasingly, as a formal liberty more or less regularly requested and granted, whose foundations lay largely in that custom. When antiquarian-minded MPs in the early Stuart Parliaments discussed freedom of speech, they tended, typically, to conflate these two elements, hence making parliamentary free speech an 'ancient liberty'. The Speaker's request was by the early seventeenth century a marker of the grant of a substantial liberty (though not, as Elton points out, a privilege), and something that could and would be appealed to in justification of outspoken debate.[60] In this sense it is a counterpart to the writ of summons, which outlined the reasons for which MPs were called to Parliament in the first place, and which was also frequently invoked in the debates of the early seventeenth century. The writ called members 'ad tractandum et consentiendum pro quibusdam arduis et urgentibus negotiis statum et defensionem regni et ecclesiae Anglicanae tangentibus [to treat and consent about difficult and urgent business concerning the state and defence of the kingdom and the Church of England]'.[61] In order properly to fulfil these duties, it was

---

[56] See Elton, *The Parliament of England*, p. 332.   [57] Ibid.

[58] *The Letters of Stephen Gardiner*, ed. by J. A. Muller (Cambridge: Cambridge University Press, 1933), p. 392, quoted in Elton, *The Parliament of England*, p. 341.

[59] Sir Thomas Smith, *De Republica Anglorum*, ed. by Mary Dewar (Cambridge: Cambridge University Press, 1982), pp. 80–1. Smith also includes as one of his four requests 'that if any should chaunce of that lower house to offend any of them being called to that his highnes court: That they might (according to the ancient custome) have the punishment of them' (p. 81).

[60] On the important difference between the terms 'privilege' and 'liberty' in this context, see Elton, *The Parliament of England*, p. 333. Elton points out that the only parliamentary privilege properly so called is that of freedom from arrest.

[61] Quoted in Russell, *Unrevolutionary England*, p. 7. See below, p. 178, for a discussion of the appeals to the writ of summons that were made in 1621.

argued, the Commons needed to have liberty of speech – just as they needed freedom from arrest, so that they were not interrupted by cases brought in the lower courts of law. It was this freedom, to the end that such 'urgent business' could be debated fully, that was secured in the Speaker's request and its granting by the monarch. As Speaker Robert Bell put it in 1571, 'for liberty of speech to be freely had (due reverence always used to your Majesty), without which it is impossible any great matter be achieved in any conference; for except the objections on every part be heard, answered and confuted, the counsel cannot be perfected'.[62]

Although the request for freedom of speech was couched in terms that admitted no reservation or qualification, this does not mean that the liberty granted was unqualified. As J. E. Neale put it – and this takes us back to the issue of definition, which I raised above – 'liberty was not licence, which still remained punishable; and the danger was that while the crown retained the right to enforce discipline in Parliament, it necessarily defined licence'.[63] 'Licence' would certainly include slandering the crown; it would more broadly also imply keeping to the limits imposed by considerations of decorum – what Lord Keeper Puckering, replying to the Speaker's request in 1593, called 'fitt obseruacion of persones, matters, tymes, places, and other needfull Circumstances'.[64] This latter condition was potentially a site of conflict: one person's decorous but frank speech might be another's outrageous breach of decorum. The Lord Keeper's reply to the Speaker, in which he granted the requests on behalf of the crown, often placed such vague conditions on the grant, indicating as much as anything else that the Commons were still not deemed to be the sole arbiters of what was liberty, what licence. In 1559, replying to Gargrave, Lord Keeper Bacon stated that 'for the third [request], which is liberty of speech, therewith her Highness is right well contented, but so as they be neither unmindful or uncareful of their duties, reverence and obedience to their sovereign'.[65]

---

[62] J. E. Neale, *Elizabeth I and her Parliaments*, volume II: *1584–1601* (London: Jonathan Cape, 1957), p. 245.

[63] Neale, 'The Commons' Privilege of Free Speech in Parliament', p. 274.

[64] Ibid., p. 279; Neale, *Elizabeth I and her Parliaments*, volume II, p. 249. The Speaker was Edward Coke, who was also Solicitor General.

[65] D'Ewes, *The Journals of all the Parliaments during the Reign of Queen Elizabeth*, pp. 16–17, quoted in Elton, *The Tudor Constitution*, p. 269; see also Bacon's similar warning in 1571: *Proceedings in the Parliaments of Elizabeth I*, ed. by Hartley, volume I, p. 199. The Speaker had occasion to remind the House of this warning on 10 April, having been reminded himself by the Attorney General. See further Norman Jones, 'Parliament and the Political Society of Elizabethan England', in *Tudor Political Culture*, ed. by Dale Hoak (Cambridge: Cambridge University Press, 1995), pp. 226–42, at p. 236.

This kind of warning became, as G. R. Elton has written, 'one of the standard *topoi* in Bacon's reply to the Speaker'.[66] In the above quotation from Bacon we can see the innovatory distinction made by Elizabeth between matters of state, which could only be discussed if they were introduced on her behalf and with her permission and 'other matters concerninge the common wealth'.[67] This distinction, effectively a highly mobile set of goalposts, was also made by James I, who warned in his opening speech in 1621 that 'you of the Lower House, I would not have you to meddle with complaints against the King, the church or state matters, nor with princes' prerogatives. The Parliament was never called for that purpose. And if among you there be any such busy body, he is a spirit of Satan that means to overthrow the good errand in hand.'[68]

Warnings from the monarch to the Commons in the Lord Keeper or Lord Chancellor's reply to the Speaker's request were also delivered in James's Parliaments. In 1614, for example, Speaker Crew requested freedom of speech in the following terms:

to the end that this weighty and important business which is now in hand may receive no rub or interruption by the diminution or severance of any part of this body we are humble suitors to your majesty to vouchsafe us the allowance of our ancient privileges and immunities . . . since in this great council there be many things of weight and consequence to be consulted of, which by the freedom of speech and debate may be best discerned and understood, we are likewise humble suitors to your Majesty for your gracious allowance *ut in libero senato loquemur libere*, not doubting but that we shall confine and circle ourselves within those lasts and limits of duty and moderation as shall be fit.[69]

Responding to this request, the Lord Chancellor, Thomas Egerton, Lord Ellesmere, declared that

His Majesty is graciously pleased to grant your three petitions . . . the first that you may speak freely assuring himself you will speak with that reverence and duty to his Majesty as becomes subjects, with such judgement and discretion as

---

[66] Elton, *The Parliament of England*, p. 342. See also the answer to the Speaker's request made in 1601: 'touching your other requests for freedom of speech, her Majesty willingly consenteth thereto, with this caution, that the time be not spent in idle and vain matter, painting the same out with froth and volubility of words, whereby the speakers may seem to gain some reputed credit by emboldening themselves to contradiction, and by troubling the House of purpose with long and vain orations to hinder the proceeding in matters of greater and more weighty importance' (30 October 1601: D'Ewes, *The Journals of all the Parliaments during the Reign of Queen Elizabeth*, p. 601, quoted in J. R. Tanner (ed.), *Tudor Constitutional Documents A.D. 1485–1603*, second edition (Cambridge: Cambridge University Press, 1930), pp. 553–4).

[67] On this distinction see Elton, *The Parliament of England*, pp. 342–3. Elizabeth wanted especially to prevent discussion of the succession.

[68] 30 January 1621: *CD 1621*, II, 12.   [69] 7 April 1614: *PP 1614*, 27–8.

becomes councillors. For you are councillors of the great council of the king-dom. Let me tell you the property of councillors which is to speak *rara, vera, et ponderosa*.[70]

In 1621, meanwhile, the Speaker's request for 'libertye of dutifull speeches' met with the response that while the Commons were granted their liberties, they should be careful not to abuse them, 'not to turne libertie of speeche into licence or breake the reverence due to a Soveraigne'.[71] As in Elizabeth's reign, these warnings came at times when there was apparent danger that liberty might well become what the crown would consider licence. In 1614 James may have had in mind the hot-tempered debates of 1610, and he was already suspicious of Parliament's propensity to drift, as he saw it, into intemperate and time-wasting speechifying. In 1621, meanwhile, there was a danger that too many members might recall the chaotic end of that last 'addled' session in 1614. These warnings are rather more vague and formulaic than the Elizabethan examples I have cited; but this may well be because James had frequent recourse to messages sent to the House in which his expectations were clarified.

From the evidence that is available from the Speakers' requests and the Lord Keepers' or Lord Chancellors' replies as recorded from the time of More to that of James I, a few conclusions may be drawn. The first – and this is a point on which even Neale and Elton agree – is that by Elizabeth's reign, and so certainly in that of James, the request for and grant of freedom of speech was a central part of the formalities surrounding the opening of Parliament. The second, which follows from this, is that by at least the beginning of Elizabeth's reign parliamentary freedom of speech was a recognised right. It had, in fact, acquired the status of an 'ancient' liberty. The right was regarded as sufficiently secure that Peter Wentworth, after having exercised it so vigorously in his speech of 1576, could draw careful distinctions in his examination by the Privy Council between his status as a private and a public person, and theirs as Privy Councillors and committees appointed by the House, and the significance of this to his freedom of speech:

Yf your honours ask me as councellors to her Majestie, you shall pardon me, I will make you no answere; I will doe noe such iniurie to the place from whence I came. For I am now no private person; I am a publicque and a councellor to the whole state in that place, where it is lawfull for me to speake my minde freely and

---

[70] Ibid., p. 29.   [71] 3 February 1621: *CD 1621*, IV, VIII, X.

not for you (as counsellors) to call me to accompt for any thing that I doe speake in the House . . . But if you aske me as committees from the House, I will then willingly make you the best answere I can.[72]

The third conclusion that can be drawn at this stage is that no matter how secure an aspect of parliamentary liberty the right to freedom of speech was at the beginning of James I's reign, it was still a limited right. And the fourth is that these limits were markedly unclear: the right to parliamentary free speech was hedged around with ambiguity and contention. Although it could be argued that the limits were clearly pointed out to members of the Commons on a regular basis, what seems more striking is the way in which exhortations to remain within the bounds of respectful discourse and to keep away from matters of prerogative were subject to interpretation. Some members in James's – and Charles's – Parliaments would argue that they needed to discuss matters of prerogative, but far more would be likely to argue that they were not aware that they had overstepped the mark: in fact, that the goalposts had been moved when they were not looking. This meant that the fear of exceeding liberty and trespassing into licence was a serious concern, and that MPs would only find out where the boundary was once they had crossed it. Once again, it was up to them – and the crown – to contend for the limits of decorum; and it is this process of definition and of the search for the proper limits of duty that constituted many of the debates that I shall now go on to consider.

THE EARLY PARLIAMENTS OF JAMES I, 1604–1610: FREEDOM OF SPEECH AND IMPOSITIONS

1604–1607

The first Parliament of James I, which sat from 1604 to 1610, saw the new king finding his way in an unfamiliar environment.[73] Although James had been welcomed on his accession with general rejoicing, as soon as Parliament met this welcome was tempered by a series of skirmishes over key matters of policy. The session began with the case of the contested election for Buckinghamshire (Fortescue and Goodwin), which had led the Commons to suspect that they were being asked to relinquish their ability to decide the outcome of elections. James was conciliatory, however, and the case ended with the compromise solution that there would be a new election. He had

---

[72] *Proceedings in the Parliaments of Elizabeth I*, ed. by Hartley, vol. 1, p. 435.
[73] On this Parliament see also Notestein, *The House of Commons 1604–1610*.

nonetheless made his position on parliamentary privilege clear (a position that never wavered), stating in a message to the House on 29 March 1604 'that he had no Purpose to impeach their Privilege; But since they derived all Matters of Privilege from him, and by his Grant, he expected they should not be turned against him'.[74] Also in relation to this case the bugbear of misinformation had been invoked in the House of Commons: the king, one member argued on 30 March, was being misled about the Commons' proceedings.[75] Every time the danger of misinformation was raised, freedom of speech was seen as being under threat, for how could speech be properly free if members thought their statements were being reported and distorted to the king? Again and again in James's and Charles's Parliaments, MPs tried to protect their proceedings from being disclosed to the monarch before they had reached any conclusions: proper counsel required that points were heard on all sides, and this would not happen if members suspected their fellows of being informers rather than participants in debate.

The remainder of this session was taken up by the issues of James's plans for the Union of England and Scotland, and his financial needs. Both of these issues raised questions of freedom of speech, often in ways that would become characteristic of the reign. Discussions about the Union began with an encouraging message from the king, in which he set up what seemed like ideal conditions for proper counsel. The message was divided into:

1. A gracious Allowance. 2. A Desire. And, 3. An Admonition.
1. His Majesty, in the Matter of Union, alloweth Freedom and Liberty of Speech to all.
2. That at the Committee they would prepare themselves to speak freely, the Depth and innermost conceit of their Hearts; and that at the Conference they would admit of the Judges to attend.
3. That they would not resolve or determine of any thing, before they heard the Reasons at large.[76]

The three elements of the message were reassuring, and no-one seems to have found it unusual that the king should allow freedom of speech specifically about the Union, having granted it generally at the beginning of the session. The House resolved to send a message of thanks to James. Only a week later, however, the Commons received a message from the king saying that they were failing to deal with the Union properly; a message that caused considerable alarm.[77] The following day it was moved 'that it

---

[74] *CJ*, I, 158.
[75] 'Moved, and urged by one . . . that, in his Conscience, the King hath been much misinformed; and that he had too many Misinformers': *CJ*, I, 159.
[76] 24 April 1604: *CJ*, I, 183–4.   [77] 1 March 1604: ibid., 193–4.

might be made known to the King, how much we take his late Letter to heart', and once again the blame was laid at the door of misinformation that was somehow reaching James.[78] In an attempt to flush out the informers, it was 'urged further, out of a fear, that the King was much misinformed, that every Man, that hath Access to the King, should purge himself of Tales, either to his Majesty, or any Privy Counsellor'.[79] In the end, the House resolved to forbear from sending their message of disappointment and from their search for misinformers – a decision that was received well by the king.[80] But members had clearly been concerned both that the king wished to control the way in which they dealt with a matter of business, and at the idea that he was misinterpreting their actions in a derogatory sense. It was thought that Privy Councillors and others with access to the king might wish, for reasons most likely to do with court factionalism, to sow discord at particular times between the king and the Commons, or certain of its members. One of the accusations levelled at the Duke of Buckingham in the remonstrance of 1626 was that he had deliberately set up the previous Parliament of 1625 to fail.[81] At the same time, to blame informers for the king's criticism of Parliament could be a means of offering indirect criticism of the king himself.[82]

The Commons' sensitivity over the way in which they were handling the Union was sharpened by the news that the Bishop of Bristol had published a book which was, according to Mr Tey, 'tending to the Derogation and Scandal of the Proceedings of the House in the Matter of the Union; answering the Objections made against the Union in Name; and taking Knowledge of many other Passages of the House touching that Matter, unmeet to be questioned by any, much less by any Member of the Higher House'.[83] A committee was formed to examine the issue, and eventually

---

[78] Ibid., p. 197.　　[79] Ibid.

[80] James sent a message to the House on 4 March 1604, saying that he was glad for their good purposes, and interpreted their forbearance positively; thanks were sent to him for the message. See *CJ*, I, 199.

[81] 'No sooner was there any motion made there of his name to this purpose, but that he, fearing that his actions might have been too laid open to the view of your most excellent Majesty and to the just censure of that which might have followed then presently, through his misinformations to your Majesty of the intentions of the said Commons (as we have just cause to believe), procured a dissolution of the said Parliament': *PP* 1626, III, 436.

[82] In this respect these accusations are related to the attacks on 'evil counsellors', which could similarly be based on real fears of the king's being led astray by his advisers or provide a means of indirectly criticising him.

[83] 26 May 1604: *CJ*, I, 226. The book was John Thornborough, *A Discourse Plainely Prouing the Euident Vtilitie and Vrgent Necessitie of the Desired Happie Vnion of the Two Famous Kingdomes of England and Scotland: by way of answer to certaine obiections against the same* (London, 1604). On this case, see R. C. Munden, 'James I and "the Growth of Mutual Distrust": King, Commons, and Reform, 1603–1604', in *Faction and Parliament*, ed. by Sharpe, pp. 43–72, at p. 62; Annabel Patterson, *Censorship and Interpretation: The Conditions of Reading and Writing in Early Modern England* (Madison: University of Wisconsin Press, 1984), pp. 73–9.

the bishop himself declared his penitence: he was asked to retract in writing.[84] The Commons were angry at what they saw as an act of defamation against them; they were also incensed that their proceedings (which were supposed to be secret) were being published to the nation, and in a partisan fashion. They felt that their dignity was infringed by being taken to task for what some might see as their frank speaking against the Union; but at the same time, they were horrified that Thornborough could have publicised their proceedings. It may seem odd that the body that was so concerned with freedom of speech should be determined to curtail the bishop's freedom to publish, but as we have seen already, parliamentary freedom of speech was a very specific kind of liberty. And there were recognised and acknowledged ways of working with what David Zaret has called the 'secrecy norms' that operated in early seventeenth-century Parliaments, of which printing a book attacking the House of Commons was not one. Members might plunder their diaries for news to send to friends or patrons in manuscript; rumours were spread, and even ballads sometimes written about what was happening in Parliament – but the bishop had gone too far. Another two cases of a similar nature arose in the same Parliament: one, in June 1604, in the midst of the Thornborough affair, was when Dr Howson, a member of the Convocation House, was accused of delivering sententious speeches about the Commons;[85] the other, which went further, was in May 1606, when Dr Parker delivered a sermon at Paul's Cross in which he attacked the Commons for their confused proceedings.[86] Bowyer called this sermon 'an Invective Oration . . . very seditious and Slanderous', and the king eventually examined Parker, although the House had wanted to be allowed to punish him themselves.[87]

The vexed question of the crown's finances and the means by which they could be improved was the second issue that led to disputes over Parliament's freedom of speech in this part of the session. Unlike the Union, which was of course a Jacobean innovation, the crown's right to purveyance (the purchase of food and transport at extremely low prices) and wardship (the right to manage the lands of those of its tenants-in-chief who inherited while they were minors) were issues inherited from the previous reign. Along with the related issue of monopolies, which had provoked fierce debate in 1601, both had been presented as grievances in the later Parliaments of Elizabeth, and they were revived in 1604. In the meantime, the crown's need for money had

[84] 1 June 1604 (committee formed): *CJ*, 1, 230; 11 June 1604 (Bacon reports from the conference on Thornborough's book; the bishop is penitent): *CJ*, 1, 236.
[85] 8 June 1604: *CJ*, 1, 235.   [86] 26 May 1606: *CJ*, 1, 312–13.
[87] *The Parliamentary Diary of Robert Bowyer 1606–1607*, ed. by David Harris Willson, reprint (New York: Octagon Books, 1971), pp. 180–1.

hardly lessened, and for the first two Parliaments of James's reign finance proved one of the greatest sticking points between king and Commons. In April 1604 a petition was sent to the king concerning the abuse of purveyance, and there was a debate on 21 May about whether the restraint of trade (i.e. monopolies) was a restriction on the liberty of the subject.[88] By June there had been a conference with the Lords about wardship, and it was clear that while James continued to reassure the Commons that he would prosecute abuses as vigorously as his predecessors had done, he was far from happy with the way in which the Lower House was dealing with this issue. Reporting from the conference, Sir Edwin Sandys 'delivered from their Lordships no other than Matter of Expostulation, Opposition of Reason to Reason, Admonition, or precise Caution, in proceeding'.[89] This, he pointed out, accorded with 'the Grounds of his Majesty's Speech subsequent, advisedly and of Purpose made upon that Occasion to the whole House, assembled by his Majesty's Direction at *Whitehall*, on *Monday* last (wherein many particular Actions and Passages of the House were objected unto them, with Taxation and Blame)'.[90] What was to be done, with the Commons criticised for their manner of proceeding by both king and Lords? The suggestion that was taken up was put as a motion by Sir Thomas Ridgeway:

that, since it appeared, his Majesty had made such an impression of Mislike of the Proceedings of the House in general, as also, that the Grounds conceived, touching Wardship, and Matters of that Nature, seemed to be so weakened and impugned; it were necessary and safe for the House, and dutiful and convenient in respect of his Majesty, instantly to advise of such a Form of Satisfaction, either by Writing, or otherwise, as might in all Humility inform his Majesty in the Truth and Clearness of the Actions and Intentions of the House, from the Beginning, thereby to Clear it from the Scandal of Levity and Precipitation; as also of the Proceedings in particular, touching the said Matter of Wardship; with this special Care, that a Matter, so advisedly and gravely undertaken and proceeded, might not die, or be buried, in the Hands of those that first bred it.[91]

The document that resulted from this motion was the Form of Apology and Satisfaction. Provoked by the disputes over the Union and the scandal of the Bishop of Bristol's book as well as by the grievances of wardship and purveyance, the Apology was intended to correct some of James's more egregious misapprehensions about the nature of Parliament; misapprehensions,

---

[88] 30 April 1604: *CJ*, I, 190; *CJ*, I, 218ff.
[89] 1 June 1604: *CJ*, I, 230. See further Rabb, *Jacobean Gentleman*, chapter 4.
[90] *CJ*, I, 230.　　[91] Ibid., I, 230–1.

the Apology argued, which had been bred by 'misinformation' and 'sinister information or counsel'.[92] The Apology was once a pillar of the Whig interpretation of the causes of the Civil War, but its stature was reduced by the work of G. R. Elton, who showed that it was never accepted by the whole House.[93] Yet, as Conrad Russell has written, 'even when we have dethroned the Apology from the status of a great constitutional document, it remains a political event'.[94]

The Apology is most famous for its rejection of the argument that the Commons 'held not our privileges of right, but of grace only, renewed every parliament by way of donature upon petition, and so to be limited'.[95] Its authors asserted that, on the contrary,

> our privileges and liberties are our right and due inheritance, no less than our very lands and goods; that they cannot be withheld from us, denied or impaired, but with apparent wrong to the whole state of the realm; and that our making of request in the entrance of Parliament to enjoy our privilege is an act only of manners, and doth weaken our right no more than our suing to the king for our lands by petition.[96]

As one of the liberties requested at the opening of Parliament, freedom of speech, according to the Apology, was a right that the Commons held in perpetuity and which was outside the control of the monarch. The assertion that the formal request for privileges is 'an act only of manners' is striking, and robs the king's grant of any power, as well as making any conditions set upon the grant seem fairly hollow. As well as making this strong case for the status of freedom of speech as a parliamentary privilege, the Apology is itself couched in terms of frank but honest counsel. This is evident from its opening description of the dangers of misinformation and of the way in which its authors have waited for some other solution before resorting reluctantly to this course of action:

> But now, no other help or redress appearing, and finding these misinformations to have been the first, yea the chief and almost the sole cause of all the discontentful and troublesome proceedings much blamed in this Parliament, and that they might be again the cause of like or greater discontents and troubles hereafter (which the Almighty Lord forbid), we have been *constrained*, as well in *duty* to your royal

---

[92] 'The Form of Apology and Satisfaction', in *The Stuart Constitution*, ed. by J. P. Kenyon, second edition (Cambridge: Cambridge University Press, 1986), pp. 29–35, at pp. 29 and 35.

[93] See Elton, 'A High Road to Civil War?'

[94] Conrad Russell, 'English Parliaments 1593–1606: One Epoch or Two?', in *The Parliaments of Elizabethan England*, ed. by D. M. Dean and N. L. Jones (Oxford: Blackwell, 1990), pp. 191–213, at p. 208.

[95] 'The Form of Apology and Satisfaction', p. 31.   [96] Ibid.

Majesty whom with faithful hearts we serve as to our dear native country for which we serve in this Parliament, to *break our silence* and *freely to disclose* unto your Majesty the truth of such matters concerning your subjects the Commons as hitherto by misinformation hath been suppressed or perverted.[97]

Truth and plainness, say the authors, are the two qualities they 'most affect' in the Apology. Again at its conclusion they emphasise that 'with dutiful minds and sincere hearts towards your Majesty, have we truly disclosed our secret intents and delivered our outward actions in these so much traduced and blamed matters' – the combination of duty and sincerity being, as we have seen in earlier chapters, a key component of good counsel.[98] And as the document draws to a close, the authors state that they have to put some final requests to James, an obligation 'which faithfulness of heart, no[t] presumption, doth press upon us'.[99] 'We stand not in place', they write, 'to speak or do things pleasing, our care is and must be to confirm the love and to tie the hearts of your subjects the commons most firmly to your Majesty'. In consequence, they pray (and the impersonal is surely significant here) 'let no suspicion have access to their fearful thoughts . . . that those which with dutiful respect to your Majesty speak freely for the right and good of their country, shall be oppressed or disgraced'.[100]

The Form of Apology and Satisfaction addressed a wide range of grievances, and I do not wish to suggest that as a document it is more concerned with freedom of speech than with those matters of policy. Rather, I want to highlight the way in which it frames its arguments and its requests in terms that appeal to the language and theory of frank counsel, at the same time as it asserts the Commons' *right* to freedom of speech as one of their 'fundamental privileges'.[101] Although the Apology was not an official document of the Commons, although many members clearly thought its authors had gone too far, and although it was never formally presented to the king, its use of the language of duty and obligation, of the constraint to speak out, and of the right to do so – its combination of loyalty and frankness – is typical of many debates and speeches throughout James's reign. Nor did the Apology simply sink without trace: a copy reached the House of Lords, and it is likely that James also saw one (the fairest contemporary manuscript is found among the Salisbury papers at Hatfield House): he may have been referring to it when in his intemperate speech at the prorogation of Parliament he warned that now the Commons had failed

---

[97] Ibid., p. 29. My italics.   [98] Ibid., pp. 34–5.
[99] Ibid., p. 35.   [100] Ibid.   [101] Ibid., p. 31.

so badly, 'the best apology-maker of you all, for all his eloquence, cannot make all good'.[102] Moreover, the Apology's resounding warning that 'the prerogatives of princes may easily and do daily grow; the privileges of the subject are for the most part at an everlasting stand' was to be a rallying cry for outspoken MPs in the 1620s.[103]

The speech that James delivered at the end of this session made no attempt to disguise his annoyance and impatience with the Commons. Sounding rather like a tetchy headmaster, he distinguished between the Lords, who he said had carried themselves 'with discretion, modesty, judgement, care and fidelity', and the Commons, to whom he announced darkly, he had 'more to say'.[104] Introducing a theme that would resound throughout his reign, the king blamed a number of disruptive MPs for derailing the Parliament, and singled out the vices of boldness and loquacity for special criticism. 'Some', he grumbled, 'had an itching humour ever to be talking, and this common saying is proper to common babblers, *in multiloquis non deest peccatum*.'[105] All in all, James said, he was disappointed with the suspicion that had been shown towards him, with 'nothing but curiosity from morning to evening to find faults with my propositions'. Compared to his experiences as king of Scotland, he was treated with hostility rather than as a 'counsellor': 'there, all things warranted that come from me; here all things suspected'.[106] The resistance that the king had experienced he regarded as coming from curiosity, rashness, and loquacity; not from any reasoned concerns about his policies. Licentiousness, he suggested, originated in the passions; freedom should be bounded by reason. And he concluded by declaring that 'I wish you would use your liberty with more modesty in time to come.'[107]

James's speech at the prorogation of the 1605 session was echoed closely in his speech at the opening of the second session of 1606, which began in November of that year and closed in July 1607. Although the sessions after the discovery of Gunpowder Plot in November 1605 were marked by much calmer relations between king and Commons, a degree of tension was still discernible around the issue of the Commons' use of their freedom of speech. James began by recalling what he saw as the excessive 'popularity' and loquacity of some members in the previous session, noting that

---

[102] 7 July 1604: *The Stuart Constitution*, ed. by Kenyon, pp. 36–7, at p. 37. See also Rabb, *Jacobean Gentleman*, pp. 106–7.
[103] 'The Form of Apology and Satisfaction', p. 32.
[104] *The Stuart Constitution*, ed. by Kenyon, p. 36.
[105] Ibid., p. 37.   [106] Ibid., p. 37.   [107] Ibid.

there is in Parliament (as there is in all Multitudes) Diversities of Spirits, as there was amongst the very Apostles themselves; and that some of them were more popular than profitable, either for the Council, or for the Commonwealth; and that there were some Tribunes of the People, whose Mouths could not be stopped, either from the Matters of the Puritanes or of the Purveyance.[108]

He went on to offer what reads like a not very heavily veiled threat, tempered by an encouraging suggestion that he would allow the Commons to deal with any members who overstepped the bounds of liberty in their speech and trespassed into licence:

He said, he would make One Admonition unto the Lower House of Parliament; *viz.* that they ought to enter into a double Consideration of themselves: One, as they were Subjects in general; another as they were specially called to be Counsellors of the Kingdom; and that the Thought of the One must not make them forget the Consideration of the other. That the Parliament was not so perpetual, but that they, being Subjects, were subject to an Account, as Kings themselves were; who, though they be exempt from any Censure or Correction, upon the Earth, yet after the Expiration of their Reigns and their Lives, must yield an Account to the eternal King: And therefore admonished them, to beware, that they were not like *Icarus*, the son of *Daedalus*; that soared so near the sun with his Wings of Wax, that his Wax melted, and down he fell . . . if any such Plebeian Tribunes should incur any offence, or commit any such Error, they would correct them for it; and judge themselves as (St *Paul* saith) that they be not judged; and that the whole Body receive not a Wound by One ill Member thereof.[109]

Here James is surely suggesting an analogy between the reigns of kings and the sessions of Parliaments: when a king dies, he is called to account before God; when a Parliament ends, its members are called to account before the king. He emphasises that their nature as counsellors is 'special', and limited by time and place, while their nature as subjects is 'general': ever-present, and the condition to which they must eventually return. The repeated invocation of 'Tribunes' (a term also used by Salisbury in the 1606 session) both continued James's identification of opposition with a small group of disruptive, rabble-rousing MPs and implied that they were prototypically republican in outlook – an assertion that, coming from James, was more derogatory than ideologically descriptive.

James was able to draw a distinction between the duty that MPs owed to their king and that which they owed to their country (usually meaning the borough or county they represented, rather than England at large). This was a distinction that many MPs saw as illusory: to them the interests of king and country should be identical. This identification was not always possible,

---

[108] *CJ*, I, 314.   [109] Ibid.

however: taxation would place a burden upon the counties, and some areas would be affected more than others. Yet professions of loyalty to the crown could equally be interpreted as servility: in March 1605/6 Sir William Skipwith urged that 'Every Man lay his Hand upon his Heart, remember the Place, from whence he comes, and give according to his Conscience.'[110] Sir Henry Hubbard accused him of flattery, and Skipwith angrily denied the charge.[111] This is a clear example of the way that members wished to control their fellows' speech and to maintain the proper discourse of counsel – a discourse from which flattery was meant to be altogether excluded, as I have shown in chapter 1. On the same subject of subsidies, there was also a suggestion that members were being threatened by their superiors: on 12 April 1606 Nicholas Fuller complained that 'I did offend some in this, That I moved we might have tyme to answer such Matters as were obiected against the Bill: And a great One told me, I had spoken that which had bene better unspoken.'[112] In the face of this attempt to control his speech, he asked for support from the Commons, going on to say 'I desire Wittnesse, and that it be remembred, That I have spoken nothing offensively: And all the House with a Generall Acclamation and Approbation of his speech, did cleere him of all fault, and allowe his speech to the Lords.'[113] Being cleared by the House should, he clearly thought, protect him from any potential punishment outside of it: this was a strategy that was used frequently in the later Parliaments of James and the early Parliaments of Charles, though it was not always successful. In Fuller's request, and in James's opening speech of November 1606, we can see responsibility being claimed by and given to the House of Commons for the punishment of its members when their frank speech went too far. This suggested, of course, that the Commons would be largely responsible for deciding when this happened, which could in turn lead to friction between them and the king.

On 16 February 1606/7, during yet another debate on the unresolved matter of the Union, Christopher Piggott delivered a bitter speech against the Scots, 'using many words of scandal and obloquy'.[114] The *Commons Journal* reports his speech in a tone of some disapproval, and records that

---

[110] 14 March 1605/6: *CJ*, 1, 284.   [111] 14 March 1605/6: *CJ*, 1, 284; 15 March: *CJ*, 1, 285.

[112] *The Parliamentary Diary of Robert Bowyer 1606–1607*, ed. by Willson, p. 121.   [113] Ibid.

[114] *CJ*, 1, 333. On this incident, see also Roger Lockyer, *The Early Stuarts: A Political History of England 1603–1642* (Harlow: Longman, 1989), p. 144. Piggott had been elected in place of Sir John Fortescue after the election debacle of 1604; see Notestein, *The House of Commons 1604–1610*, p. 78. He is memorialised in John Hoskyns's poem 'The Parliament Fart' (on which see further below, pp. 242–3): 'Quoth Sir Edward Hoby alledged with the spigot, / Sir, if you fart at the Union, remember Kit Piggott' (Baird W. Whitlock, *John Hoskyns, Serjeant-at-Law* (Washington, DC: University Press of America, 1982), p. 290).

there was general shock felt by the House, but that Piggott was not censured because it was felt that proceeding with business was a more pressing concern. It is worth noting that this is the Clerk's interpretation of the silence with which the speech was met – a silence that could also be interpreted as sympathetic.[115] Three days later, however, the speech was recalled and the House was informed of the king's annoyance at MPs' failure to punish Piggott.[116] It was decided that his punishment should be left to the House, and he was sent to the Tower and discharged from his seat.[117] Less than two weeks later, the Commons decided that he should be released from imprisonment because of illness, and James agreed to allow them to do as they saw fit.[118] Piggott's case shows the extent to which the exercise of and jurisdiction over freedom of speech were matters for negotiation between king and Commons. Initially the Commons decided that in this case getting on with the debate was more important than stopping to censure a member (whether or not this was because they sympathised with his views is unclear): James clearly thought otherwise. Having been told that they had slipped up, the Commons were willing to return to a speech that it seems they may anyway have thought excessive; but on the condition that they should be left to deal with it and allowed sole rights of punishment. This was an example of negotiation working unusually smoothly.

Much of the rest of this session, until the adjournment in July, was taken up by the Union, and it was on this subject that more issues about freedom of speech arose. James continued to urge on the Commons in their slow progress towards a position from which a statute could issue, delivering speeches on 31 March and 2 May that combined encouragement and criticism.[119] In the later speech he ended by advising 'that you beware of all fantastical Spirits, all extraordinary, and colourable Speeches; that there be no Distractions, nor Distempers, among you' – and that they should hurry up.[120] The Commons were again worried that the king was receiving information about their proceedings which not only caused his annoyance at the speed of their progress, but also led him to try to dictate the nature of their debates. On 6 May it was agreed that they would take three points to the king to clear this up: first, 'that his Highness would not suffer himself to be traduced by any private Suggestions or Reports; but either by Mr. Speaker, or by some other Means, be pleased to receive Information

---

[115] See Gardiner, *History of England*, volume 1, pp. 330–1. [116] 16 February 1606/7: *CJ*, 1, 335.

[117] *CJ*, 1, 336. Piggott apparently took his expulsion very seriously, Sir Edwin Sandys remembering in the 1610 session that he had described it as a 'judgement greater than if they had struck off his head' (*CJ*, 1, 480–1, quoted in Rabb, *Jacobean Gentleman*, p. 186).

[118] 28 February 1606/7: *CJ*, 1, 344. [119] *CJ*, 1, 357–63 (31 March); 368 (2 May). [120] *CJ*, 1, 368.

from the House itself, of their own Meaning, as also of the Meaning of any particular Man'; secondly, 'that his Majesty would be pleased to give Leave to such Persons as have expressly been blamed or taxed by his Majesty, for their Speeches in the House, to clear themselves in his Majesty's Hearing and Presence; as likewise all shall hereafter be said to offend in the same Kind'; and lastly, 'that he will also be pleased, by some gracious Message, to make known to the House, that his princely Meaning was, and is, that they should, with all Liberty and Freedom, and without Fear, deliver their Opinions in the Matter in Hand, and so proceed according to their best Judgements'.[121] The next day the Speaker delivered a message from the king intended to offer some reassurance: 'touching freedom of speech,' it declared, 'he should not think him worthy of his place, that did not speak freely what he thought of the Matter in hand, so it were bounded with Modesty and Discretion'.[122] Modesty and discretion: here were two qualities on whose definition it could be very difficult to agree. Their limits would be tested even more strenuously in the next session of James's first Parliament.

As this session drew to a close, there was further discussion of whether the monarch was able to restrict discussion in the House, after the Speaker had delivered a message from James saying that he did not want to be bothered with a petition from the merchants.[123] Finance would prove to be the greatest sticking point of the next session, but the ways in which discussions about freedom of speech had been framed in relation to both the grievances of wardship and purveyance and the issue of the Union (plans for which disappeared from view after the 1606/7 session) would be drawn on and expanded in later meetings.

1610

In the final session of James's first Parliament, freedom of speech became the subject of angry debate between king and Commons. The issue to which it was most directly attached was the king's right to impose extraordinary and extra-parliamentary duties on imports and exports (commonly called 'impositions'), but it was also raised as part of a wider defence of the liberties of the subject and questioning of the limits of the royal prerogative. The session was intended – at least by Lord Treasurer Salisbury – to provide a partial solution to the king's financial problems with the scheme

[121] *CJ*, I, 370. These points seem to have originated with Lewknor.
[122] 7 May 1607: *CJ*, I, 371.
[123] 17 June 1607: *CJ*, I, 340. See also Rabb, *Jacobean Gentleman*, pp. 133–5.

for a Great Contract; but these plans were derailed by a series of objections, by the king's lukewarm support for his minister, and by the refusal of the House to work on the Great Contract to the exclusion of their concerns about new impositions.[124] Even while the Commons were engaging in negotiations about the Contract and meeting in conference with the Lords, the anxiety they had felt in the last session about the privacy of their proceedings and the king's surveillance of their proceedings appears to have cast a shadow over business. Writing to Trumbull from Calais, Taverner suggests an extreme level of concern about the likelihood that critical speeches by MPs would be reported to James; this, he says, 'hath brought so base a fear amongst them, no man dareth speak freely. But they have it now in speech to deliver their voices by lot, as in Venice.'[125] Allowing for a degree of exaggeration, this still presents a picture of a hamstrung Commons, responding to fear with silence. This was to prove far from the case.

The first explosion over free speech was, in fact, provoked by the actions of a non-member – not a bishop, as in 1604, but the Regius Professor of Civil Law at Cambridge, John Cowell. On 23 February 1610, John Hoskyns brought the Commons' attention to Cowell's book *The Interpreter*, which had been published in 1607.[126] According to Hoskyns, the book (a law dictionary) argued that 'the King gives us Leave to make Laws of Favour' and was derogatory of Parliament and the common law.[127] Hoskyns was especially concerned about the passages under the headings of 'Subsidy', 'Parliament', and 'King.'[128] Nor was the book unique: Hoskyns 'produced several treatises containing as much as Dr. Cowell's book, all sold *impune*; among the rest was Blackwood's book, which concluded "that we are all slaves by reason of the Conquest" '.[129] *The Interpreter* put a strong case for England as an absolute monarchy, and for the liberties of the subject as deriving from the grace of the king rather than from right (the latter position sounding fairly close to some of James's own statements).[130] The book was considered by the Committee for Grievances, and at a conference between the

---

[124] The Contract initially requested a grant of £600,000 in supply and £200,000 in annual support, in return for which the king would relinquish some of his most unpopular prerogative revenues, including purveyance but excluding wardship. See Lockyer, *The Early Stuarts*, pp. 173–82 at p. 174.

[125] March 30 1610: *HMC Downshire*, volume II, pp. 86–7, quoted in *PP 1610*, II, 46 n. 2.

[126] John Cowell, *The Interpreter: Or Booke containing the Signification of Words* (Cambridge, 1607). On this case, see Sommerville, *Royalists and Patriots*, pp. 113–19.

[127] 23 February 1609/10: *CJ*, I, 399.

[128] These passages, along with that on 'Prerogative', were also the ones cited by Richard or Henry Martin at the conference with the Lords on 2 March: see *PP 1610*, I, 25.

[129] William Petyt, *Miscellanea Parliamentaria* (London, 1681), p. 66, quoted in *PP 1610*, II, 33.

[130] See Cowell, *The Interpreter*, sigs. 2Q1ʳ, 3A3ᵛ; Sommerville, *Royalists and Patriots*, pp. 114–15.

Commons and the Lords.[131] Having got this far, the Commons were on shaky ground, procedurally. Being a non-member, Cowell had no right to freedom of speech; equally, though, what exactly could he be punished for? He had not committed slander or defamation in any way that would pass muster in a court of law; and even had he done so, Parliament was not a court that could hear such an action. His fault, according to Hoskyns and others, was that he had disseminated a dangerous ideological position and, in Coke's words, attempted to remove the *lapis angularis* of the commonwealth: that legislation was performed by the king in Parliament not simply as a matter of form.[132] Distasteful as some of these ideas might be, it was not clear that they came within parliamentary jurisdiction. All these points were put by Cecil in a speech to the House of Lords on 5 March.

The Lords, who in any case had not expressed any antagonism to Cowell's book, and to one of whose members, Richard Bancroft, it had been dedicated, agreed to search for precedents and have another meeting with the Commons.[133] At this point, however, the king stepped in and, declaring that Cowell 'is too bold with the common law . . . mistaketh the dignity of parliament' and that 'for this matter to treat of his power and prerogative, he holdeth not fit to be called into *problème*', eventually issued a proclamation condemning the book, banning its sale and reading, and calling in the copies that had already been sold.[134] However, as J. P. Sommerville has argued, we should beware of finding in James's actions a sign of sympathy with the Commons' objections to Cowell: the king wanted above all to prohibit discussion of his prerogative, while the Commons had wanted Cowell's theories of government punished.[135] The Commons' attempt to curtail absolutist rhetoric had failed, one could say, while James had once again made clear his belief that some matters were above the capacity of his subjects and should not be discussed.

The Cowell case was unusual in concerning a non-member, although attempts by the House of Commons to control the speech of those outside it would occur again in 1621. It was the subject of impositions, along with the negotiations over the Great Contract, that provoked both the most outspoken speeches of this session and the strongest defences of parliamentary freedom of speech, as well as leading members to discuss in some detail

---

[131] For the latter, see *PP 1610*, I, 24–5.   [132] Ibid., 24.

[133] Ibid., 27; Sommerville, *Royalists and Patriots*, p. 116.

[134] Cecil reporting the king's words in the House of Lords, 8 March 1610: *PP 1610* I, 29; Sommerville, *Royalists and Patriots*, pp. 116–17.

[135] Sommerville, *Politics and Ideology*, pp. 117–19.

the relationship between their parliamentary liberties and privileges and
the liberties of the subject more generally conceived (the two had been
audaciously described as identical in the Apology of 1604).[136] As in James's
first sessions, one of the king's concerns was that the Commons should deal
efficiently with the business for which they had been called, and in a speech
to both Houses on 21 March 1610, he made it clear that this was to redress
his financial needs.[137] Perhaps remembering the problems of the previous
session, he went out of his way to stress that he was being frank and open
with his Parliament, announcing that 'I have called you this day together
to make you a present of a crystal whereby you may see the King's heart.'[138]
Part of James's frankness consisted in explaining what should be outside
the consideration of his subjects: with reference to Cowell's book, but not
exclusively, he announced that 'as in divinity it is blasphemy to dispute of
God's power, so it is treason for subjects to dispute of a king's power'.[139] As
for grievances, he had some further advice to give: 'first, you may meddle
with the abuse of my commission but not with my power of government,
for I have been a king too long now to be taught my duty, having governed
a kingdom this thirty-seven years. Secondly, not with those things which I
received from my predecessors and I possess *mode maiorum*.'[140] Nor should
Parliament create grievances or lead the people astray: 'I desire you in your
grievances that it may be the grief of the people and not your own particular grievances and not to buzz those things into the peoples' heads which
they never thought grievous.'[141] This was a suspicious speech, for all its
conciliatory descriptions of the king's dependence on the law, and it ended
with a warning that just as the Commons disliked being misinterpreted, so
did James:

Thus have I according to my promise delivered to you a glass of the king's heart,
and as glass may be, my ways chiefly hurt, so may my speech. First if you place
a glass in the wrong light so as you misconstrue my meaning, secondly with foul

---

[136] 'Now concerning the ancient rights of the subjects of this realm, chiefly consisting in the privileges
of this House of Parliament'; 'which assertions . . . tending directly and apparently to the overthrow
of the very fundamental privileges of our House, and therein of the rights and liberties of the whole
commons of your realm of England . . .': 'The Form of Apology and Satisfaction', p. 31.

[137] *PP 1610*, II, 59–63. For other accounts of the speech, see ibid., 44–52; *CJ*, I, 413; James I, *The
Workes* (London, 1616), sigs. Xx6ʳ–Zz4ᵛ. James explains that he is in financial need in the section
on 'Calling of Parliament', *PP 1610*, II, 61–2.

[138] Ibid., p. 59.

[139] Cf. the version in James I, *The Workes*, sig. Yy2ʳ: 'as to dispute what God may doe, is Blasphemie
. . . So it is sedition in Subiects, to dispute what a king may do in the height of his power: But iust
Kings wil euer be willing to declare what they wil do, if they wil not incurre the curse of God. I
wil not be content that my power be disputed vpon: but I shall euer be willing to make the reason
appeare of all my doings, and rule my Actions according to my Lawes.'

[140] *PP 1610*, II, 61.   [141] Ibid., 61.

hands or with the breath so may my words by railing speeches be slandered and abused; the last and worst, if it be let fall and broken. So the greatest neglect of my words that can be is to let it lie dead and not follow my advice.[142]

What exactly the king's prerogative covered, and what was a reasonable grievance, turned out to be two more examples of contested definitions. The judgement in Bate's case in 1606, on impositions on currants, looked to James like a licence to impose: to some members of the Commons it provided no such general precedent, and they decided to scrutinise impositions. This led to a serious dispute about the Commons' right to debate freely, and to choose the subjects of debate (something James had already tried to qualify in his speeches). On 11 May 1610 the Speaker delivered a message from the king 'to this effect, that we should not entertain into our consideration any disputation touching the prerogative of the king in the case of impositions for that was determined by judgement in the proper court [i.e. in the Exchequer] and could not be undone but by error'.[143] This peremptory instruction provoked two extended and outspoken debates in the Commons: the first about whether the Speaker should be acting as a messenger from the king to the Commons as well as vice versa, and the second about the king's rights over his subject's property.[144] Thomas Wentworth gave an immediate rebuff to the king's belief that impositions were an open-and-shut case, now completely shut to the Commons: he pointed out that the king was once again misinformed, as no-one was trying to have the judgement in Bate's case reversed.[145] Rather, as it was an individual case it did not bind anyone else, and was subject to dispute in any court of law – 'and shall all other courts be at liberty notwithstanding this judgement to dispute the law and shall this court be barred and tied not to dispute it?'[146] More than this, 'is not the king's prerogative disputable?' To say otherwise was not just foolish but dangerous, Wentworth argued: 'nay if we shall once say that we may not dispute the prerogative, let us be sold for slaves'.[147] Wentworth's language here sounds extreme, but it was seriously meant, and part of a much larger argument about the subject's rights over his property, as Quentin Skinner has shown.[148]

Compared to these serious legal arguments, the Commons' discussion of the precise nature of the Speaker's role and responsibility might at first seem rather trivial. Yet there were good reasons why this was the next matter that

---

[142] Ibid., 62–3.   [143] Ibid., 82.

[144] For these debates and the aftermath of Bate's case more generally, see Sommerville, *Royalists and Patriots*, pp. 140–4.

[145] *PP 1610*, II, 82.   [146] Ibid., 82.   [147] Ibid., 83.

[148] See Quentin Skinner, 'Classical Liberty, Renaissance Translation and the English Civil War', in Skinner, *Visions of Politics*, volume II: *Renaissance Virtues*, pp. 308–43.

was raised after Wentworth's speech, and why the House spent time on it in committee. As well as being suspicious that since the king was out of town, the Speaker's message had in fact come from the Council (in which case the House would treat it as 'no message at all'), the Commons were unhappy with the Speaker being used as the king's mouthpiece. Elizabethan precedents were adduced to show that the Speaker was a one-way messenger system unless the Commons had sent him to the king in the first place.[149] The king sent another message, asserting that he had indeed sent the first and that he could 'no longer forebear by my [i.e. the Speaker's] mouth to command you to give over all such arguments or directions, as may any way tend to the examination of his power and prerogative'.[150] The question of the Speaker's role occupied the House for almost another week, with the king asking if the House intended to start refusing messages from him. Sir Henry Montagu, the Recorder of London, attempted to solve the issue by distinguishing between the Speaker as a public person and Sir Edward Phelips as a private man: as the former he could not bring a message from the king, but as the latter he might. Christopher Brooke and John Hoskyns thought this was an impossible distinction, however. Eventually, on 19 May an anodyne message was sent to the king reassuring him that the Commons were not attempting to challenge the king, but simply retaining 'those due respects from our Speaker which appertain unto us'.[151] At issue in these debates was the Commons' desire to have the Speaker continue to act as their messenger and as an officer of the Lower House. Their anxiety arose mainly because of the nature of the message that the Speaker was delivering, which was effectively a gagging order: it seemed to some ominous if the Speaker could be used to silence the Commons on behalf of the king, when he would also have to act as the Commons' intermediary with James.

A tug-of-war had begun over the linked issues of the Speaker's right to deliver the message and the contents of the message itself, as several members wished to discuss the latter as well as the former. As the committee for grievances was considering the 'great grievance of impositions',[152] this was almost inevitable; but James wanted to have a response to his question (whether the Commons were going to stop receiving his messages) before they actually dealt with the implications of what he had ordered.[153] Noy, Wentworth, Hoskyns, and Brooke all argued that the House should be allowed to debate impositions. Noy thought that the king's message made

---

[149] 11 May 1610: *PP 1610*, II, 84; 12 May: ibid.   [150] 13 May 1610: ibid., 86.
[151] 19 May 1610: ibid., 99.   [152] Sir Herbert Croft, 18 May 1610: *PP 1610*, volume II, 93.
[153] 19 May 1610: ibid., 96.

the House not only toothless but voiceless too: 'this message,' he explained, 'implies in it a question (so) whether there be such a negative power to prohibit us from disputing? . . . If we may not say this is our right, if we may not complain, because we are commanded not to complain; then we must bear any apparent wrong, if a commandment come to us not to dispute it.'[154] Wentworth declared his confidence that there were none in the House who, like Cambises' counsellors, told the king that they had a law that he could do what he wished, and as a result were 'branded with that note of infamy to all posterity'.[155] Hoskyns was sure that 'our answer should be that we may dispute it. We may look into it to inform ourselves though not to judge it.'[156] And he was unhappy with the idea that there were *arcana imperii* that were beyond the scope of subjects; this seemed a potentially blasphemous idea: 'as to the phrases of infinite and inscrutable, they be things that belong to heaven and are not upon earth and he that looks for them here upon earth, may miss them in heaven'.[157]

While all this discussion was to the Commons a vital defence of their right to free debate, to James it seemed like so much impudent hot air. On 21 May he delivered a speech to both Houses that was his angriest so far. Not only were the Commons not getting on with the 'principal errand', but they were questioning what a king might do and disputing his prerogative.[158] He bluntly explained that all kings had the right to lay impositions, and that to attempt to curtail this right would be to reduce a king to the condition of a Duke of Venice.[159] The Commons needed to remember that as subjects they were bound to obey, whatever the nature of their monarch: 'if you have a good king you are to thank God, if an ill king he is a curse to the people but *preces et lachrimae* were ever their arms'.[160] James was speaking theoretically, but his words were far from reassuring as he developed his theme: 'you cannot so clip the wing of greatness. If a king be resolute to be a tyrant, all you can do will not hinder him.'[161] Only towards the end of his speech did the king offer what must have been intended as reassurance, announcing that he would not lay impositions without consulting Parliament but offering the rider that this was an act of graciousness, not an obligation: 'many things I may do without parliament, which I will do in parliament, for good kings are helped by parliament not

[154] 18 May: ibid., 93.
[155] Ibid., 93–4; see Herodotus, *The History*, trans. by David Grene (Chicago: University of Chicago Press, 1987), 3.31, pp. 224–5.
[156] *PP 1610*, II, 94.   [157] Ibid., 94. For Brooke, see ibid.
[158] Ibid., 100–7 at 101, 101–2. For other accounts see ibid., 87–9, and *Parliamentary Debates in 1610*, ed. by S. R. Gardiner, Camden Society, first series 81 (London: 1861), pp. 34–6.
[159] *PP 1610*, II, 103.   [160] Ibid.   [161] Ibid.

for power but for convenience that the work may seem more glorious'.[162] This was a long way from the idea of Parliament as the place of counsel that was implied by the writ of summons.

James's speech linked his power to impose with his desire that Parliament should stop discussing his prerogative, and MPs also identified the link. Speaking the day after James's harangue, Wentworth made the case for imposition only being lawful with the assent of Parliament (citing Fortescue), and for the Commons' right to discuss the prerogative; although 'the king referred us to his speech in print wherein 'tis said to be sedition to dispute what a king may do', if this was indeed the case then 'all our law books are seditious, for they have ever done it'.[163] James Whitelocke agreed, and argued that the king had now claimed a general right to impose, which had to be questioned: 'if we let this pass *sub silentio* all posterity is bound by it and this will be as great a record as can be against them'.[164] Anticipating points of Thomas Hedley's celebrated speech later in the session, Whitelocke went on to identify three distinguishing features of England that he considered would be under threat if the king's prerogative to impose were allowed:

one is that we are masters of our own and can have nothing taken from us without our consents; another that laws cannot be made without our consents, and the edict of a prince is not a law; the third is that the parliament is the storehouse of our liberties. All these are in danger to be lost by this power, for *de modo et de fine non constat nobis*. We know not how this may stretch.[165]

Bacon attempted to head off the argument that a petition of right should be sent to the king by showing that both Elizabeth and Mary had restricted debate in Parliament, but he was rebuffed with the answer that his precedents were irrelevant. The reason that Parliament should have the right to debate impositions was that they were matters of *meum et tuum*, of property rights.[166] This was a significant point: the Commons acknowledged that they could 'treat by way of advice but may be inhibited' on the subject of the succession, on matters personal to the monarch, and in questions of 'war, peace and coin', since these 'concern us not directly, but in a generality and by consequence'.[167] The petition was drawn up and delivered to the king. Prepared by a subcommittee led by Sir Edwin Sandys, the petition reiterated points made by Wentworth at the start of the session: the Commons had no desire to 'impugn' the king's prerogative, nor did they wish to have the judgement in Bate's case reversed; but they did want to be allowed

---

[162] Ibid., 105. [163] 22 May 1610: ibid., 108. [164] Ibid., 109.
[165] Ibid. [166] Ibid., 110–12. [167] Ibid., 112.

freedom to debate the subject of impositions, while there was a fear that Bate's case would be used as a precedent and 'extended much further, even to the ruin of the ancient liberty of this kingdom, and of your subjects' right of propriety of their lands and goods'.[168] Only once these fears were dispelled could what James had called the 'principall errand' be treated.

The petition was well received by the king, who said that the Commons' concerns had been based on a misunderstanding of his message and his speech (though it would take a subtle reader to have interpreted it as being a request for the House to wait until the king came back to Westminster before discussing impositions, as James argued had been intended). He also 'protested he never meant to take away any of our liberties which he hoped we would not abuse',[169] and in a rather surprising volte-face allowed free discussion of impositions as well as promising free access to his presence for ten or twelve MPs to come in 'homely' fashion and discuss their intentions.[170] James was right to think that cultivating an affable form of majesty would encourage his subjects. But if he thought that his openness and generosity would mean that impositions would cease to occupy the Commons, he was wrong. June saw the most outspoken attacks on the notion that the king could impose by his prerogative, with Nicholas Fuller speaking on the 23rd and Hedley's speech on the 28th. I do not have space here to deal with the ideological implications of these important speeches, of which Hedley's in particular has been studied in considerable detail by scholars.[171] What is striking about the position taken in relation to impositions by Wentworth and Hedley is, as Markku Peltonen and Quentin Skinner have shown, the extent to which they deploy the neo-roman language of republicanism derived from their reading of the *Digest*, and of Cicero, Livy, and Sallust. They use this vocabulary to argue that the very existence of the king's right to impose means that the subject's property is no longer his own, because that property is now subject to the king's will. One's property is one's 'living', and if the king has the power to take away one's property at his will, then the means of one's life is subject to the will of the king. For the means of one's life – one's 'living' – to be subject to the will of another is what it means to be a slave, according to the classical authorities upon which this argument depended; hence, if the

[168] *CJ*, I, 431–2. See also Pauline Croft, 'Fresh Light on Bate's Case', *Historical Journal* 30 (1987): 523–39; Rabb, *Jacobean Gentleman*, p. 154.
[169] 25 May 1610: *PP 1610*, II, 115, 116.   [170] Ibid., 116.
[171] See especially Markku Peltonen, *Classical Humanism and Republicanism in English Political Thought 1570–1640* (Cambridge: Cambridge University Press, 1995), pp. 220–8, and Skinner, 'Classical Liberty, Renaissance Translation and the English Civil War', p. 320. See also Sommerville, *Royalists and Patriots*, pp. 85–7, 89–92.

king has power over one's property one is already *ipso facto* a slave.[172] It is this condition of slavery that men like Hedley and Wentworth feared and from which they wished to defend themselves. It is easy to see how vital the right freely to debate impositions is in all of this: if there was no right to dispute impositions then the king could do as he wished with his subjects' property (as we have seen many MPs arguing), which in turn meant that they had surrendered – or been deprived of – their liberty. Failure to offer frank counsel to the ruler was also regarded as a mark of servitude, as I have shown in chapter 1 above; thus the exercise and defence of freedom of speech were signs of liberty as well as ways of maintaining it.

In 1610 the links between parliamentary freedom of speech and the liberties of the subject were asserted in a far more sophisticated way than they had been in 1604. As the negotiations over the Great Contract faltered and, eventually, failed, MPs continued to speak out on matters as diverse as the iniquity of sermons claiming extreme powers for the king and denigrating the common law,[173] subsidies,[174] and (probably the cause of the Parliament's dissolution) the Scots.[175] Lewknor's speech in November is fascinating for its parrhesiastic framing strategies, from his opening meditation on the opposing dangers of speaking and remaining silent, to his concluding protestation of fidelity. Arguing that the poorer sort should be spared the burden of extra taxation, he began by rejecting cowardly and slavish silence:

'tis sometimes a good choice not to choose at all and 'tis a hard choice when a man must either speak with danger or against his conscience. I know that *terror regis est quasi rugitus leonis* and a word ill taken, though not evil spoken, may blot out the memory of many well-deserving actions, yet *tacere nolo*. And 'tis an argument of exceeding baseness for a man not to speak his mind when his country requires his aid, and therefore I will plainly, freely and openly deliver my opinion.[176]

---

[172] For these arguments, see Skinner, 'Classical Liberty, Renaissance Translation and the English Civil War'; Skinner, 'John Milton and the Politics of Slavery', in Skinner, *Visions of Politics*, volume II: *Renaissance Virtues*, pp. 286–307.

[173] Martin on 14 November 1610: *PP 1610*, II, 327–8.

[174] Notably Lewknor on 16 November 1610: ibid., 332–5.

[175] On 23 November 1610, Hoskyns claimed that 'the royal cistern had a leak', and that Parliament would be quicker to deal with supply if it was not thought that too much money was going to James's Scottish followers: *PP 1610*, II, 344. Boderie reported that feeling against the Scots was so fierce that he feared a Sicilian Vespers against them, a notion that was notoriously echoed by John Hoskyns in 1614 (on which see below): Antoine Lefèvre de Boderie, *Ambassades de la Boderie en Angleterre sous le règne de Henri IV et la minorité de Louis XIII depuis les années 1601 jusqu'en 1611*, 5 volumes (Paris, 1750), vol. v, pp. 510–11, quoted in *PP 1610*, II, 345 n. 4.

[176] 16 November 1610: ibid., 332.

After his *exordium*, Lewknor digresses to reflect again on the duty of counsellors and on princes' need for frank counsel, using a pair of *sententiae*: 'I am somewhat perplexed to deliver my opinion resolutely, and yet since no kind of men have more need of free, sincere, and open-hearted advice than princes, and miserable is the prince from whom that is kept back, I hold it now a fit time to speak plainly and let the King know the voice of his commons.'[177] In his conclusion, he asks a favour of his audience, no doubt thinking of those outside the House as well as of his fellow MPs:

I now am to make a request to you that no evil exposition be made of anything I have said, for I know well that words reported again, as they have another sound, so they are many other times reported so that they have another sense. But I protest to God that no affectation of popularity nor any other respect hath moved me now to speak, but a true desire to discharge my conscience and my duty to the King and to my country.[178]

In another copy of this speech, Lewknor invokes the writ of summons in recalling the end to which Parliaments are called – 'which is that man should therein with all liberty freely deliberate, advise, and conclude matters importing the general good of the commonwealth'.[179] From the Apology of 1604 to the petition of 1610, this first Parliament of James's reign had established many of the terms in which debates on freedom of speech would be conducted for the next twenty years and more. In the next session the discontent that had simmered on both sides would break out into open hostility.

1614: THE ADDLED PARLIAMENT

Three years after the formal dissolution of his first Parliament in April 1611, James I called new elections, and members assembled at Westminster again in February 1614.[180] Still troubled by his financial wants, the king hoped that this new session would offer the substantial assistance he required without the ill-feeling and mutual suspicion that had characterised the conclusion of the last one. In his opening speech to Parliament, he declared optimistically that

---

[177] Ibid., 333.   [178] Ibid., 334.   [179] BL MS Harley 4228, fol. 16: *PP 1610*, II, 400.
[180] On this Parliament see principally Moir, *The Addled Parliament of 1614*; Conrad Russell, *The Addled Parliament of 1614: The Limits to Revision*, The Stenton Lecture 1991 (Reading: University of Reading, 1992); Stephen Clucas and Rosalind Davies (eds.), *The Crisis of 1614 and the Addled Parliament: Literary and Historical Perspectives* (Aldershot: Ashgate, 2003).

a king [as opposed to a tyrant] knows his subjects can never have so good access unto him, speak so freely and safely, and have means to lay open the just complaints and griefs of his subjects as in parliament; and this parliament, I hope, shall be called the parliament of love.[181]

He went on to promise that he would speak to the Commons directly and not through the intermediaries of the Speaker or his servants. Despite his friendly words and good intentions, though, the Parliament was distinguished by a failure of communication not only between the king and the Commons but between members of the Lower House themselves. Less than two months later, in the face of paranoia about the misreporting of speeches and threats of dissolution, John Hoskyns pointed out that 'this was titled a parliament of love but the arguments that are made are rather of fear'.[182] Many of his fellow MPs made speeches that seriously suggested James was acting more like a tyrant than a king and that they were in danger of being enslaved.

This breakdown of communication centred around the desire of many MPs to counsel the king, and the incompatibility of this desire with the king's intentions for the session. It was a session notable for a series of speeches that excited the displeasure of either king, Lords, or Commons, and for the continued defence in the Commons of the parliamentary right – and duty – to speak frankly. The Parliament may have been no Parliament at all but an assembly, and the threats to their powers perceived by some of its members may have been exaggerated, but the debates concerning freedom of speech and its limits were important, and addressed serious matters of constitutional theory. This was noted by Sir Henry Wotton when, amid the hasty dissolution of the Parliament, James sent John Hoskyns, Thomas Wentworth, Christopher Neville, and Sir Walter Chute to the Tower for their outspokenness in the last days of the session. In a letter to Sir Edmund Bacon, Wotton acerbically described their speeches as 'better becoming a Senate of Venice, where the treaters are perpetual princes, than where those that speak so irreverently are so soon to return (which they should remember) to the natural capacity of subjects'.[183] Echoing the language used by the king in 1610, this comment suggests that contemporaries recognised that MPs were challenging the absolute distinction between their parliamentary privileges and the duties of 'subjects'. The continuity of language suggests that not much had changed between 1610 and 1614, and it is true

---

[181] 5 April 1614: *PP 1614*, 19.   [182] 3 June: ibid., 422–3.

[183] Logan Pearsall Smith, *The Life and Letters of Sir Henry Wotton* (London: Oxford University Press, 1907), volume II, p. 37.

that the issue of impositions had refused to lie down and die: it was raised repeatedly in 1614. Although James offered some honeyed words, he also admitted frankly that 'this parliament is principally called to relieve my wants', and the beginning of the session was marked by suspicions that he had plans to mould a sympathetic assembly by using 'undertakers' to manage business in the Lower House.[184]

Matters which addressed the freedom of speech properly to be accorded to MPs arose repeatedly during the brief life of the Parliament. There were five specific speeches or sets of speeches that were considered to be scandalous by the Commons or the king – or at least noted to have caused considerable discomfort. The first was Richard Martin's speech on 17 May. Martin was in the Commons to speak as counsel for the Virginia Company, along with a delegation from the Lords, but (as the anonymous diarist notes), 'he, contrary to all men's expectations, beginning with Virginia, came into another subject both in taxing the House in general and also some particular men'.[185] Chamberlain describes Martin 'taxing [the Commons] for their slow proceeding, for their disorderly carriage, and schooling them what they should do, with divers odd glances'.[186] Despite this speech being the 'most offensive and injurious to the House' that Sir Edward Montagu had ever heard, Martin was 'not interrupted because it was agreed by the House before he came in to hear him in silence'.[187]

The second scandalous speech was only heard at second-hand in the Commons, but despite – or it may be because of – this caused even more upset than Martin's brainstorm. It in fact consisted of three separate comments by Bishop Richard Neile of Lincoln, uttered on 21, 23, and 24 May, that a joint conference of Lords and Commons on the subject of impositions should not be entertained because – as Mervyn reported him –

to question the King's prerogative in imposing was like a disease called *noli me tangere* and in touching that matter we did not only cut off a branch but strike at the root of the imperial crown . . . he said he knew our spirits and thought it not fit to hear us, for the Lords should hear nothing but undutiful and seditious speeches of us.[188]

---

[184] On 'undertakers' – men who would 'manage' the Parliament to make it more amenable to the king's needs – and Sir Henry Neville's policy advice to the king, see Moir, *The Addled Parliament*, pp. 12, 15, 68–9, 97–113. Neville's 'Advice' is reproduced in *PP 1614*, 247–53.

[185] Anonymous notes, MS 0.2.7, Trinity College, Cambridge: ibid., 279.

[186] John Chamberlain, *Letters*, ed. by N. E. McClure, 2 volumes (Philadelphia: The American Philosophical Society), volume I, p. 531.

[187] *PP 1614*, 276. No complete copy of Martin's speech appears to have survived; see ibid., 271, n. 25.

[188] Ibid., 348. For the individual comments, see *HMC Hastings MSS*, volume IV, pp. 249, 253, 259, quoted in Moir, *The Addled Parliament*, pp. 117, 118, 122.

A committee was quickly selected to investigate and report on the matter.

On 21 May, the same day that Bishop Neile was applying his horticultural analogies to the Commons, Thomas Wentworth – described by Wotton as a 'silly and simple creature'[189] – applied some distinctly uncomfortable scriptural passages to the discussion of impositions, notably Daniel 11:20 ('Then shall stande up in his place in the glorie of the kingdome, one that shall rayse taxes: but after fewe dayes hee shall bee destroyed, neither in wrath, nor in battell') and referred to the murder of Henri IV (who had indeed used impositions, as Sir Henry Wotton had noted in support of James).[190] These comments seem to have provoked Neile's second outburst. Wentworth ended, in either a hapless attempt to prevent analogical reasoning or an even more sinister ultimatum, depending on one's interpretation, by saying 'but by far be it from my Lord the King that aught so should befall him'.[191] Unsurprisingly, both James and the French ambassador were incensed by the speech.

The fourth speech was delivered by Sir Walter Chute on 1 June, and suggested that there were multiple financial abuses which acted as a drain on the 'main cistern' of the king's coffers as well as declaring that 'they that practiced with the King to have no parliament would also labour to dissolve it' and suggesting that supply and dissolution should come only after redress of grievances.[192] The last set of speeches are the most notorious, and came on 3 June: Christopher Neville borrowed from Bishop Neile's sylvan thesaurus, asking 'would the King take from us the cedars of freedom and liberty under which the subjects of England were shadowed, and shroud us with these shrubs of bills of grace?', and went on to describe Neile himself as one of a fearsome mongrel species: 'their master's spaniels but their country's wolves'.[193] John Hoskyns's notorious speech attacking James's Scottish favourites and hinting at a massacre through a reference to the Sicilian Vespers followed soon after, and four days later the session was over.[194]

---

[189] Wotton, *Life and Letters*, volume II, p. 37.
[190] *PP 1614*, 313, 316, 317; Geneva Bible version of Daniel 11:20 quoted from Moir, *The Addled Parliament*, p. 116. See *PP 1614*, 315 for Wotton's comparative examples of imposing kings.
[191] Ibid., 316.   [192] Ibid., 408.
[193] Ibid., 420. On Neville's speech, see Skinner, 'Classical Liberty, Renaissance Translation and the English Civil War', p. 321.
[194] *PP 1614*, 422–3; on this speech see the perceptive comments of Russell, *The Addled Parliament of 1614: The Limits to Revision*, pp. 23–5, esp. p. 25. See also Chamberlain to Carleton, 8 June, 1614: Chamberlain, *Letters*, volume I, pp. 537–8. On Hoskyns's involvement in this Parliament, see Whitlock, *John Hoskyns, Serjeant-at-Law*, pp. 427–68.

In each of the cases outlined above, the Commons were concerned to maintain that it was they who could deem a speech excessive or scandalous and, if necessary, punish the speaker. Martin's speech was in no sense an assertion of any right to freedom of speech, but it *was* regarded as an insult to the House and he was censured by the Commons and called to the bar to be admonished and to excuse his actions.[195]

The Neile affair was, similarly, a case of an insult by a non-member, but was treated much more seriously, both because it was transmitted by rumour and because of the threat it offered to friendly relations between two of the three components of Parliament, the Lords and Commons. Discussions in and out of committee went on until the end of the session, with the main point of debate being whether Neile should be investigated by the Lords, acting on advice from the Commons, or by the king. Certainly one of these had to be relied upon, since the Lower House had no jurisdiction over the Upper, nor vice versa. On 26 May Sir Edwin Sandys, noting that the case was 'as weighty as any ever came here concerning the liberties of this and the higher House of Parliament', argued that 'to go immediately to the King wrongs the liberties of the Upper House', while Sir Roger Owen worried that 'if the King may punish him now for an offense to our House, so he may do one of ours'.[196] The committee's vote finally went narrowly in favour of going to the king, but not before many verbal attacks on both the bishop's person and on his office, and a decision on the part of the committee to forbear any other business until a satisfactory message had been received from the Lords.[197] Neile had slighted the Commons' good intentions in their discussion of impositions and was thus likely, Hoskyns thought, to 'make discord between the king and his people'.[198]

Wentworth, meanwhile, having provoked the bishop by his speech on 21 May, made his apology on the day that the latter's remarks were first discussed in the Commons: apologising for his remarks, he was cleared 'by a general acclamation' of the House.[199] He was nonetheless investigated by the Council at the end of the session and briefly imprisoned, possibly to placate the French ambassador.[200] Here, as with the speeches on 3 June, a conflict between the king's and the Commons' jurisdiction over outspokenness becomes apparent. The day before the dissolution Sir Guy Palmes brought a motion effectively to assert and shore up this jurisdiction, saying that

---

[195] *PP 1614*, 271–87.   [196] Ibid., 355, 356, 357.   [197] See Moir, *The Addled Parliament*, p. 125.
[198] 25 May: *PP 1614*, 349.   [199] 25 May: ibid., 340, 348–9.
[200] Sir Henry Wotton wrote to Sir Edmund Bacon that the ambassador had lodged a complaint about Wentworth's speech (8 June 1614; Wotton, *Life and Letters*, volume II, p. 37).

since it was said the parliament should be so soon dissolved, in respect of some reports cast forth that divers of the House should be called into question after the parliament, he wished if there were any that could accuse any member of the House to have spoken any unbeseeming words of the King that they might here be charged with them, and either purge themselves or receive punishment.[201]

The Speaker thought this dubious, since nobody was actually named, but Hoskyns acknowledged that 'it concerned him in particular'; Sir John Savile reminded the House that 'the ancient course in parliament was that if any man's speech had been excepted against, the Queen sent to the House and accused the party, and the House punished him'.[202] Wotton then attempted, it seems, to bring this discussion to some sort of conclusion, and to do so in the Commons while it was still possible, asking Hoskyns to explain what he meant by referring to the Sicilian Vespers.[203] Hoskyns's reply hardly sounds satisfactory: he said that 'he had no private intent in it and he thought the story was known to many and he meant it general'.[204] Later, he was to amplify this excuse, claiming that he had been working entirely from a script given to him by Lionel Sharp and Sir Charles Cornwallis: when he was investigated by the Privy Council after the end of the session and asked to explain his reference to the Sicilian Vespers, he said he had a 'hint thereof, and afterwards a general information, from Dr *Lionel Sharp of Cambridge*'.[205] Chamberlain, in addition, asserted that 'Hoskyns was emboucht, abetted, and indeed plainly hired with monie to do that he did.'[206] This seemed to implicate Sharp and Cornwallis's patron, the Earl of Northampton, who certainly had some interest in seeing the Parliament fail (and who notoriously drove through London in triumph when it was dissolved), but Northampton's involvement has been effectively questioned by Linda Levy Peck.[207] However lame his explanation, Hoskyns was then cleared upon the question put to the House. Neville and Sir Edward Giles went on to reply to rumours of accusations against them, but their replies do not survive in any of the records. Of course, none of these manoeuvres was successful in keeping these speeches a matter for and in the House, and the four members were soon incarcerated: this apparent assault on parliamentary liberty was to become a *cause célèbre* in the next Parliament and beyond.

As well as wishing to protect their jurisdiction over speeches deemed to be excessive or insulting, many MPs in 1614 continued to assert Parliament's

---

[201] *PP 1614*, 426.   [202] Ibid., 428.   [203] Ibid.   [204] Ibid.
[205] Quoted in Whitlock, *John Hoskyns, Serjeant-at-Law*, p. 459.
[206] Chamberlain, *Letters*, volume 1, p. 540.
[207] Linda Levy Peck, *Northampton: Patronage and Policy at the Court of James I* (London: George Allen and Unwin, 1982), pp. 208–10.

conciliar function: to present it as their right as well as their duty to advise the king. The importance of counsel was acknowledged by James in his opening speech:

> so I trust to meet with you at Michaelmas, at which time I will promise you to ask you nothing (and so assure your countries) but say: my masters come, let us consult what is good for the commonwealth and what laws are fit either to be added, amended, or taken away and you in all humble manner to inform me what is amiss and fit to be amended in the commonwealth.[208]

Although the Parliament never saw Michaelmas, this is evidence of James's awareness both of his MPs' desire to fulfil their role as counsellors and of the importance of at least attempting the appearance of patience. On 12 April Sir George More reminded his fellow members that they were 'sent hither from all the commons of the kingdom; our principal care to speak for the commonwealth that continually speaks to us', and that there was 'health' in 'the multitude of counsellors'.[209] Responding to these kinds of arguments, and to the Commons' return to the question of impositions, the king delivered a speech to the Lower House on the afternoon of 4 May. Stating that 'there is not in the world so great a counsel as yours, both in the quantity and quality',[210] James again blamed misunderstanding on both sides for the 'harsh parting of the last parliament', and described his reliance on counsel in general and on the counsel of wise and experienced counsellors in particular.[211] He had retained those whom he inherited from Elizabeth: unlike Rehoboam he would not listen to young and rash counsellors.[212] But these very counsellors advised him that it was within his prerogative to impose: could they be wrong? Attempting to offer some comfort, he vowed that he would never lay impositions on 'home-bred commodities' (i.e., on exports) – but 'to bar me from my right, to rob my crown of so regal a prerogative, to show your wills for that you cannot obtain resting in my power, is mere obstinacy'.[213] This was cold comfort to some of James's audience: their counsel was praised, but the king had characteristically made it clear that in the matter of impositions they had to rely on him to act as a good king. Prayer and tears were the only options available should he or his successors not do so – to challenge the prerogative 'mere obstinacy'. This was not all: the king had words of warning that should this Parliament fail like the last, he would do without the Commons' counsel: 'I confess that my best strength and safety is placed in the love of my people. But if

---

[208] *PP 1614*, 19.   [209] Ibid., 64.   [210] Ibid., 140.
[211] Ibid. By contrast, Sandys had argued on 12 April that the fault was mainly on one side: there was, he said, 'great wrong done the last Parliament by misreporting the speeches of many members of this House' (*PP 1614*, 68).
[212] Ibid., 141–2.   [213] Ibid., 142.

you will not show it, yet I am born your king and must live, but you must not look for more parliaments in haste. And if for my relief I be forced to stretch my prerogative the world then will see where the fault has been.'[214]

The obstinacy persisted, however, and the Commons proceeded with James's licence to offer their counsel while they could. On the day after the king's speech MPs proceeded to investigate James's claims about his imposing power. Sandys marshalled precedents against the king's right to do so, noting that 'some other princes had imposed but never claimed any right'.[215] 'This liberty of imposing', he went on, recalling the arguments of 1610, 'held to trench to the foundation of all our interests. That makes us bondmen, gives use but no propriety.'[216] Whitelocke denied James's claim that impositions were a 'flower of the prerogative': there had been none from the reign of Edward III until that of Mary, 'so if a flower, a long winter, not budding in 160 year[s]'.[217] Even as they debated impositions, the members reminded themselves of their right to do so and worried about the king's likely reaction. If there was a conference with the Lords on the subject, it was no use having the king in attendance, said Mr Whitson, for if he was there 'none dare reply'. Hoskyns argued that Parliament had to proceed with business at its own pace and in its own order: they had been 'called to give counsel not to give money'; giving supply, he pointed out, was not mentioned in the writ of summons as one of Parliament's functions.[218] Nor should they be afraid or take notice of threats that if they did not give supply Parliament would not be called: 'this House never in fear; no cause of fear of not calling of parliament. The King gains by them, not the subject.'[219] It seems to have been Mr Hyde who drew the Commons' attention to the fact that 'it was the resolution of the last parliament that it is in the King's power to call a parliament, but when they are assembled it is freely to consult of what they shall determine themselves; for if they should be bound to treat of what the King list, there is no freedom'.[220] Armed with the encouragement of this day's debates, the committee for grievances prepared materials for a conference with the Lords, and Sir Robert Cotton granted MPs access to his collection of parliamentary records to search for precedents.[221]

It was in opposition to this conference that Neile made his notorious speeches. The conference was delayed and, ultimately, was never to take place, but the Lords' delay over it and Neile's comments caused the

---

[214] Ibid., 144.   [215] Ibid., 146.   [216] Ibid., 147.   [217] Ibid., 149.
[218] Ibid., 152.   [219] Ibid.   [220] Ibid., 159.
[221] Sir Edwin Sandys reported from the committee on 12 May: ibid., 211–14; cf. the account at ibid., 223–7. A letter was sent to Cotton on 13 May (ibid., 232), and his reply was read on 20 May, when Hoskyns was appointed one of the members sent to search the library (ibid., 297).

Commons to dig their heels in over impositions. From this moment on, at the end of May, it was impossible that the king's supply should be granted soon, and on 3 June James sent a message to the House to tell them that 'unless we forthwith proceed to treat of his supply he will dissolve the parliament'.[222] This was the message that provoked the desperate speeches of Hoskyns, Strode, Fuller, Whitson, and Hyde, as well as a debate about whether the Commons could offer the king a subsidy to fend off the threat of dissolution.[223] A message sent in reply to the king's ruled this out, however, explaining that 'till therefore it shall please God to ease us of these impositions wherewith the whole kingdom does groan, we cannot without wrong to our country give your Majesty that relief which we desire'.[224] This sealed the Parliament's fate, and on 7 June it was dissolved. In the last hours of its existence, those opposed to impositions continued to press their case. Their attempts to exercise their right freely to debate what seemed the most pressing issues for the commonwealth were being curtailed, they thought, and as they had explained in 1610, this meant that the king's right to impose without Parliament was effectively confirmed. Sir Edwin Sandys put the case as he saw it:

There were, he said, 2 things that did hinder us from proceeding for the King's supply: one for the liberty of the House, another for the liberty of the kingdom. The mischief is now of the sudden dissolution, a great wrong to his Majesty and the whole state. The difficulty of this parliament consisted in righting the King and his people. That there is nothing more grievous to every loyal heart than thus to have it break up; but to conclude the liberty of the kingdom thus by it were an unestimable wrong to the kingdom, and if the King would give us assurance against the impositions but for his own time, what should we have of his posterity.[225]

During the Parliament of 1614 the Commons and the king struggled again over questions of definition: their 'forbearance' from business seemed to James like 'cessation';[226] their defence of the right to debate impositions seemed to him like a plot to deny him his income. The instability of evaluative terms is evident in Wotton's explanation of Hoskyns's imprisonment: he was, he wrote,

in for more wit, and for licentiousness baptized freedom. For I have noted in our House, that a false or faint patriot did cover himself with the shadow of equal moderation, and on the other side, irreverent discourse was called honest liberty; so as upon the whole matter, 'no excesses want precious names'.[227]

---

[222] Ibid., 413.   [223] See ibid., 414–24.   [224] Ibid., 425.
[225] Ibid., 430–1.   [226] 27 May 1614: ibid., 374.
[227] Wotton, *Life and Letters*, volume II, p. 37. On the rhetorical technique of redescription that Wotton is complaining of – and employing – here (*paradiastole*), see Skinner, *Reason and Rhetoric*, chapter 4; Skinner, 'Moral Ambiguity and the Renaissance Art of Eloquence', *Essays in*

The lines of communication were thoroughly addled by the end: James was simply not speaking the same language as Sandys and his fellow MPs. Although conspiracy theories abounded after the dissolution of Parliament,[228] to many in 1614 there really did seem to be a crisis of liberty, and it is vital to take seriously Sandys's conviction that even if he was not imprisoned, to be 'bound to treat of what the King list' would place him and his fellow MPs in a condition of bondage as harsh as that suffered by Hoskyns and his companions in the Tower, and much more enduring.

1621: FREEDOM OF SPEECH DEFINED AND DEFENDED

Some historians have denied that the debates on freedom of speech in 1604 to 1610 and 1614 have substantial ideological significance, preferring to see them as individual tussles over single issues. I have tried to show that they were much more than that. When it comes to the Parliament of 1621, most students of the period agree that freedom of speech became as important an issue as almost anything else, especially in the second session, which sat from 20 November to 18 December.[229] It is, however, impossible properly to understand why these debates happened in the way that they did, and what exactly the Commons were concerned about if we do not appreciate the importance of, and the developments to be found in, James's first two Parliaments.

The first session: January–June 1621

It was seven years since the last Parliament when MPs assembled in 1621, and in the meantime open hostility had broken out in continental Europe between Protestant and Roman Catholic forces.[230] James's own son-in-law, Frederick of Bohemia, was at the centre of the struggle for the Palatinate. At the same time, negotiations were taking place over a possible marriage for Charles, Prince of Wales, with the Infanta of Spain. There was a widespread

---

Criticism 44:4 (October 1994): 267–92; Skinner, 'Thomas Hobbes: Rhetoric and the Construction of Morality', *Proceedings of the British Academy* 76 (1991): 1–61.

[228] For an example of the theory that the Parliament had been deliberately undermined by Northampton and his faction, see Chamberlain to Carleton, 30 June, 1614; Chamberlain, *Letters*, volume 1, p. 540.

[229] On this Parliament see Zaller, *The Parliament of 1621*; Russell, *Parliaments and English Politics*, chapter 2; Brennan Pursell, 'War or Peace? Jacobean Politics and the Parliament of 1621', in *Parliament, Politics and Elections*, ed. by Kyle, pp. 149–78.

[230] On this session, see Christopher Thompson, *The Debate on Freedom of Speech in the House of Commons in February 1621* (Orsett: Orchard Press, 1985).

expectation that the Parliament had been called because James was preparing for war, although he made it clear that it was the negotiations for peace that were at issue. Once again, he needed money – for his own wants, and to relieve the Palatinate. A benevolence had failed to raise anything like the sums needed, and Parliament was, in a sense, a last resort.[231] Anti-Catholic feeling was rife, and outspoken informal counsel was being spread from the pulpits, the press, and in manuscript libels: Thomas Scott's *Vox Populi or Newes from Spayne* was published in 1620, and in December of that year James had the Bishop of London forbid his clergy from speaking on the Spanish Match or 'any other matter of State'.[232] Despite this, the following Sunday 'a younge fellow at Paules-crosse upon his text (thou shalt not plough with an oxe and an asse) spake very freely'.[233] On 24 December James issued a proclamation 'against excesse of Lavish and Licentious Speech of matters of State'.[234]

Although the opening of the 1621 Parliament was reasonably calm, it would have been surprising if the memory of the last session and the recent proclamation had not been in some members' minds. In his opening speech James tried to set some ground-rules for this meeting, thinking no doubt about 1614: 'this lesson', he said, 'I would give you, especially you of the House of Commons, which is, that when ye shall meet together, the consideration of the preciousness of the time and weightiness of the matter might keep you from wasting the time in long speeches'.[235] He also offered a briefing on his constitutional theory that put Parliament firmly in its place, and the king there with it: 'a parliament in general is a thing composed of a head and a body; the head is the monarch that calleth it, the body is as the three states called together by that head . . . kings and kingdoms were before parliaments, and are relatives'.[236] As to the question of what Parliament could reasonably discuss, the answer was what the king asked them to discuss.[237] The Parliament was called for two reasons, 'to sustain me in my urgent necessities' and to give aid to the Palatinate.[238] There was no time for the kind of debate that had characterised the last session, said James, warning the Commons that 'I would not have you to meddle with complaints against the King, the church or state matters, nor with princes' prerogatives. The parliament was never called for that purpose.

---

[231] See Zaller, *The Parliament of 1621*, pp. 17–18. [232] See above, chapter 2, pp. 104–5.

[233] Chamberlain to Carleton, 22 December 1620: Chamberlain, *Letters*, volume II, p. 331. On Scott see further chapters 2 above and 4 below; on manuscript libels and James's proclamations, see chapter 4.

[234] 'A Proclamation against excesse of Lavish and Licentious Speech of matters of State', Whitehall 24 December 1620, in *Stuart Royal Proclamations*, volume I, ed. by Larkin and Hughes, pp. 495–6.

[235] 30 January 1621: *CD 1621*, II, 3. [236] Ibid., II, 3. [237] Ibid., II, 4. [238] Ibid., II, 7, 9.

And if among you there be any such busy body, he is a spirit of Satan that means to overthrow the good errand in hand.'[239] He went on to try to draw a line under the experiences of the first two Parliaments of his reign:

There hath been great expectation about this parliament. I have had two kinds of parliaments, the one when I came first into England, when I was an apprentice and so unexperienced, governors in the *quondam* time being more skilful by long experience, and so many things might then be amiss which I have endeavored to amend, considering there are two sorts of speakers which I would inhibit, first, lion-like speakers that dare speak of anything that appertains to princes, secondly, fox-like that seem to speak one thing and intend another, as to bring the king in dislike with his subjects. After this came in a strange beast called Undertakers. They took much upon them, and though some principal men about me were content to believe it, yet I myself never would.[240]

Granting the Speaker's request for 'libertye of dutifull speeches' (an interesting phrasing) at the opening of Parliament four days later, the king advised the Commons not to misuse their privilege, 'not to turne libertie of speeche into licence or breake the reverence due to a Soveraigne'.[241] Again, James wanted to remind MPs that reason should instruct them in their duties, and that therefore they could simply not be licentious if they were dutiful.

Even as they moved relatively quickly to commit the subsidy bill that would help James in his desire to be prepared for military action, in the first two weeks of the session MPs turned their attention to freedom of speech. Unlike in 1604 to 1610 and 1614, when the debates had been provoked by the MPs' desire to discuss specific policy issues (the Union; impositions) and the king's reluctance to let them do so, in 1621 freedom of speech was raised quickly and in response to the events of the last Parliament as well as to the king's proclamation and speech.[242] On the first day of business in Parliament, Monday 5 February 1620/1, Sir Edward Giles 'moved for a petition to the king for freedom of speech, and that those that spake extravagant in the House might be punished by the House and not after Parliament, in regard of the late proclamation'; a motion that was seconded by Sir Robert Phelips, arguing that 'we should desire to be made free men before we can bee fitt to be Counsellours'.[243] Sir Edward Coke supported

---

[239] Ibid., II, 12.
[240] Ibid. The king repeated his strictures on 'lion-like' and 'fox-like' speakers on 3 February at the presentation of the new Speaker, Sir Thomas Richardson: *CD 1621*, II, 15.
[241] Ibid., IV, 8, 10.
[242] The debates on freedom of speech during the period 3–15 February are summarised in Bod. MS Rawl. B.151, which I discuss at length in chapter 4 below. The passages treating this Parliament are reproduced in *CD 1621*, VI.
[243] Ibid., II, 17; ibid., IV, 12.

the idea of a petition, and twice cited Strode's case in 4 Hen. VIII, while Thomas Crew reminded his fellow MPs that 'we had freedom of speech last parliament, yet we know what followed. And therefore we should entreat his Majesty that if anything here be spoken amiss, it may be here only censured and not hereafter.'[244] Sitting as a Committee, the House considered the idea of a petition, with arguments on both sides.[245] Throughout the discussion, both in and out of Committee, Secretary Calvert insisted that the Commons were wasting their time: the privilege had already been granted, he protested, so why should they ask for it to be confirmed? Eventually he conceded that 'you do well to stand upon your privileges though I see not yet how they are impeached; but if any doubt by reason of the proclamation, I think it best to go to the King by petition'; but they were missing the point: 'I think that proclamation was intended against such as make ordinary table talk of state matters in taverns and alehouses, and not against parliament men.'[246] Sir George More agreed that privileges should only be brought into question 'in case of a breach as was suspected the last parliament', but this allusion to 1614 only succeeded in provoking Sir Robert Phelips, who said that 'if ever privileges were broken it was the last parliament upon those men who, the next day after the parliament was dissolved, were committed to the Tower'.[247] The day concluded with a subcommittee being appointed to draw up a petition and to report back in the Court of Wards the following afternoon; meanwhile, 'the other two parts [of the Committee's business, i.e. grievances and supply] being twins, it was not thought fit to enter upon until answer were brought from his Majesty concerning liberty of speech'.[248]

The issue was returned to in a rather scrappy way on 9 February, when Sir Thomas Roe brought the subcommittee's draft to the committee on grievances.[249] Glanville objected to the whole idea of such a petition, but was told in no uncertain terms by Coke, a stickler for procedure, that he was out of order for speaking against a question that had already been settled. Sir Edwin Sandys, who had not been at the debate on the 5th, said that the matter should not have been referred to a committee without being debated more fully, and it was recommitted to the House.[250] The fullest debates took

---

[244] Ibid., ii, 23–4.

[245] The Committee of the Whole was also to consider whether to petition the king for the better use of the recusancy laws, and what the House should do about supply and the redress of grievances: ibid., ii, 24.

[246] Ibid., ii, 19, 25.   [247] Ibid., ii, 25.   [248] Ibid., ii, 27.

[249] The draft is recorded in ibid., iv, 37.

[250] Ibid., ii, 52. Sandys's absence had been noted on the 6th, when Samuel Sandys excused him on the grounds that he was away on Virginia Company business; this did not impress Sir Edward Giles, who asked testily whether Virginia should keep him from England (ibid., ii, 28).

place on 12 February, when Coke began by giving an outline of the general rules governing freedom of speech in the House and suggesting some ways of defining its limits. He described an ascending scale of frankness, in five points. First, he said, it should always be bound by decorum: 'every man's discretion and wisdom must be a rule to himself that so he do not propound things unreasonable or out of order';[251] secondly, it was true that 'we have a freedom of speech to speak what we think good for government either in church or commonweal and what are the grievances', but members were too prone to bring in excessively general points.[252] Why not make sure that every MP proposing business supplies a 'model' for it, so that time was not wasted?[253] The third kind of freedom was recklessness, and should be censured by the House; the fourth was 'when men out of faction will bring in a design to trouble the state': this should be dealt with by the House, but might not be within its competence if it concerned foreign affairs.[254] The fifth and final kind of freedom of speech that needed to be dealt with was treasonous speech, and this had always been acknowledged as being outside the jurisdiction of the Commons. If these ground rules were adopted, the House having enjoyed a proper debate on the subject, Coke saw no need to take the issue further: 'the freedom of this House is the freedom of the whole land,' he said, 'and if this freedom, being proposed, should have been rejected, we might justly have been blamed' – but it had not been rejected. Calvert agreed: they had done enough, and should get on with 'the matters of the commonwealth'.[255] This was not enough for some members, though, and Poole made the declaration that is cited as this chapter's epigraph, while More and Phelips returned to the events of the last Parliament, much to the discomfort of Coke and Calvert.[256] This time they both agreed that a petition was necessary, but Coke argued that a bill would be a better way of proceeding; Crew replied that a bill would only come into effect after the session was over.[257] The House agreed that a committee would decide how to go to the king.[258] On 15 February, however, Calvert delivered a message from the king that assured the House of as much freedom of speech as any of his predecessors had allowed and hoped that they would punish anyone who exceeded their liberty; satisfied with this gesture, the Commons sent a message of thanks to James and ensured that his precise words were written in the Clerk's book.[259]

The king's message put an end to the debates about a petition for freedom of speech, but issues concerning the House's privilege appeared in

---

[251] Ibid., II, 56. [252] Ibid. [253] Ibid., II, 57. [254] Ibid., *CJ*, I, 517. [255] *CD 1621*, II, 57.
[256] Ibid., 58, 59; *CD 1621*, IV, 39–40. [257] Ibid., II, 62. [258] Ibid., 63.
[259] Ibid., 83–4. For James's message, see ibid., VI, 289–90; ibid., VII, 575.

other guises during the first session of this Parliament. In several of these cases the Commons came into conflict with the king on precisely the questions of jurisdiction that Coke had raised in his speech of 12 February. On the same day that the message arrived, a Lincoln's Inn lawyer and MP, Shepherd, spoke out against an act for punishing abuses of the Sabbath, 'taxing the House, saying that they made laws which were gins and snares for papists but not so much as a mousetrap for a puritan, etc.'[260] He was told to withdraw from the House and later expelled. In April and May the House stepped onto somewhat thinner ice when they attempted to punish a non-member, Edward Floyd, for speaking disrespectfully about the king's daughter and son-in-law after their defeat at the White Mountain.[261] Patriotic outrage swept the case along, with punishments of various degrees of severity being suggested, but the king stepped in to question the Commons' right to punish the speech of a non-member without any more evidence than hearsay.[262] At a meeting with the king Speaker Richardson explained why the Commons had tried to punish Floyd, and James replied that while he thought their zeal was commendable they were both exceeding their rights and wasting time:

you will wrong ourselves and your successors in challenging an omnipotency or in erecting a judicature which is not known how far it may reach. And the time of the year grows hot. The health of your bodies will crave a recess. Therefore work like bees to bring honey both to the king and the people and trouble not yourselves with genealogies, as Saint Paul said unto Timothy, that is with frivolous and unprofitable questions and disputes.[263]

Eventually the king punished Floyd with the advice of the Lords, but some MPs were unhappy with the way that the limits of their powers had been exposed, Alford declaring that 'our liberties are more shaken than ever, and now to be baffled'.[264] This was a difficult point to press, since there was no evidence that the Commons could traditionally punish non-members, as I have discussed above. It is therefore important to note the enthusiastic support that such proposed innovations received: many members in the House seemed to want their power over speech to be extended as well as defended.

One of the most weighty matters of this session was the investigation into a series of financial and other abuses, most notably the control and granting of monopolies. The holders of the patents for alehouses and for gold and silver thread (Sir Giles Mompesson, who was also an MP, and Sir Francis

---

[260] Ibid., ii, 82.   [261] Ibid., 335.   [262] 2 May 1621: ibid., 337.
[263] Ibid., 342–3.   [264] Ibid., 345.

Michell, respectively) were prosecuted and punished, with the Commons testing the limits of their jurisdiction again.[265] The Lord Chancellor, Francis Bacon, was accused of taking bribes, and prosecuted through the revival of the medieval practice of impeachment, with both Houses of Parliament cooperating.[266] Abuses in the Court of Chancery were also looked into, as were the affairs of the Merchant Adventurers. The investigations into patents seemed likely at one stage to lead as far as Buckingham, who had risen into his position as the king's favourite since the Parliament of 1614.[267] In almost all of these cases the Commons, or one of its members, had reason to assert or defend their right to freedom of speech, and it is impossible to see them as entirely independent of the debates at the beginning of the session. In the course of a general attack on Mompesson on 21 February, Sir Francis Seymour said that he could not believe that the referees of the patents that had been issued were without fault – a suggestion that could lead to very high places, and to figures like the Duke of Buckingham's brothers. Conrad Russell has shown that Seymour was probably part of a cabal mobilised against Buckingham; whether this was so or not, he claimed on 28 February that he had been questioned for raising the issue of the referees, and later asked to be cleared by the House from speaking too freely.[268] The fact that Seymour was attempting to undermine Buckingham and acting as part of a court-based faction did not mean that he should be allowed to be silenced: whether the Commons knew of his agenda is irrelevant to the issue of his freedom of speech. The House also began investigations into the Court of Chancery in March, with members framing their speeches with protestations of their duty to speak frankly even about and to some of the 'great ones' of the land.[269] James supported the Commons in their pursuit of several of the grievances that arose in this first session, allowing the impeachment of Bacon, but he became increasingly impatient with them as time wore on.[270] The speech he delivered on 20 April warned

---

[265] On popular reactions to Mompesson's prosecution and banishment, see Richard Cust, 'Politics and the Electorate in the 1620s', in *Conflict in Early Stuart England*, ed. by Cust and Hughes, pp. 134–67, at p. 142; chapter 4 below.

[266] On the revival of impeachment, see Colin G. C. Tite, *Impeachment and Parliamentary Judicature in Early Stuart England* (London: Athlone Press, 1974).

[267] On the investigation into patents, see Russell, *Parliaments and English Politics*, pp. 98–111.

[268] Russell, *Parliaments and English Politics*, p. 109; *CD 1621*, II 146; II May 1621: ibid., 359. Seymour was cleared, even as Calvert tried to reassure him that it was unnecessary. In April the king had put Yelverton into the Tower for comparing Buckingham with Hugh le Despencer, the favourite of Edward II, but he had been freed when the Lords complained that this was a breach of their privileges since they had been pursuing charges against him. See Zaller, *The Parliament of 1621*, pp. 120–3.

[269] E.g. Neville on 17 March: *CD 1621*, II, 240; Coke on 27 April: ibid., 327.

[270] See Russell, *Parliaments and English Politics*, pp. 109–12.

MPs that 'time was precious', and that they risked wasting it on too many petty complaints, while Calvert delivered messages from James on 1 and 14 May telling them that he disliked their discussion of baronets and that information about the Merchant Adventurers was privileged.[271] It seemed as though James's support of the Commons' claim to freedom of speech was confined to those areas that he was happy to see investigated. Combined with the length of the session so far, these matters led to James's decision to inform the Commons at the end of May that he planned to adjourn or prorogue Parliament on 2 June and reconvene it 'about Allhallowtide'.[272] The House reacted with horror and 'passionate speeches';[273] but what was the cause of their passion? Partly, no doubt, it was because they realised that very little business had been achieved in the way of legislation, and that they might meet with a cold welcome if they returned to their countries having granted two subsidies and not dealt thoroughly with grievances. Partly, though, it also seems to have been the case that some MPs thought their freedom of speech was itself being curtailed by this adjournment: that is, they linked their ability to stay in session with their right to consult about the great and weighty matters of the kingdom. A third reason for their alarm was a fear of being punished for speeches uttered during the session (the spectre of 1614 again): if the Parliament was adjourned by commission, then a prorogation could follow and parliamentary privileges would lapse, whereas they would remain 'live' during an adjournment.[274] Sandys, Alford, and Jephson were all cleared by the House of having spoken anything unfitting, but Sandys, along with the Earl of Southampton and John Selden, were arrested on 16 June.[275] Sandys and Southampton were suspected of having planned to open direct negotiations with Frederick and Elizabeth, but the claim that Sandys's punishment was not for anything said or done in Parliament was regarded with scepticism.

Russell has described the debates on freedom of speech in February 1621 as 'very lukewarm';[276] but this treats them too much in isolation from the rest of the session. These debates cannot be separated from the way in which the Parliament then went on to pursue accusations of corruption in a host of institutions, or from what was surely an ongoing dispute about the extent to which conditions could be placed on the Commons' liberty of speech by the king. As Christopher Thompson has written, 'the debates between the

---

[271] *CD 1621*, II, 303–4, 333, 365.   [272] 28 May 1621: ibid., II, 398.
[273] 29 May 1621: ibid., 406.   [274] See Zaller, *The Parliament of 1621*, p. 136.
[275] *CD 1621*, II, 421 (Sandys and Alford: 2 June); 426 (Jephson: 4 June); Zaller, *The Parliament of 1621*, p. 139; Gardiner, *History of England*, volume IV, p. 133 (arrests).
[276] Russell, *Parliaments and English Politics*, p. 92.

5th and 15th February, 1621 clearly showed that the House of Commons was not prepared to accept the limitations on its freedom of speech initially set out by the King and the Lord Chancellor'.[277] Throughout the first session of the Parliament of 1621, the Commons made it clear that they would resist any further attempt to restrain their liberty of speech: in the second session they put this resistance into practice.[278]

The second session: November–December 1621[279]

The second session of the Parliament of 1621 barely lasted a month, but in this short time some of the most important debates on freedom of speech in all the early Stuart Parliaments took place. At first it seemed that the session would be rather calm than otherwise: in his opening speech Lord Keeper Williams gave explicit sanction to the Commons to discuss foreign affairs; indeed, he instructed them that the session was called in order to deal with war.[280] Even this could have been seen as ominous, however: the Commons had proved unenthusiastic about the conflict in the first session, and being commanded about the business they should discuss had not gone down very well in previous assemblies. In addition, the Lord Keeper seasoned his speech with a warning that 'the form of proceedinge must be ancient and not Moderne, without importune Herangues, malitious divertions'.[281] Despite his instructions and warnings, the Commons at first dealt with domestic matters, and seemed more inclined to debate what they saw as the excessively lenient treatment of English Catholics than the possible war against Spain. Only Alford questioned the implications of Williams's address for the Commons' liberty of speech, noting that the proclamation against lavish or licentious speech had been reissued during the recess.[282] He wondered how easily the sudden call for counsel could sit with apparent restrictions on parliamentary speech: 'we are not a fit parliament to treat of these great matters for the Palatinate and the rest are matters of state, but there is a proclamation to forbid us to treat of state matters'.[283] Not only that; misinformation still dogged the Commons, he claimed, and attempts to clear members of excessive speech had failed: no-one should

---

[277] Thompson, *The Debate on Freedom of Speech*, p. 15.
[278] For this argument, see ibid., p. 16.
[279] For claims by Gondomar about the extent of his involvement in the failure of this session, see the letter to the Infanta Isabella printed in Pursell, 'War or Peace?', pp. 165–78.
[280] 21 November 1621: *CD 1621*, IV, 423–5.   [281] Ibid., 425.
[282] The proclamation had been reissued (with revisions) on 26 July 1621; see *Stuart Royal Proclamations, volume I*, ed. by Larkin and Hughes, pp. 519–21.
[283] 23 November 1621: *CD 1621*, II, 441.

be imprisoned for 'speaking his mind freely here for his country's good', but 'Mr. Hoskins was freed here yet committed. Sir Edwin Sandys was freed here yet restrained.'[284] All Calvert could do was (rather wearily, one suspects) reiterate that the proclamation did not apply to Parliament but to alehouses and taverns – 'I hope this is neither alehouse nor tavern' – and to assure the House that Sandys was not committed for Parliament business.[285] Sandys's arrest was raised again on 1 December, when several members, including Spencer and Mallory, tried to pursue the question of what state their liberties were left in by this peremptory act of punishment. It is clear from these speeches that even at this stage of the session MPs were jealous of their freedom and alert to any attempts to restrain it. Spencer declared that 'our privileges are broken which are and ought to be dearer to us than our lives', while Mallory reminded the House of its responsibility to posterity: 'we are intrusted for our country. If we lose our privileges, we betray it; if we give way to this [Sandys's imprisonment], we lose our privileges and losing them we deserve to be hanged.'[286] Several members, including Sandys's brother Sir Samuel Sandys, tried to close down the discussion, believing that it was provocative: to others this could simply look like the kind of servile fear that restraints on speech would necessarily foster.[287]

It was not the case of Sandys, however, but a motion put by Sir George Goring that provoked the outright battle over free speech. On 29 November Goring moved that the Commons' advice on war should take the form of a resolution that would be sent to the king. It should declare that 'if the King of Spain withdraw not his forces from the Palatinate and come not to the King's proposition, let us petition for war against him and we will assist [the king]'.[288] This motion was added to the petition for the proper use of the recusancy laws, with an added petition for Prince Charles to be married to a Protestant: it returned to the House on 3 December. In reply to the misgivings of some MPs, it was argued that the Commons were doing exactly as Williams had asked, and giving counsel about war; moreover, they were not prescribing action to the king but, as Brooke put it 'we only present a humble petition desiring his Majesty to think of the fittest course, less than which we cannot do'.[289] Throughout their debate, the Commons regarded the statements on war and the prince's marriage as all of a piece

---

[284] Ibid.   [285] Ibid.   [286] Ibid., 483–4.
[287] Ibid., 485–6.   [288] Ibid., 474; v, 225.
[289] Ibid., II, 494. See pp. 487–98 for the debate on the petition. Phelips remembered that 'The kinge sayd to us at Whitt Hall, Speake freely unto me, Lett me trulie knowe what is good for my people' (ibid. v, 230).

with the recusancy petition of which they were part. As Coke put it, while marriages and alliances were certainly *arcana imperii*, this was not a petition of right requiring an answer (which he would not have supported), but a petition of grace, and the writ of summons was their guide in determining whether the Commons should offer counsel on the threat of Catholicism, foreign and domestic: 'the king calleth the Parliament *pro magnis arduis et urgentibus negociis nos statum et defensionem ecclesiae concernentibus etc.* Now judge if ever cause were more urgent than this or did concern the state, kingdom and commonwealth. *Ecclesiam Anglianam* [*sic*] are the words of the writ and doth not this concern religion?'[290] A humble excusing clause was even added to the end of the document.[291]

This is not the place to deal with the origins of Goring's motion. Zaller has shown that he was acting on Buckingham's instructions, and that it is likely that the duke was either attempting to break relations between king and Parliament (as he would later be accused of having done in 1624) or trying to cover all the bases at a time when both war and Charles's marriage were still open questions.[292] Whatever the faction-based motive for the motion, its results were explosive. Somehow James (who was at Newmarket) heard (or, most likely, saw a draft) of the petition before it was even delivered to him and sent a furious letter to the House through the Speaker. As he had in previous sessions, he accused a small number of firebrands of reaching beyond their station:

we have heard by divers reports, to our great grief, that our distance from the Houses of Parliament caused by our indisposition of health hath emboldened some fiery and popular spirits of some of the Commons to argue and debate publicly of matters far above their reach and capacity, tending to our high dishonour and breach of prerogative royal.[293]

The Commons were not to meddle with 'mysteries of state', to discuss the Prince's marriage, or to speak disparagingly of the King of Spain; and they should know that 'we think ourself free and able to punish any man's misdemeanours in Parliament, as well during their sitting as after'. What Phelips called 'this soul-killing letter'[294] sent the House into a state of angry dismay, with Hakewill quoting the Apology of 1604: 'the prerogatives of

---

[290] Ibid., II, 497.
[291] 'This is the sum and effect of our humble declaration which (no way intending to press upon your Majesty's most undoubted and regal prerogative) we do with the fullness of all duty and obedience humbly submit to your most princely consideration': ibid., 498.
[292] Zaller, *The Parliament of 1621*, p. 152.
[293] J. R. Tanner, *Constitutional Documents of the Reign of James I A.D. 1603–1625, with an historical commentary* (Cambridge: Cambridge University Press, 1930), p. 279.
[294] *CJ*, I, 658.

kings increase but our privileges are at an eternal stand'.[295] Members recalled that the only reason they had addressed foreign policy was that they had been 'incited' by the Lords, and that there were many precedents for the Commons petitioning the king about prerogative matters.[296] Coke was not alone in worrying about how far the king meant to take his restriction: 'wee must talke of no matters of government nor of matters that have their due motion in other Courts. This troubles me. I knowe not how farr this maye be stretched.'[297] Still alarmed at the evidence that their proceedings were being (as they saw it) misreported to the king, the House resolved to send a second petition to the king explaining that they had looked into the matters contained in their previous petition because they saw them as connected with the defence of the Palatinate. Now they asked him to send a reply only to the main body of that first petition, dealing with the recusancy laws. But they also needed to confront the king's abridgement of their rights, and begged for them to be confirmed in a sentence whose length and whose qualifying clauses perhaps point at the degree to which frankness and duty seemed to be slipping apart:

> your Majesty, by the general words of your letter, seemeth to restrain us from intermeddling with matters of government, or particulars which have their motion in courts of justice, the generality of which words in the largeness of the extent thereof, – as we hope beyond your Majesty's intentions, – might involve those things which are the proper subjects of parliamentary action and discourse; and whereas your Majesty's letter doth seem to abridge us of the ancient liberty of parliament for freedom of speech, jurisdiction, and just censure of the House, and other proceedings there; wherein, we trust in God, we shall never transgress the bounds of loyal and dutiful subjects; a liberty which we assure ourselves so wise and just a King will not infringe, the same being our undoubted right and inheritance received from our ancestors, and without which we cannot freely debate nor clearly discern of things in question before us, nor truly inform your Majesty, wherein we have been confirmed by your Majesty's former gracious speeches and messages; we are, therefore, now again enforced humbly to beseech your Majesty to renew and allow the same, and thereby take away the doubts and scruples your Majesty's late letter to our Speaker hath brought upon us.[298]

This petition struggles to combine assurances of the Commons' faith in James's good intentions with assertions of their rights: the words 'seemeth' and 'seem' are repeated; the Commons are sure that 'so wise and just a

---

[295] 5 December 1621: *CD 1621*, II, 501.

[296] Digges, Phelips, and Coke reminded the House that the Lords had encouraged discussion of foreign affairs: ibid., 503, 504; ibid., v, 233. Crew and Wentworth cited precedents: ibid., II, 503.

[297] Ibid., v, 233.

[298] Edward Nicholas, *Proceedings and Debates in the House of Commons in 1620 and 1621*, 2 volumes (Oxford, 1766), volume II, pp. 289–300.

King' as James could not *really* be infringing their freedom; it is only the
confusion that they find themselves in about the real meaning of his message
that 'enforces' the Commons to ask the king to renew their privileges. At
the same time, though, alongside these escape clauses (providing an escape
for James, not the Commons) is a thoroughly determined assertion of the
Commons' rights that declares in a subclause that they are 'our undoubted
right and inheritance received from our ancestors, and without which we
cannot freely debate nor clearly discern of things in question before us'.
The petition was approved on 8 December, but having dispatched it the
Commons were uncertain whether they should carry on with their business:
as the second petition asked, how could they achieve anything if their liberty
of speech was curtailed? If they were not allowed to discuss the prerogative
then how could they have the conference that the Lords wanted on the
monopolies bill? Phelips explained that 'if we have not liberty of speech,
we have not power to make laws'.[299] The king only made matters worse
by sending a message in advance of a reply to the petition that urged the
House to continue with their business and not to fear for their privileges.
Phelips noted that 'our liberties are hereby strooke at', while Crew said that
'wee are in a terrible Dilemma either to forfeit our liberties by dealinge
onlie in such busines as the kinge shall appoint, or to disobey the kings
command. This is a great wound to our priviledges.'[300] Freedom of speech
was being identified increasingly with the Commons' – and the peoples' –
liberty more generally conceived.

   A much greater wound was inflicted when the king's answer was finally
read in the House on 14 December. Where the Commons' second petition
had tried to blend conciliation with assertiveness, the king bluntly put them
straight on all the issues they had raised. They had claimed not to trespass
on his prerogative in the apologetic clause of their first message, but in fact
they had done little else, he said. To claim that because they were asked to
vote supply for a possible war they were able to advise him about it was
absurd: would a merchant be licensed to counsel the king if he had lent him
money to pay the troops? And as for their privilege of freedom of speech,
'we cannot allow of the style, calling it "your ancient and undoubted right
and inheritance", but could rather have wished that ye had said that your
privileges were derived from the grace and permission of our ancestors and
us (for most of them grow from precedents, which shews rather a toleration
than inheritance)'.[301] He did conclude by promising to be as careful of their

[299] 10 December 1621, *CD 1621*, II, 508.   [300] 12 December 1621: ibid., V, 235.
[301] The king's answer of 11 December 1621, to the petition of 9 December, in Tanner, *Constitutional
Documents*, pp. 283–7, at p. 286.

privileges as any of his ancestors: but James's idea of what this care consisted in was clearly different from that of many MPs. Despite the acerbic tone of this message, the Commons were so relieved at the king's promise that religion would be maintained, and so glad of any assurance about their liberties that they expressed almost as much gratitude as annoyance. But the following day the implications of James's theory of rights (with which many MPs must by now have been familiar) were noted, with considerable alarm. Mallory noted that 'the King hath sent a gracious answer but we are worse than afore, for he saith our privileges are not by inheritance and that we must not trench into his prerogative'; Phelips complained that nothing had changed since James's first Parliament, when the king had also argued that privileges were only derived from grace.[302] Crew wanted the offending section of the king's message to be read again so that everyone could be clear exactly what was being proposed in it: he argued that in contrast to James's assertion, 'our privileges are by law from our ancestors and are our due'. A protestation along the lines of the 1604 Apology was required, he went on to suggest, and in it the Commons should maintain that their liberties were by inheritance: 'if we should yield that they are permissive, the walls would witness the contrary as in Magna Carta'.[303] Coke likewise said that 'I will not dispute with my Maister for his words, but when the king says he can not allowe our liberties of right, this strikes at the roote. We serve here for thousands and ten thowsands.'[304] For Coke, Parliament's representative status meant that if MPs' liberties were attacked, so were those of the people. The matter was referred to a committee. On Monday 17 December the king, on the advice of Lord Keeper Williams, sent yet another message, this time intended to be conciliatory.[305] But the Commons were so sensitive by now to the constitutional implications of James's words that his attempt to allow that there were in fact some privileges of 'undoubted right', as well as those of grace, was seen for the false concession it was. Because the only privileges of 'undoubted right' that he acknowledged were those confirmed by 'law or statute', anything that was derived from precedent or custom was ruled out. Furthermore, as Zaller writes, since statutes required the consent of the crown to become law, 'this argument preserved intact the principle that all privileges, whether permanent or permissive, derived ultimately from the power of the Crown'.[306] As for his previous message's response to the phrase 'undoubted right and privilege', James explained that 'the plain truth is that we cannot with patience endure our subjects to use such anti-monarchical

[302] 15 December 1621: *CD 1621*, II, 521–2, 524.   [303] Ibid., 525.
[304] Ibid., v, 240.   [305] For the message, see ibid., II, 528–30.
[306] Zaller, *The Parliament of 1621*, p. 173.

words to us concerning their liberties'. The Commons, he advised, should get on with their business 'cheerfully', 'rejecting the curious wrangling of lawyers upon words and syllables'.[307] Words and syllables were not such trivial matters as James pretended to think, however, and MPs were aware of this. Phelips riposted that he did not love curiosity of syllables and words 'but in our liberties', and it had been precisely on questions of definition, of precedent, and of the interpretation of key words like 'right', 'inheritance', and 'grace' that the arguments about freedom of speech were based, from James's first Parliament onwards. The Commons refused to admit that their liberty of speech, and thus their ability and obligation to counsel the king, derived from his grant, which could be removed at any point. To concede this point would make them not just toothless (there was little evidence that they wanted to bite the king's ankles in any case), but voiceless, the kind of council that could, in Bacon's words, only 'sing him a Song of *Placebo*'.[308] They would be subject to the king's will and thus, effectively, slaves. Hakewill argued that the king's attempt to abrogate the privileges to his own power was mistaken: 'the privileges of this howse are the principall parte of the Lawe of the land . . . and therefore we hold them not by grace but by Lawe and right'.[309] The request for privileges at the opening of each Parliament was unfortunate, he said: it was only a 'matter of good manners', and the Commons' liberty of speech was a right before it began to be petitioned for.[310] Perhaps it should be left out. He went on to quote the Apology of 1604, urging that a committee should produce a similar document, and was supported by Strode, Coke, Alford, and Wentworth.[311]

The king's final message arrived in the House on 18 December, threatening the Commons that if they did not complete the laws they had been working on (the bill for the continuance of statutes and the General Pardon), their 'slackness' would force him to end the session. This last attempt to prescribe the Commons' business only encouraged them in their work to frame a protestation to assert and protect their liberty of speech. Precedents were cited to show that there was no commandment that the Commons should not treat of specific subjects, no 'negative bound'; Crew complained that the writ of summons had been ignored, and Coke demanded that MPs should 'speak of war and peace and marriage' as they found occasion to

---

[307] *CD 1621*, II, 529–30.

[308] Francis Bacon, 'Of Counsell', in *The Essayes or Counsels, Civill and Morall*, ed. by Michael Kiernan (Oxford: Clarendon Press, 1985), pp. 63–8, at p. 68. See chapter 1 above.

[309] Quoted in Zaller, *The Parliament of 1621*, pp. 173–4. [310] *CJ*, I, 667.

[311] *CJ*, I, 667: 'An humble Declaration to his Majesty, that we hold our Privileges as our Inheritance. Readeth Part of the Apology, made in this Point, in the first Parliament of the King. – A Committee for Privileges; and yet to go on with Business.'

do so.[312] Sir Nathaniel Rich put the case clearly, providing a brief *narratio* of the situation before making the crucial distinction between liberty and licence:

> let us first recollect what liberties have bene impeached and then to provide the remedie. Concerninge freedom of speech, that hath bene impeached in matter and manner. Meddle not with this business, goe to this busines first (by which wee are restrayned from the choise of our busines). When I speake of freedome of speech, I meane not Licentiousnes and exorbitancie, but speech without servile feare or, as it were, under the rodde.[313]

The Protestation drawn up by the House and entered into the *Commons Journal* resolved into only a few pithy sentences all the principles concerning the nature of their freedom of speech on which they would not budge. It began by asserting that the Commons' liberties were 'the undoubted birthright and inheritance of the subjects of England', repeating the very terms that had so infuriated James. Quoting the writ of summons, it went on to state that 'the arduous and urgent affairs concerning the king, state and defence of the realm, and of the Church of England' were 'proper subjects and matters of counsel and debate in parliament': unlike the Apology, the Protestation thus specified the subjects that Parliament could treat, giving it a great scope of interest, and in citing the writ it bolstered its claims with a document that James had himself approved at the opening of every Parliament.[314] In treating these matters, every MP had freedom of speech, and Parliament was able to decide the order of its own business: there was to be no more instruction about what the Commons should be doing with their time. Finally, every MP had freedom from punishment for their speech, unless that punishment came from the House itself. Were a member to be questioned in any way then the case should be presented to the king by the Commons as a whole before the king gave 'credence to any private information'.[315] The Protestation challenged James on virtually every point with which he had criticised the Commons: it gave the lie direct to his constitutional theory as outlined in his various messages in 1621 and before. Nor did it simply demand freedom to debate: as Zaller notes, it claimed the right of 'freedom of speech to propound, treat, reason and bring to conclusion' the matters before the Commons – to make decisions, and to pass laws. The Protestation was unlike the Apology in many ways, but they differed most importantly in their status as documents. The Apology shows

---

[312] *CD 1621*, II, 539, 540–41, 541.   [313] Ibid., V, 242–3.
[314] See Zaller, *The Parliament of 1621*, p. 181.
[315] For the text of the Protestation, see *The Stuart Constitution*, ed. by Kenyon, pp. 42–3.

us what some MPs were thinking about freedom of speech in 1604; it gives us an insight into the possible ways in which that right was conceived. The Protestation, though, was approved by the House and entered into the *Commons Journal*: it came after many days of debate in the House, and as the result of the explicit debate between the king and the Commons about the origin and nature of the rights of Parliament. It set down as an official declaration of the House the position that 'the liberties, franchises, privileges and jurisdictions of parliament are the undoubted birthright and inheritance of the subjects of England': the liberties of the House were identified with the liberties of the subject, and an alternative source for the freedom of that people from the grace of the king was thus asserted. Asserted, and not requested. In the Commons' Protestation of 1621 freedom of speech is the foundation of the subject's liberties.

After he announced the dissolution of Parliament on 19 December, James replied to the Protestation by tearing it from the *Commons Journal*. This act, along with the imprisonment of Coke, Phelips, Pym, Hakewill, and Mallory after the dissolution, demonstrated to John Chamberlain that '*vanae sine viribus irae*, and that there is no disputing nor contesting with supreme authority'.[316] Russell has written that in December 1621 the Protestation was 'a powerless piece of paper, a last vain protest by a dying Parliament'.[317] This is certainly how James wanted it to be seen, as he confirmed in a bitter proclamation explaining the reasons for the Parliament's dissolution that was published on 6 January 1621/2.[318] The king showed that his power to control the Commons' speech was undiminished by the Protestation: the act of removing their words from the official record of their proceedings was a material demonstration of this. However, the Commons in 1621 demonstrated that their position on freedom of speech had hardened even as attempts to control it increased. There was no organised opposition to the king or his policies, but – perhaps more importantly – a constitutional theory in direct opposition to James's was outlined in the course of the Commons' description of free speech as their undoubted right and as vital to the operation of counsel.[319] Again, the neo-roman distinction between

---

[316] Chamberlain to Carleton, 19 January, 1622: *Letters*, volume II, p. 421.

[317] Russell, *Parliaments and English Politics*, p. 142.

[318] 'A Proclamation declaring his Majesties pleasure concerning the dissolving of the present Convention of Parliament', Westminster, 6 January 1622, in *Stuart Royal Proclamations*, volume I, ed. by Larkin and Hughes, pp. 527–34; see footnote 16 above.

[319] D'Ewes and Chamberlain expressed some of the anxiety that the ending of the session provoked, with D'Ewes writing in his Journal on 2 January 1621/2 that 'our talke of his Maiesty was very broad, both for imprisoning Sir Edward Cooke and also for his intention to breake upp the parliament to the great discontent of all his truly religious and loyal subiects', and Chamberlain writing to

free men and slaves was vital to this theory: if freedom of speech was only granted by grace of the crown, and was therefore a privilege that could be rescinded by the mere decision of the crown (as opposed to a right), then MPs were left at the mercy of the crown in what they said: they were in a condition of servitude.

1624–1628: NEW COUNSELS AND EVIL COUNSELLORS

1624–1626: the 'grievance of grievances'

The last Parliament of James I and the first two Parliaments of his son took place under the growing shadow of war. Although the Commons appeared in 1624 to be greatly relieved that they had been recalled at all after the angry dissolution of 1621, they soon turned their attention to what they saw as the dangers of bad counsel – an endemic problem, they thought, but one that was concentrated in the figure of the Duke of Buckingham. Throughout these three sessions, freedom of speech was treated almost exclusively in relation to the question of counsel and its competing sources. Many of the arguments introduced drew heavily on the theories of counsel that I have already described in chapter 1. Evil counsel, as I have shown, was seen as dangerous by its propensity to draw the prince from the path of virtue; yet focusing on it could also be used as a way of offering indirect criticisms of a prince's own weakness – his willingness to listen to bad counsel, and inability to identify it as flattery rather than frankness, was a sign that his virtue was already flawed. Charles I in particular was aware of this latter point, and was sensitive to the implications of attacks on his favourite, as became very clear in 1626.

James's last Parliament began auspiciously, with an apparent concession from the king in his opening speech over the liberties of Parliament. He declared that the Parliament had been called to advise him on the treaties with Spain, the match for Charles, and the Palatinate, explicitly allowing that these were proper subjects for discussion in the House. He also sanctioned Coke's interpretation of the writ of summons in the 1621 Protestation.[320] Accommodations had been reached between some of the most outspoken members of the 1621 Parliament and Buckingham and Charles, who wanted to manage this Parliament into a position of bellicosity appropriate

---

Carleton on 16 February that 'the times are daungerous and the world growes tender and jealous of free speach'. See *The Diary of Sir Simonds D'Ewes (1622–1624)*, ed. by E. Bourcier (Paris: Didier, 1974), pp. 55–6; Chamberlain, *Letters*, volume II, p. 423.

[320] *CJ*, I, 670; see also Russell, *Parliaments and English Politics*, p. 155.

to the determination they felt about war with Spain, after the collapse of the negotiations for the Spanish Match.[321] In these circumstances, with a Parliament ready to get on with passing bills in order to take something home to the country and wipe out the memory of 1621, and a sufficient degree of anti-Spanish feeling to get some kind of a war under way, freedom of speech took a back seat.[322] The only explicit and lengthy discussion of it took place on 27 February, when Eliot, Alford, and Seymour spoke out. Eliot raised the issue of the imprisonments after the last session, arguing that it was misreporting and misreporting alone that had caused the hostility between the king and Parliament. Alford said that he agreed, but wanted to put off Eliot's motion for a 'Tie of Secrecy' until 'Time serves'; then he would support an act to confirm the Commons' privileges.[323] Seymour asked for a review of the Protestation of 1621, suggesting that it should be re-entered in the *Commons Journal*, and wanted the members who had been imprisoned to clear up the question of whether they had been punished for Parliament business. Coke agreed that freedom of speech was 'the Quintessence of the other Four Essences', but his recommendation to proceed with a petition of grace to preserve the House's liberties was, along with Seymour's suggestions, referred to a committee, from which it did not return. Freedom of speech was hardly raised again, with most members wanting to look forward rather than back.[324] Even the question of impositions was followed up without reference to parliamentary privilege, and James did not attempt to restrict the discussion.[325] In 1624 the Commons saw no clear and present danger threatening their freedom of speech, and were concerned to pass some legislation; at the same time, their quietness may have been the sign of a realisation that, in the aftermath of 1621, their options were limited. They could, it appeared, either have Parliaments or they could argue about freedom of speech and be dissolved. Their responsibilities to their countries weighed upon them: how could they be proper counsellors and representatives if they were sent home without achieving anything? This was, in fact, an argument that James himself had used. In 1624 they were able to reach an accommodation; this would be less possible as they saw the dangers of evil counsel growing under the new king.

---

[321] See ibid., pp. 148–53.

[322] However, for the argument that the Parliament of 1624 was not as pro-war as some revisionist accounts have suggested, see Michael B. Young, 'Buckingham, War, and Parliament: Revisionism Gone Too Far', *Parliamentary History* 4 (1985): 45–69. See also Mark E. Kennedy, 'Legislation, Foreign Policy, and the "Proper Business" of the Parliament of 1624', *Albion* 23:1 (Spring 1991): 41–60.

[323] *CJ*, I, 719.   [324] Ibid., Russell, *Parliaments and English Politics*, pp. 161–2.

[325] 8 April 1624: *CJ*, I, 758.

James I died in March 1625, and on his death Parliament was automatically dissolved. When Charles I recalled Parliament in June 1625, he made
his intentions for the session quite clear: he needed money for war, and he
needed it quickly. If the Commons needed any further encouragement to
be swift, he rather tactlessly went on to say, they should bear in mind the
current plague epidemic.[326] After a month the session was adjourned, and
reconvened in Oxford because of the plague still raging in London; it was
during this second sitting of the Parliament that members began properly
to address the problem of evil counsel that some of them saw as behind
the calling of Parliament. Seymour even argued that they had been set up
to fail, arguing that 'he knew no ground of this meeting unless some out
of private ends seek to put dissension between the King and his people,
and gave this advice out of ignorance or malice rather than out of any care
of the commonwealth'.[327] Asked for money to support a war that was not
yet actually being fought, MPs argued that almost all the troubles they had
suffered over the previous few years had originated in bad counsel – and
it soon became clear that the target they aimed at was Buckingham. The
king, it was suggested, put his faith in too few counsellors – and, as the
Book of Proverbs had it, 'in the multitude of counsellors there is safety'.[328]
Phelips said that the treaties with Spain, the Spanish Match, and the war

all together proceed from the counsels of those who brought his Majesty to be in
love with the deceitful face of friendship, to be seduced by the practices of that
subtle, artificial, fox-like people. He remembers with comfort that he was one of
those who suffered in that cause when we were under that ill planet by which some
man were made so powerful, that we were harassed in our liberties and imprisoned
in our person, from which himself was delivered without injuring the liberty of
the House in words or writing, and taxed with nothing but only with speaking
against the Spanish match.[329]

In his account of the Parliament Sir John Eliot gave a fuller version of
Phelips's speech, in which a comparison with the decline of Rome into
tyranny makes the dangers of bad counsel even clearer:

counsels were there [in the state] monopolized, as the general liberties elsewhere.
That the whole wisdom was supposed to be comprehended in one man. That
he, being master of the favor, was likewise master of all business. *Nihil unquam
prisci et integri moris*, as Tacitus notes in the declination of the Romans, *sed exuta
aequalitate omnia unius iussa aspectare.*

---

[326] 18 June 1625: *PP 1625*, 192.   [327] 5 August 1625: ibid., 393–4.
[328] Proverbs 11:14 (King James Version); this is quoted on fol. 1ʳ of Huntington MS HM 30887, 'A
Discourse of the Priuiledge and Practice of the High Court of Parliament in England collected out
of the Common Lawes of this Land &c.', an early seventeenth-century manuscript, part of which
was printed in William Hakewill, *Modus tenendi Parliamentum* (1660).
[329] *PP 1625*, 396.

There were other similarities with the current situation, in which the Commons found themselves to be counsellors without the power to counsel: 'though there were many councillors in name, that few retained the dignity *aequales magis quam operis*, as Paterculus has it of the like, though their reputation might be somewhat yet that their authority was but small and their affections as much captived as their greatness'.[330] Coke made certain that the source of evil counsel was unmistakable, alluding to Buckingham's engrossing of high offices and stating directly that the office of Lord Admiral should be held by someone 'of great experience and judgement'.[331] When Edward Clarke objected to these attacks, he was censured by the House: the Commons were jealous of their right to criticise evil counsellors and warn the king.[332] On 10 and 11 August the attacks grew fiercer, with Coke bringing up precedents for the punishment of evil counsellors. He argued that there were two leaks that would sink any ship of state: 'a bottomless sieve' and 'solum et malum consilium'. Both currently assailed England, with the bad counsel consisting in part in the request for more subsidies after the Commons had already given.[333] Sir Guy Palmes invoked the precedent of Empson and Dudley, perhaps the most notorious of evil counsellors, who were hanged for their actions.[334] On 11 August Buckingham was finally referred to by name, by Seymour – as Eliot wrote, 'this first direct nomination of the Duke . . . took off all vizards and disguises in which their discourses had been masked'.[335] On the following day Parliament was dissolved. The attacks on Buckingham had not had the full support of the House, but even Sherland, who warned the Commons that it was unclear how a counsellor could be sanctioned without the approval of the king, maintained the necessity of giving frank counsel. Arguing for the better prosecution of the recusancy laws, he gave a powerful historical example:

Henry the Fifth was a wise and potent prince, not inferior to any since the Conquest, and yet what did his subjects unto him? In the first year of his reign they found a remissness in the execution of the laws. Upon which they spoke plain language and prayed him then, in parliament, to put the laws in execution better than his father had done. Which, though sharp, was good and wholesome counsel and followed by that King, which likewise if his Majesty will now do he may enjoy like honor and prosperity and be both loved at home and feared abroad.[336]

---

[330] Sir John Eliot, *Negotium Posterorum*, in ibid., 542. [331] Ibid., 403.

[332] Clarke made his objection on 6 August; he made his submission and was cleared on the 8th: ibid., 413, 424.

[333] 10 August 1625: ibid., 446.

[334] *PP 1625*, p. 451. Russell suggests that this allusion was the cause of Palmes's being pricked as a sheriff in 1626 and thus prevented from sitting in Parliament: *Parliaments and English Politics*, p. 268.

[335] *PP 1625*, 563. [336] Ibid., 566.

At the end of the Parliament of 1625 Phelips had responded to a suggestion for 'the acquitting of those who were likely to be questioned for that which they had spoken' by pointing out that this had done little good in the past, as he could witness from personal experience.[337] So it proved to be in the aftermath of that Parliament; though punishment this time came in the form of exclusion from the House by being appointed sheriff: Coke, Seymour, and Palmes, as well as Phelips, were all dealt with in this way.[338] Buckingham hoped this might defuse the campaign against him, but he was over-optimistic. In fact, in the next Parliament the Commons used their perceived control over supply to bargain for the duke's prosecution.[339] The campaign against Buckingham was by now a common project of the Commons and his opponents at court; I will not discuss the complexities of this campaign in any detail here, but focus rather on the way in which the Commons continued to press for the removal of an evil counsellor and, in doing so, to deploy the inseparable languages of counsel and freedom of speech.

Although the Commons began their attack on Buckingham in 1626 tentatively – perhaps, as Russell suggests, through 'alarm at their own temerity' – from the start they continued to employ the language of evil counsel in their debates about the favourite.[340] On 25 February Wilde listed the causes of the kingdom's evils: 'The misemploying of our monies the misguiding of our great action the miscounselings and ill counseling, the refusing of the cordial counsel of parliament. We are not to judge things by their events, but when great things are managed by single counsel or private respects, they are to be looked into.'[341] On 10 and 11 March the proceedings gathered pace, with Clement Coke's speech on the precedence of domestic over foreign oppressions and Dr Turner's delivery of six 'queries' about the duke.[342] The king sent a message accusing Coke and Turner of having uttered seditious words, which in turn provoked the House into a defence of their liberty to offer frank counsel. When called upon to explain himself, Turner justified his speech by asserting that he 'spoke not for any particular ends but out of loyalty and sincerity for the good of his country', and gave precedents for taking action against someone on the basis of 'common fame'.[343] When Sir William Walter argued on 20 March that the cause of

[337] 12 August 1625: ibid., 476.   [338] See Russell, *Parliaments and English Politics*, p. 268.
[339] Notably in the proposed Remonstrance to the king: see *PP 1626*, II, 436–41.
[340] Russell, *Parliaments and English Politics*, p. 273.
[341] *PP 1626*, II, 149.   [342] Ibid., 250, 261–2.
[343] Ibid., 299. The argument in favour of common fame as a justifiable basis for prosecution was supported by reference to the case of Bishop Neile in 1614, and that of the Duke of Suffolk, de la Pole, under Henry VI.

the kingdom's evils was that 'all the King's counsel rides upon one horse', he described the key qualities of good counsellors (drawing on Exodus 18:21). They should be drawn from the full range of the nobility, not 'upstarts and a night's growth'; they should not delegate their own duties to others; they should not 'incline to false worship' (a clear dig at Buckingham's Catholic relations); they should not flatter; they should shun bribery; there should be many of them ('where there is abundance of counsel, there is peace and safety'); they should only deal with minor affairs; and they should not be young men.[344] Walter's eight key points are commonplaces of the literature of counsel, and show how these general strictures could be applied to a specific case: as a result, Buckingham was shown to be the very epitome of the bad counsellor.

As the Commons continued their discussions of Buckingham's abuses, the king called both Houses to Whitehall. The speech delivered on his behalf by the Lord Keeper, Sir Thomas Coventry, levelled a familiar charge against the Commons: that what they called liberty was in fact licentiousness. Certain members were using the pretence of parliamentary liberty to violate the king's honour and his 'regal rights'. Coventry said that 'his Majesty does not forget that the parliament is his council and therefore it ought to have the liberty and freedom of a council, but his Majesty also understands the difference between counselling and controlling, between liberty and abuse of liberty'. The Commons were to cease proceedings against Buckingham immediately.[345] After the Lord Keeper had finished, the king suggested that unless the Commons became more amenable to his demands for supply, their opportunities to counsel would be thoroughly curtailed: 'remember', he said, 'that parliaments are altogether in my power for the calling, sitting, and continuance of them. Therefore as I find the fruits either good or evil they are for to continue or not to be.'[346] Although Buckingham tried to palliate the House in a conference with the Lords the following day, denying that the king was putting an ultimatum to the Commons, this was hard to believe, and several members spoke out against the perceived threat to their liberties. It was agreed that a remonstrance was necessary.[347] The remonstrance, which was delivered to the king on 5 April, blamed misinformation for Charles's annoyance. It also explained that the House

---

[344] Ibid., 324. Copies of Walter's speech circulated in manuscript separates; see ibid., 324, n. 25.
[345] 29 March 1626: ibid., 392.   [346] Ibid., 395.
[347] See ibid., 400–34. On 30 March Eliot said that 'the King commands us no[t] touch upon that great man; if this granted, our privilege gone. Has not the examination of all subjects been done in this place? . . . For supply, not now to think of it, for if our privileges denied we can debate neither this nor anything else' (404).

had dealt with the speeches of both Turner and Clement Coke – any possible offence had been explained to the Commons' satisfaction. More importantly, the Commons needed to be able to investigate the duke of Buckingham: it was their right, and it was for the good of the kingdom:

> it has been the ancient, constant, and undoubted right and usage of Parliaments to question and complain of all persons, of what degree or quality soever, found grievous in commonwealth and who have abused the trust and power committed to them by their sovereign; a course not only approved in your late father's days but by frequent precedents in the times of your most famous progenitors appearing in histories. Without which liberty no private man, no servant to a king, perhaps no councillor, can be a means to call great officers into question for their misdemeanours, without exposing himself to great enmity. But the commonwealth might languish under this pressure without redress. And whatsoever we shall do accordingly this Parliament, we doubt not but it shall redound to the honour of your crown and welfare of your subjects.[348]

The king refused to respond to the remonstrance, and adjourned the House for Easter. In the period immediately after this recess it appears that there was some hope of a compromise, and on 29 April Charles even allowed the Commons to proceed with their action against Buckingham.[349] The case of the Earl of Bristol in the House of Lords had led to additional accusations being levelled against the duke, however – including that of having poisoned James I with a plaster or potion. When Digges and Eliot spoke at the conference with the Lords about the articles of impeachment that would be preferred, they mentioned this suspicion. Eliot even compared Buckingham at length to the notorious Sejanus, a touchstone for evil counsel (and also accused of rising to power as a poisoner).[350] Incensed at this comparison, and at the implication that he might have been an accessory to his father's murder, Charles committed both Digges and Eliot to the Tower; the Commons was in uproar at this latest assault on their liberties.[351] Sir Dudley Carleton's attempt to calm the situation by warning the House that in other countries 'when they changed their parliamentary liberty into tumultuary endeavors, it was changed by the sovereign to another form of government' and that 'new counsels' would be sought if they continued only increased the anger felt by MPs.[352]

Charles understood that the attack on Buckingham was an implicit criticism of him – as D'Ewes wrote, Eliot's comparison of the duke to Sejanus

---

[348] Ibid., 433–4.
[349] See Russell, *Parliaments and English Politics*, pp. 293–306; *PP 1626*, III, 98 (James's message).
[350] Ibid., pp. 220–4. Eliot's parallel with Sejanus is at p. 223.
[351] Digges was released on 15 May, and Eliot on 19 May.   [352] 12 May 1626: ibid., 241–2.

'must intend himself [the king] Tiberius', and this was hardly flattering.[353] He was unwilling to accept the Commons' separation of their criticisms of his favourite from application to the king, as James had done in the case of Bacon in 1621, and this broke down one of the only mechanisms by which the Commons could express serious grievances about misgovernment. They reacted suspiciously to Charles's claim that Eliot was punished for matters 'extrajudicial to this House', and saw the imprisonments as a direct restriction on their freedom of speech.[354] Wilde saw the king's prerogative as virtually wiping out the liberties of Parliament, rather than existing in a condition of 'reciprocal relation and respect', as should be the case. He argued that the Speaker's request for freedom of speech at the opening of Parliament was a formal confirmation of an existing right, not a true request that could be granted or withheld: 'a proclamation does not make a law, but declare[s] a law; and the coronation does declare the right of succession. So our Speaker does not pray our liberty of speech from the King but declares it.'[355] Sir George More argued that to have their freedom of speech restrained would reduce the Commons to a condition of servitude, invoking arguments we have seen in earlier Parliaments: 'the great happiness of the subject and the honor of the King: that he rules over free men not bondmen. *Ergo* this House has always been careful to preserve their liberties.'[356]

Even as proceedings against the Earls of Bristol and Arundel went slowly ahead in the House of Lords, the Commons pressed for another confirmation of the liberties that seemed so vulnerable – and the likelihood of supply being voted became more unlikely than it had ever been. In the ongoing debates over the House's freedom of speech the liberties of Parliament were again identified with the 'liberty of the whole kingdom',[357] and even before the king had sent a message forbidding the Commons from writing to the University of Cambridge to discourage them from electing Buckingham as Chancellor another remonstrance was considered necessary.[358] This was the document in which Buckingham was blamed for the dissolution of the previous Parliament; it also laid all the grievances of the kingdom at his door, and complained of the imprisonment of Digges and

[353] D'Ewes to Stuteville, 11 May 1626: Thomas Birch (compiler), *The Court and Times of Charles the First*, 2 volumes (London: H. Colbourn, 1848), volume 1, p. 101.

[354] 16–17 May 1626: *PP 1626*, 111, 265 (king's use of 'extrajudicial'), 269–78. Eliot was questioned about being seen in the vicinity of Gray's Inn, and having met foreign ambassadors, both of which charges he denied (see 265, n. 4).

[355] 17 May 1626: *PP 1626*, 111, 271.   [356] Ibid., 277.

[357] Sir Nathaniel Rich, on 22 May 1626: ibid., 304.

[358] See ibid., 302–432. The king's message was sent on 6 June (380).

Eliot and the language of 'new counsels'. Buckingham, it said, was 'of all other our most insupportable grievance', and until he was removed there could be no hope of the country's health.[359] The remonstrance was delivered to Charles on 14 June. He promised an answer to it the following morning, but instead on the 15th Parliament was dissolved. The next day, the king issued a proclamation forbidding the 'publishing, dispersing, and reading' of the remonstrance.[360]

In 1626 the Commons focused their attention on the Duke of Buckingham's evil counsel, which was regarded as leading the king and the kingdom into danger. The campaign against the duke was orchestrated by those around the Earl of Pembroke and, as such, was an instance of the factional politics that characterised the age. Yet at the same time, this attack on an over-mighty subject involved serious assertions of the Commons' right to act as counsellors themselves and, as a result, their right to freedom of speech. This was not simply a strategy for pursuing the aims of noble patrons of some members: the arguments that were advanced, the language that was deployed, and the concerns aired by MPs, were all familiar from previous Parliaments, and they show that by this point many in the Commons saw their liberties – and perhaps the very institution of Parliament – as under serious threat. It will not do to blame the failure of the Parliaments of the 1620s on the Commons' inability to offer good counsel: they saw no means by which they could do so.[361] Charles I acted in a more peremptory fashion than his father had, and he eschewed James's tendency to enter into arguments with his Parliament over constitutional theory. The Commons, on the other hand, continued to draw on precedents that had been appealed to, or even established, in the previous twenty-five years. They would do this again in 1628, in the aftermath of the Forced Loan and in the face of the Five Knights' Case, devoting much of that Parliament to a full-scale defence of English liberties based on the neo-roman theories of property that had been advanced in 1610.[362] The Parliament of 1628 began

---

[359] Ibid., 436–41, quotation at 441.

[360] Ibid., 446–9. For the proclamation, see *Stuart Royal Proclamations*, ed. by Larkin and Hughes, volume II, pp. 93–5.

[361] See Kevin Sharpe, 'Introduction: Parliamentary History 1603–1629: In or out of Perspective?', in *Faction and Parliament*, ed. by Sharpe, pp. 1–42.

[362] When Charles imposed the Forced Loan in 1626 seventy gentlemen were imprisoned for refusing to subscribe. Five of them went further and issued writs of *habeas corpus*, demanding to know why they had been detained – if they were told that it was for refusing to pay the Loan, then their trial would, they hoped, be a test of the Loan's legality. However, they were simply told that they had been detained by the king's special command, as was the crown's right in matters of national security. The judges refused to pass judgement in the face of this, and remanded the defendants in custody pending a further hearing, thus avoiding endorsing either the knights' refusal to pay or

with determined defences of parliamentary freedom of speech and assertions of the importance of counsel from Seymour, Phelips, and Digges.[363]
This chapter does not analyse that Parliament in detail, since after the ini-
tial debates freedom of speech was eclipsed by much wider discussions of
the liberties of the people. As I have argued, though, freedom of speech
was a concern that led many MPs to identify their liberties with those
of the commonwealth at large. Along with the increasing fear of popery
fostered by the rise of the Arminian or anti-Calvinist party in the Church
of England, this attention to the liberties of the people – and especially to
those concerned with their property – led ultimately to the drafting of the
Petition of Right in 1628, and to Charles's decision in 1629 to rule without Parliament. It also led to what was perhaps the most striking material
expression of the struggle over parliamentary speech since James erased the
1621 Protestation from the *Commons Journal*: the extraordinary scene of
the Speaker being held down in his seat while Eliot read his Protestation
against 'new counsels' at the end of the 1629 Parliament.[364]

CONCLUSION

In many ways, the story of Parliament in the period that I have discussed
here is one of discontinuity: as Russell states, 'the mood and the atmosphere of 1621–4 is completely different from that of 1626–8.'[365] Relations
between James I and his Parliaments were always more harmonious than
those between Charles I and his: in the later period England was at war,
there were serious religious divisions at home, and many perceived a drift
towards arbitrary government. The same could of course be said about the
way in which freedom of speech was debated and defined in the Parliaments
of the years from 1603 to 1629: the nature of the debates varied according to
the concerns that faced MPs. Yet at the same time there is both continuity
and development in ideas about parliamentary freedom of speech. It is during this period that a liberty whose limits were ill-defined and the request
for which was still a recent innovation was tested, discussed, defined, and
defended to an unprecedented degree. MPs used ideas drawn from both

the crown's actions in imposing the Loan. Solicitor General Heath attempted to have a judgement
in favour of the crown inserted in the records of the King's Bench after the fact, which could then
have been appealed to as a precedent, but Parliament was recalled before this could take place. See
Lockyer, *The Early Stuarts*, pp. 223–4; Richard Cust, *The Forced Loan and English Politics, 1626–1628*
(Oxford: Clarendon Press, 1987).

[363] 22 March 1628: *CD 1628*, II, 53–75.
[364] For this document, see *The Stuart Constitution*, ed. by Kenyon, p. 71.
[365] Russell, *Parliaments and English Politics*, p. 419.

medieval theories of government and the humanist reading with which many would have been familiar to argue for their status as counsellors, and for the necessity of freedom of speech to good counsel. They invoked neo-roman theories of freedom and unfreedom to show how the right to speak freely was intimately linked to their other rights both as members of Parliament and as subjects. One of the most striking aspects of the many debates about freedom of speech in this period is the way in which the liberties of Parliament are increasingly identified with the liberties of the subject: at times it seems as though one is not merely intended to underpin the other, but is meant to be extended to the other.[366] This would lead to the almost inconceivable notion that Parliament was arguing that all Englishmen could be counsellors, and speak frankly to the king. It is unlikely that many MPs would have endorsed such a notion, but if 'all Englishmen' was restricted to 'propertied Englishmen', then we may not be too far from the truth. MPs increasingly saw themselves as 'representatives of the people'; at the same time, many of their contemporaries had been brought up on the notion that the commonwealth was kept in good health by a 'multitude of counsellors' in several walks of life. Having begun by noting that Parliament was exceptional in having a formal right to free speech, perhaps it is best to end by emphasising the evidence that is present throughout this chapter that parliamentary free speech, and the arguments that supported it, were remarkably continuous with the theories and practices outlined in other fora. What is more, this was not a one-way process: the language of the debates and the arguments advanced in favour of the subject's liberties did not remain within the walls of Westminster. MPs went home to their countries when Parliament was not sitting, and because of this, as well as a sophisticated process of manuscript 'publication' of news, this material reached interested writers and readers around the country, who set it alongside their own thoughts and other collections of texts in a process of political analysis. Parliamentary notions of free speech were considered as part of a much broader process of political engagement, as I will show in the next chapter.

---

[366] On the identification of parliamentary privileges with the liberties of the subject, see J. P. Sommerville, 'Parliament, Privilege, and the Liberty of the Subject', in *Parliament and Liberty*, ed. by Hexter, pp. 56–84.

CHAPTER 4

'A very paschall fit for Rome': freedom of speech and manuscript miscellanies

The Question of Libells, extends it selfe (I conceive) to manuscripts, as well as Prints; as beeing the more mischievous of the Two: for they are com[m]only so bitter, and dangerous, that not one of forty of them ever comes to yᵉ Presse, and yet by yᵉ help of Transcripts, they are well nigh as publique.

Sir Roger L'Estrange[1]

THE MANUSCRIPT CULTURE OF THE EARLY SEVENTEENTH CENTURY

Sir Roger L'Estrange's complaint, voiced in a document presented to the House of Lords in 1675, is testimony to the power and longevity of manuscript as a medium throughout the seventeenth century, as well as to one of its most popular uses: the dissemination of libels. By the time L'Estrange was writing, printing had been established in England for two centuries, but this 'revolution' in book production took place in the context of a thriving culture of scribal publication, and developed alongside that culture rather than supplanting it.[2] As H. R. Woudhuysen has put it, 'the printing press changed the world, but writing by hand went on'.[3] There were many reasons in the early seventeenth century why a text might be written in manuscript rather than printed. Few of them have much to do with the once-influential notion of the 'stigma of print', which argued that aristocratic authors regarded the printed book with disdain, associating it with trade and with a breadth of readership for which they had no

---

[1] 'Mr L'Estraings Proposition concerning Libells, &c.', 11 November 1675, quoted in Harold Love, *The Culture and Commerce of Texts: Scribal Publication in Seventeenth-Century England* (Amherst: University of Massachusetts Press, 1998), p. 74.

[2] On the printing revolution, see Elizabeth L. Eisenstein, *The Printing Press as an Agent of Change*, 2 volumes (Cambridge: Cambridge University Press, 1979).

[3] H. R. Woudhuysen, *Sir Philip Sidney and the Circulation of Manuscripts, 1558–1640* (Oxford: Clarendon Press, 1996), p. 11.

desire.[4] One very important reason for texts being written and distributed in manuscript was that, for the educated, such writing and exchange was a way of life. This may seem somewhat basic and circular as an argument, but it benefits from being restated. The education offered by the grammar schools and the universities in this period put a high premium on writing by hand, not only, or perhaps even primarily, in the sense of composition, but in the senses of addition (manuscript annotation of printed books) and transcription (the collection of commonplaces).[5] This education also trained pupils in the writing of familiar letters on classical models, a central part of manuscript culture and social relations more broadly.[6] The writing of manuscripts, whether in response to printed or other manuscript texts or as an independent activity, was a habit, a part of one's life, in the sixteenth and seventeenth centuries, just as was the writing of verse; and both are perhaps equally difficult for us to imagine now.

Within this culture there might be many possible reasons for a specific text being circulated in manuscript rather than print, and when considering these it is vital to remember that, as Harold Love has put it, 'scribal transmission might be chosen without any sense of its being inferior or incomplete'.[7] Love's use of the term 'scribal publication' is designed to emphasise that manuscript was not simply a form used for preliminary drafts or for the production of single copies. Scriveners produced multiple copies of texts in a fashion we could see as analogous to the increasingly prevalent use of 'print on demand' by academic publishers today. Manuscript offered other advantages, the most important of which to this chapter are, first, its freedom from official control, allowing potentially dangerous texts (or even those that had previously been suppressed in print) to circulate relatively freely and, second, the opportunity to make personal copies of texts that could be built up into a collection – although even this freedom had its

---

[4] See J. W. Saunders, 'The Stigma of Print: A Note on the Social Bases of Tudor Poetry', *Essays in Criticism* 1 (1951): 139–64. For an extensive modification of this view, see Steven W. May, *The Elizabethan Courtier Poets: The Poems and their Contexts* (Asheville: Pegasus Press, 1999).

[5] On annotation, see for example Lisa Jardine and Anthony Grafton, '"Studied for Action": How Gabriel Harvey Read his Livy', *Past and Present* 129 (November 1990): 30–78; on commonplacing, see Peter Beal, '"Notions in Garrison": The Seventeenth Century Commonplace Book', in *New Ways of Looking at Old Texts: Papers of the Renaissance English Text Society, 1985–1991*, MRTS 107, ed. by W. Speed Hill (New York: Mediaeval and Renaissance Text Society, 1993), pp. 131–47; Mary Thomas Crane, *Framing Authority: Sayings, Self, and Society in Sixteenth-Century England* (Princeton: Princeton University Press, 1993). For the humanist pedagogical background, see R. R. Bolgar, *The Classical Heritage and Its Beneficiaries* (Cambridge: Cambridge University Press, 1954), pp. 265–75.

[6] See Jonathan Gibson, 'Letters', in *A Companion to English Renaissance Literature and Culture*, ed. by Michael Hattaway (Oxford: Blackwell, 2000), pp. 615–19; James Daybell (ed.), *Early Modern Women's Letter Writing, 1450–1700* (Basingstoke: Palgrave, 2001).

[7] Love, *The Culture and Commerce of Texts*, p. 35.

limits. The pioneering work of scholars like Love and Woudhuysen has demonstrated both the socially inclusive nature of manuscript as a form and the importance of tracing the circulation of manuscript texts amongst diverse communities: aristocratic and gentle, female and artisanal, urban and rural. Nonetheless, misconceptions persist about the aristocratic nature of the form, and about the static nature of 'coteries'; writing about Spenser's *A View of the Present State of Ireland*, Andrew Hadfield can still assert that 'manuscripts were generally produced by or on behalf of aristocrats'.[8] While this may be true of professionally produced single copies of individual texts, it ignores one of the most important forms of scribal publication; what Love calls 'user publication'. 'User publication', in contrast to 'author publication' or 'entrepreneurial publication', took place when an individual copied a text for his or her own use, and was probably the most common way in which manuscripts were disseminated.[9]

My focus in this chapter will be on 'user published' texts, but one kind of 'entrepreneurially published' text will be crucial to it. This is the large body of political material copied commercially by scriveners working in the capital and distributed around the country; it includes both newsletters and 'separates' containing parliamentary reports.[10] As Love has written, this kind of material was 'copied in larger quantities than any other kind of scribally published text'.[11] Gentlemen had long-standing arrangements with scriveners to provide letters containing news from the capital on a regular basis, while reports on business in Parliament were provided in a similar way. In addition, individual speeches were distributed by their authors and others (indeed, in some cases it seems clear that speeches were distributed in manuscript that were never actually delivered in Parliament).[12] In the years before the regularly printed newsbook, this was probably the best means of obtaining information about current affairs.[13] Even when an individual's motives in collecting and responding to texts were not allied to a republican

---

[8] Andrew Hadfield, 'Censoring Ireland in Elizabethan England, 1580–1600', in *Literature and Censorship in Renaissance England*, ed. by Hadfield (Basingstoke: Palgrave, 2001), pp. 149–64, at p. 152.

[9] See Love, *The Culture and Commerce of Texts*, pp. 47–89.

[10] Ibid., pp. 13–22.   [11] Ibid., p. 9.

[12] For example, Huntington MS 1554 is a collection of parliamentary material which includes letters written between 4 May 1606 and 10 February 1627; three speeches by James I in the 'Addled' Parliament of 1614; Francis Bacon's 'humble submission' of 1621; speeches at the 1625 session that was held at Oxford, and a journal of the proceedings in Parliament from 13 April to 5 May 1640; Bod. MS Eng. hist. d.89 is a record of proceedings in the Parliaments of 1623, 1626, and 1628, and of the impeachment of the Duke of Buckingham in 1626: it was written *circa* 1628.

[13] See F. J. Levy, 'How Information Spread Among the Gentry, 1550–1640', *Journal of British Studies*, 21 (1982): 1–24, esp. p. 21; Richard Cust, 'News and Politics in Early Seventeenth-Century England', *Past and Present*, 112 (August 1986): 60–90; Joad Raymond, *The Invention of the Newspaper: English*

or 'oppositional' agenda, the very practices of transcription or annotation are acts that place him or her in a critical and active relationship to the civic world. We can see this in the case of Sir William Drake, whose reading practices have been so thoroughly excavated by Kevin Sharpe.[14] As Sharpe is at pains to point out, Drake was a loyal landowner whose reading and annotation of a large number of classical and contemporary texts was anything but revolutionary; but through that reading and annotation he developed a civic identity inaccessible to someone who was merely a passive receiver of information or knowledge. To develop such an identity required a degree of knowledge about and critical involvement in political affairs. This is, in part, why the model of the counsellor presented in an influential humanist text like Elyot's *The Book named The Governor* is of someone close to the court, even if not living in it. In this chapter I argue that the collection of news, parliamentary reports, and verse libels – among other kinds of text – in manuscript by people who were both geographically and socially separated from the 'centre' of politics allowed the ideas about freedom of speech that I have been describing to circulate relatively widely in early Stuart society. This collection of material was, in fact, motivated in part by a desire to participate in civic culture and to make the kinds of claim for a right to free speech that I have discussed in the previous chapters.

VERSE LIBELS AND MANUSCRIPT MISCELLANIES IN EARLY STUART ENGLAND

News that was disseminated in manuscript within and beyond the capital in early Stuart England took a variety of forms. One of these was the newsletter, written by either a professional scrivener, a regularly paid informant (who would not necessarily have been a professional scribe) or by a friend of the recipient (as in the case of John Chamberlain's voluminous correspondence with Sir Dudley Carleton). Another was the verse libel – a scurrilous, satirical, and often *ad hominem* treatment of actual events or of the political or moral failings of an individual or group. These different forms of 'news' often existed side by side in the minds or on the pages of individuals in the early seventeenth century, despite – or perhaps because

Newsbooks, 1641–1649 (Oxford: Clarendon Press, 1996); Ian Atherton, 'The Itch Grown a Disease: Manuscript Transmission of News in the Seventeenth Century', in *News, Newspapers and Society in Early Modern Britain*, ed. by Joad Raymond (London: Frank Cass, 1999), pp. 39–65; Alastair Bellany, *The Politics of Court Scandal in Early Modern England: News Culture and the Overbury Affair, 1603–1660* (Cambridge: Cambridge University Press, 2002), chapter 2.

[14] See Kevin Sharpe, *Reading Revolutions: The Politics of Reading in Early Modern England* (New Haven: Yale University Press, 2000).

of – their differences in decorum and, often, the degree of judgement they offered on the events they recounted. Both forms could, however, be dangerous to both their authors and their recipients, should they be deemed too outspoken, and could court a prosecution for libel or defamation. In 1621, Parliament initiated investigations into the abuse of patents and monopolies and other fiscal misdemeanours. By the end of March, the growing list of offenders included the Lord Chancellor, Francis Bacon. Amid the growing scandal, Samuel Albyn was writing newsletters to his patrons, and on 28 March he gave an account of the current state of affairs in relation to Bacon, having attended the king's speech to the assembled Houses of Parliament:

> [the king] seemed very grasius to the Lord Chanselor and I was in a place whear a very wise gentleman offered 20 Angles to 10 that he would continue his place. He shewed Reasons which yf you ware at shope or at an alle house I should perhaps tell you but for my eares not wright you at this tyme.[15]

Albyn was clearly concerned that any reported speculation as to Bacon's safety (his support by Buckingham, perhaps, who was soon also to be subject to investigation, or his expectation of the king's or the Prince of Wales's favour) could prove rash. While exchanging gossip in a shop or an alehouse was probably safe, to repeat it in a letter might end in his suffering the punishment dealt out to seditious libellers – the cropping of his ears. Noting that the 'wise gentleman' was in a minority and that 'in the generall oppinion [Bacon] is thought to bee utterly lost and Ruinated for ever', Albyn ended his letter with an apology for not sending any of the more satirical reactions to recent events – but this time not for fear of punishment: 'I would haue written you the coppies of certayn Lybles against Sir francis michell who is yet in ye towre Siʳ francis bacon who is in his sty at york House & Sir gills mompesson who is I know not wher but I am sleepi & cannot.'[16]

Libel and political news are side by side in Albyn's mind, then (even if one ultimately wins out on the page); and their proximity in this period has been recognised in recent scholarship.[17] Libels were written in response to the fall

[15] Samuel Albyn to [?John Rawson], BL MS Harley 383, fols. 13–14, quoted in *CD 1621*, VII, 591.

[16] Ibid., fol. 14ʳ. The letter is subscribed '10 acloke at night'. *CD 1621* erroneously prints 'towne' for 'towre'; the manuscript is admittedly hard to read here, but the fact that Michell was sent to the Tower after appearing before the Commons on 23 February supports my reading; see Conrad Russell, *Parliaments and English Politics 1621–1629* (Oxford: Clarendon Press, 1979), p. 105. Albyn ends his letter by promising that 'my Lord Chancellor's Letter to the Lords & sum other thing I will shew you when you come'.

[17] See Pauline Croft, 'The Reputation of Robert Cecil: Libels, Political Opinion and Popular Awareness in the Early Seventeenth Century', *Transactions of the Royal Historical Society* 6:1 (1991): 43–69; Adam

from favour or death of prominent public figures, to especially noteworthy events (such as the Spanish Match negotiations or Buckingham's disastrous mission to the Ile de Rhé), and as commentaries on the state of the nation. They were written from a wide range of political or religious positions, and we should be wary of identifying the form with a coherently 'oppositional' or anti-government outlook. Libels were written against puritans, for instance, and on behalf of Roman Catholics. In 1605, in the aftermath of Gunpowder Plot, the diarist Walter Younge noted that

> while these things were handling there were divers pasquils and libels cast abroad in London by a certain papist against the Earl of Sarum, Sir Robert Cecil, charging him to be the only mouth which kindled the king's displeasure against the Roman Catholics, wishing him to desist if he tendered his own life and safety.[18]

Libels, especially when brief and easily memorised (many rely on heavy end-rhymes), could be circulated orally; like other forms of news, however, they were very often disseminated in manuscript, either alone or in the context of a letter.[19] Like other forms of news, too, they were frequently copied into manuscript miscellanies. These miscellanies were a vital component of early modern manuscript culture: unlike the more formal commonplace book, their contents were not arranged under headings or topics, although some do have principles of organisation that go beyond the mere copying of material as it comes to the hand of the compiler. The commonplace book was a storehouse of quotations and of knowledge that was designed

---

Fox, 'Ballads, Libels and Popular Ridicule in Jacobean England', *Past & Present* 145 (November 1994): 47–83; M. Lindsay Kaplan, *The Culture of Slander in Early Modern England* (Cambridge: Cambridge University Press, 1997); Alastair Bellany, '"Raylinge Rymes and Vaunting Verse": Libellous Politics in Early Stuart England, 1603–1628', in *Culture and Politics in Early Stuart England*, ed. by Kevin Sharpe and Peter Lake (Basingstoke: Macmillan, 1994), pp. 285–310; Bellany, 'A Poem on the Archbishop's Hearse: Puritanism, Libel, and Sedition after the Hampton Court Conference', *Journal of British Studies* 34 (April 1995): 137–64; Bellany, 'Libels in Action: Ritual, Subversion, and the English Literary Underground, 1603–1642', in *The Politics of the Excluded, c. 1500–1850*, ed. by Tim Harris (Basingstoke: Palgrave, 2001), pp. 99–124; Bellany, *The Politics of Court Scandal in Early Modern England*; Adam Fox, *Oral and Literate Culture in England, 1500–1700* (Oxford: Oxford University Press, 2000), chapter 6; Andrew McRae, 'The Literary Culture of Early Stuart Libelling', *Modern Philology* 97:3 (2000): 364–92; McRae, *Literature, Satire, and the Early Stuart State* (Cambridge: Cambridge University Press, 2004).

[18] *The Diary of Walter Younge, Esq.*, ed. by George Roberts (London: Camden Society, 1868), pp. 2–3. For a dramatic treatment of this practice, see Christopher Marlowe, *Edward II*, 2.2.176–7, where Mortimer tells Edward 'Libels are cast against thee in the street; / Ballads and rhymes made of thy overthrow' (Christopher Marlowe, *Dr Faustus and Other Plays*, ed. by David Bevington and Eric Rasmussen (Oxford: Oxford University Press, 1995), p. 352).

[19] John Chamberlain mentions enclosed libels in some letters to Sir Dudley Carleton, as well as copying one in the middle of a letter to Carleton of 4 August 1620; see *The Letters of John Chamberlain*, ed. by N. E. McClure, 2 volumes (Philadelphia: American Philosophical Association, 1939), volume II, p. 315 (posthumous libel on the Earl of Oxford); p. 518 (enclosed libel mentioned).

for use in the construction of an oration, letter, or piece of writing;[20] the miscellany was a personal compilation of texts that could all have similar motives behind their collection or be copied for a wide range of reasons.[21] The commonplace book was usually put together over an extended period of time; though some miscellanies are the product of a family's interests over a century or more, others were compiled in a matter of weeks or months.[22]

When studying manuscript miscellanies, it is not always easy – or even possible – to be certain why a compiler has copied a text. This problem is at the centre of my discussion, later in this chapter, of manuscripts containing poems by John Hoskyns. Compilers rarely provide explanations of their motives, and therefore much is down to interpretation, especially where little is known about a manuscript's provenance. It might be thought that a basic and universal condition for the copying of a poem is that the copyist enjoyed it, but even this is not certain, notably in the case of libels and other political texts. For example, at the head of some libels he copied in 1640 the Suffolk parson John Rous wrote, 'I hate these following railing rimes, / Yet keepe them for president of the times.'[23] Newsworthiness (a complex idea in itself), an interest in controversy, or a desire to keep track of what the 'opposition' was up to could all be reasons for taking down a text. On the other hand, it is important not to stress the political to the exclusion of other motives (especially the aesthetic), even in the case of libels. John Donne complained that those he had received on Sir Robert Cecil after the latter's death were poor specimens: 'Nothing in my L. of *Salisburies* death', he wrote, 'exercised my poor consideration so much, as the multitude of libells . . . all of which are brought into these parts, are so tastelesse and flat, that I protest to you, I think they were made by his friends.'[24] It is also difficult to separate motives from opportunities

---

[20] On commonplace books, see Beal, '"Notions in Garrison"'. Part 1 of Folger MS V.a.130, which belonged to Thomas Medcalf, was originally laid out as a commonplace book, ruled and with alphabetical headings; there are a few entries, but it was soon abandoned; part 11 is a miscellany in verse and prose; Bod. MS Rawl. poet. 117 was transformed from a legal commonplace book into a verse miscellany by its main copyist and first owner, Christopher Wasse (d. 1690).

[21] On manuscript miscellanies, see Arthur F. Marotti, *Manuscript, Print, and the English Renaissance Lyric* (Ithaca: Cornell University Press, 1995).

[22] On family-based manuscript collections, see Marotti, *Manuscript*. Folger MS V.b.210 was compiled between 6 April and 17 November 1604; it contains copies of several texts that had been printed in the previous few years, including Nicholas Breton's *Pasquils Mad-Cap. And his Message* (London, 1600), as well as relations of the arrest and execution of Thomas Howard in 1571–2 and 'The Earle of Arundell's letter to Q. Eliz. Anno 1586'.

[23] John Rous, *Diary of John Rous, Incumbent of Santon Downham, Suffolk, from 1625 to 1642*, ed. by M. A. E. Green (London, 1856), p. 140.

[24] Donne, probably writing to Sir Henry Goodyer, July 1612; John Donne, *Letters to Severall Persons of Honour* (London, 1651), sigs. N^r–N^v.

when establishing how and why an item appeared in a manuscript. A poem might well be copied out because the scribe found it witty, but equally it might not have come to that scribe's attention in the first place unless scribe and poet moved in the same circles. Political sympathies may be consistent with, or be subservient to, school, college, university, Inns of Court, or parliamentary links of a more social kind. The reputation of the author may be a spur for copying; but often texts in both verse and prose are unattributed. Several manuscript collections are copied more or less wholesale from another single manuscript, either unchanged or with additions, omissions, or rearrangements in ordering.[25] Generic coherence is rarely a feature of miscellanies: though collections devoted exclusively to the political, or to particular genres of poetry do exist (Donne's elegies originally circulated in manuscripts, or sections of manuscripts, entitled 'Liber Elegiarum'), miscellanies are usually by definition heterogeneous in their contents.

In order to understand the way in which manuscript miscellanies function, it is vital to read their contents against one another, and to read the miscellanies as collections rather than considering the texts they contain as discrete items. Especially in the work of textual editors, individual texts have tended to be extracted from miscellanies without any sense of their context: the nature of the collection as a whole, where the text is placed in it, or the identity or apparent biases of the compiler. In the case of libels, this fosters a reading that sees them as local and responsive rather than as continuous with broader political issues and with a sense of civic engagement. If we instead consider the miscellany *in toto*, both libels and parliamentary debates can be seen as part of a wider concern about the counsel that was allowed to reach the king and the range of information that was allowed to reach his people – precisely the kinds of argument that I have shown to be central to the idea of free speech in this period.

The heterogeneity of their contents can, I think, give us clues to the ways in which manuscript miscellanies participated in the debates over free speech with which I am concerned. In this chapter I will describe this engagement with issues of free speech by first reconsidering the status of libellous verse in early Stuart England. I will then offer a case study of a particularly important manuscript, and finally I will trace the transmission of poems by John Hoskyns, alongside libels and other political materials, in manuscript miscellanies of the early seventeenth century.

---

[25] For examples, see Mary Hobbs, *Early Seventeenth-Century Verse Miscellany Manuscripts* (Aldershot: Scolar Press, 1992); Hobbs, 'Early Seventeenth-Century Verse Miscellanies and their Value for Textual Editors', *English Manuscript Studies* 1 (1989): 182–210.

LIBELS AND FREEDOM OF SPEECH

Scholars have recently argued forcefully for the importance of libellous verse to our understanding of political debate in the early seventeenth century.[26] Aside from these notable exceptions, however, the study of such verse has too often accepted the perspective of those who tried to restrict and control it, and lost sight of the perspective of those who composed it. Libels and the intentions and effects of libel law must play a large part in any discussion of freedom of speech in early Stuart England; but they must both also be seen in the context of the manuscript miscellanies into which libels were copied. In attempting to understand the real significance of libels for early Stuart ideas about freedom of speech, I will take issue with what I regard as the three currently dominant arguments about libels and libel law. These are, first, that libels were dangerous acts of individual free expression which were almost always quashed by a repressive state. Samuel Albyn's hesitancy in his letter quoted above supports this position, as do the dreadful images of a few other cases, both historical and literary – John Stubbs's loss of his right hand for publishing the *Gaping Gulf* in 1579, or Malfont's tongue nailed to a tree in *The Faerie Queene*, for example.[27] M. Lindsay Kaplan has argued that the paradigms offered by slander legislation were so pervasive as to condition both 'state' and 'popular' understanding of transgressive language.[28] This reading, though, is based on a misunderstanding of the law of slander and an anachronistic understanding of free speech. The second argument is that libels were local and immediate responses to events that can tell us little more than what the political temperature was in a certain brief period. On the face of it this is unexceptionable. Yet far from being the flimsy straws that tell you how the wind is blowing, the power of libels was long-lasting, and their application more various than has usually been allowed.[29] Since libels are so often personal attacks, it has recently been argued that they eroded a 'civility of trust' that served to knit early modern society together.[30]

---

[26] See Thomas Cogswell, 'Underground Verse and the Transformation of Early Stuart Political Culture', in *Political Culture and Cultural Politics in Early Modern England*, ed. by Susan D. Amussen and Mark Kishlansky (Manchester: Manchester University Press, 1995), pp. 277–300 and works by Bellany and McRae cited in note 17.

[27] See Edmund Spenser, *The Faerie Queene*, ed. by A. C. Hamilton (Harlow: Longman, 1977), Book v, Canto IX, stanzas 25–6, p. 592.

[28] Kaplan, *The Culture of Slander.*

[29] John Selden's celebrated description: 'though some make slight of Libells, yet you may see by them how the wind sitts . . . More solid things doe not shew the Complexion of the times so well as Ballads and libells' (*Table Talk of John Selden*, ed. by F. Pollock (London: Quaritch, 1927), p. 72).

[30] See Debora Shuger, 'Civility and Censorship in Early Modern England', in *Censorship and Silencing: Practices of Cultural Regulation*, ed. by Robert C. Post (Los Angeles: Getty Research Institute for the

According to this third argument, libel law and censorship were necessary protections against (usually untrue and certainly irrelevant) slights on the honour of public persons. Working on the assumption that if you throw enough mud then some will stick, libel-writers refused to adhere to the rules of decorous political debate and chose to play dirty. Critics who pursue this argument are certainly right to note the insulting nature of libels, and their disregard for truth. It is also true that many of the cases of defamation and slander prosecuted show that an attempt had been made to injure reputation. However, J. H. Baker has shown that common law actions on the case for words, or defamation (and the scope of the offence as it was conceived from the first judgement, in 1517), relate most clearly to temporal loss rather than to loss of fame or credit.[31] In addition, Sheila Lambert emphasises that cases of *scandalum magnatum*, or the slandering of a magistrate, were most often brought not by the crown, protecting its officers, but by private individuals.[32]

More important still, I suggest that these positions all fail to take account of the justifications for libelling, and the place of the libel in the possibilities for political comment and analysis open to the population of early Stuart England. Only by considering these aspects of libelling, and by looking at the miscellanies in which so many libels found a home, can we properly understand the complex relations between freedom of speech, libel, and the form of the manuscript miscellany.

Rather than being primarily attacks on persons, libels acted as an unofficial means of counsel to which individuals might have recourse when more acknowledged fora, such as Parliament, appeared to have failed or to have been restrained by the crown – as took place in 1614. When libels are read alongside the other contents of the miscellanies into which they were copied, it becomes clear that parliamentary proceedings and scandalous comment were considered to be continuous, or at least similar in

---

History of Art and the Humanities, 1998), pp. 89–110. I am grateful to David Norbrook for bringing this article to my attention. Shuger pursued a parallel argument in 'Roman Catholicism, Roman Law, and the Regulation of Language in Early Modern England (*c.* 1558–1641)', a paper delivered at the West Coast Law and Literature Conference, University of Southern California, 13 May 2002. I am grateful to Debora Shuger for detailed and generous discussions of this subject. For a similar argument about the politically polarising effects of manuscript news, see Cust, 'News and Politics'.

[31] J. H. Baker, 'Defamation', in *An Introduction to English Legal History*, third edition (London: Butterworths, 1990), pp. 495–508. On the law of defamation see further Roger B. Manning, 'The Origins of the Doctrine of Sedition', *Albion* 12:2 (1980): 99–121; J. A. Sharpe, *Defamation and Sexual Slander in Early Modern England: The Church Courts at York* (York: University of York, 1980).

[32] Sheila Lambert, 'State Control of the Press in Theory and Practice: The Role of the Stationers' Company before 1640', in *Censorship and the Control of Print in England and France 1600–1900*, ed. by Robin Myers and Michael Harris (Winchester: St Paul's Bibliographies, 1992), pp. 1–32.

the purpose to which they could be put by their readers. The part played by manuscript miscellanies in the culture of early modern free speech also becomes apparent when we consider instances where printed books – sometimes ones which had been proscribed – are copied into their pages. In the early years of James's reign, for instance, I will show that John Stubbs's *Gaping Gulf* was not regarded primarily as an historical instance of state restriction of the press. Rather, the book, its censorship, and the way in which both should be construed were objects of urgent deliberation among men who were trying to work out how to have truly political debate in a monarchy.

I have shown in chapter 3 how parliamentary debates over freedom of speech expressed a desire on the part of MPs to be allowed to offer counsel to the king and to point out when they thought he was receiving bad counsel from others. They were also, I concluded, part of an attempt on the part of members to make sure that it was they who set the boundaries for expression, and not the king. How did libelling fit into this contest over the definition and extent of the right to counsel frankly, and to keep such frank counsel within the House of Commons? Often the same individuals who were pressing for the right – or duty – of the House of Commons to advise the king were also penning or sharing acid attacks on the ministers who they felt were leading him astray.[33] In the writings of the time, these salacious verses are frequently referred to as 'pasquils', and that description can lead us to some insights concerning their nature and their use. The term refers to the custom of affixing anonymous satires to a classical statue that was re-erected in Rome in 1501.[34] The statue was known as Pasquino, hence the extension of the terms 'pasquinade' or 'pasquil' to the satires

---

[33] Authorship is often difficult to determine in the case of libels, which were usually anonymous, but there are some instances of libels attributable to MPs, including John Hoskyns's poem on Bacon's fall, 'Great Verulam is very lame', and the communally produced 'Parliament Fart', attributed to Hoskyns by Aubrey but also supposed by one copyist to have been written by 'Ned Jones, Dick Martin, Hopkins [*sic*] and Cr Brooke' (BL MS Add. 23229, fols. 16ʳ–17ᵛ). Both of these poems are discussed further below.

[34] On Pasquino and the Italian tradition, see Mary Lahan, *Pasquin et Marforio* (Paris, 1861); R. and F. Silenzi, *Pasquino. Cinquecento pasquinate* (Milan: Bompiani, 1932); Mario dell'Arco, *Pasquino e le pasquinate* (Milan: A. Martello, 1957); Anne Reynolds, 'Cardinal Oliviero Carafa and the Early Cinquecento Tradition of the Feast of Pasquino', *Humanistica Lovaniensia* 34A (1985): 178–208; Reynolds, 'The Classical Continuum in Roman Humanism: The Festival of Pasquino, the *Robigalia*, and Satire', *Bibliothèque d'Humanisme et Renaissance* 49:2 (1987): 289–307. On the relation between public pasquilling and private defamation in early modern Italy, see also Peter Burke, *The Historical Anthropology of Early Modern Italy. Essays on Perception and Communication* (Cambridge: Cambridge University Press, 1987), chapter 8, esp. p. 109. On the spread of this tradition throughout Europe and its use by an important but neglected English humanist, see Catherine Mary Curtis, 'Richard Pace on Pedagogy, Counsel and Satire', unpublished PhD diss., University of Cambridge (1996), esp. pp. 207–20.

themselves.[35] Replies to these *pasquinate* were then attached to another statue dubbed Marforio. This practice was well known to the northern European humanists of the early sixteenth century, and Richard Pace, an English writer who was in Rome in the year that the first *Carmina* of Pasquin were published, was highly influenced by it in writing his *Julius exclusus*.[36] In the 1530s Sir Thomas Elyot wrote that 'there be . . . Pasquilles in Englande as well as in Rome',[37] and he popularised the term and the form of the pasquil for an English audience in his *Pasquil the Playne* (1533) – a book he described as 'a mery treatise, wherein plainnes and flatteri do come in trial'.[38] Elyot makes a direct association between the practice of pasquilling and the humanist debate over the proper responsibilities of a counsellor to his prince, a debate that his text does not just discuss detachedly but in which it is deeply implicated. In writing *Pasquil*, Elyot, who opposed Henry VIII's attempt to divorce Katharine of Aragon, tried to persuade the king's counsellors that they could best serve their master not by flattering and acceding to his whims but by decorously admonishing him. 'Pasquil' thus becomes the name of an honest and frank-speaking counsellor, concerned to ensure the welfare of the country before his own advancement or his prince's comfort. More broadly, Elyot's works offer a fine example of the links between pasquilling and counselling: in *The Book named The Governor*, published two years before *Pasquil the Playne*, he had laid down an education programme for an entire generation of perfect counsellors.[39]

Instances of the public posting of pasquils and libels abound in the late sixteenth and early seventeenth centuries.[40] Texts were placed in the hand of Queen Elizabeth's statue at Westminster and on the coffin of Archbishop

[35] The statue still stands, in a piazza named after it, and continues to be used by Romans for the posting of political comments and verses; at the time of writing, reactions to Prime Minister Silvio Berlusconi's visit to Washington, DC and his relations with President George W. Bush adorn Pasquino.

[36] See Curtis, 'Richard Pace', pp. 211–14. Curtis writes that 'for Pace, Pasquino's verse may have fulfilled the needs for prudent counsel, accommodated to circumstances, and conveyed in figured and direct speech' (p. 212).

[37] Thomas Elyot, *Of the Knowledeg whiche maketh a wise man* (London, 1533), sig. A5. Elyot is stressing that the message of his work – which is concerned with the importance of plain speaking and the virtues that are necessary to the commonwealth – should be taken as general rather than specific. His mention of Pasquil alongside Gnatho, Dionysius of Syracuse, Harpocrates, Aristippus, and Plato is significant.

[38] Thomas Elyot, *Pasqvil the playne* (1533), title page.

[39] A later, and rather different, instance of the term is in Thomas Watson's poem 'My Love is Past. A Pasquine Pillar Erected in the Despite of Love', from his *The ΕΚΑΤΟΜΠΑΘΙΑ, or Passionate Centurie of Loue* (1582): this is a pattern poem which ingeniously depicts the plinth and torso of Pasquino, as well as the attached text. See Thomas Watson, *English Poems*, ed. by Albert Chatterly (Norwich: Marion Hopkins, 2003), p. 191.

[40] See Walter Younge's use of the term 'pasquil' above, p. 201.

Whitgift;[41] 'let fall in the gallery at Whitehall' (in the case of the Roman Catholic tract *Balaam's Asse*);[42] or (after the committal of Eliot, Selden, and the five members to the Tower in 1629) deposited in 'the Dean of Paul's [John Donne] his yard before his house'.[43] In 1623, John Chamberlain reported to Dudley Carleton that 'the poet Owens monument in Powles begins to serve for a Pasquin to any merrie or malicious companion that fasten daylie some odde rime or other foolish paper upon yt'.[44] Sometimes these acts of fly-posting were mentioned when a libel was subsequently copied into a miscellany.[45] The posting of a libel could also be part of a wider campaign of dissent, as occurred in Berkshire in 1604/5. The Justices of the Peace wrote to Cecil that

we received letters from the Privy Council dated 28 February last for the examination of a very strange, irreligious and intolerable outrage lately committed by some ill-affected persons in breaking open the door of the church of Enborne, tearing in pieces the Communion Book and Ecclesiastical Canons lately published, and casting abroad a libel in contempt of religion established in his Majesty's dominions.[46]

The potential offered by the practice of posting libels or pasquils for the spreading of propaganda and deceit, rather than safe outspokenness, is explored in Act I, scene 3 of Shakespeare's *Julius Caesar* (c. 1599), where

---

[41] Bod. MS Malone 23, fol. 32; Bellany, 'A Poem on the Archbishop's Hearse'.

[42] Thomas Larkin to Sir Thomas Puckering, 16 March 1618/19, in Thomas Birch (compiler), *The Court and Times of James the First illustrated by authentic and confidential letters from various public and private collections*, two volumes (London, 1848), volume II, p. 147. On the aftermath of the delivery of *Balaam's Asse* and the execution of its author, Williams, see Larkin to Puckering, 4 May 1619, in Birch (compiler), *The Court and Times of James the First* II, 157; Chamberlain to Carleton, 8 May 1619, in *The Letters of John Chamberlain*, volume II, p. 235. Chamberlain noted that at his execution Williams 'saide he was sory that he had written so sawcilie and unreverently, but pretended he had an inward warrant, and a particuler illumination to understand certain hard passages of Daniell and the Revelation, which made him adventure so far'. On an earlier *Balaam's Asse* (possibly the same text?), written in 1613 by one John Cotton, see Cyndia Susan Clegg, *Press Censorship in Jacobean England* (Cambridge: Cambridge University Press, 2001), pp. 100–1, and *HMC Ancaster*, pp. 365–85 (examination of Cotton and Archbishop Abbot's notes on the text).

[43] Diary entry of Archbishop William Laud, 29 March 1629, *The Works of the Most Reverend Father in God, William Laud D.D.*, ed. by William Scott and James Bliss (Oxford, 1847–60), volume III, p. 210, cited in Love, *The Culture and Commerce of Texts*, p. 82.

[44] Chamberlain to Carleton, 25 October 1623; *The Letters of John Chamberlain*, volume II, p. 518.

[45] See note 41 above.

[46] The Justices of the Peace of Berkshire to Viscount Cranborne, dated from Newbury, 15 March 1604/5; *HMC Salisbury* 17 (1605), pp. 58–9. The JPs go on to suggest that they will use palaeographical evidence to try to establish authorship of the libel: 'we think it fit that we had the libel itself, which (as we understand) was left with your Honour, that comparing hand with hand we may the better find out the libeller' (p. 59). Cf. Archbishop Abbot's notes on the 1613 *Balaam's Asse*, which suggest that scriveners had been asked to compare the hand in the tract with that of its putative author, John Cotton: Clegg, *Press Censorship in Jacobean England*, p. 100.

Cassius asks Cinna to lay a series of papers where Brutus will come across them (including, tellingly, 'upon old Brutus' statue', thus associating the papers with Brutus' republican family history).[47] Brutus is the one who listens to anonymous counsel which is in fact flattery disguised as popular sentiment, while Caesar foolishly turns a deaf ear to the frank advice of Artemidorus.[48]

The dangers of using libelling as an unofficial means of counsel were pointed up by Sir Edward Coke in his celebrated report *de Libellis famosis*, based on the case of *Attorney General* v. *Pickering* in 1605. Libel, Coke declared, should not be used even to indicate real injustice or corruption,

for in a settled state of government the party grieved ought to complain for every injury done him in an ordinary course of law, and not by any means to revenge himself, either by the odious course of libelling, or otherwise.[49]

But this 'ordinary course of law' was not, of course, open to the 'party grieved' if that party was conceived as the people at large, except through the presentation of grievances in Parliament. If it was felt that this course was failing (and, as I have shown, James appeared to regard the presentation of grievances as a distraction from the Commons' main task of voting him subsidies), then an extraordinary course might be pursued, and libels often make claims – implicit and explicit – to be speaking for a wider community. In a letter probably to Sir Henry Goodyer written in July 1612, John Donne makes the point (with notable caution) that libelling is sometimes necessary:

I dare say to you, where I am not easily misinterpreted, that there may be cases, where one may do his Countrey good service, by libelling against a live man. For, where a man is either too great, or his Vices too generall, to be brought under a judiciary accusation, there is no way, but this extraordinary accusing, which we call Libelling.[50]

Having speculated that if only the number of libels that appeared on Cecil after his death had been written while he was alive 'they might then

---

[47] William Shakespeare, *Julius Caesar*, 1.iii.142–6, in *The Riverside Shakespeare*, ed. by G. Blakemore Evans (Boston: Houghton Mifflin Company, 1974), p. 1111. I am grateful to Lucinda Platt for drawing my attention to this example.

[48] Shakespeare, *Julius Caesar*, 11.iii; 111.i.3–12, in *The Riverside Shakespeare*, pp. 1116, 1117. On the public posting of libels, see further Bellany, *The Politics of Court Scandal*, pp. 107–8; Andrew Gordon, 'The Act of Libel: Conscripting Civic Space in Early Modern England', *Journal of Medieval and Early Modern Studies* 32:2 (Spring 2002): 375–97.

[49] Sir Edward Coke, 'The Case *de Libellis famosis*, or of Scandalous Libels', in *The Reports of Sir Edward Coke, in English*, 7 volumes (London, 1776–7), volume v, p. 126.

[50] Donne, *Letters*, sigs. N^v–N2^r. Note that Donne goes on to condemn libels against the dead as 'unexcusable' (sig. N2^r).

have wrought upon him',[51] Donne goes on to note that libelling has been reported to have had a demonstrably good effect on one contemporary figure: 'I have heard that nothing hath soupled and allayed the D. of *Lerma* in his violent greatnesse, so much as the often libels made upon him.'[52]

Francis Bacon, in his *History of the Reign of Henry VII* (1622), likewise associated libels with the restriction of other redress and of free speech more generally. The *History* is very much concerned with the problems of counsel, and Bacon describes the atmosphere of paranoia that followed the impeachment of Stanley for uttering seditious words qualified with a conditional clause. His punishment, writes Bacon,

was matter of great terror amongst all the King's servants and subjects; insomuch as no man almost thought himself secure, and men durst scarce commune or talk one with another, but there was a general diffidence everywhere; which nevertheless made the King rather more absolute than more safe. For bleeding inwards and shut vapours strangle soonest, and oppress most.

Hereupon presently came forth swarms and vollies of libels (which are the gusts of liberty of speech restrained, and the females of sedition), containing bitter invectives and slanders against the King and some of the council.[53]

Bacon is far from wholeheartedly endorsing libelling here – libels are, he says, the 'females', or mothers, of sedition. But he sees them, unequivocally, as the result of fear and of restraint of speech, suggesting by a deft use of the body politic analogy that this restraint would lead to sickness in the nation and danger to the king – much more danger than would have resulted from allowing his subjects a certain latitude in what they could say.[54] A work from the mid-1590s that has only recently been attributed to Bacon similarly links libelling with the attempt to offer informal counsel, but there Bacon is less equivocal in his condemnation of the practice. He writes there that 'these malitious Pamphlettes are *thought to be* the flying sparks of trewthe forcibly kept downe and choked by those which are possessed of the state inasmuchas they cary with them a presence, and Countenaunce of liberty of speech' (my italics).[55] Bacon describes libelling as 'a corrupt and

---

[51] Ibid., sig. N^v.   [52] Ibid., sig. N2^r.

[53] Francis Bacon, *The History of the Reign of King Henry VII*, ed. by Brian Vickers (Cambridge: Cambridge University Press, 1998), p. 115.

[54] In 1621 a similar case was brought against seditious words couched in a conditional clause, an unidentified correspondent writing to the Revd Joseph Mead on 1 March that 'this week, at Winchester, was a poor silly fellow solemnly executed, for saying, if the king should change the religion, he would be the first one to cut his majesty's throat' (Birch (compiler), *The Court and Times of James the First*, volume II, p. 233).

[55] Francis Bacon (?), 'An aduertisement towching seditious writings' (Public Record Office, SP 12/235/81), transcribed in Brother Kenneth Cardwell, 'An Overlooked Tract by Francis Bacon', *Huntington Library Quarterly* 65:3 and 4 (2002): 421–33, at p. 431.

*per*verse practise of evill subiectes', who are frequently motivated by their discontent about 'some ambitious hopes of theirs which haue been abortiue and blasted' (there are echoes here of A.D.B.'s complaints about anti-court writings).[56] In contrast to his suggestion in *Henry VII* that restricting liberty of speech might provoke libels, in the 'Aduertisement' Bacon recommends that from the point of view of the prince it is important to balance the relative merits of ignoring 'seditious' writings against the 'perill' of leaving their authors 'to that creditt which they by all Cunnynge worke and erect vnto themselues'.[57]

Members in the Commons themselves identified the link between libelling and the attempt to counsel or the desire for redress, and saw the need to discuss the problems it could cause: in the 1610 session the presentation of libels was considered as part of the long-running work on grievances. They were recognised as an unofficial way of protesting against apparent injustice, or pointing out corruption, but cautious members saw that they could undermine the work the House was undertaking on pre-senting a limited list of his subjects' grievances to the king: on 27 March 1610 Edwin Sandys, hardly a known flatterer of James, moved that the Com-mittee for Privileges 'consider how to prevent the Preferring of Grievances, like Pasquils, and yet to preserve the Liberties of the House'.[58] On the other hand, any attempt to suppress them or punish the supposed authors could, if the authors were MPs, be seen as an assault on parliamentary freedom of speech.

The widespread and sophisticated use of the language of counsel in rela-tion to libels should alert us to the dangers of reductionist readings of them that claim they are of limited interest because they merely deal in political commonplaces or, as Richard Cust puts it, in 'popular stereotypes, such as the good lord or evil counsellor'.[59] As I have shown in chapter 1, these 'stereotypes' were not popular in the early seventeenth century sim-ply because they were hoary and familiar. Rather, like all commonplaces, they both draw on and contribute to a vital and fruitful language, in which an argument can take place about the qualities that would make a 'good lord or evil counsellor'. A manuscript miscellany in which libels were copied and read alongside other forms of political news could become a forum for the analysis of political events and, as Alastair Bellany has argued, demanded and fashioned an active reader, 'allowing the reader-writer to compare reports, revise accounts and juxtapose libellous charges to

---

[56] Bacon (?), 'An aduertisement', pp. 431, 432. On A.D.B.'s *The Covrt of the Most Illustrious and Most Magnificent James, the First* (1619), see chapter 1 above.

[57] Bacon (?), 'An aduertisement', p. 433.   [58] *CJ*, I, 415.   [59] Cust, 'News and Politics', pp. 238–9.

soberly expressed allegations'.[60] In Bellany's terms, 'commonplacing turned the reader from a passive recipient into an active judge of scribal news material'.[61]

I will discuss manuscript miscellanies that combine political material with verse libels further below. Other combinations are also germane to my purpose here, however. Folger MS V.a.402, compiled in the 1620s by Brian Cave, shows an interest in political events of the 1620s, and juxtaposes letters and speeches with fictional texts.[62] Although it does not contain any verse libels, the manuscript does have a transcript of Scott's *Vox Populi* (fols. 32ʳ–56ʳ), which accords with a notable emphasis on texts treating international politics and, especially, relations with Spain. Cave has also copied Thomas Alured's letter to Buckingham advising against the Match (fol. 57ʳ), Spinola's oration to his army (fol. 20ʳ) and 'a letter of the king of Bohemia's ambassador to the lord lieutenance', dated 1620 and asking for monetary assistance (fol. 9ʳ). In addition, there are transcripts of James's speech in Parliament on 16 January 1620/1 and the answer of the Lord Chancellor (that is, Bacon) (fols. 25ʳ; 31ʳ) and of the Commons' Protestation, dated 18 December 1621 (fol. 66ʳ). The last text in the manuscript is a relation 'concerning the plaister & potion' given to James and said by some to be poisoned (and possibly the work of Buckingham): the relation refutes the charge and argues that it was a perfectly decent remedy that had nothing to do with the king's death (fol. 68ᵛ). Fiction masquerading as fact (*Vox Populi*) is thus read in the context of verbatim report (James's speech; the Protestation). We cannot know whether Cave, or any other readers of the pamphlet, took Scott's propaganda-fuelled, supposedly fly-on-the-wall account of Gondomar's council meeting for the truth. We can see, however, that Cave is amassing a range of texts on related matters and reading them with and against each other. What his conclusions were, again, we cannot know; but we can see him exercising his reason in the pages of his miscellany.

Huntington MS 46323 is a manuscript associated with the Calverly family of Yorkshire, and from its contents appears to have been compiled in the 1620s.[63] The first nineteen folios are taken up with verse, and the rest of the book is filled with law notes written in two columns cross-wise on the page, starting from the other end of the volume. The notes are in a different hand from the poetry, but there is one interesting connection, with the second copyist transcribing a section of a law book concerned with libelling only a

---

[60] Bellany, *The Politics of Court Scandal*, p. 114.   [61] Ibid.

[62] Cave has signed the manuscript in two places; at fol. 1ᵛ rev. he has written '1626: scriptum̲ est: Bri: Cave: forts', while at fol. 2 he has written 'Qui sapit pauca loquetur – Brian Cave'.

[63] On this manuscript, see Marotti, *Manuscript*, p. 42; Peter Beal (compiler), *Index of English Literary Manuscripts*, volume I: *1450–1625*. Part I: *Andrewes-Donne* (London: Mansell, 1980), 1.2.15; 2.1.557.

few pages after the first hand has copied out virulent anti-Spanish poems. The first copyist transcribes Michael Drayton's 'To his coy love, a canzonet' ('I pray thee leaue loue mee noe more', fol. 3^v), Donne's 'The Sunne Rising' (here entitled 'Ad Solem', as it is in several manuscripts, fol. 4^r), and Sir Henry Wotton's 'Ode on ye Queene of Bohemia' ('you meaner beauties of ye night', fol. 4^v), before moving on to more politically sensitive material. One of the anti-Spanish poems begins

> All the news that now is told
> Is of the <Spanish> ^golden^ Lady
> The Pope will not allow king James
> To bee her owne Sweet Daddy

and ends with the plea 'God send o^r Charles safe home againe / And let her worship tarry'.[64] Another (beginning 'Poor silly wight that carkes all the night') is similarly hopeful of an end to the marriage negotiations, though perhaps less sanguine, ending

> But yet dare I say and so will I pray
>   God saue vs from Spanish infection
> The Devill and the Pope the Masse and the Rope
>   And all their Priestly correction
> God grant her to proue true of her loue
>   As he of his royall desert
> And as for their gold to say I dare be bold
>   Wee shall nere need the helpe of Cart.
>   (fol. 11^r)

Both of these poems set speculation about the nature of the marriage negotiations and, especially, the trustworthiness of the Spanish against more personal petitions for the safety of the country. The second of them suggests that the Match is part of a large-scale papal plot for the reconversion of England, as *Vox Populi* had also argued.[65] Mixing news, rumour, and opinion, they combine the public and the individual voice and thus, in the pages of a manuscript miscellany, co-opt the copyist into the debate in which they are engaging.[66] The libels in this manuscript are consistently critical of the pacific policies of the period from 1618 to 1623, and display

---

[64] Huntington MS 46323, fols. 9^v; 10^r.

[65] See [Thomas Scott], *Vox Populi or Newes from Spayne* (n.p., 1620), sig. B2^r.

[66] The manuscript also contains a copy of the libel / counsel poem addressed to James and sometimes attributed to Robert Herrick, 'The King's Five Senses' (fols. 15^r–15^v), which is found in the politically dominated Herrick manuscript in the University of Texas at Austin. See Norman K. Farmer, Jr. (ed.), 'Poems from a Seventeenth-Century Manuscript with the Hand of Robert Herrick', *The Texas Quarterly* 16:4 (Winter, 1973), supplement, and McRae, *Literature, Satire and the Early Stuart State*, pp. 75–82 (who argues convincingly for its attribution to William Drummond of Hawthornden).

a scepticism about the motives of foreign powers – another anti-Spanish poem remembers the Armada and fears a repeat of 1588 but with less assurance of English success (fol. 11^r), while one against the French worries about the powers of the Guises and the weakness of the king (fols. 17^r–18^v). The last anti-Spanish poem in the collection was written after Charles's return from Spain without the Infanta, and is unequivocal in its celebration of this conclusion to the story:

> The Sonne of o^r most noble King
> He went to Spaine to fetch a thing
> I hope that you haue heard of it before, before, before
> But they kept such adoe about her
> That he's come home againe without her
> And I am verye glad therefore, therefore, therefore.
>
> (fol. 16^r)

Put together these libels provide a running – if one-sided – commentary on the Spanish Match and testify to the popular anxiety surrounding it. Their outspokenness on the subject – even their temerity in discussing such an important piece of combined domestic and foreign policy – could have caused trouble for their authors and their recipients, especially after the two proclamations 'against excess of Lavish and Licentious Speech of matters of State' of 24 December 1620 and 26 July 1621. These proclamations, which were issued in the wake of widespread discussion of events in Europe (notably Frederick's defeat at Prague) and of the Spanish Match, and attacks on the Spanish Ambassador Gondomar (including Scott's *Vox Populi*), commanded subjects

> to take heede, how they intermeddle by Penne, or Speech, with causes of State, and secrets of Empire, either at home, or abroad, but containe themselves within that modest and reverent regard, of matters above their reach and calling, that to good and dutifull Subjects appertaineth; As also not to give attention, or any manner of applause of entertainement to such discourse, without acquainting some of Our Privie Councell, or other principall Officers therewithall, respective to the place where such speeches shall be used, within the space of foure and twentie houres, under paine of imprisonment, and Our High displeasure.[67]

Sceptical of the tendency of libellers to represent themselves as writing for the king's own good and against the evil counsellors that allegedly surrounded him, this first proclamation concluded with a warning:

---

[67] 'A Proclamation against Excess of Lavish and Licentious Speech of Matters of State', Whitehall 24 December 1620, in James F. Larkin and Paul L. Hughes (eds.), *Stuart Royal Proclamations*, volume 1: *Royal Proclamations of King James I 1603–1625* (Oxford: Clarendon Press, 1973), pp. 495–96, at p. 496.

Neither let any man mistake Us so much, as to thinke, that by giving faire, and specious attributes to Our Person, they can cover the scandalls, which they otherwise lay upon Our Government, but conceive, that Wee make no other construction of them, but as fine, and artificiall glosses, the better to give passage to the rest of their imputations and scandalls.[68]

These two proclamations emphatically restricted freedom of speech even as the first claimed that 'Wee doe well allow of *convenient* freedome of speech' (my italics),[69] and it is hard to see them as stemming only, or primarily, from a desire to protect the reputations of individual persons. Even if, as recent commentators have argued, such proclamations did not see any tightening or formalisation of print censorship, they certainly represented a serious attempt officially to restrain discussion of state matters.[70] They both encouraged auditors or recipients of 'licentious' words or works to turn state's evidence and report what they had heard to the authorities under pain of severe punishment.[71] This was essentially an extension of the offences covered by the statute of *scandalum magnatum*, or the slandering of a magistrate, first enacted in the Statute of Westminster of 1275 (3 Edw. I, c. 34), especially in the understanding of what was meant by 'publication';[72] the extension followed Coke's arguments in *Attorney General* v. *Pickering*,

---

[68] Ibid.

[69] Ibid., p. 495. 'Convenient' here means 'appropriate' or 'becoming'; see *OED*, under convenient, senses 4 and 5 (both obsolete, but still current in the seventeenth century).

[70] See Lambert, 'State Control of the Press in Theory and Practice', who argues that the purpose of the 20 December proclamation was 'only to assure the Spanish Ambassador that the state was doing its best, as in duty bound, to give him proper protection. There is no general tightening of censorship here' (p. 20); cf. Clegg, *Press Censorship in Jacobean England*, pp. 185–7.

[71] The second proclamation ends by announcing

Wee doe further charge and command, not onely Our Officers and Ministers, but all other our loving Subjects, as they tender Our pleasure, and will answere the contrary, that they use all diligence to discover and bring to Justice, all such as shall offend in either kind [by speaking or writing, or by entertaining or concealing 'licentious speech']; letting all men know, that Wee will extend the like severitie towards the remisnesse of such, who shall conceale, as against the boldnesse of audacious Pennes and Tongues, so unrespective of duetie to Government.

(Larkin and Hughes, *Stuart Royal Proclamations*, p. 521.)

[72] The statute declares that

forasmuch as there have oftentimes been found in the country [devisers] of tales whereby discord or occasion of discord has many times arisen between the king and his people or great men of this realm, for the damage that hath and may therefore ensue, it is commanded that from henceforth none be so hardy to cite or publish any false news or tales whereby discord or occasion of discord or slander may grow between the king and his people or the great men of the realm.

(Cited in J. F. Stephen, *A History of the Criminal Law of England*, 3 volumes (London: Macmillan, 1883), volume II, pp. 301–2.) On the statute and its development, see Manning, 'The Origins of the Doctrine of Sedition', pp. 111–12.

and was consistent with discussions held in the court of Star Chamber in 1599. There the Lord Keeper, Thomas Egerton, had announced

it may be some may thinck that to be hearers or present at such sedicious discourses or to knowe of the making and contriving of such libells is a small offence or none at all, but that the fault will lye wholy vpon the Devisors and Doeres thereof; But lett none be deceaved, for whosoever dothe but *perbere aures*, and doe conceale and not discover such talkeres and discoursers, and such sedicious libellores, hearing or being privie thereof[?] they cannot be deemed, but as maynteyneres and favoureres of the same, and to be punished as severely, as the principall Actors.[73]

The second copyist in Huntington MS 46323 provides a (probably unintentional) commentary on the potential dangers attendant on the first copyist's fondness for anti-Spanish libels, drawing on this legal history. In the midst of the law notes he has transcribed, it seems from Coke's *Reports*, a section on 'Libellers', which reads as follows:

A man finding a libell against a private man, must presently burne it or deliver it to some Magistrate. 2. If against a Magistrate or Publick person, to deliver it to some Magistrate that by examination the author may be found out. 3. Libellers (it seemeth) may be bound to their good behaviors as disturbers of the Peace, whether they be contrivers, procurers, or publishers of the libels; for such libelling and defamation tendeth to the raising of quarrels and effusion of bloud, and speciall occasions to the breach of the Peace. 4. Libelling is by scandalous writings, by book, ballad, epigram, or rime; 2. by scandalous words, as jests, taunts, or songs. 3. by hanging up of pictures or signes of reproach neere the place where the party traduced doth converse most, as gallowes, cucking stoole, pillorie, hornes, or such like. (fol. 48ᵛ rev.)[74]

These examples give some sense of the way that manuscript miscellanies gathered politically sensitive material and provided a space in which their compilers could collect examples of others' free speech. They did this in the context of increasing concerns about the effects of such material and of proclamations and law cases that denied its claims to be part of counsel, instead deeming it 'licentious and bold', 'unfitting', and 'an offence against

---

[73] PRO SP 12/273, fol. 61ʳ, cited in Kaplan, *The Culture of Slander*, p. 24. On the history of slander and defamation, see (in addition to works cited in n. 31 above) Stephen, *A History of the Criminal Law of England*, volume II, pp. 298–309; W. S. Holdsworth, 'Defamation in the Sixteenth and Seventeenth Centuries', *Law Quarterly Review* 159 (July 1924): 302–15; *Law Quarterly Review* 160 (October 1924): 397–412; *Law Quarterly Review* 161 (January 1925): 13–31; Sir John Spelman, *The Reports of Sir John Spelman*, ed. by J. H. Baker, 2 volumes (London: Selden Society, 1977–8), volume I, pp. 236–48; *Select Cases on Defamation to 1600*, ed. by R. H. Helmholz (London: Selden Society, 1985).

[74] Cf. Coke, 'The Case *de Libellis famosis*', p. 125.

the law of God'.[75] I want now to return to the case of *Attorney General* v. *Pickering* and to one of the texts that was at the heart of that case. I will examine this text as it appears in a manuscript miscellany that displays a thoroughgoing engagement with issues of free speech, counsel, and libel; this case study will provide material evidence for the claims I have so far been making in more general terms.

DEFINING LIBEL IN 1605

The landmark case of *Attorney General* v. *Pickering* in 1605 plays a crucial part in the connection between counselling and libelling. In his report on the case, Coke resolved several points, of which one of the most important was – as has been recognised – the identification of a libel against a magistrate with a criticism of the monarch who appointed him. He explained why this was necessary in the following terms:

if [a libel] be against a magistrate, or other publick person, it is a greater offence [than if against a private man]: for it concerns not only the breach of the peace, but also the scandal of government; for what greater scandal of government can there be than to have corrupt or wicked magistrates to be appointed and constituted by the King to govern his subjects under him? and greater imputation to the state cannot be, than to suffer such corrupt men to sit in the sacred seat of justice, or to have any meddling in or concerning the administration of justice.[76]

On the face of it, Coke's statement supports Debora Shuger's argument that libels were intended to undermine authority by the foul means of insinuation and association.[77] If we consider it from the position of would-be frank counsellors, however, its significance is rather different. Coke's report seriously diminished their ability to present themselves as loyal servants of the crown through the extreme medium of libelling its servants or calling for their removal.[78] The case and the report are not just important for the

---

[75] 'A Proclamation against excesse of Lavish and Licentious Speech of matters of State', Ashby, 26 July 1621, in Larkin and Hughes, *Stuart Royal Proclamations*, volume I, p. 520; Coke, 'The Case *de Libellis famosis*', p. 125.

[76] Coke, 'The Case *de Libellis famosis*', p. 125. Cf. the report of Coke's speech in Star Chamber during the case, where he said that 'allthoughe the libelle be true & ye person infamous, yet it is a great offence. & by ye Course of lawe a lybelle is founde an olde sinne. for ye state & gouernmente is delyuered to ye magistrate, & therefore any priuate deliuery or wrytinge of a lybelle is a greate offence: yea, to see it, heare or report it' (William Paley Baildon (ed.), *Les Reportes del Cases in Camera Stellata 1593 to 1609. From the Original MS of John Hawarde* (privately printed, 1894), p. 225). Cf. also Bacon (?), 'An aduertisement': 'to defame a private man is indeede to him a losse Invaluable, but to deface a prince or gouvernor dissolveth and subverteth the state' (p. 432).

[77] See note 30 above.   [78] Cf. Bellany, 'A Poem on the Archbishop's Hearse', p. 163.

restating and redefinition of libel law: the occasion and the nature of the case, and Coke's motives in his restating, are equally worthy of note.

The case against Lewis Pickering was for libelling Queen Elizabeth and Archbishop Whitgift by placing a scandalous poem on the latter's hearse; but Pickering was only prosecuted after he was implicated by Thomas Bywater.[79] Pickering, a Northamptonshire gentleman and a graduate of the puritan-dominated Emmanuel College, Cambridge, had been close to the king since joining in the desperate rides north of many hopeful courtiers after Elizabeth's death in 1603.[80] Bywater was a Cambridge graduate – also with links to Emmanuel – who after ordination had failed to be preferred to any living and became an itinerant preacher; he 'preached such schismatical doctrines as he was suspended from preaching',[81] but he had served as chaplain to Lord Hunsdon and tutor to Lord Sheffield's children.[82] In February 1605, he presented a tract to the king as James was out hunting at Ware; his rooms were subsequently searched, and a copy of the libel on Whitgift was found.[83] Coke examined Bywater, and ascribed his actions and puritan attitudes to the disaffection of one passed over for preferment, but also raised the more threatening possibility of a puritan conspiracy, saying that 'it was plotted by Biwater & his complices that in there sermons & praiers they showlde stirre the people to a desyre of reformacyon, w[ch] is not tolerable in a monarchie but in a Democracie'.[84]

Pickering's libel, as the object of a Star Chamber prosecution and the origin of Coke's Report, has thus far been studied at the expense of Bywater's tract. I want here to redress the balance, and consider the latter as it appears in a manuscript miscellany copied well after Bywater's rash delivery of

[79] See Bellany, 'A Poem on the Archbishop's Hearse', pp. 137–41.

[80] Pickering was admitted to Emmanuel in 1587 (Sarah Bendall, Christopher Brooke, and Patrick Collinson, *A History of Emmanuel College* (Woodbridge: The Boydell Press, 1999), p. 80); on his ride to Edinburgh and his presence in James's entourage around 1604 as one of several 'men who could interpret the mind of the puritans to the king and his to them', see Patrick Collinson, *The Elizabethan Puritan Movement* (Oxford: Clarendon Press, 1967), p. 450; Bellany, 'A Poem on the Archbishop's Hearse', pp. 141–4.

[81] From Coke's 'Anatomy' of Bywater, *HMC Salisbury* 16, 35.

[82] Bywater graduated BA from Christ's College, Cambridge, in 1592/3, and MA in 1596 (John Peile (compiler), *Biographical Register of Christ's College, 1505–1905*, 2 volumes (Cambridge: Cambridge University Press, 1910) I, 197). He was at Emmanuel College in 1601 (Bendall, Brooke, and Collinson, *A History of Emmanuel College*, p. 80). On Bywater's relations with Lord Hunsdon and Lord Sheffield, see *HMC Salisbury* 16, 83; 108–9.

[83] The exact date of the presentation to James has been unclear (see Bellany, 'A Poem on the Archbishop's Hearse', p. 140, n. 8): the unique copy discussed below dates it to 20 February 1604/5, which is congruent with letters by James Montagu and the earl of Worcester written on 23 and 25 February that mention the tract. See Bod. MS Rawl. B.151, fol. 96[v]: 'presented and given to the king with his own hand, the 20.th of febr: at Ware. 1604'. On this manuscript, see further below.

[84] *Les Reportes del Cases in Camera Stellata*, ed. by Baildon, p. 225.

his work. For Bywater has not only effectively been sidelined in historical accounts of these events; after being examined by Coke and Cecil he was sent to the Tower of London and, after sending a series of increasingly desperate pleas for mercy to Cecil and the Privy Council, he disappears from the historical record.[85] Although presented in a single copy directly to the king, Bywater's book was called 'a very Paschall fitte for Rome' by Coke and 'the most saucy and dangerous thing that ever I saw' by James Montagu.[86] Taking a closer look at his tract can help us to see quite how broad the definition of a libel or pasquil could be, as well as demonstrating the enduring interest and use of such texts by politically engaged individuals.

READING AND WRITING LIBELS IN SHROPSHIRE, 1618–1627

At the end of the second decade of the seventeenth century, in Shropshire, the godly minister Robert Horn (1565–1640) was compiling a manuscript miscellany. The miscellany – now Bodleian Library MS Rawlinson B.151 – is a quarto, bound in contemporary vellum;[87] the pages are densely packed in a fairly small hand, accommodating roughly 205,000 words on its 105 folios. Unlike many miscellanies, where details about the compiler and the location of compilation remain obscure, Horn's inscriptions tell us that MS Rawlinson B.151 was transcribed at Clunbury, Ludlow, and Westhope in Shropshire between the years 1618 and 1627. Horn matriculated at Magdalen Hall, Oxford, in 1581, proceeding to take his BA in 1584 and his MA in 1587. He was chaplain of Magdalen Hall between 1585 and 1595; in 1596 he was presented as rector of Ludlow parish by the Earl of Essex, soon getting into trouble for zealous behaviour such as failing to wear a surplice and refusing to make the sign of the cross at baptism.[88] In the 1620s Horn corresponded with the godly Sir Robert Harley, who lived relatively close to Ludlow, at Brampton Bryan – and for whom John Hoskyns may have written his

---

[85] See *HMC Salisbury*, vol. XVII, pp. 213, 320 459. Pickering wrote to the Privy Council that he had no intention of publishing his libel, but had only given a copy to Bywater on the condition that he kept it secret, that his acquaintance with Bywater was recent and intermittent, and that he was in the king's favour; he was released from the Tower in 1605 and his fine waived (*HMC Salisbury (Cecil)*, volume XVII, pp. 620–1, 623.

[86] *Les Reportes del Cases in Camera Stellata*, ed. by Baildon, p. 225; *HMC Salisbury*, volume XVII, p. 65.

[87] See *Catalogi Codicum Manuscriptorum Bibliotechae Bodleianae* (1862), volume V (i), p. 502.

[88] On Horn see *DNB*, under Horn, Robert; Michael Faraday, *Ludlow 1085–1660. A Social, Economic and Political History* (Chichester: Phillimore, 1991), p. 71; on Horn and the manuscript, see also David Colclough, ' "The Muses Recreation": John Hoskyns and the Manuscript Culture of the Seventeenth Century', *Huntington Library Quarterly* 61:3 and 4 (1998): 369–400, at pp. 386–9.

rhetorical handbook, *Directions for Speech and Style* around 1599.[89] Between 1613 and 1632 Horn published eight works: sermons and expositions of portions of Scripture, and an edition of *Three Sermons Preached by . . . Doctor Eedes* (London, 1627).[90] The sermons support Horn's reputation for 'godliness': in one of his collections, *Certaine Sermons, of the Rich Man and Lazarus* (London, 1619) he draws on du Plessis Mornay to describe the time in which he and his parishioners are living as 'an age and time, wherein *vngodlinesse*, which . . . was wont but to whisper men in the eare, and lispingly to speake between the teeth, doth now most boldly, and without all blush of shame, with open mouth, call vpon both Bench and Pulpit for protection'.[91] Horn goes on to lament that 'it is a corrupt time and state where the poore are not provided for, but by begging at doores', and, drawing attention to the number of sturdy beggars filling the highways, asks 'doth not this both preache to our eares, and proue to our faces, that somewhat in the Church, and somewhat in the Common-wealth is out of course?'[92]

MS Rawlinson B.151 is dominated by texts connected with matters of freedom of speech and counsel. As well as being the repository of the only known copy of Bywater's tract, it contains the 1624 proclamation against popish and puritanical books (fol. 2^r);[93] Sir Philip Sidney's letter to Queen Elizabeth, from 1579 (fols. 3^r–6^r); the letter from Sir Charles Cornwallis to King James explaining his involvement in the inflammatory speeches of 1614 (fols. 6^r–7^v); Scott's *Vox Populi* (1620) (fols. 19^v–30^r; see figure 1) and one of only two extant copies of his *Sir Walter Rawleigh's Ghost* (1626) (fols. 50^r–54^r); the speech purportedly by Archbishop Abbot against the Spanish match (fol. 54^r); the letter from Thomas Alured to Buckingham on the

[89] On Horn's correspondence with Harley, see Jacqueline Eales, *Puritans and Roundheads: The Harleys of Brampton Bryan and the Outbreak of the English Civil War* (Cambridge: Cambridge University Press, 1990), pp. 48–9 and n. 15, citing BL Portland MS Loan 29/119. Harley was bound with Hoskyns when he entered Middle Temple on 24 October 1599; for arguments suggesting that he was the most likely addressee of the *Directions*, see Louise Brown Osborn, *The Life, Letters and Writings of John Hoskyns* (New Haven: Yale University Press, 1937), pp. 106–7; Baird W. Whitlock, *John Hoskyns, Serjeant-at-Law* (Washington: University Press of America, 1982), pp. 137–8.

[90] Horn's published works are *Life and Death. Foure sermons. Also points of instruction for the ignorant* (London, 1613); *The Christian Governor, in the common wealth, and private families (Gods gentle remembrance)* (London, 1614); *Points of Instruction for the Ignorant. As also, an exposition of the ten commandments and the Lords prayer* (a reprint with additions of part 2 of *Life and Death*) (London, 1617); *Certaine Sermons, of the Rich Man and Lazarus* (London, 1619); *The Shield of the Righteous: Or the Ninety First Psalm, Expounded* (London, 1625); *A Caveat to Prevent Future Judgements* (London, 1626) and *The History of the Woman of Great Faith. Treatised and Expounded* (London, 1632).

[91] Horn, *Certaine Sermons*, sig. A2^r.   [92] Ibid., sigs. D4^v–E^r; E^r.

[93] 'A Proclamation against Seditious, Popish, and Puritanicall Bookes and Pamphlets', Nottingham, 15 August 1624, in Larkin and Hughes, *Stuart Royal Proclamations*, volume 1, pp. 599–600.

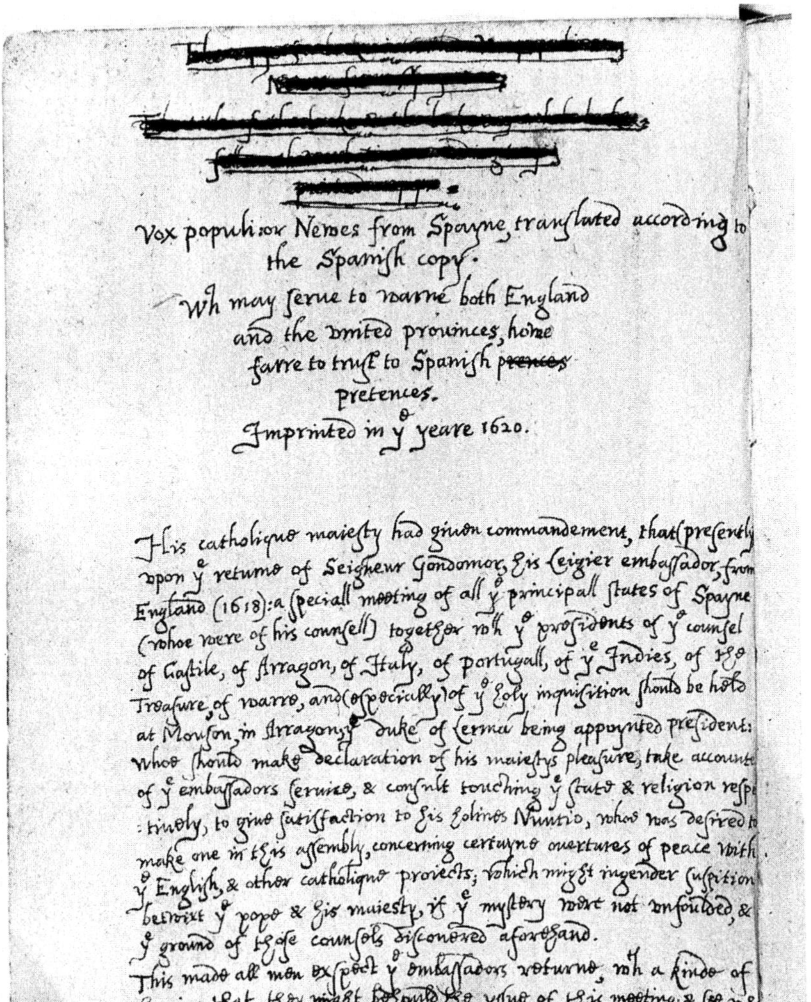

Figure 1. Thomas Scott, *Vox Populi* (1620), transcribed by Herbert Jenks in Bodleian Library Oxford MS Rawlinson B.151, fol. 19ᵛ.

same subject (fols. 17^v–19^r); records of proceedings in the Parliaments of 1610, 1621, 1624, 1625, 1626, and 1628; records of the proceedings against Buckingham in 1626 (fols. 76^v–77^r; 78^v; 83^r–84^r; 86^r) as well as Buckingham's 'relation' and a 'briefe' of it (fols. 103^v; 60^r–60^v); a letter from Thomas Morton, then Bishop of Coventry and Lichfield, to 'the Ministers of his diocese in the county of Salop, concerning a contribution for the ffrench protestants in England' (fols. 97^r–97^v); and several poems by the notoriously outspoken John Hoskyns: his libel on Bacon's fall in 1621, 'Great Verulam is very lame' (fol. 102^v), his verses to his son warning of the dangers of frank speech, 'Sweet Benjamin, while thou art yong' (fol. 103^r), and 'A Dreame', which portrays Hoskyns's wife pleading for her imprisoned husband (fol. 103^r; headed 'Mr. Hoskins his dreame in the Tower. 1614.').

The links between these texts show that the manuscript demands to be read as a collection, and that the juxtaposition of apparently disparate materials is in fact part of Horn's political agenda. Not only Horn's agenda, though: MS Rawlinson B.151 was a communal production, and contains tangible evidence of the way communities of readers were constituted through the circulation of texts. Both of the works by Thomas Scott were transcribed by Horn's younger neighbour in Shropshire, Herbert Jenks (he has signed them), who had graduated BA from Lincoln College, Oxford, in May 1620 and later attended Lincoln's Inn.[94] Given Jenks's links with Oxford and, later, the Inns of Court, this instance of text-sharing hints at a potentially extensive network of readers and writers with a range of geographical or institutional affiliations; we have to recognise the limitations of the physical evidence we have for the nature and extent of such communities. Jenks may well have been only one of several individuals from whom Horn received, or with whom he shared, texts: MS Rawlinson B.151 was used by Notestein, Relf, and Simpson as one of the sources for *Commons Debates in 1621*, and they suggest that for his parliamentary information Horn used a combination of separates and 'inside information' in the form of letters or notes from an MP with whom he was in correspondence.[95]

---

[94] Joseph Foster (ed.), *Alumni Oxonienses: The Members of the University of Oxford, 1500–1714*, 4 volumes (1892), volume II, p. 807. Jenks was admitted to Lincoln's Inn on 25 June 1631, and was called to the Bar on 29 January 1639 (*The Records of the Honourable Society of Lincoln's Inn*, volume I: *Admissions from A.D. 1420 to A.D. 1799* (Lincoln's Inn, 1896), p. 214; William Paley Baildon (ed.), *The Records of the Honourable Society of Lincoln's Inn. The Black Books* (1897), volume II, p. 350). I have found no trace of him between his graduation from Oxford and his admission to the Inn.

[95] See *CD 1621*, I, 100–1; passages from the manuscript are reproduced in *CD 1621*, VI, 365–428. Bod. Rawl. B.151 was also used by Foster for her copy of Nicholas Fuller's speech in 1610: see *PP 1610*, II, 405–41, citing MS Rawl. B.151, fol. 8^r.

He also used printed materials where possible.[96] Horn also received supplementary information about the 1621 Parliament after his main copying was done; additional passages appear later in the manuscript with cross-referencing to the main texts.[97] It appears that MS Rawlinson B.151 was only one of perhaps several such manuscripts with similar contents that Horn compiled: at one point he refers back to records of the 1614 Parliament in another 'written book' (fol. 13ᵛ).[98] Given Horn's interest in freedom of speech, it would be fascinating to see what he gathered from that difficult session, but unfortunately the book is probably lost.

Horn copied many of his texts as soon as they were available, and they were of obvious immediate relevance to one interested in current affairs. Scott's pamphlets, for instance, spoke explicitly to debates current in the 1620s – primarily the potential dangers of England's relations with Spain and James's reluctance to go to war.[99] Horn was also interested in texts from the past, though, and in the ways that they could be used to interpret the present.[100] As well as Sidney's letter to Queen Elizabeth advising against her marriage to the Duc d'Alençon,[101] he copied extracts from John Stubbs's *Gaping Gulf*, on the same subject (fols. 15ᵛ–17ᵛ). No mention is made of Stubbs's fate, nor is there any attempt to place the work in its historical context, beyond dating it at the beginning. Instead Horn has a marginal note, also at the beginning, which reads 'Against marrying wᵗʰ Papists by Protestants': the text is thus fitted into a running commentary on the Spanish Match and the dangers of inter-confessional unions (it is worth

---

[96] Horn often notes that a piece is 'since printed' – see, for instance, his copies of the king's letters to the Speaker in 1621 (fols. 41ᵛ, 45ᵛ) and his answer to the Commons' Petition (fols. 43–5).

[97] See, e.g., fol. 46, where the letter 'A' refers to the beginning of notes on the 1621 Parliament.

[98] 'There was a Parliamᵗ, Anno 1614; wherin nething proceded. the kings first speach therin look in the former written book.'

[99] On which subjects see also Horn's copies of letters exchanged by James and his son-in-law, Frederick of Bohemia (fols. 54ᵛ–56), a list of 'Reasons conceaued by the House of Commons for their reason of diswading the king from proceeding any further in his treatyes wᵗʰ Spayne,' and – to give a balanced view of the topic – a set of 'pretended advantages for the Match wᵗʰ Spaine. by secretary winwood' (fols. 98–9).

[100] Cf. his epistle to the reader in *Three Sermons Preached by . . . Doctor Eedes*: 'they [the sermons] concerne the times we liue in as directly and particularly as if they had bin set vnto them by the Preacher' (sig. A2ʳ).

[101] Horn's copy of this text – so sketchy as to count more as a paraphrase than as a transcription – has been dismissed by editors as of little value. However, it is precisely the effect of such ongoing dissemination and re-contextualisation that I want to suggest is of considerable importance to our understanding of manuscript culture in this period. See Sir Philip Sidney, 'A Letter Written by Sir Philip Sidney to Queen Elizabeth, touching her Marriage with Monsieur', in Sir Philip Sidney, *Miscellaneous Prose of Sir Philip Sidney*, ed. by Katherine Duncan-Jones and Jan Van Dorsten (Oxford: Clarendon Press, 1973), pp. 39–41. Duncan-Jones and Van Dorsten do note the telling changes that have been effected to the letter, pointing out that 'Strong anti-papist sentiments are added to the piece' (p. 41).

noting that it is followed immediately by Alured's letter to Buckingham). A 'libel' (Stubbs's pamphlet was often described thus) is revealed to have enduring political power, and its arguments (for Horn at least) to be ones of principle rather than personality – just as Stubbs himself argued. At the end of the extract, Horn shows that his book was designed to generate debate, urging us to look for the letter 'A' in the margin, where he has squeezed in a short exercise in arguing *in utramque partem*. Responding to Stubbs, he writes

Object. we finde the Jews often to match wth the Gentils as Boaz with Ruth, ruth. 4. 13, and the match allowed. – Answ. when the Lord gaue his law against such marriages, he specially excepted, if they wold renounce superstition, and embrace true religion, as Ruth did. Ruth. 1. 16. deut. 21. 12. 14. gen. 34. 15. 16. ps. 45. 10. 11. (fol. 17^v)

Writers like Stubbs, who were concerned to assert their status and fulfil their obligations as frank counsellors and who were rendered so vulnerable by Coke's conclusions in his report on libels, loom large in Horn's polit-ical miscellany. I want to return now to Thomas Bywater's tract, another example of direct advice to the monarch that Horn transcribed some time after its delivery (see figure 2).[102] We can only speculate as to how the text made its way from the manuscript delivered to James in 1605 and then read by members of the Privy Council, to Horn's miscellany in Shropshire in the early 1620s. We know that manuscript copies of Scott's *Vox Populi* were produced commercially by scriveners in the months after its publica-tion,[103] but Bywater's tract would not have been available to scriptoria in the same way, nor would it have had the widespread notoriety that made Scott's pamphlet a *succès de scandale* in print or manuscript. It is difficult to work from negative evidence: though no separates or other transcripts of Bywater's tract are known of, it is possible they survive unnoticed; and even if they do not, it is usually assumed that our extant manuscript archive from this period represents only a tiny fraction of what was written. However, I would hazard that we have to imagine a much more informal transmission for Bywater's tract, among a smaller reading constituency. Whatever the explanation, its appearance in Horn's manuscript highlights once more the vigour of the culture of scribal publication, and the way in which it fostered the dissemination and preservation of libellous texts over time and space.

---

[102] Horn copied Bywater's tract on 11 and 12 March 1621 (fol. 96^v).

[103] See Love, *The Culture and Commerce of Texts*, pp. 75, 96–7. Folger MSS V.a.223 is a manuscript separate of *Vox Populi*, while in Folger MS V.a.363 it is one of only two texts, running from fol. 12^r–fol. 34^v (the other text is John Hepwith's poem 'The Callidonian Forrest', beginning 'Whilome divided, from the maine Land stood', printed in 1641 (fols. 36^r–63^r)).

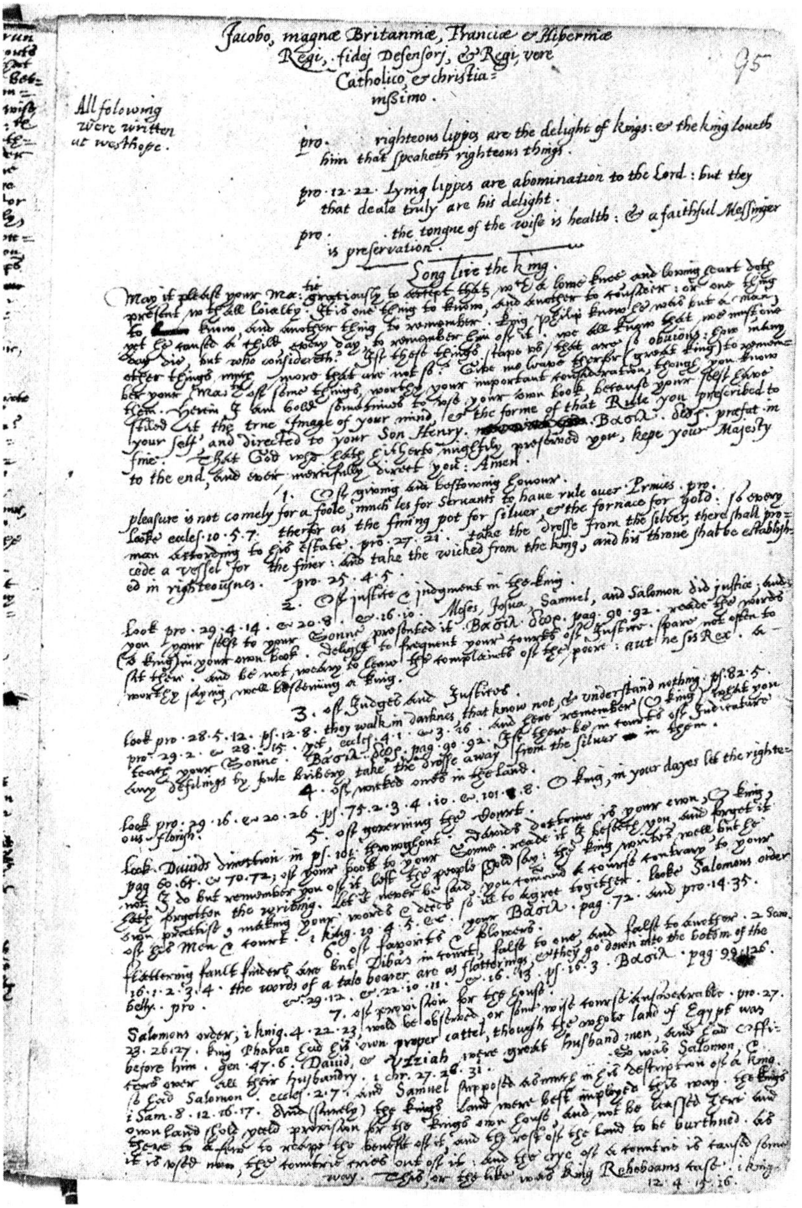

Figure 2. Thomas Bywater's tract presented to King James I in 1605, Bodleian Library MS Rawlinson B.151, fol. 95^r.

The burden of Bywater's work is that the king, while he knows how best to govern and has shown this in his book *Basilikon Doron*,[104] is both forgetful of his own principles and led astray by bad counsel.[105] Bywater, as his loyal and honest servant, is bound to remind him of where he is going wrong, and he does so by citing passages of Scripture alongside passages of *Basilikon Doron*, from his brief preface to the end of the tract. The text is headed with three quotations from the book of Proverbs that set the tone for the work as a whole: 'righteous lips are the delight of kings: and the king loveth him that speaketh righteous things' (16:13); 'Lying lippes are abomination to the Lord: but they that deale truly are his delight' (12:22) and 'the tongue of the wise is health: & a faithful Messinger is preservation' (an amalgam of 12:18 and 25:13). Many of the sections of Bywater's tract insist upon the importance of the king having an open and communicative relationship with his people, and on the dangers of being led astray. His section on 'governing the court' is typically outspoken, and even refers to Psalm 101, where David resolves to 'cut off' 'whoso privily slandereth his neighbour':

look. Dauids direction in ps. 101 throughout. Davids doctrine is your own, O king, pag. 60. 64. & 70. 72; of your book to your sonne. reade it I beseech you, and forget it not. I do but remember you of it, lest the people shold say: the king writes well, but he hath forgotten the writing. Let it never be said, you com͟mand a court contrary to your own practise, making your words & deeds so ill to agree together. looke Salomons order of his Men & court. 1 king. 10. 4. 5 &c. your Βασιλ. pag. 99, 126. (fol. 95ʳ)

I Kings 10:4–5 does not give a very clear idea of Solomon's court, but it is sufficient to provoke the Queen of Sheba into exclaiming in admiration, 'thy wisdom and prosperity exceeded the fame which I heard; Happy are thy men, happy are these thy servants, which stand continually before thee, and that hear thy wisdom' (I Kings 10:7–8). Most notable here, perhaps, is Bywater's repeated use of heavy-handed escape clauses such as 'lest the people shold say' and 'let it never be said': he denies responsibility for saying what would be truly outspoken while in fact articulating it, and at the same time associates his views with a much larger community.

---

[104] First printed, in an edition of seven copies, in 1599; reprinted in 1603 in Edinburgh and London, and later in the *Workes* (1616). See King James VI and I, *Political Writings*, ed. by J. P. Sommerville (Cambridge: Cambridge University Press, 1994), pp. xviii–xix, xxx.

[105] The text opens 'may it please your Ma:ᵗⁱᵉ graciously to accept that wᶜʰ a lowe knee, and loving heart doth present with all loialty. It is one thing to knowe, and another to consider: or one thing to know, and another thing to remember' (fol. 95ʳ).

In sections on 'favourites & folowers' and 'Councellours & their counceils' Bywater contrasts the pliability and insinuations of the flatterer with the sometimes harsh words of the counsellor, drawing on the traditions examined in chapter 1 above. He reminds James that counsel requires deliberation rather than a hasty response:

flattering fault finders are but Zibas in court, false to one and false to another. 2 Sam. 16. 1. 2. 3. 4. the words of a tale bearer are as flatterings, & they go down into the botom of the belly. pro. [large gap in text] & 29. 12. & 22. 10. 11. & 16. 13. ps. 16. 3. Βασιλ. pag. 99. 126.
. . .
look. pro. 20. 18. & 15. 22. & 20. 5. & 14. 15. Councelours counsel pro and contra: therfor what they say is to be weighed as in a balance; not lightly to be receaued, nor with like lightnes to be cast of. Ahitophels not to be trusted too farre, for they will prove false with the times: 2 Sam. 15. 31: but Daniels and Josephs are best councellours for a king: dan. 6. 1. 4. gen. 41. ch: or, if not these, yet an Hushaj is better than an Ahitophel. 2 Sam. 15. 32. 33. 34. &. 17. 6. 7. (fols. 95ʳ–95ᵛ)

The list of biblical references treating the value of wise and mature counsel and the dangers of youthful or flattering counsellors is impressive, and Bywater begins to sound almost like a commonplace book: indeed, the force of his argument is in part the result of this forest of citations.[106]

The need for the prince to be accessible was a recurrent topos in the literature of counsel, and James's increasing preference for reserved majesty elicited considerable criticism through the course of his reign. Bywater emphasises the importance of direct counsel and casts the alternative – the pyramid of communication via ministers and courtiers – in effective confessional terms, as an example of Roman Catholic corruption: 'Be open and affable to every rank of honest & good persons,' he advises, 'for intercession to Saints is idolatry. Βασιλ. pag. 46. you know your own words.' Moreover, he explains, continuing the religious metaphor – and punning on the sense of 'angel' as a gold coin worth about ten shillings – such mediation is financially corrupt, 'because these Saints must have adoration, as well as intercession; and we must bring Angels vnto them in this devotion. the sufferance of such superstition will eclipse the kinges glory. O king: giue not your glory vnto others, nor your praise to grauen images. Esa. 42. 8' (fol. 96ʳ).[107]

---

[106] Coke even referred to Bywater's book as 'the slanderous commonplaces' (*HMC Salisbury*, volume XVII, p. 114).

[107] The pun was picked up by the Earl of Devonshire: 'because Mr Bywater teaches me that the saints of the Court must not only have adoration but intercession, though I cannot do it by angels who are perfect, yet I have sent you six suckling rabbits of Wansteed, which I am sure are innocent' (to Viscount Cranborne (Cecil); *HMC Salisbury*, volume XVI, p. 430).

The financial and the ecclesiastical are treated at greater length in Bywater's sections on 'Taxes and Subsidies' and 'Popery and purity'. The latter resonates with the sentiments of the 'godly' after the compromises of Hampton Court, Bywater asserting that

Popery wonderfully hath encreased, & doth, since your Ma:^ties coming to the scepter of England; and it is worse wth the Puritan, better wth the Papist then ever in the late good Queens dayes. Imprisonment of good Ministers is as ordinary, or more, then of Papists. all favour is shewed to the dumbe Ministery, and much favour unto Popery: but disgrace & disfavour to zelous & faithful Ministers. (fol. 95^v)

He goes on to demand, alluding to the 'blind guides' of Matthew 23:24, 'Is not this to straine out a gnat, & to swallow a camel?' There are direct challenges in this section to the increasingly concerned attempts on the part of James and his Council to distinguish between the 'moderate' and 'radical' godly and to exclude the latter from consideration as true members of the Church.[108] Bywater puts the question of inter- and intra-confessional definition starkly:

the Papist is Arch-enemy to the Puritan: quaere (therfor) if the Puritan be not the best Protestant. the papist can agree well inough with the common Protestant: see cathol. supplicat. pag. 16: quaere (therfor 2^ly) if the common Protestant be not the worst Protestant. The Puritan so called (for I speake vt vulgus) desireth nothing but what is in your Ma:^ties own words & writings: Βασιλ. pag. 43. wch is that all churches in your dominions be planted with godly & sufficient Pastors; and that the doctrine & discipline of the Church be in purity after Gods word. And here, let not the errors of some in Scotland prejudge us your Loving Subjects & Ministers here in England: we are not as they were: we do not as they did. (fol. 95^v)

As for taxes and subsidies, Bywater allows that they 'are lawful, yet Asa his oppression is unlawful: 2 chr. 16. 10: and, neither Asa's oppression, nor Rehoboam's imposition will prosper'. 'When warres are raised, and other extraordinary matters do compell you,' he goes on, 'you may raise Subsidies. but do it as rarely as you can: and when you do it, employ it all about the right use, & not sinisterly. be therein yourself *fidus depositarius*. Βασιλ. pag. 99. happy are the people that haue such a king' (fol. 95^v).

Reporting the delivery of Bywater's tract to James at Ware, James Montagu (the Dean of the Chapel) wrote to Archbishop Bancroft that 'he spares neither the king, Councillor nor Court but teaches the king in every

---

See Bellany, 'A Poem on the Archbishop's Hearse', pp. 143–4; Kenneth Fincham and Peter Lake, 'The Ecclesiastical Policies of James I and Charles I', in *The Early Stuart Church*, ed. by Kenneth Fincham (Basingstoke: Macmillan, 1993), pp. 23–50, esp. 25–8.

point his duty'.[109] The tract is divided into numbered sections in Horn's miscellany, and these give a good idea of the scope of these 'points':

1. Of giving and bestowing honour;
2. Of justice & judgement in the king;
3. of Judges and Justices;
4. of wicked ones in the lawe;
5. of governing the Court;
6. of favourites & folowers;
7. of provision for the house;
8. of taxe and subsidies;
9. of Councellours & their counceils
10. of nobles & great ones
11. of Leagues and peace
12. of Popery and purity
13. of formality & ceremonies
14. of reverence at the word & prayer
15. of hearing Preachers
16. of Swearing
17. of Sport & pleasure
18. of restraint of accesse to the kings face
19. of discipline, or church goverment
20. of greevances of the people.   (fols. 95ʳ–96ᵛ)

Throughout his tract, Bywater presents himself in the common language of such texts as speaking for the community at large in the voice of a frank and friendly adviser. He ends by stressing that he is only fulfilling what he considers to be his responsibilities, writing

thus I have plainly, as I cold, and faithfully I doubt not, discharged the duty of a good & Loyal Subject to the Lord my king, for the honour of the Lord my God, the good of my countrey, and peace of myne own soule. Let my Lord the king be gracious vnto me, accepting this fruit of my love & loyalty, and pardoning my fault, if any be. (fol. 96ʳ)

For Horn, transcribing over fifteen years later, the text was an example not just of godly writing but of frank counsel, to be employed, considered, and redeployed in a deliberative context. He is less interested in Bywater's fate than in his presentation as a loyal but unhappy subject forced to speak out. This is not, however, how the tract was received by either James or his Council. They launched a detailed investigation into Bywater's contacts

---

[109] James Montagu, Dean of the Chapel, to the Archbishop of Canterbury, 23 February 1604/5, in *HMC Salisbury*, volume XVII, p. 65.

and history, proceeding by Coke's examination of him (as recorded in the 'Anatomy', quoted above) and by seeking letters or depositions from anyone connected with him. The bookseller from whom Bywater had bought the blank paper sextodecimo into which the tract was written testified that he was a more or less regular customer (while trying to make the casual nature of this relationship clear).[110] Lord Hunsdon, who had employed Bywater as his chaplain, was enjoined to search Bywater's chamber, and in his letter to Cranborne reporting that this had been done also distanced himself from any knowledge of Bywater's offence.[111] Lord Sheffield's letter to Cranborne is more revealing, describing Bywater's conduct when he was 'schoolmaster' to Sheffield's children, 'about some 20 years past'.[112] Bywater, it seems, had spent more time in zealous admonition than he did in the schoolroom, for he wrote and presented a tract to his employer:

being, as he seemed to me, religiously bent to follow the preaching of the Word I was willing to further him till at the last his zeal began to be so hot that before he had ever given me any private admonition of those faults he supposed to be in me he wrote a book and presented it to me, even as he did this to the King; wherein he very sharply reproved [me] for my great faults, of which I know and confess for some of them I was justly taxed, and yet they were but following hunting and hawking too much. But for most of them he reproved me as falsely as I make no doubt he has done the King and the State. Whereupon, though I would say little, he being a minister of the word of God, thinking it might proceed from his unadvised zeal, yet finding him to grow more precise every day insomuch that he would maintain to my face that both hawks and hounds, which I did then and do now moderately delight in, were not ordained by God for man's recreation but for

---

[110] See the deposition of Richard Boyle, 4 March 1604/5, in *HMC Salisbury (Cecil)*, volume xvii, p. 82:

> I have known [Bywater] a year or thereabouts. I never had any dealings with him, save that he has now and then bought a book of me. To my remembrance I never bound any books for him but only a little small paper book of white paper, and to my remembrance I ruled it also, and this I bound the lat summer, since which time I never saw the book. There was no writing in the book, for he spake to me to make the book of paper and it was in 16.

[111] See *HMC Salisbury*, volume xvii, p. 83, Lord Hunsdon to Viscount Cranborne, 4 March 1604/5:

> I have received a letter from the Privy Council by Mr. John Corbett; thereby finding their favours towards me in sending him to make search in Mr. Bywater's chamber, who was my chaplain, I have performed the contents so far as my health would suffer me; and when I could stay no longer, appointed one of my men to stay with him, until he had satisfied himself of all Mr. Bywater's books and papers. For Mr. Bywater's fault what it is, God knoweth, for I do not know, but it seems he hath been busier than becomes his vocation. Had I known he had been so hot brained that he could not contain himself within the compass of that I hired him for, he should never have been my chaplain.

[112] *HMC Salisbury (Cecil)*, volume xvii, p. 108: Lord Sheffield to Viscount Cranborne. Sheffield must be exaggerating the number of years that have passed.

adorning the world with creatures of such sorts, some for the earth and some for the heavens.[113]

This advice did not go down well; Sheffield goes on, 'as soon as with conveniency I could provide me of another I rid myself of him'.[114] The paths of employer and recalcitrant servant were to cross again, however, when Bywater buttonholed Sheffield at Parliament. As he was shown the book Bywater had been working on, we can imagine Sheffield's reaction as that of one of Donne's speakers in the *Satires*, taken aside by a bore recognisable from the Horatian tradition, but suddenly more dangerous:[115]

he came to me the last Parliament, and presented to me a certain paper book which he desired me to look over, and told me, if my remembrance fail me not very much, that he had presented the like of it to the King at his first coming into England, which speech of his made me the willinger to see it. But having received it I never read above one half leaf of it, but seeing it tend to such reformations in the church as I knew were distasteful to the State and nothing pleasing to myself, at his next coming I delivered it to him again, using very few words, for I was very weary of his company. I saw by that little I read he aimed at so unfitting things, yet finding in some part of that I read something touching a learned ministry as also some amendment to be wished touching the abuses in the spiritual courts; and remembering that the King in his religious care of the State had wished us in the Parliament to proceed in those things; in either of which I think there is [not] any good Christian but would wish some amendment; the unfittingness of that it seemed to me he aimed at, as also the good intention of the King and the State well known to me touching those two points forenamed, drew this answer from me briefly – for I had no mind to have many words with him – that there would be something done in those things that were necessary to be reformed, of which the King to my knowledge had a great care, but now the Parliament was near an end and therefore the time served not. This was the briefest answer I could at that time think of, which if it be by his delivery otherwise taken than I meant it I am sorry, but this I protest was the truth.[116]

---

[113] Ibid.   [114] Ibid.
[115] See John Donne, *Satire IV*, ll. 119–20; 129–33:

> He, like a priviledg'd spie, whom nothing can
> Discredit, Libells now 'gainst each great man.
>   . . .
> I more amas'd than Circes prisoners, when
> They felt themselves turne beasts, felt my selfe then
> Becoming Traytor, and mee thought I saw
> One of our Giant Statutes ope his jaw
> To sucke me in

> (*Donne's Poetical Works*, ed. by H. J. C. Grierson, 2 volumes (Oxford: Clarendon Press, 1912), volume I, p. 163)

[116] *HMC Salisbury*, volume XVII, p. 109.

Sheffield was obviously worried, though he was later reassured by Cranborne that the king did not blame him.[117] He had good reason to be concerned, since Bywater was prosecuted severely and outside of Star Chamber.[118] James, and the ministers who pursued the investigation, were convinced (or determined to be) that Bywater was part of a larger conspiracy, as can be seen from Coke's comment quoted above (p. 218). Certainly from the summer of 1603 there was a more or less organised puritan campaign to persuade the king that the godly were a significant and influential part of the church, supported by petitions to Parliament.[119] After the compromises of Hampton Court, a number of disaffected godly people attempted to warn the king about the need for further reformation and what they saw as his deflection from pro-puritan policies by his advisers.[120] Behind these campaigns was a belief that the godly were obliged to speak out and to counsel the king, and that in his turn he should listen to their counsel. At issue in the development of Jacobean ecclesiastical policy, in the reception of such acts of godly counselling and, especially, in Bywater's case, were questions of definition. When was a puritan 'moderate' and when 'radical'?[121] When was a campaign a conspiracy? When was counsel loyal advice and when was it sedition? The Privy Council, well aware of the need to spin the news, described Bywater as a 'seditious sectary'[122] and decided that his case needed to be seen as an attempt to undermine the government, not as an attempt to offer conscientious counsel on matters indifferent. Writing to James, probably in March 1604/5, they laid out their plan:

the best way that we for the present mean to proceed in is speedily to remove him to the Tower, as an argument to declare him guilty of a further offence, than for any private error or audacity. Next, we will so use it as the whole scope of his perilous projects may be made notorious (though not expressly divulged) to the end that those which would suppose that he is punished for his disobedience in matters of

---

[117] Lord Cranborne to Lord Sheffield, ibid., p. 124.

[118] At Pickering's trial, Coke declared ominously that 'this Court Can not proceede wth Bywater: he drawes deeper' (*Les Reportes del Cases in Camera Stellata*, ed. by Baildon, p. 225).

[119] See Collinson, *Elizabethan Puritan Movement*, pp. 452–4; B. W. Quintrell, 'The Royal Hunt and the Puritans, 1604–1605', *Journal of Ecclesiastical History* 31:1 (January 1980): 41–58, who discusses the importance of Northamptonshire puritan gentry.

[120] Such petitions had been proffered from the beginning of James's reign. The 'Poore mans peticion to the Kinge' (dated May 1603 and presented to James at Theobalds) is transcribed in BL MS Add. 22601, the subject of a forthcoming study by Maria Reardon. It is also found in BL MSS Add. 29607 (the miscellany of Randle Holme; fol. 17^r) and Harley 1925 (the miscellany of Nicholas Throckmorton-Carew; fols. 1^v–2^r). I am grateful to Maria Reardon for this information.

[121] See Bellany, 'A Poem on the Archbishop's Hearse', pp. 143–4.

[122] The Council to the king, ?March 1604/5, draft with corrections by Cranborne, in *HMC Salisbury*, volume XVII, p. 123.

ceremony may well understand it to be for other pernicious courses, conceived by him to the disturbance of the State.[123]

In some ways, of course, the Council were right: Bywater wanted to claim that he was speaking on behalf of a group, not acting for his private interest. But for them, such claims were by definition seditious and incompatible with monarchy, while for Bywater they were the duty of a loyal subject. For the Council this wider group was a shadowy puritan pressure group; for Bywater it was the people broadly conceived. By prosecuting Bywater according to their plan, the Council went on to argue, possible objections from a wider constituency of fickle and critical subjects would be anticipated:

the corrupt humour of many, who are always apter to scandalise the constant proceedings of state, than to discredit those who never can like the present government, may be so prevented that your Majesty's well affected subjects may be satisfied that such men's unconformity proceeds not for any scruple in matters indifferent or tenderness of conscience, as is suggested, but from some inward and malicious design as would by consequence bring it to question at last, whether it be indifferent for your Majesty to govern in a Monarchy, or be subject to a Presbytery.[124]

This is the course of action that led to Bywater's imprisonment for at least a year and a half – and, we might speculate, to his death in confinement. But it is difficult to see either his tract or Horn's miscellany as attempts to undermine a smooth-running 'civility of trust'. Bywater certainly exceeds his warrant as a preacher, especially a suspended one. But as Thomas Scott was fond of reminding his readers, 'necessitie supplie's the place of an ordinary calling'.[125] Bywater was drawing on a strong tradition of belief in prophetic outspokenness as licensed by God: according to this tradition (discussed in chapter 2), to remain silent was a far greater offence than to speak out. This does not mean that we should consider his tract as the acceptable face of libelling, and regard Pickering's libel as an insult too far. Rather, they exist on a continuum of political comment and analysis, and show the range of ways in which counsel might be delivered, depending partly on the degree of influence that an individual felt he possessed. And this is precisely how such texts were perceived by many contemporary readers – readers like Robert Horn – even if the king and his Privy Council thought otherwise.

Bywater's tract is both given an interpretative context by, and provides such a context for the other texts collected by Horn. Far from being an

---

[123] Ibid.   [124] Ibid.   [125] [Thomas Scott], *Vox Dei* (n.p., n.d. [1624]), sig. D[r].

opportunistic collection of any available news, as miscellanies are sometimes described, MS Rawlinson B.151 is a tool for the analysis of such news. Records of parliamentary proceedings note debates on freedom of speech, church government and foreign policy.[126] As well as the prose works that I have discussed so far, Horn has transcribed verse, in the form of libels and other poems, related to his engagement with matters of counsel and free speech. Towards the end of the volume, a long way after the copies of proceedings in the 1621 Parliament, he has copied a libel on Sir Giles Mompesson that rejoices lustily and punningly in the prosecution by the Commons and Lords of the abuser of patents:[127]

> S^r. Giles Mompesson, & ^S^r Fr:^ Mich<e>il
> [marg: March. 1621.]
> The tottering state of transitory things
> like to a Jade takes on, casts, kicks, & flings:
> that he who's this ^day^ Dominus fac totum,
> may, next day, be thought but a Man of Gothum.
> (Imposture-like) oppression hath been
> by inward putrefaction (long) unseen,
> till ripenes burst it, and good times did hy
> to bring some fit, some special remedy.
> a foile there is, a conquest in our costs,
> not of an host of men, but Man of Hosts.
> So, gentle Hosts; the happy day is com;
> Michel is not respected, Giles is mom.
> Drink healths, make bonefires, wash your merry throtes:
> mourn all in sack: and give your horse more otes.
> Sr Giles did think't no wisdom to abide;
> nor by St Giles his church, with his, to ride.
> brave hosts, your Lord of hosts is fled for feare;
> who might have staid, and ta'n his hanging here.
> but now the speach of Lame Giles proves a lye:
> for, if Sr Giles were Lame, how cold he flye?
>
> (fol. 102^v)[128]

---

[126] See, for instance, fol. 46^r, 'Additions of some passages in the former Parliament before their first recesse at Easter. 1621.', where 'freedom of speech' appears as one of the marginal notes.

[127] On the revival of parliamentary judicature in 1621 and the joint prosecution of Mompesson and others, see chapter 3 above.

[128] I have also found copies of this poem in Folger MSS V.a.345 (p. 126) and V.a.103 (fol. 73). On Folger MS V.a.345 see further below, and Arthur F. Marotti, 'Folger MSS V.a.89 and V.a.345: Reading Lyric Poetry in Manuscript', in *The Reader Revealed*, compiled and edited by Sabrina Alcorn Baron, with Elizabeth Walsh and Susan Scola (Washington, DC: Folger Shakespeare Library, 2001), pp. 45–57. Folger MS V.a.103 also contains an anagram on Mompesson that draws on the commonplace

The impeachment of Bacon in the same year receives a modicum of balanced commentary, with the popular poem in Bacon's favour, 'When you awake, dull Britans, and behold' (fol. 102^r), set alongside Hoskyns's 'Great Verulam is very lame' (fol. 102^v), which begins a short sequence of works by Hoskyns concerned with freedom of speech and with his imprisonment in the Tower after the dissolution of the 'Addled' Parliament of 1614.[129] The next of these poems after the Bacon piece is more personal, and directly concerns Hoskyns's confinement. It is in the form of a dream-poem, a well-tried method of distancing a text's potentially sensitive content from its author, but the allegory of 'A Dreame' is far from opaque, presenting the pathetic spectacle of three generations of Hoskyns's family – his mother, his pregnant wife, and his son – lamenting in front of the cave in which he is kept prisoner. Hoskyns has here been completely silenced, to underscore the reason for his incarceration: 'he smild, he sighd, then smote his brest, / as if he meant – God knowes the rest' (fol. 103^r; see figure 3).[130] The personal impact of Hoskyns's imprisonment seems to be the main force of the poem, with the old woman declaring that his family will die without him:

> 'Tis not the rule of sacred hest
> to kill the old one in the nest;
> as good be killed as from them hid,
> who die wth grief o God forbid.

But this domestic pathos is merely the spur for the wife's cutting analysis of the reasons for Hoskyns's punishment and the structural problems in the political realm that it reflects. The son, acting as stooge, asks innocently 'My father never was vnkind, / who lets him (then) to speake his mind? / . . . / o mother, say, who can do this?' Her answer asserts Hoskyns's good intentions as a counsellor and glances at the king's limitations:

---

equation of him with Empson in Henry VII's reign ('Mom Persons / More Empsons', fol. 73^r) and a quatrain based on the final line of this poem:

> The Proverbe of lame Gyles is false I say
> Had Gyles beene lame he had not runne away;
> Sr Gyles thought fit no longer to abide,
> For feare hee by St Gyles his church should ride. (fol. 73)

The compiler has also transcribed libels on Cecil, Frances Howard, and Somerset. On libels about Mompesson, see also McRae, *Literature, Satire and the Early Stuart State*, pp. 38–9.

[129] For this Parliament, and Hoskyns's part in it, see chapter 3 above.

[130] The poem also appears in BL MSS Add. 4130 (fols. 92^v–94^v); Add. 4149 (fols. 211^r–213^r); Add. 21433 (fols. 145^v–147^r); Add. 25303 (fols. 162^r–163^r); Harley 6947 (fols. 252^r–3^r); Bod. MSS Ashmole 36–7 (fol. 213^r); Ashmole 781 (pp. 129–31); Malone 19 (pp. 71–3). It is printed (from BL MS Harley 6947) in Osborn, *The Life, Letters and Writings of John Hoskyns*, pp. 206–8.

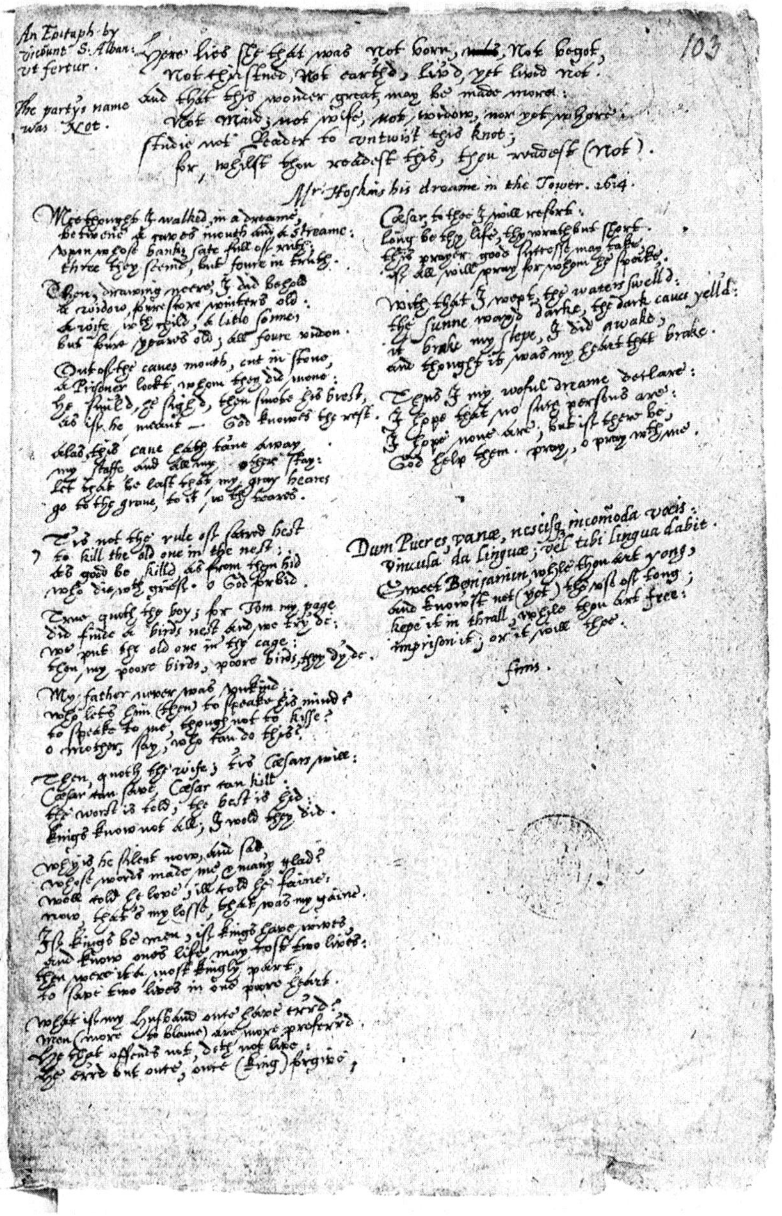

103

An Epitaph by vicount S. Alban: ut fertur.

The partys name was Not.

Here lies he that was Not born, [illegible], Not begot,
Not christned, Not earthd, livd, yet lived Not.
And that this wonder great may be made more:
Not Maid; not wife, not, widow, nor yet whore.
Studie not Reader to untwist this knot;
for, whilst thou readest this, thou readest (Not).

Mr Hoskins his dreame in the Tower. 1614.

Methought I walked, in a dreame,
betweene a caves mouth and a streame:
Upon whose banks sate full of ruth,
three they seemd, but foure in truth.

When, drawing neere, I did behold
a widow, fourescore winters old:
a wife, with child, a litle sonne,
but foure yeares old; all foure undon.

Out of the caves mouth, cut in stone,
a Prisoner lookt, whom they did mone:
he smild, he sighd, then smote his brest,
as if he meant — God knowes the rest.

Alas, this cave hath tane away
my staffe and all my other stay:
let that be last that my gray heares
go to the grave, to it, with teares.

Tis not the rule of nature best
to kill the old one in the nest;
as good be killd as from them hid
who die with griefe. o God forbid.

True quoth the boy; for Tom my page
did finde a birds nest, and we tryde:
we put the old one in the cage:
then, my poore birds, poore birds, they dyde.

My father never was unkinde:
who lets him (then) to speake his minde?
to speake to me, though not to kisse?
o mother, say, who can do this?

Then, quoth the wife; tis Caesars will:
Caesar can save, Caesar can kill.
the worst is told; the best is hid:
kings know not all; I would they did.

Why is he silent now, and sad,
whose words made me many glad?
well told he love; ill told he faine:
now that's my losse, that was my gaine.

If kings be men, if kings have wives,
and know ones life may cost two lives:
then were it a most kingly part,
to save two lives in one poore heart.

What if my husband once have errd?
men (more to blame) are more preferrd.
he that offends not, doth not live:
he errd but once, our (King) forgive,

Caesar, to thee I will resort:
long be thy life, thy wrath but short.
this prayer good Hostesse may take,
we all will pray for whom she spake.

With that I wept, the waters swelld:
the sunne waxd darke, the dark cave yelld:
it brake my slepe, I did awake,
and thought it was my heart that brake.

Thus I my woful dreame declare:
I hope that no such persons are:
I hope none are, but if there be,
God help them. pray, o pray with me.

Dum Puer es, vanae, nesciusque incomoda vocis:
Vincula da linguae; vel tibi lingua dabit.
Sweet Benjamin while thou art yong,
and knowst not (yet) the use of tong;
kepe it in thrall, while thou art free:
imprison it; or it will thee.

finis.

Figure 3. John Hoskyns, 'A Dreame' and 'Dum puer es, vanae' in English and Latin, Bodleian Library MS Rawlinson B.151, fol. 103r.

Then, quoth the Wife; 'tis Caesars will,
Caesar can save, Caesar can kill.
the worst is told, the best is hid.
kings know not all; I wold they did.

. . .

What if my Husband once have err'd?
Men (more to blame) are more preferr'd.
He that offends not, doth not live:
He err'd but once, once (king) forgive.

The poem was very popular, in its full twenty-stanza state, in shorter versions such as that in MS Rawlinson B.151 (which has thirteen stanzas), and in a cut-down version which combined the last two lines of the first stanza above with the whole of the final one.[131] Seven copies of one or the other version state that it was presented to the king by Hoskyns's wife, Bodleian Library MS Rawlinson D.160 adding the optimistic but erroneous sidenote that 'vpon ye sight of it the Kings ma:^tie most graciously granted her suite and her husband was forth with released' (fol. 3^v).[132]

The third and final poem by Hoskyns in MS Rawlinson B.151 is that addressed to his son, more rueful in tone than 'A Dreame'. It appears here as both a Latin distich and an English quatrain (see figure 3):

Dum Puer es, vanae, nescisque incommoda vocis
Vincula da linguae; vel tibi lingua dabit.

Sweet Benjamin, while thou art yong,
and know'st not (yet) the vse of tong,
kepe it in thrall, while thou art free:
imprison it; or it will thee.[133]

---

[131] This extract is found in BL MS Egerton 923 (fol. 11^r); Bod. MSS Ashmole 781 (p. 131); Eng. poet. e.14 (fol. 88^r rev.); Malone 16 (p. 20); Rawl. D.160 (fol. 3^v); Sancroft 53 (pp. 50 and 52); Corpus Christi College, Oxford, MS 327 (fol. 23^v); Folger MSS L.a.992 (a single leaf; verso) and V.a.262 (p. 90).

[132] Copies that describe the poem being delivered to the king by Benedicta Hoskyns are BL MS Egerton 923; Bod. MSS Ashmole 781; Eng. poet. e. 14; Malone 16; Rawl. D. 160 and Sancroft 53. Chamberlain went along with the ascription to Mrs Hoskyns, writing to Carleton on 23 February 1615 that 'Hoskins and his comperes are still in the Towre and no speach of theyre releasing, though Hoskins wife that is a poetesse hath ben a longe suitor, and presented the king with a petition in rime which I here send you' (*The Letters of John Chamberlain*, volume I, pp. 581–2).

[133] The poem is found, in one or other of these two forms, in fourteen other manuscripts: BL MSS Add. 4130 (fol. 93^v); Add. 10309 (fol. 148^r); Add. 21433 (fol. 147^r); Add. 25303 (fol. 163^r); Bod. MSS Ashmole 36–7 (fol. 213^r); Malone 19 (p. 149); Rawl. D. 727 (fol. 94^v); Rawl. poet. 26 (fol. 2^v); Rawl. poet. 117 (fol. 16^r); Corpus Christi College Oxford MS 327 (fol. 23^v); National Library of Wales, Carreglwyd Papers, A 830, series II, p. 218; Folger MSS V.a.162 (fol. 56^r); V.a.262 (p. 90); and Huntington MS HM 116 (p. 66).

This poem is notable for its almost paradoxical articulation of the importance of self-silencing. It also derives from an early Tudor tradition of warnings addressed to disobedient sons, often foretelling their deaths; here, though, this topos is reoriented to offer an implicit critique, rather than an endorsement, of the harsh authority under which the son will suffer.[134]

Horn's miscellany is unusual in the amount of information it gives about dates of transcription (which follow almost every item), and in the amount of information we can retrieve about its compiler. There are, as I have discussed above, many potential reasons for an item's being copied into a miscellany: in the case of Hoskyns's appearance in MS Rawlinson B.151 it is worth bearing in mind the geographical proximity of Hoskyns's home town and parliamentary seat of Hereford to Horn's bases in Shropshire.[135] Yet Hoskyns is also a prominent figure in the culture of free speech in early Stuart England, and it is clear that Horn too was participating in that culture, in the pages of his book. MS Rawlinson B.151 shows particularly clearly how the manuscript miscellany facilitated political analysis, commentary, and reflections on the art, duty, and dangers of counsel by juxtaposing texts gathered in a range of ways from a wide variety of sources. Approaching the archive in a different way, and turning from a case-study of an individual manuscript to a case-study of the transmission of an individual's works can provide further insights into the negotiations between free speech, counsel, libel, and political commentary in this fascinating medium.

COLLECTING JOHN HOSKYNS IN THE EARLY SEVENTEENTH CENTURY

Examining the transcription of poems and other works by John Hoskyns in early seventeenth-century manuscript miscellanies, it becomes clear that his reputation as a proponent and defender of free speech in Parliament was a spur to the collection of his writings. It also adds to our understanding of the way that collections build up a body of information and commentary on political events;[136] the kind of information that I have suggested is crucial

---

[134] See, for instance, Ralegh's poem to his son, 'Three thinges there bee that prosper vp apace' (*The Poems of Sir Walter Ralegh*, ed. by Agnes Latham (London: Routledge and Kegan Paul, 1951), p. 49); cf. (with variant in the last lines) *The Poems of Sir Walter Ralegh: A Historical Edition*, ed. by Michael Rudick, Renaissance English Text Society, seventh series, no. 23 (Tempe, AZ: Arizona Center for Medieval and Renaissance Studies in conjunction with Renaissance English Text Society, 1999), p. 125. I am grateful to Lorna Hutson for directing me to this tradition.

[135] For other instances of Hoskyns's appearance in manuscript, see pp. 241–8 below.

[136] A very clear example of the juxtaposition of news and libellous comment, from a slightly later period, can be found in Folger MS V.a.192, which is divided into two parts. This collection contains, in

to the development of a civic identity and to the notion of free speech in this period. Thus here, first I expand the brief sketch I have already offered of Hoskyns in Parliament and convey a sense of his reputation as a frank speaker and as a poet, and second, I use his works as an alternative route through the mass of manuscript material containing libels.

John Hoskyns's career followed the classic pattern of the time for a man of his social position:[137] he was educated at Westminster, Winchester, and New College, Oxford, going on to read for the Bar at Middle Temple.[138] He then entered Parliament, sitting in the House of Commons for the first time in 1604, and attending every session until his death except that of 1621.[139] Continuing to practise the law, he was made a judge in 1621 and a serjeant-at-law in 1623.[140] As I have argued above, all of these institutions fostered textual networks which were frequently intertwined: individual texts, or even whole miscellanies were exchanged and shared between their members – and individuals were, like Hoskyns, frequently members of more than one.[141] Rhetorical and compositional skills were taught intensively to students at schools like Winchester with the intention that they should become habitual, and Hoskyns wrote verse regularly throughout his life. The earliest texts of his to survive are Latin verses written at Winchester.[142] Most of his poems are occasional, ranging from witty (and serious) epitaphs and elegies to scurrilous attacks on political figures, such as 'Great Verulam is very lame'. Hoskyns's reputation as a frank speaker began early: at New College in 1592 he was appointed *terrae filius*, an orator who was licensed to make satirical speeches, but was expelled soon afterwards because, as Aubrey says, 'he was so bitterly Satyricall', exceeding even the bounds of

---

the first part, records of parliamentary proceedings, speeches in the Privy Council and petitions to the king from around 1639–40: it was probably compiled somewhat after the events described. In the second section, in the same hand as part one, are found two contrasting poems on Bacon's fall: the first is Hoskyns's 'Great Verulam is very lame' (fol. 6ʳ rev.), and the second is 'When you awake dull Brittayns and behold' (fols. 6ʳ–12ʳ rev.).

[137] The Hoskyns family were reasonably wealthy landowners in Herefordshire; see Whitlock, *John Hoskyns*, pp. 5–16.

[138] There is no firm evidence to support Aubrey's claim that Hoskyns spent a year at Westminster before going on to Winchester (where his attendance is confirmed), but Whitlock is happy to admit its plausibility. See *Aubrey's Brief Lives*, ed. by Oliver Lawson Dick (Harmondsworth: Penguin, 1962), p. 245; Whitlock, *John Hoskyns*, pp. 23–8.

[139] For Hoskyns's participation in these Parliaments, see chapter 3 above.

[140] See Whitlock, *John Hoskyns*, pp. 560–2; 587. John Donne preached the sermon (now lost) after the rain-sodden procession to the serjeants' feast; Chamberlain to Carleton, 25 October 1623, *The Letters of John Chamberlain*, volume II, p. 518.

[141] On texts shared between collections, and their institutional affiliations, see Hobbs, *Verse Miscellany Manuscripts*, esp. chapter 8.

[142] See Osborn, *The Life, Letters and Writings of John Hoskyns*, pp. 168–9; Whitlock, *John Hoskyns*, pp. 34–6.

his licence.[143] After he was released from the Tower following his imprisonment in 1614, Hoskyns chose discreetly to stay away from the next session
of Parliament, but he was nonetheless frequently invoked as a martyr to
the cause of free speech and continued to write satirical verse, even court-
ing a charge of *scandalum magnatum*.[144] Writing to Carleton in February
1617 about the host of libels circulating on Buckingham, Chamberlain
mentioned that 'Hoskins the lawier is in a laberinth beeing brought into
question for a rime or libell (as yt is termed) made some yeare and a halfe
agon. Yf he find not the better friends yt is feared he shalbe brought into
the Starchamber and then he is undon.'[145] Whitlock conjectures that the
poem that provoked this investigation was one that, once more, addresses
the dangers of speaking; and that ties speaking, (over)hearing, and secrets
of state – *arcana imperii* – together as threats to a courtier's life:

> He that hath heard a Princes Secrecy
> hath his Deaths Wound, & let him loke to dye
> For Princes Hearts can*n*ot Endure Longe
> to be obnoxious to a Servants Tongue.
> Noe Counsell but mans life will some way show it
> then in some Case as good Doe ill as Know it.[146]

Hoskyns was notorious for his outspokenness, but this was a notoriety that
he to some extent deliberately courted. Although his reputation cannot
always be established as the reason for Hoskyns's poems being copied into
manuscript, in several cases a compiler can be seen to be putting the verse
to political use in this way.

Hoskyns's contemporary literary reputation was considerable, and is
another strong reason for his appearance in miscellanies. Aubrey recounts
the story of Hoskyns's son Benedict approaching Ben Jonson and asking to
be taken into his literary circle and 'adopted' as his 'sonne'; Jonson refused
because, he said, 'I dare not; 'tis honour enough to be your Brother: I

---

[143] *Aubrey's Brief Lives*, p. 246. See Whitlock, *John Hoskyns*, pp. 81–2 and David Norbrook, 'Rhetoric, Ideology and the Elizabethan World Picture', in *Renaissance Rhetoric*, ed. by Peter Mack (Basingstoke: Macmillan, 1994), pp. 140–64, at p. 152. Whitlock suggests that the speech that lost Hoskyns his fellowship was against the tomb of Christopher Hatton.

[144] Hoskyns made a special journey from London to Hereford, his former seat, in November 1620, to ensure that his name was not submitted as one of the members (Whitlock, *John Hoskyns*, p. 555). His case was alluded to by Sir Robert Phelips on 5 and 12 February 1621, by Alford on 5 February and by unspecified 'others' on 23 November 1621. See *CD 1621*, II, 25, 59; iv, 13, 433.

[145] Chamberlain to Carleton, 8 February, 1617; *The Letters of John Chamberlain*, volume II, p. 52.

[146] The attribution is conjectured by Whitlock from the poem's proximity to other Hoskyns poems in British Library MSS Harley 6038 and Harley 1221, and from the fact that in the former manuscript it is signed 'J. H.'; see Whitlock, *John Hoskyns*, pp. 490–1 and n. 40.

was your Father's sonne, and 'twas he that polished me.'[147] Jonson was not alone in enjoying Hoskyns's editorial favours, says Aubrey – when in the Tower, he was a neighbour of Sir Walter Ralegh, and acted as 'Sir Walter's *Aristarchus*, to review and polish [his] stile'.[148] Anthony à Wood went so far as to describe Hoskyns as 'the most ingenious and admired poet of his time', and one poem now ascribed to him was for many years included in the Donne canon.[149] Possibly a member of the so-called 'Mermaid Club', Hoskyns's 'acquaintance were all the Witts then about the Towne' – among them John Donne, Sir Henry Wotton, and Sir Benjamin Rudyerd.[150] Above all, Hoskyns was, like many other writers of his time, a manuscript poet, even allegedly collecting all his verse in a single manuscript – a volume that was, perhaps unsurprisingly, lost.[151] Several of his poems were published in his lifetime – all epitaphs, elegies, or commendatory verses, most of them in Latin – but many more circulated as separates and in miscellanies.[152] The wide extent of this circulation was noted by Hoskyns's twentieth-century

---

[147] *Aubrey's Brief Lives*, p. 246. Cf. pp. 252–3 (Aubrey's Life of Jonson).

[148] Ibid., pp. 246–7.

[149] Anthony à Wood, *Athenae Oxoniensis*, ed. by Philip Bliss, 2 volumes (London, 1815), volume II, col. 626. The poem previously attributed to Donne is 'Absence'; see Osborn, *The Life, Letters and Writings of John Hoskyns*, pp. 192–3; 285–6 n.

[150] *Aubrey's Brief Lives*, pp. 246–7. All study of the Mermaid Club (whose existence remains open to question) has been based on the third letter in Thomas Coryat, *Thomas Coriat Traveller for the English Wits: Greeting* (London, 1616). The most influential article on the subject is I. A. Shapiro, 'The "Mermaid Club"', *Modern Language Review* 45 (1950): 6–17. See also Pascal Brioist, 'Que de choses avons nous vues et vécues à la Sirène', in *Culture et société dans l'Europe moderne et contemporaine*, ed. by Dominique Julia (Florence: European University Institute, 1992), pp. 89–132; Whitlock, *John Hoskyns*, pp. 385–92; Michelle O'Callaghan, *The 'Shepheards Nation': Jacobean Spenserians and Early Stuart Political Culture, 1612–1625* (Oxford: Clarendon Press, 2000), pp. 73–7; David Norbrook, *Poetry and Politics in the English Renaissance*, revised edition (Oxford: Oxford University Press, 2002), p. 190.

[151] Aubrey claims that Hoskyns 'had a booke of Poemes, neatly written by one of his Clerkes, bigger then Dr Donne's Poemes, which his sonn Benet lent to he knowes not who, about 1653, and could never heare of it since' (*Aubrey's Brief Lives*, p. 247). Also lost are Hoskyns's Greek Lexicon (completed up to the letter M) and Plutarchan autobiography (*Aubrey's Brief Lives*, pp. 246, 247).

[152] Camden published a collection of epitaphs including several by Hoskyns in the *Remains*, but his attributions are probably unreliable in some cases (William Camden, *Remaines . . . Concerning Britaine* (London, 1605), p. 56; see Whitlock, *John Hoskyns*, pp. 51–3). Eight elegies were published in the New College volume in commemoration of Sir Philip Sidney, *Peplvs* (Oxford, 1587), pp. 14–27; an elegy for Sir Christopher Hatton was published in *Oxoniensivm Στεναγμός* (Oxford, 1592) (though Osborn, *The Life, Letters and Writings of John Hoskyns*, p. 283, points out that this volume may never have been publicly issued); an elegy on Elizabeth appeared in the Oxford volume *Oxoniensis Academiae Funebre Officium* (Oxford, 1603), pp. 140–1; celebratory verses on James's accession were published in *Academiae Oxoniensis Pietas Erga Serenissimvm & Potentissimvm Iacobum* (Oxford, 1603), p. 168. Commendatory verses were published in William Gager, *Ulysses Redux* (Oxford, 1581); Rowland Vaughan, *Most Approved, and Long Experienced Water-Workes* (London, 1610), sig. D2[v]; Thomas Coryat, *Coryat's Crudities Hastily Gobbled vp in Five Moneths Trauells* (London, 1611), sigs. e5[r]–e6[v] (also appearing in Coryat, *The Odcombian Banqvet* (London, 1611), sigs. H[v]–H3[r]); John

editor, Osborn, while one effect of Baird Whitlock's thorough biographical research was further to expand the number of manuscripts known to contain works by Hoskyns. Still more copies were noted in the course of work by James L. Sanderson and Peter Beal.[153] I have located copies of poems by Hoskyns unnoticed by these scholars in the Folger Shakespeare Library and the Henry E. Huntington Library, and it is likely that more will be found in other archives. Since Osborn and Whitlock were concerned, respectively, to establish copy-texts or locate information about Hoskyns's life, neither one paid detailed attention to the manuscripts in which his poems appeared.

It is, as always when dealing with manuscript miscellanies, both important and difficult to establish how and why Hoskyns's poetry might have come to be copied. Sometimes it can be a simple case of misattribution in the course of a scribe's desire to have as full a collection as possible of an author's verse.[154] Individual texts might have different meanings for different readers: for example, Hoskyns's well-known poem 'The Parliament Fart', enduringly popular throughout the seventeenth century,[155] could be

Owen, *Epigrammatum Joannis Owen Cambro-Britanni, Oxoniensis*, etc. (Leiden, 1620), sig. A2^r. 'Absence' was printed (unattributed) in Francis Davison's *A Poetical Rapsody* (London, 1602). See further Osborn, *The Life, Letters and Writings of John Hoskyns*, chapter 10 and notes.

153 See James L. Sanderson, 'An Edition of an Early Seventeenth-Century Manuscript Collection of Poems (Rosenbach MS 186 [1083/15])', unpublished PhD diss., University of Pennsylvania, 1960, who notes twenty-seven copies of Hoskyns's poem 'The Parliament Fart'; Beal, *Index of English Literary Manuscripts*, volume 1, Part 1, pp. 126–8, who notes thirty-seven copies of the elegy on Anne Prideaux sometimes attributed to William Browne of Tavistock. Beal does not give Hoskyns an entry in the *Index*.

154 'Absence' appears in BL MS Stowe 961, a collection described as 'Dr. J. Donne Poems' (fol. 80^v) as well as in the Bridgewater MS of Donne's poems (Huntington MS EL 6893, fol. 36^r) and in a collection of Donne poems in part II of Huntington MS HM 198 (fol. 34^r); Hoskyns's mock love-poem to the Lady Jacob is attributed to Donne in Richard Archard's miscellany, Folger MS V.a.124, fols. 36^r–38^v, which contains other Donne poems; the popular elegy on Anne Prideaux ('Nature in this small volume') appears in British Library MS Lansdowne 777 (fol. 60^v), the autograph collected verse of William Browne, but is not signed by him, unlike most of his poems (see Whitlock, *John Hoskyns*, p. 633, n. 89); in Bod. MS Eng. poet. e.97 the same poem is attributed to William Strode (p. 54); in Bod. MS Firth e.4 it appears with verse by Thomas Randolph (p. 110). It is important to remember that attributions to Hoskyns – as to other poets of the time – remain open to question, being based as they are on selected manuscript evidence of varying reliability.

155 The twenty-seven known copies of the poem are: BL MSS Add. 58215 (fols. 19^v–18^v rev.); Add. 4149; Add. 1030 (fols. 123^r–4^r); Add. 23229; Add. 30982 (fols. 33^r–33^v); Sloane 1489 (fol. 25^r); Sloane 2023 (fol. 59^r); Stowe 962; Bod. MSS Douce f. 5 (fol. 28^r); Ashmole 36–7 (fol. 131^r); Malone 23 (p. 1^v); North b. 24 (fol. 28^r); Rawl. poet. 160 (fol. 157^v); Rawl. poet. 26 (fol. 7^r); Rawl. poet. 117 (fol. 196^r rev.); Rawl. poet. 172 (fol. 8^r); Sancroft 53 (p. 53); Tanner 306 (two copies: fols. 254^r, 256^r, and 255^r); Corpus Christi College Oxford MS 328 (fol. 94^v); Cambridge University Library MS Add. 8447 (the 'Rainsford MS'); Huntington Library MS HM 198, part 1 (pp. 3–4); Folger MSS V.a.160 (p. 79); V.a.275 (p. 101); V.a.322 (p. 226); V.a.339 (fol. 248^v); J.a.2 (fol. 81^r); The Philip H. and A. S. W. Rosenbach Foundation, Philadelphia, MS 1083/15 (the 'Crawford MS'). The poem was printed in *Facetiae. Musarum Deliciae: or, the muses recreation, conteining severall pieces of poetique wit*

written out and read as an insider's joke for fellow-parliamentarians, a satirical swipe at the Lords (the fart was Henry Ludlow's response to the chief messenger from the Upper House), or even an anti-parliamentary jibe, depending on the circumstances of its copying and its local context.[156] British Library MS Add. 25303 is a salutary case, suggesting at least four possible kinds of copying. Firstly, there are strong parliamentary links: it was put together for Robert Bowyer, a parliamentary colleague of Hoskyns,[157] and contains six of the latter's poems as well as his 'Fustian Answer made to a Tufftaffeta Speech'.[158] Oxford associations are also present, however – there are poems by King, Carew, Corbet, and Duppa among others. But the manuscript has many poems that are linked to the Inns of Court or are by Inns authors like Robert Ellice, Henry Blount, and John Vaughan, and shares over 104 poems with British Library MS Add. 21433, another Inns-based collection.[159] Lastly, there may very well be a more specifically political interest behind the manuscript's inclusion of Hoskyns's two poems 'To his Son Benedict Hoskyns' and 'A Dreame', indicated by the transcription of the libel / counsel poem 'The King's Five Senses' elsewhere in the manuscript.[160]

---

by Sir J. M. and Ja: S. 1656, ed. by Sir John Mennis, 2 volumes (London, 1817), volume I, p. 55 and *Le Prince d'Amour or the Prince of Love with a Collection of Several Ingenious Poems and Songs By the Wits of the Age* (London, 1660), pp. 93–9. Whitlock, *John Hoskyns*, pp. 288–92, gives an edition of the poem working from BL MS Stowe 962 and Cambridge University Library MS Add. 8447 (the 'Rainsford MS'). On the latter manuscript, see Peter Davidson, 'The Rainsford Family Notebook', *Notes and Queries* 31 (229) (June 1994): 2, 247–50. Copies of the short 'Epitaph of the Parliament Fart' ('Reader I was borne and tride') appear in sixteen manuscripts: BL MSS Add. 15227 (fol. 79[r]); Add. 30982 (fol. 157[v]); Egerton 2421 (fol. 2[v]); Sloane 1792 (fol. 95[r]); Stowe 962; Bod. MSS Rawl. poet. 71 (p. 4); Rawl. poet. 153 (fol. 28[r]); Rawl. poet. 160 (fol. 158[v]); Sancroft 53 (p. 56); Corpus Christi College Oxford MS 328 (fol. 94[v]); Folger MSS V.a.97 (p. 128); V.a.162 (fol. 86[r]); V.a.170 (p. 65); V.a.245 (fol. 61[r]); V.a.339 (fol. 231[v]); Huntington MS 116 (p. 111).

[156] Marotti, *Manuscript*, suggests that the poem's 'continued popularity . . . through the mid-seventeenth-century compilers of anthologies was probably related to Royalist political cynicism and distrust of Parliament as an institution' (p. 115). A possible example of this kind of copying is in Folger MS V.a.160, probably compiled in the 1630s and 1640s by Matthew Day of Windsor (d. 1661). The final piece in the volume is Denham's 'Cooper's Hill' (pp. 95–107), and there are poems by Herrick and Randolph, as well as loyal verses 'Vpon the Commotion in Scotland & his Ma[ties] armes for the suppressing of it' (pp. 73–6). On 'The Parliament Fart' see also O'Callaghan, *The 'Shepheards Nation'*, pp. 76–7.

[157] Whitlock, *John Hoskyns*, pp. 110–11.

[158] On this speech see Osborn, *The Life, Letters and Writings of John Hoskyns*, pp. 98–102. It also occurs in Bod. MS Malone 16 (fols. 74[v]–75[r]) and Huntington MS HM 1338 (fols. 146[r]–146[v] rev.). The poems are the mock love poem to the Lady Jacob; 'On Dreames' (fol. 138[v]); the epitaph on Sir Walter Pye (fol. 151[r]); 'A Dreame' (fols. 162[r]–163[r]); 'To his Son Benedict Hoskyns' (in both Latin and English, fol. 163[r]) and 'Nature in this small volume' (fol. 163[r]).

[159] On this manuscript's place in an Inns of Court textual tradition, see Hobbs, *Verse Miscellany Manuscripts*, pp. 90–3.

[160] See p. 213, n. 66 above.

Where it is possible to infer reasons for the transcriptions of Hoskyns's poems into a manuscript (from indications given by the rest of the contents, or from notes appended by the compiler), the following categories appear to be most significant, although they tend to overlap: collections of epitaphs; groups of 'witty' verse (for instance, punning pieces such as 'The Parliament Fart', which may also be libellous); Oxford associations; Inns of Court associations; Wykehamist associations; and political collections. There is one instance in which a poem by Hoskyns seems to be copied for his Welsh links, and one in which a poem is copied with other poems about love.[161]

Looking at those miscellanies where Hoskyns's poems have been copied for their political comment, or for their association with a celebrated frank-speaker or wit, expands the argument I have made earlier in this chapter about the link between libel, free speech, and manuscript. The miscellanies in this, final section show further how a collection like Bodleian MS Rawlinson B.151 is only one instance of the culture of collecting information and comment where issues of frank speaking and counsel loom large. This is not to subsume all comment on specific events or scandals into the larger category of 'free speech' so much as to argue that one of the significant motives to collecting such material was, as I put it at the beginning of this chapter, the desire to make oneself capable of participating in a civic culture – and that one result might have been that such a culture was brought, fitfully, into being.

Although none of them provide the wealth of information about their compiler that illuminates the context of a manuscript like Bodleian Rawlinson B.151, there is a large group of manuscript miscellanies that share an interest in Hoskyns's poems with an ongoing concern with political events. Folger MS V.a.162 is a miscellany in two hands, compiled some time in the 1630s.[162] It contains a number of poems dating from Elizabeth's

---

161 Bod. MS Don. c. 54, the manuscript of Richard Roberts, a Welsh judge, contains a copy of Hoskyns's Latin 'Convivium philosophicum' at fols. 21^r–22^r; a legal, not specifically Welsh link may be the reason for Hoskyns's presence. On this manuscript see *The Poems of Sir John Davies*, ed. by Robert Krueger (Oxford: Clarendon Press, 1975), p. 438. BL MS Add. 25707 (the 'Skipwith MS' of Donne's verse: Δ21 in Beal's list of Donne manuscripts; referred to as *A25* by editors) contains an excerpt from the elegy on Sir Albertus Morton and his wife ascribed to Hoskyns by Whitlock and the copyist of BL MS Harley 6038 ('Here lye two bodies happy in their kinds') at fol. 100^v, among poems by King and Carew and headed 'An Epitaph of two Louers'. On this poem, see Whitlock, *John Hoskyns*, pp. 613–15.

162 The inscription 'Stephen Wellen' on fol. 1^r seems to be in the same hand as the first and last parts of the miscellany (fols. 1^v–26^v and 81^r–97^r), while the section from fols. 27^r–80^v begins with the inscription 'Hen: Allworth'. There is a 'sonnett on ye new yeare 1639' at fol. 22^v.

reign, as well as verse by Herbert and material relating to Oxford.[163] It also displays a strong interest in Jacobean political scandals. Among poems on the Spanish Match[164] and libels on Frances Howard and Robert Carr,[165] Buckingham,[166] and Sir Giles Mompesson (fol. 53[r]) the compiler has copied Hoskyns's poem to his son (fol. 56[r]), the epitaph to 'The Parliament Fart' (fol. 86[r]) and the 'Fustian Answer' (fols. 68[r]–69[r]), as well as some of his witty verses.[167] There is also a copy of the quatrain written in the aftermath of the 1614 imprisonments:

> The Councell by committing foure
> Have sent eight humors to the tower
> Hoskins the Poet merrily sad
> Sharpe the divine soberly madd
> Cornwallis the statesman is popishly precise
> And Chute the Caruer is foolishly wise.
>
> (fol. 32[r])[168]

A few pages before Hoskyns's poem to his son we find Sir Walter Ralegh's address to his (fol. 38[v]; discussed above, p. 238 n. 134). Despite the wide range of genres and subjects collected by the two compilers of this volume, its regular inclusion of libels and other political verses from the very beginning is surely testimony to a desire on their part to build up a bank of information and comment on public events and their private, often scandalous origins or effects.

Folger MS V.a.345 is another manuscript with Oxford (and especially Christ Church) links that mixes some Elizabethan verse with libellous political material of the early seventeenth century.[169] A collaborative production in several hands, the manuscript seems to have belonged to one D. Doughte. Again, the contents are very miscellaneous, ranging from songs by Dowland

---

[163] Shakespeare's sonnet 71 appears at fol. 12[v], while the song from Act 4 scene 1 of *Measure for Measure*, 'Take oh take those lipps awaie', is at fol. 20[r]; Herbert's 'The Altar' is at fol. 12[v] and 'Redemption' is at fol. 15[v]; among several Oxford-related items are epitaphs on Ben Stone (fol. 27[r]) and 'M[r] Owen Burser of Christ [Church]' (fols. 28[r]–28[v]).

[164] Fols. 29[v]–30[v], 46[r]–48[v], 66[v]–68[r], 73[r]–73[v], 79[r]–79[v].

[165] Fols. 33[r], 35[r], 37[v], 50[v], 62[v], 63[v].   [166] Fols. 35[v], 73[v], 80[r].

[167] The other poems by Hoskyns are the mock love-poem to the Lady Jacob (fol. 39[r], attributed to Mr Poulden, of New College Oxford), 'Mr Permenter stands at the Center' and 'As at a banquet' (fol. 59[v]), and 'A zealous Lock-Smith dy'd of late' (fol. 88[v]).

[168] This poem also appears in a variant form in Bod. MS Rawl. poet. 26 (fol. 2[r]) and BL MS Sloane 2023 (fol. 60[v]); in both Hoskyns is identified as a lawyer instead of a poet. See Whitlock, *John Hoskyns*, pp. 492–3, n. 14.

[169] On this manuscript, see Marotti, 'Folger MSS V.a.89 and V.a.345', in *The Reader Revealed*, and Marotti *Manuscript*, pp. 32, 142, 155–8, 159, 172–3, 327–8.

(pp. 19, 65–6) to poems about Oxford characters or subjects (for instance, 'Vpon Mr Sanborne Sheriff of Oxfshir', pp. 14–16; 'Do^r: Corbet on Tom ye great bel of C:C:', pp. 20–2), bawdy verse (for example, 'A vertuous Lady sitting in a muse', p. 29) and poems by Thomas Bastard, to libels on Cecil (pp. 36, 110), Frances Howard (p. 290), Buckingham (p. 315), and Bacon (pp. 25, 127). One of the two libels on Bacon is Hoskyns's 'Great Verulam is very lame' (p. 127), and the manuscript also contains five more of his poems.[170] The compilers' interest in libellous politics is also apparent from copies of 'The King's Five Senses' (pp. 59–61, here attributed to James Johnson) and a poem on the extravagant monument to Sir Christopher Hatton. This latter offers a sardonic commentary on the lavish treatment of royal favourites (even in death) in comparison with loyal (and in Sidney's case, outspoken) subjects, and is a topic on which Hoskyns may also have exercised his sharp tongue.[171]

Huntington MS HM 198 is, again, in several hands, and is made up of two distinct miscellanies bound together.[172] The first was compiled for Edward Denny,[173] around 1630 and contains Hoskyns's 'The Parliament Fart' (pp. 3–4) and 'On Dreames' (p. 174). The second, compiled in the second quarter of the seventeenth century, contains a number of poems by Donne and a large amount of devotional material of a distinctly Roman Catholic flavour, including twenty-nine sonnets by Sir Toby Matthew (pp. 88–95).[174] Part one of the manuscript contains a good deal of political and libellous material, including libels on Frances Howard (pp. 19–21, 33–4), Buckingham (pp. 44–6, 96, 156; as well as his 'Rodomanthato' to the Commons, pp. 157–8), and Northampton ('The Great Archpapist Learned Curio', p. 164), 'The King's Five Senses' (pp. 30–2), and the Commons' 'Humble Petition' to the dead

---

[170] These are 'Of a Cosener' (p. 49, attributed to Bastard), 'An Epitaphe on Mr Sandes' (p. 75), 'Here lye two bodies happy in their kinds' (p. 103), 'Song vppon a bellowes mender' (p. 150), and 'A zealous Lock-Smith dy'd of late' (p. 273).

[171] See above, p. 240 n. 143; the poem, at p. 50, begins 'S^r francis [Walsingham] and Sr Philip [Sidney] haue no tombe': for an edition, see David Norbrook and H. R. Woudhuysen (eds.), *The Penguin Book of Renaissance Verse 1509–1659*, revised edition (Harmondsworth: Penguin, 1993), p. 97. It is also found in Alexander B. Grosart (ed.), *The Dr Farmer Chetham MS*, 2 volumes, Camden Society, old series no. 89 (Manchester: Chetham Society, 1873), volume II, p. 180.

[172] On this manuscript see further L. A. Beaurline, 'An Editorial Experiment: Suckling's *A Sessions of the Poets*', *Studies in Bibliography* 16 (1963): 43–60; C. M. Armitage, 'Identification of New York Public Library Manuscript 'Suckling Collection' and of Huntington Manuscript 198', *Studies in Bibliography* 19 (1966): 215–16.

[173] The compiler should not be confused with the eponymous Earl of Norwich, d. 1630; see Beal, *Index*, volume I, Part I, p. 253, arguing *contra* C. M. Armitage, 'Donne's Poems in Huntington Manuscript 198: New Light on "The Funeral"', *Studies in Philology* 63:5 (October 1966): 697–707.

[174] See Anthony G. Petti, 'Unknown Sonnets by Sir Toby Matthew', *Recusant History* 9:3 (October 1967): 123–58. On the dating of the manuscript I follow a typescript note by W. A. Ringler dated 17 May 1977 contained in the information file for this manuscript at the Huntington Library.

Queen Elizabeth (pp. 62–3). There is also a copy of the verses on Bacon, 'When you awake dull Brittayns and behold' (pp. 37–40).

The 'Dr Farmer Chetham MS' contains two speeches by Bacon as well as 'Great Verulam is very lame' (I, pp. 60–72), indicating an interest in achieving a breadth of coverage on the disgraced Lord Chancellor, and other political texts include the arraignment of Essex and parliamentary reports from 1621 (I, pp. 1–30; II, pp. 206–13). The Oxford-linked Bod. MS Douce f.5 also contains copies of Hoskyns's 'Great Verulam is very lame' (fol. 37ᵛ) and of 'The Parliament Fart' (fols. 28ʳ–29ʳ). Other political texts include four popular pieces on the Duke of Buckingham: 'Rex and Grex' (fol. 5ʳ); 'Art thou returned againe wᵗʰ all thy faults' (fols. 5ᵛ–6ᵛ), on his return from the disastrous expedition to the Ile de Rhé; 'Verses made on George Duke of Buckingham stabbed at Portsmouth by Felton in forme of a Dialogue' (fols. 13v–14); and 'Verses on the duke setting forth to Spaine' in 1623 (fol. 21ᵛ).[175] There is also an elegy on Sir Philip Sidney – which in the early seventeenth century could look very much like nostalgia for a bygone martial Protestantism (fols. 15ʳ–15ᵛ) – and a libel on Frances Howard (fol. 33ᵛ). Another such manuscript, with an Oxford connection and apparent political agenda, is Bodleian MS Malone 19. The manuscript is in a single hand with the exception of two pieces on the last two pages, which are clearly much later. It is one of the chief sources of Hoskyns's poems, containing nine of them, including 'A Dreame' (pp. 71–3); 'Sic luo, sic merui' (p. 148) and 'My little Ben now thou art young' (p. 149).[176] As well as the Oxford-related texts (such as poems on or by Ben Stone of New College), there are many items relating to the political events of the 1610s and 1620s: poems satirising James I, including one on his religious policy ('The Parliament sittes with Synode of wittes', p. 14) and one on his refusal to help Prince Frederick ('Whiles thy sonnes rash vnlucky armes attempt', p. 20); poems attacking the Spanish Match (pp. 21–35); libels on Buckingham and the Earl of Somerset, Robert Carr (p. 38); and the (not quite perfect) anagram popular at the time of the latter's marriage to Frances Howard:

> Anªgram.|
> ffrancis Howard
> Car findes a whore.|
> (p. 53)

---

[175] On government attempts to deal with the unrest over the expedition to the Ile de Rhé, see Cogswell, 'Politics and Propaganda', *passim*.

[176] The other Hoskyns poems are 'Reader I would not haue the mistake' (p. 95); the mock love-poem to the Lady Jacob (p. 105); 'Even as the waves of brainlesse butter'd fish' (p. 137); 'As a louse as we cracke' (p. 148); 'Mr Permenter stands at the Center' (p. 149), and 'Of Sr Tho. Gressam' (p. 150).

Bodleian Library MS English poetry c.50 contains 'Great Verulam is very lame' (fol. 32^v) as well as two other poems on Bacon's fall (fols. 7^v; 13^r), and several on Buckingham, either concerning the Ile de Rhé expedition or his assassination (fols. 13^v; 24^v; 26^r; 27^r–29^r). Bodleian Library MS Ashmole 781, meanwhile (written in a single hand between *c.* 1620 and 1631), contains separate copies of 'A Dreame' in full and in its reduced version (with an addition by Quarles), along with the letter from Cornwallis to King James (pp. 108–11); letters from Essex to Queen Elizabeth and the 'buzzing bees complaint' ascribed to the former (pp. 80–3; 132–4); 'Sr Geruas Ellowis Livtenant of the Tower his Appologie toutching his knowledge of Sr Tho: Overburie his death' (pp. 51–5); and verses on Cranfield's fall (p. 136). There are several pieces relating to King James's project of uniting England and Scotland, with the opposition to which Hoskyns was closely involved.[177] These include a text headed 'The generall state of ye Scottish Common-wealth with ye causes of their often mutinies and other discords. Authorities in matters of state' (pp. 19–25)[178] and a letter from James to Parliament on the Union and 'Objections against the change of the name and stile of England and Scotland' (pp. 87–8; 113–14).[179]

These are a few of the manuscripts in which Hoskyns's political poems appear with other material dealing with public events,[180] and this survey should give some idea of how frequently such manuscripts put together texts from different genres treating similar political subjects. It shows that libels are not merely copied for their lubricious insights into the private lives of public persons, but are used to amass opinion and information which may then be sifted by their transcribers. Thus compilers of miscellanies used their texts as something like a tool of political analysis. To make this argument more conclusive we need much more concrete information about the men and women who did the compiling, but the two approaches I have offered to the material – a single case-study and a broader survey – lay its foundations. Considered in the context of arguments about the limits of and opportunities for counsel, libelling, and the collecting of libels in manuscript miscellanies, cannot easily be seen as attempts to break down a culture of consensus, or civility. Instead they should be seen as one part of a range of responses to political events, and as a means of both unofficial

---

[177] See Whitlock, *John Hoskyns*, pp. 192–211.

[178] This text appears in a fair copy in BL MS Cotton Caligula BV art. 18 and CIX art. 275.

[179] Hobbs, *Verse Miscellany Manuscripts*, p. 125, identifies links between this manuscript and Folger MS V.a.96; Huntington Library MS HM 172; Harvard fMS Eng. 626; and BL MS Harley 6918.

[180] Others that might be considered are BL MSS Add. 10309; Add. 30982; Harley 1221; Harley 6038; Bod. MSS Eng. poet. e.14; Rawl. D. 160; Rawl. poet. 117; and Huntington MS HM 116.

protest and political deliberation. If we read libels as attacks on civility, then we risk ignoring vitally important traditions of popular (and not so popular) comment and analysis, from the vernacular ballad to the classical satire, to the pasquil. We also risk forgetting that the rhetorical culture of early Stuart England was not dominated by deliberative and forensic forms of argument, but by epideictic rhetoric.[181] In other words, the readers of libels were living in a culture where the formal exercise of praise and blame, *laudatio* and *vituperatio*, was a part of everyday life. From formal orations in University colleges to panegyrics and libels, auditors and readers were used to assessing insults in terms that did not always have the law of defamation as their end-point. Part of the special nature of rhetoric under a monarchy or principiate, this predominance of epideictic rhetoric was a sign of both weakness and strength: weakness, in that it signalled the separation of rhetoric from the exercise of citizen activity in the Senate; strength, in that it provided individuals with a means of vigorously participating in political culture outside of such civic fora.[182] Compilers of miscellanies and many authors of libels would have been raised in a tradition that trained them to read with an ear to *vituperatio* as a formal effect. This does not mean that they read libels as versions of academic exercises (although this was certainly one possible way of reading them), but that they read them in a context in which the praise of virtue and the censure of vice was commonplace, and an important part of one's identity as both *homo rhetoricus* and *vir civilis*. This took place outside the Houses of Parliament, but in a close relation to the debates that were conducted there. Individuals who were, or felt they were, deprived of a place in which effective counsel could be offered or in which they could safely fulfil their duties as outspoken counsellors both penned libels against ministers of the state and collected them with other kinds of information and advice from the present and the recent (and not-so-recent) past. Whether they were, like John Hoskyns, members of Parliaments in which freedom of speech, and of the subject, were both seen as increasingly under threat and debated hotly, or, like Robert Horn, ministers of God following the demands of conscience and the example of

---

[181] See Norbrook, *Poetry and Politics*, revised edition, p. 69: 'under a monarchy the orator, the master of persuasive, "deliberative" rhetoric, had to become a courtier and use the "demonstrative" rhetoric of praise and blame'. For the following brief discussion of epideictic rhetoric, I am indebted to conversations with Lawrence D. Green and Rita Copeland.

[182] Although there is naturally some crossover, epideictic rhetoric sometimes being appropriate for both political (deliberative) and legal (forensic) oratory; see Richard A. Lanham, *A Handlist of Rhetorical Terms*, second edition (Berkeley and Los Angeles: University of California Press, 1991), pp. 164–5; Brian Vickers, *In Defence of Rhetoric*, corrected edn (Oxford: Clarendon Press, 1997), pp. 21–3; 54–62.

biblical *parrhesia* in their local community, they used libellous texts and the resources of manuscript circulation as part of their civic armoury.

As I have argued throughout this book, the desire to counsel was the foundation of the notion of free speech in early Stuart England. It was not an abstract desire for freedom of expression, nor a local desire to smear the honour of individuals, but a desire rooted in the context of political debate as it took place in Parliament and in the pages of manuscript miscellanies compiled around the country. This desire was behind the appeal in Parliament to statutes legislating for regular assemblies and for the privilege of free speech. One of its means of justification was silenced in the 1605 case against Pickering, but it continued to form and inform the composition and transmission of the political libels of the period. As it developed in this period, the law of defamation disallowed freedom of speech arguments congruent with those I have described. To accept the terms of that law does a disservice to the range of arguments about frank counsel and its possibilities that took place inside and outside Parliament. Libel, law, and the theory of counsel were vital components of a vigorous debate around the definition of the loyal subject or good counsellor taking place in early Stuart England, and by participating in such debate individuals in turn questioned the definition of free speech and remade their political language.

Epilogue

There's no such thing as free speech, and it's a good thing, too.

Stanley Fish[1]

Stanley Fish's characteristically provocative statement is not intended to suggest that freedom of speech, as a concept that lies at the heart of ideas of personal and civic liberty, is a mere chimera. Nor is he suggesting that we should stop arguing about it. Rather, he is challenging the idealisation (even reification) of free speech as a stable, universal, and ahistorical category. If such a category did exist, Fish argues, then debates that test the relative claims of different individuals or groups to speak freely would indeed have to cease. He presses, throughout his work on this subject, for ongoing and vigorous debate, and for a conception of free speech that is attentive at all times to history.

One of the aims of this study has been to show how broad a range of traditions people in early Stuart England drew on when they argued about free speech. From rhetorical handbooks, treatises on counsel, Scripture, and parliamentary precedent they derived theories of what it meant to possess the right to speak frankly – or to be deprived of it – and lessons in how to practise it effectively. More importantly, though, I have shown what was done with those traditions in the local conditions in which these people lived. There is certainly no single theory of free speech in the period that I consider here; as much of this book has suggested, notions – and instances – of free speech emerged though debate and disagreement, not through clear consensus or *a priori* political theories. Yet in each of the areas I have examined, freedom of speech was regarded as a defining characteristic of the truly free individual and state, and as a moral imperative. While the rhetorical figure of *parrhesia* may appear to lose its teeth somewhat in the

---

[1] Stanley Fish, *There's No Such Thing as Free Speech and It's a Good Thing, Too* (Oxford: Oxford University Press, 1994); see especially chapter 8. See also Fish, *The Trouble with Principle* (Cambridge, MA: Harvard University Press, 1999).

period under discussion, the argument that members of the commonwealth are citizens, not subjects, and that as such they – or their representatives – need properly to be free is urged more and more strongly. This can be seen most clearly in the case of Parliament, where demands for freedom of speech and references to the representative function of the body often shored up neo-roman conceptions of liberty. But it is no less present in the writings of a godly loyalist like Thomas Scott, or even in the packed pages of Robert Horn's manuscript miscellany. This study deliberately eschews a Whiggish narrative of progress from repression to freedom (this is simply not what the record shows us); however, it does describe a culture in which notions of civic life were profoundly informed by republican texts and theories, and in which many individuals conceived of themselves as part of a larger community whose rights might be under threat and certainly needed to be maintained and defended.

Rhetoric – public speech – had many faces in the early seventeenth century. However, from the academic exercises of the schoolroom, with its figure-spotting and double-translation, to the forensic argument of the law courts, the sacred exhortation of the pulpit, the now virtually inaudible oratory of Parliament and the sometimes anxious, sometimes vitriolic, art of epideictic, rhetoric's forms and its history served as continual reminders of the power of language. Rhetoric was traditionally represented in personified form as armoured, and bearing a sword. This did not only imply that language could be used to attack one's foes, but that it could defend one against enemies. It also implied that in speaking out one took on a public role; the role of the active citizen. Writers, MPs, and churchmen in early Stuart England therefore laid claim to that role as they asserted their right to free speech and as they participated in the political life of the realm, even if their participation consisted in the amassing and comparing of texts in a miscellany. Their notion of free speech was married, as I have indicated, to a belief in the necessity of political participation and representation (and their ability to provide it), which in turn was embedded in a positive conception of liberty, imagined not – as it would be circumscribed by Thomas Hobbes – as the absence of restraint but as a condition in which it is the whole body of the people that governs and makes laws.[2] Such a theory of liberty lay behind the establishment of the English Republic, but it was, as Quentin Skinner has shown, ultimately eclipsed, and lies dormant even in twenty-first-century Western democratic societies.[3]

---

[2] See Quentin Skinner, *Liberty before Liberalism* (Cambridge: Cambridge University Press, 1998), esp. pp. 59–60; Thomas Hobbes, *Leviathan*, ed. by Richard Tuck, rev. edition (Cambridge: Cambridge University Press, 1996), esp. pp. 145–54.

[3] Skinner, *Liberty before Liberalism*, pp. 59–120.

This melancholy observation brings us to the present moment. Writing a chapter in the history of a right such as freedom of speech, that is so central to our own conceptions of liberty and, indeed, to our ideas of what a subject is in the modern Western world, inevitably raises serious ideological questions. What are the implications of the arguments I make here for current liberal (and post-liberal) treatments of free speech? The free speech legislation in operation today in what we regard as democratic societies, based on documents such as the First Amendment to the Constitution of the United States of America, the Universal Declaration of Human Rights, or the European Convention on Human Rights, and the jurisprudence that has followed this legislation, relies on a conception of freedom of speech that asserts its universal and inalienable nature. Some formulations of the right do allow for state restriction of speech in qualifying clauses, the European Convention stating that

The exercise of these freedoms, since it carries with it duties and responsibilities, may be subject to such formalities, conditions, restrictions or penalties as are pre-scribed by law and are necessary in a democratic society, in the interests of national security, territorial integrity or public safety, for the prevention of disorder or crime, for the protection of health or morals, for the protection of the reputation or rights of others, for preventing the disclosure of information received in confidence, or for maintaining the authority and impartiality of the judiciary.[4]

In some rather striking ways, this coincides with early modern notions of freedom of speech and its limits as described in this book, even if such notions were a long way from being enshrined in law. But the modern liberal idea of free speech as expressed in First Amendment law, which – with good intentions – does not in principle allow for such limitations, has tended to be an idealising one that, as Stanley Fish has argued, depends on decontextualising and dehistoricising speech acts. Thus each individual's or group's right to speech is to be protected, no matter what the history of that individual or group. Yet it might be possible to imagine that speech from a group or an individual with a history of being discriminated against

---

[4] Article 10, clause 2 (1950). The rights and freedoms guaranteed by the Convention were incorporated into UK law by the Human Rights Act 1998. Cf. 'Congress shall make no law respecting an estab-lishment of religion, or prohibiting the free exercise thereof; or abridging the freedom of speech, or of the press; or the right of the people peaceably to assemble, and to petition the government for a redress of grievances' (First Amendment to the Constitution of the United States, 1791; no qualifying clause); 'Everyone has the right to freedom of opinion and expression; this right includes freedom to hold opinions without interference and to seek, receive and impart information and ideas through any media and regardless of frontiers' (Universal Declaration of Human Rights, Article 19, 1948; qualified in clause 2 of Article 29: 'In the exercise of his rights and freedoms, everyone shall be subject only to such limitations as are determined by law solely for the purpose of securing due recognition and respect for the rights and freedoms of others and of meeting the just requirements of morality, public order and the general welfare in a democratic society').

should be less subject to restriction than that from a group or individual with a history of discriminating against others. Otherwise there is a danger of accepting the condition described by Herbert Marcuse as 'repressive tolerance'; as Marcuse writes, where freedom and happiness are at stake 'certain things cannot be said, certain policies cannot be proposed, certain behavior cannot be permitted without making tolerance an instrument for the continuation of servitude'.[5] This is the argument that lies behind the institution of campus speech codes in the United States, and the chaos that has resulted from them is a sign of just how difficult our current modes of thinking about free speech find such arguments.[6] Speech is often expected to take its place in the 'marketplace of ideas', and to find there (in a jarring mixture of metaphors) a level playing field; but the marketplace has its own history, and some speech is always already more privileged than the rest. My argument is not that we should automatically embrace the censorship of particular expressions; rather, like Fish, I suspect that a study of the history of free speech arguments should make us more willing to argue out the cases for restriction or permission on somewhat different, but no less ethical, political, and principled grounds. These would continue to aspire to treat freedom of speech as a right constitutive of free states, but would question the elevation of free speech to the status of a principle that takes precedence over the well-being of people, or even over truth itself (as is the case with Holocaust denial). Such a conception of free speech would also require us to recover a sense of the citizen as an active participant in the making of legal decisions concerning the right to expression to an extent far greater than is current even in supposedly representative democracies.

Studying the way that early Stuart people argued about freedom of speech and its decorum shows us how important context has been in the history of the right. At the centre of the debates discussed in this book, however, has been the conviction that claims to freedom of speech entail a belief in the necessity of citizen participation in the decisions made by states. One of the ways that we can continue to test the decisions that we make about freedom of speech, and the criteria that we use to make them, is by exploring how we came by the languages that we use in imagining and exercising our rights. In order to do this, we need a series of chapters in the discontinuous history of rights. This book is intended to be a contribution to that larger project.

[5] Herbert Marcuse, 'Repressive Tolerance', in Robert Paul Wolff, Barrington Moore, Jr., and Herbert Marcuse, *A Critique of Pure Tolerance* (Boston: Beacon Press, 1965), pp. 81–117 at p. 88.
[6] See, for example, Judith Butler, *Excitable Speech: A Politics of the Performative* (London: Routledge, 1997), pp. 1–41, 71–102.

Bibliography

MANUSCRIPTS

LONDON, BRITISH LIBRARY

Additional   4130 Miscellany in verse and prose
4149 Transcripts of State Papers by Ralph Starkey
10309 Collection of characters and poems
15227 Poetical miscellany
21433 Poetical miscellany
22601 Poetical miscellany
23229 Collection of manuscript fragments
25303 Miscellany in verse and prose
25707 The 'Skipwith MS'
29607 Randle Holme's miscellany
30982 Daniel Leare's miscellany
Cotton   Caligula BV Political papers
Caligula CIX Political papers
Egerton   923 Poetical miscellany
2421 Poetical miscellany
Harley   383 Letter collection
1221 Miscellany in verse and prose
1925 Nicholas Throckmorton-Carew's miscellany
5106 Presentation MS of Bacon's *Essayes*
6038 Miscellany in verse and prose
6947 Poetical miscellany
Lansdowne   777 Autograph collected verse of William Browne
Sloane   1792 Poetical miscellany
Stowe   302 Peter Wentworth's speech
961 'Dr. J. Donne Poems'
962 Poetical miscellany

LONDON, INNER TEMPLE LIBRARY

Petyt MS 538/17   Peter Wentworth's speech

MANCHESTER, CHETHAM'S LIBRARY

MS Mun. A4.15 (formerly 8012)   Miscellany in verse and prose

OXFORD, BODLEIAN LIBRARY

Ashmole	36, 37 Loose papers bound together
	781 Miscellany in verse and prose
Don.	c.54 Collection of Richard Roberts
Douce	f.5 Poetical miscellany
English history	d.89 Parliamentary proceedings 1623, 1626, 1628
English poetry	c.50 Poetical miscellany
	e.14 Poetical miscellany
	e.97 Miscellany in verse and drama
Firth	e.4 Poetical miscellany
Malone	16 Miscellany in verse and prose
	19 Miscellany in verse and prose
	23 Poetical miscellany
Rawlinson	B.151 Robert Horn's miscellany
	D.160 Miscellany in verse and prose
	D.727 Poetical miscellany
Rawlinson poetry	26 Miscellany in verse and prose
	71 Poetical miscellany
	117 Christopher Wasse's miscellany
	153 Poetical miscellany
	160 Poetical miscellany
	172 Collection of separate manuscripts
Sancroft	53 Archbishop Sancroft's miscellany
Tanner	306 Poetical miscellany

SAN MARINO, HENRY E. HUNTINGTON LIBRARY

HM	198, parts I and II Poetical miscellany
	116 Poetical miscellany
	1338 Miscellany in verse and prose
	1554 Parliamentary letters and speeches, 1606–40
	46323 Poetical miscellany and law notes
EL	6893 Poems by John Donne (The Bridgewater MS)

WASHINGTON DC, FOLGER SHAKESPEARE LIBRARY

V.a.	97 Poetical miscellany
	103 Poetical miscellany
	124 Richard Archard's miscellany
	130 Thomas Medcalf's commonplace book and miscellany
	160 Matthew Day's miscellany
	162 Poetical miscellany

170 Poetical miscellany
192 Parliamentary speeches; poetical miscellany
223 Separate of *Vox Populi*
245 Poetical miscellany
262 Poetical miscellany with legal notes
275 Poetical miscellany
308 Poetical miscellany
322 Poetical miscellany
339 Joseph Hall's commonplace book (with Collier forgeries)
345 Poetical miscellany in several hands
363 Copy of *Vox Populi*
402 Brian Cave's miscellany (prose)
V.b. 210 Miscellany in verse and prose
J.a. 2 Miscellany of verse and prose
L.a. 992 Letter from Thomas Warwick, with Hoskyns quatrain on verso

PRIMARY SOURCES

Anon. *A Briefe and True Relation of the Murther of Mr. Thomas Scott Preacher of Gods Word and Batchelor of Divinite. Committed by John Lambert Souldier of the Garrison of Utricke, the 18. of Iune. 1626. With his Examination, Confession, and Execution* (London, 1628).

Anon. *A Godly dyalogue & dysputacyon betwene Pyers Plowman, and a popysh preest concernyng the supper of the Lorde no lesse frutefell then necessarye to be noted of al Christen men specyally considering the great controuerses & varyaunces had therin now in your tyme* (n.p., 1550).

Anon. *I playne Piers which can not flatter a plowe man men me call my speche is fowlle, yet marke the matter howe thynges may hap to fall* (London, 1550).

A.D.B. *The Covrt of the Most Illvstrious and Most Magnificent James, the First; King of Great-Britaine, France, and Ireland, &c.* (London, 1619).

à Wood, Anthony. *Athenae Oxoniensis*, ed. by Philip Bliss, 2 volumes (London, 1815).

Academiae Oxoniensis Pietas Erga Serenissimvm &t Potentissimvm Iacobum (Oxford, 1603).

Aeschylus. *Agamemnon*, trans. by Richmond Lattimore, in *Aeschylus I: Oresteia* (Chicago: University of Chicago Press, 1953).

Aristotle. *Ethics*, trans. by J. A. K. Thomson, rev. by Hugh Tredennick (Harmondsworth: Penguin, 1976).

  On Rhetoric: A Theory of Civic Discourse, trans. by George A. Kennedy (New York: Oxford University Press, 1991).

  The Politics, ed. by Stephen Everson (Cambridge: Cambridge University Press, 1988).

Ascham, Roger. *The Scholemaster*, ed. by John E. B. Mayor (London: George Bell and Sons, 1907).

Aubrey, John. *Aubrey's Brief Lives*, ed. by Oliver Lawson Dick (Harmondsworth: Penguin, 1962).

Bacon, Francis. *A Critical Edition of the Major Works*, ed. by Brian Vickers (Oxford: Oxford University Press, 1996).

De sapientia veterum (London, 1609).

The Essayes or Counsels, Civill and Morall, ed. by Michael Kiernan (Oxford: Clarendon Press, 1985).

The History of the Reign of King Henry VII, ed. by Brian Vickers (Cambridge: Cambridge University Press, 1998).

A Wise and Moderate Discourse, concerning Church-affairs (London, 1641).

The Wisedome of the Ancients, trans. by Sir Arthur Gorges (London: John Bill, 1619).

Works, ed. James Spedding, Robert Leslie Ellis, and Douglas Denon Heath, 14 volumes (London: Longman, 1857–74).

Baildon, William Paley (ed.). *The Records of the Honourable Society of Lincoln's Inn. The Black Books* (1897).

(ed.). *Les Reportes del Cases in Camera Stellata 1593 to 1609. From the Original MS of John Hawarde* (privately printed, 1894).

Beal, Peter (compiler). *Index of English Literary Manuscripts*, volume 1: *1450–1625*. Part 1: *Andrewes-Donne* (London: Mansell, 1980).

Bellarmine, Robert. *Matthei Torti Presbyteri, & Theologi Papiensis Responsio ad Librum Inscriptum, Triplici Nodo, triplex cuneus, sive Apologia pro Iuramento fidelitatis: adversus duo Brevia Papae Pauli V. & recentes litteras Cardinalis Bellarmini ad Georgium Blackuellum Angliae Archipresbyterum: Qua ostenditur, Iuramentum illud ab hostibus fidei Catholicoe excogitatum, iniquissime a subditis Catholicis, sub gravissima bonorum omnium amissionis, perpetuorumq. carcerum poena, postulari atq. exigi.* (Cologne, 1608).

Birch, Thomas (compiler). *The Court and Times of Charles the First*, 2 volumes (London: H. Colbourn, 1848).

The Court and Times of James the First illustrated by authentic and confidential letters from various public and private collections, 2 volumes (London: H. Colbourn, 1848).

Bowyer, Robert. *The Parliamentary Diary of Robert Bowyer 1606–1607*, ed. by David Harris Willson, reprint (New York: Octagon Books, 1971).

Breton, Nicholas. *Pasquil's Mad-cap. And his Message* (London, 1600).

Calendar of the Manuscripts of the Most Honourable the Marquess of Salisbury. K.G. (London: His Majesty's Stationery Office, 1940).

Camden, William. *Remaines . . . Concerning Britaine* (London, 1605).

Cardwell, Brother Kenneth. 'An Overlooked Tract by Francis Bacon', *Huntington Library Quarterly* 65: 3 and 4 (2002): 421–33.

Cardwell, Edward. *Documentary Annals of the Reformed Church of England*, 2 volumes (1839).

Castiglione, Baldassare. *The Book of the Courtier*, trans. by Sir Thomas Hoby, ed. by Virginia Cox (London: Dent, 1994).

[Cavendish, William]. *Horae Subseciuae, Observations and Discourses* (London, 1620).

Chamberlain, John. *The Letters of John Chamberlain*, ed. by N. E. McClure, 2 volumes (Philadelphia: American Philosophical Association, 1939).

Cicero. *Brutus and Orator*, trans. by G. L. Hendrickson and H. M. Hubbell (London: Heinemann, 1939).

De inventione, De optimo genere oratorium, Topica, trans. by H. M. Hubbell (London: Heinemann, 1949).

De officiis, trans. by Walter Miller (London: Heinemann, 1913).

De oratore, trans. by E. W. Sutton and H. Rackham, 2 volumes (London: Heinemann, 1942).

Pro Sexto Roscio Amerino, in *Cicero IV: The Speeches*, trans. by John Henry Freese (London: Heinemann, 1930).

The Speeches, trans. by N. H. Watts (London: Heinemann, 1931).

[Cicero]. *Ad C. Herennium, de ratione dicendi (Rhetorica ad Herennium)*, trans. by Harry Caplan (London: Heinemann, 1954).

Coke, Sir Edward. 'The Case *de Libellis famosis*, or of Scandalous Libels', in *The Reports of Sir Edward Coke, in English*, 7 volumes (London, 1776–7).

Coryat, Thomas. *Coryat's Crudities Hastily Gobbled vp in Five Moneths Trauells* (London, 1611).

The Odcombian Banqvet (London, 1611).

Thomas Coriat Traveller for the English Wits: Greeting (London, 1616).

Cowell, John. *The Interpreter: Or Booke containing the Signification of Words* (Cambridge, 1607).

Cox, Leonard. *The Arte or Crafte of Rhetoryke* (London, ?1530).

Cressy, David and Lori Anne Ferrell (eds.). *Religion and Society in Early Modern England* (London: Routledge, 1996).

Davies, Sir John. *The Poems of Sir John Davies*, ed. by Robert Krueger (Oxford: Clarendon Press, 1975).

Davison, Francis. *A Poetical Rapsody* (London, 1602).

Day, Angel. *The English Secretary, or Methode of writing of Epistles and Letters: with a declaration of such Tropes, Figures, and Schemes, as either vsually or for ornament sake are therin required. Also the parts and office of a Secretarie, Deuided into two bookes* (London: P. S. for C. Burbie, 1599; facsimile with introduction by Robert O. Evans, Gainesville, FL: Scholars' Facsimiles and Reprints, 1967).

Demosthenes. *The Three Orations of Demosthenes chiefe Orator among the Grecians, in fauour of the Olynthians, a people in Thracia, now called Romania: with those his fower Orations titled expressely & by name against Philip of Macedonie: most needefull to be redde in these daungerous dayes, all of them that loue their Countries libertie, and desire to take warning for their better auayle, by example of others*, trans. by Thomas Wilson (London: Henrie Denham, 1570; facsimile Amsterdam: Theatrum Orbis Terrarum, 1968).

Works, trans. by J. H. Vince, 7 volumes (London: Heinemann, 1930).

D'Ewes, Simonds. *The Autobiography and Correspondence of Sir Simonds D'Ewes, Bart., During the Reigns of James I and Charles I*, ed. by James O. Halliwell (London, 1845).

The Diary of Sir Simonds D'Ewes (1622–1624), ed. by E. Bourcier (Paris: Didier, 1974).

The Journals of all the Parliaments during the Reign of Queen Elizabeth, both of the House of Lords and House of Commons (London, 1682).

Diogenes Laertius. *Lives of Eminent Philosophers*, trans. by R. D. Hicks, 2 volumes (London: Heinemann, 1925).

Donne, John. *Donne's Poetical Works*, ed. by H. J. C. Grierson, 2 volumes (Oxford: Clarendon Press, 1912).

Ignatius His Conclave, ed. by T. S. Healy, SJ (Oxford: Clarendon Press, 1969).

Letters to Severall Persons of Honour (London, 1651).

Sermons, ed. by George Potter and Evelyn M. Simpson, 10 volumes (Berkeley: University of California Press, 1953–61).

Eedes, Richard. *Three Sermons preached by . . . Doctor Eedes* (London, 1627).

Elton, G. R. (ed.). *The Tudor Constitution: Documents and Commentary*, second edition (Cambridge: Cambridge University Press, 1982).

Elyot, Thomas. *The Book named The Governor*, ed. by S. E. Lehmberg (London: Dent, 1962).

The Doctrinal of Princes (1533), in *Four Political Treatises by Sir Thomas Elyot* (Gainesville, FL: Scholars' Facsimiles and Reprints, 1967), pp. 1–39.

Of the Knowledeg whiche maketh a wise man (London, 1533).

Pasqvil the playne (London, 1533).

Erasmus, Desiderius. *Apophthegmes that is to saie, prompte, quicke, wittie and sententious saiynges, of certain emperours, kynges, capitaines, philosophiers and oratours, aswell Grekes, as Romaines, bothe veraye pleasaunt & profitable to reade, partely for all maner of persones, & especially gentlemen. First gathered and compiled in Latine by the ryght famous clerke Maister Erasmus of Roterodame. And now translated into Englyshe by Nicolas Vdall* (London, 1542).

The Education of a Christian Prince and Panegyric for Archduke Philip of Austria, trans. by Neil M. Cheshire, Michael J. Heath, and Lisa Jardine, ed. by Lisa Jardine (Cambridge: Cambridge University Press, 1997).

Parallels. Parabolae sive similia, trans. and annotated by R. A. B. Mynors, in *Collected Works 23: Literary and Educational Writings I: Antibarbari / Parabolae*, ed. by Craig R. Thompson (Toronto: University of Toronto Press, 1978).

Estienne, Robert. *Thesaurus Linguae Latinae*, 3 volumes (Lugduni, 1573).

Euripides. *Bacchae*, trans. by William Arrowsmith in *Euripides V: Three Tragedies* (Chicago: University of Chicago Press, 1959).

Hippolytus, trans. by David Grene, in *Euripides I: Four Tragedies* (Chicago: University of Chicago Press, 1955).

Ion, trans. by R. F. Willetts, in *Euripides III: Four Tragedies* (Chicago: University of Chicago Press, 1958).

The Phoenician Women, trans. by Elizabeth Wyckoff, in *Euripides V: Three Tragedies* (Chicago: University of Chicago Press, 1959).

Farmer, Norman K., Jr. 'Poems from a Seventeenth-Century Manuscript with the Hand of Robert Herrick', *The Texas Quarterly* 16:4 (Winter, 1973), supplement.

Fenner, Dudley. *The Artes of Logike and Rhetorike, plainlie set foorth in the Englishe tounge, easie to be learned and practised: together with examples for the practise of the same, for Methode in the gouernment of the familie, prescribed in the word of God: And for the whole in the resolution or opening of certaine parts of Scripture, according to the same* (Middleburg, The Netherlands: Richard Schilders, 1584; facsimile in *Four Tudor Books on Education*, intro. by Robert D. Pepper, Gainesville, FL: Scholars' Facsimiles and Reprints, 1966).

Fortescue, John, Sir. *On the Laws and Governance of England*, ed. by Shelley Lockwood (Cambridge: Cambridge University Press, 1997).

Foster, Joseph (ed.). *Alumni Oxoniensis: The Members of the University of Oxford, 1500–1714*, 4 volumes (1892).

Fraunce, Abraham. *The Arcadian Rhetorike* (London: Thomas Orwin, 1588; facsimile Menston: Scolar Press, 1969).

The Arcadian Rhetorike, ed. by Ethel Seaton (Oxford: Basil Blackwell, 1950).

Gager, William. *Ulysses Redux* (Oxford, 1581).

Gardiner, S. R. (ed.). *Parliamentary Debates in 1610*, Camden Society, first series 81 (London, 1861).

Gardiner, Stephen. *The Letters of Stephen Gardiner*, ed. by J. A. Muller (Cambridge: Cambridge University Press, 1933).

Gower, John. *The Complete Works of John Gower*, ed. by G. C. Macaulay, 4 volumes (Oxford: Clarendon Press, 1899–1902).

Greenslade, S. L. (trans. and ed.). *Early Latin Theology: Selections from Tertullian, Cyprian, Ambrose and Jerome*, The Library of Christian Classics no. 5 (London: SCM Press, 1956).

Greville, Fulke. 'A Dedication to Sir Philip Sidney', in *The Prose Works of Fulke Greville, Lord Brooke*, ed. by John Gouws (Oxford: Oxford University Press, 1986), pp. 3–135.

Grosart, Alexander B. (ed.). *The Dr. Farmer Chetham MS*, 2 volumes, Camden Society, old series no. 89 (Manchester: Chetham Society, 1873).

Guevara, Anthony of. *The Diall of Princes*, trans. by Thomas North (London, 1557).

Hakewill, William. *Modus Tenendi Parliamentum* (1660).

Helmholz, R. H. (ed.). *Select Cases on Defamation to 1600* (London: Selden Society, 1985).

Herodotus. *The Famous Hystory of Herodotus*, trans. by B. R. [1584], The Tudor Translations, second series 6 (London: Constable and Co., 1924).

The History, trans. by David Grene (Chicago: University of Chicago Press, 1987).

Historical Manuscripts Commission Report on the Manuscripts of the Earl of Ancaster (London: His Majesty's Stationery Office, 1907).

Hobbes, Thomas. *Behemoth: The History of the Causes of the Civil Wars of England*, in *The English Works of Thomas Hobbes of Malmesbury*, ed. by William Molesworth, 11 volumes (London, 1839–45).

Leviathan, ed. by Richard Tuck, revised edition (Cambridge: Cambridge University Press, 1996).

Horace. *Ars poetica*, trans. by H. Rushton Fairclough (London: Heinemann, 1942).

Horn, Robert. *A Caveat to Prevent Future Judgements* (London, 1626).

Certaine Sermons, of the Rich Man and Lazarus (London, 1619).

The Christian Governour, in the common wealth, and private families (Gods gentle remembrance) (London, 1614).

The History of the Woman of Great Faith. Treatised and Expounded (London, 1632).

Life and Death. Foure sermons. Also points of instruction for the ignorant (London, 1613).

Points of Instruction for the Ignorant. As also, an exposition of the ten commandments and the Lords prayer (a reprint with additions of part 2 of *Life and Death*) (London, 1617).

The Shield of the Righteous: Or the Ninety First Psalm, Expounded (London, 1625).

Isocrates. *Works*, trans. by George Norlin, 3 volumes (London: Heinemann, 1928–9).

James VI and I. *Triplici nodo, triplex cuneus. or An Apologie for the Oath of Allegiance, Against the two Breves of Pope Paulus Quintus, and the late Letter of Cardinal Bellarmine to G. Blackwel the Arch-priest* (London, 1607).

Triplici nodo, triplex cuneus. Sive Apologia pro Iuramento Fiedelitatis. Adversus duo Brevia P. Pauli Quinti, & Epistolam Cardinalis Bellarmini, ad G. Blackvellum Archipresbyterum nuper scriptam (London, 1607).

Political Writings, ed. by J. P. Sommerville (Cambridge: Cambridge University Press, 1994).

The Workes (London, 1616).

Jewel, John. *The Works of John Jewel*, ed. by J. Ayre (Cambridge, 1850).

Jonson, Ben. *Juvenal and Persius*, trans. by G. G. Ramsay, rev. edition (London: Heinemann, 1940).

Volpone and Other Plays, ed. by Lorna Hutson (Harmondsworth: Penguin, 1998).

Kenyon, J. P. *The Stuart Constitution 1603–1688: Documents and Commentary*, second edition (Cambridge: Cambridge University Press, 1986).

Larkin, James F. and Paul L. Hughes (eds.). *Stuart Royal Proclamations*, volume 1: *Royal Proclamations of King James I 1603–1625* (Oxford: Clarendon Press, 1973).

Latimer, Hugh. *Sermons and Remains*, ed. by George Elwes Corrie, 2 volumes (Cambridge: Cambridge University Press, 1844–5).

Laud, William. *The Works of the Most Reverend Father in God, William Laud D.D.*, ed. by William Scott and James Bliss, 3 volumes (Oxford, 1847–60).

Lefèvre de Boderie, Antoine. *Ambassades de la Boderie en Angleterre sous le règne de Henri IV et la minorité de Louis XIII depuis les années 1601 jusqu'en 1611*, 5 volumes (Paris, 1750).

Le Prince d'Amour or the Prince of Love with a Collection of Several Ingenious Poems and Songs By the Wits of the Age (London, 1660).

Lincoln's Inn. *The Records of the Honourable Society of Lincoln's Inn*, volume 1: *Admissions from A.D. 1420 to A.D. 1799* (London: Lincoln's Inn, 1896).

Lipsius, Justus. *Six Bookes of Politics or Civil Doctrine*, trans. by William Jones (London, 1594).

Lycosthenes. *Apothegmata* (Paris, 1560).

Machiavelli, Niccolo. *Nicholas Machiavel's Prince*, trans. by E[dward]. D[acres]. (London, 1640).

    The Prince, ed. by Quentin Skinner and Russell Price (Cambridge: Cambridge University Press, 1988).

Malherbe, Abraham J. *Moral Exhortation, A Greco-Roman Sourcebook* (Philadelphia: The Westminster Press, 1986).

Marlowe, Christopher. *Dr Faustus and Other Plays*, ed. by David Bevington and Eric Rasmussen (Oxford: Oxford University Press, 1995).

Mennis, Sir John (ed.). *Facetiae. Musarum Deliciae: or, the muses recreation, contening severall pieces of poetique wit by Sir J. M. and Ja: S. 1656*, 2 volumes (London, 1817).

Middleton, Thomas. *A Game at Chess*, ed. by J. W. Harper (London: Ernest Benn, 1966).

More, Thomas. *Utopia*, in *The Complete Works of St Thomas More*, fourteen volumes (New Haven: Yale University Press, 1960–97), volume IV, ed. by Edward Surtz, SJ and J. H. Hexter (1965).

    Utopia, ed. by George M. Logan and Robert M. Adams (Cambridge: Cambridge University Press, 1989).

    Utopia with Erasmus' The Sileni of Alcibiades, ed. and trans. by David Wootton (Indianapolis: Hackett, 1999).

Mulcaster, Richard. *Positions Wherein those Primitive Circumstances be Examined, which are necessarie for the training vp of children, either for skill in their booke, or health in their bodie* (London: Thomas Vautrollier for Thomas Chare, 1581).

Mum and the Sothsegger. Ed. by M. Day and R. Steele, Early English Text Society, old series no. 199 (London: Oxford University Press, 1936).

Nicholas, Edward. *Proceedings and Debates in the House of Commons in 1620 and 1621*, 2 volumes (Oxford, 1766).

Norbrook, David and H. R. Woudhuysen (eds.). *The Penguin Book of Renaissance Verse 1509–1659*, revised edition (Harmondsworth: Penguin, 1993).

Osborn, Louise Brown. *The Life, Letters and Writings of John Hoskyns* (New Haven: Yale University Press, 1937).

Owen, John. *Epigrammatum Joannis Owen Cambro-Britanni, Oxoniensis* (Leiden, 1620).

Oxoniensis Academiae Funebre Officium (Oxford, 1603).

Oxoniensivm Στεναγμός (Oxford, 1592).

Peacham, Henry. *The Garden of Eloquence* (London: H. Jackson, 1577; facsimile, Menston: Scolar Press, 1971).

    The Garden of Eloquence (London: H. Jackson, 1593; facsimile, Gainesville, FL: Scholars' Facsimiles and Reprints, 1954).

Peile, John (compiler). *Biographical Register of Christ's College, 1505–1905*, 2 volumes (Cambridge: Cambridge University Press, 1910).

Peplvs (Oxford, 1587).

Petyt, William. *Miscellanea Parliamentaria* (London, 1681).

Philodemus of Gadara. Περὶ παρρησίας, *De libertate dicendi*, ed. by A. Olivieri (Leipzig: Teubner, 1914).

Plato. *The Apology*, in *The Last Days of Socrates*, trans. by Hugh Tredennick (Harmondsworth: Penguin, 1969), pp. 45–76.

Gorgias, trans. by Walter Hamilton (Harmondsworth: Penguin, 1960).

The Republic, trans. by H. D. P. Lee (Harmondsworth: Penguin, 1955).

Plutarch. *Moralia*, trans. by Frank Cole Babbitt, 14 volumes (London: Heinemann, 1927).

The Philosophie, commonlie called, the Morals, trans. by Philemon Holland (London: Dent, n.d., ?1911).

Proceedings in the Parliaments of Elizabeth I, ed. by T. E. Hartley, 3 volumes (Leicester: Leicester University Press, 1981–1995), volume 1: *1558–1581*.

Puttenham, George. *The Arte of English Poesie* (London: Richard Field, 1589; facsimile, Amsterdam: Theatrvm Orbis Terrarvm, 1971).

The Arte of English Poesie, ed. by Gladys Willcock and Alice Walker (Cambridge: Cambridge University Press, 1970).

Quintilian. *The Orator's Education* [*Institutio oratoria*], ed. and trans. by Donald A. Russell, 5 volumes (Cambridge, MA: Harvard University Press, 2001).

R., I. [John Russell]. *The Spy. Discovering the Danger of the Arminian Heresie and Spanish Trecherie* (Strasburg, 1628).

Ralegh, Sir Walter. *The Poems of Sir Walter Ralegh*, ed. by Agnes Latham (London: Routledge and Kegan Paul, 1951).

The Poems of Sir Walter Ralegh: A Historical Edition, ed. by Michael Rudick, Renaissance English Text Society, seventh series no. 23 (Tempe, AZ: Arizona Center for Medieval and Renaissance Studies in conjunction with Renaissance English Text Society, 1999).

Report on the Manuscripts of the Marquess of Downshire (London: His Majesty's Stationery Office, 1924).

Roper, William. *The Lyfe of Sir Thomas More, Knighte*, ed. by E. V. Hitchcock, Early English Text Society, original series 197 (London: Oxford University Press, 1935).

Rous, John. *Diary of John Rous, Incumbent of Santon Downham, Suffolk, from 1625 to 1642*, ed. by M. A. E. Green (London, 1856).

[Scott, Thomas]. *The Belgicke Pismire: Stinging the Slothfull Sleeper, and awaking the Diligent to Fast, watch, Pray; and worke out their owne Temporall and Eternall Salvation with Fear and Trembling* (London, 1622).

The Belgicke Souldier: Dedicated to the Parliament. Or, Warre was a Blessing (Dort, 1624).

Boanerges. Or The Humble Supplication of the Ministers of Scotland, to the High Court of Parliament (Edinburgh, 1624).

Digitvs Dei (n.p., n.d. [1623]).

Englands Ioy, for svppressing the Papists, and banishing the Priests and Iesuites (n.p., 1624).

The High-Waies of God and the King (London, 1623).

Robert Earle of Essex his Ghost, Sent from Elizian: To the Nobilitie, Gentry, and Commvnalitie of England ('Paradise', 1624).

Sir Walter Rawleigh's Ghost, or Englands Forewarner (Utrecht, 1626).

Symmachia: or, a True-Loves Knot. Tyed, betwixt Great Britaine and the Vnited Prouinces (n.p., n.d. [1624]).

Vox Dei (n.d. [1624]).

Vox Populi or Newes from Spayne (n.p., 1620).

Vox Regis (London, 1624).

Selden, John. *Table Talk of John Selden*, ed. by F. Pollock (London: Quaritch, 1927).

Shakespeare, William. *The Rape of Lucrece*, ed. by John Roe (Cambridge: Cambridge University Press, 1992).

The Riverside Shakespeare, ed. by G. Blakemore Evans (Boston: Houghton Mifflin Company, 1974).

Sherry, Richard. *A Treatise of the Schemes and Tropes Gathered out of the Best Grammarians and Orators* (London, 1550).

Sidney, Sir Philip. *Miscellaneous Prose of Sir Philip Sidney*, ed. by Katherine Duncan-Jones and Jan Van Dorsten (Oxford: Clarendon Press, 1973).

The Old Arcadia, ed. by Katherine Duncan-Jones (Oxford: Oxford University Press, 1985).

Silenzi, R. and F. *Pasquino. Cinquecento pasquinate* (Milan: Bompiani, 1932).

Smith, Logan Pearsall. *The Life and Letters of Sir Henry Wotton*, 2 volumes (Oxford: Clarendon Press, 1907).

Smith, Sir Thomas. *De Republica Anglorum*, ed. by Mary Dewar (Cambridge: Cambridge University Press, 1982).

Sophocles. *The Women of Trachis*, trans. by Michael Jameson, in *Sophocles II: Four Tragedies* (Chicago: University of Chicago Press, 1957).

Spelman, Sir John. *The Reports of Sir John Spelman*, ed. by J. H. Baker, 2 volumes (London: Selden Society, 1977–8).

Spenser, Edmund. *The Faerie Queene*, ed. by A. C. Hamilton (Harlow: Longman, 1977).

The Shorter Poems, ed. by Richard A. McCabe (Harmondsworth: Penguin, 1999).

S.R.N.I. [John Reynolds]. *Votivae Angliae* (Utrecht, 1624).

Vox Coeli, or Newes from Heaven ('Elisium', 1624).

Starkey, Thomas. *A Dialogue between Pole and Lupset*, ed. by T. F. Mayer, Camden Society, fourth series no. 37 (London: Royal Historical Society, 1989).

Stubbs, John. *John Stubbs's Gaping Gulf with Letters and Other Relevant Documents*, ed. by Lloyd E. Berry (Folger Shakespeare Library: University Press of Virginia, 1968).

Susenbrotus, Johannes. *Epitome troporum ac schematvm et grammaticorum & rhetorum* (London: Gerard Dewes, 1562).

Tacitus. *Annals*, trans. by John Jackson, 3 volumes (London: Heinemann, 1937).

Dialogus de oratoribus, in *Agricola, Germania, Dialogus*, trans. by M. Hutton and W. Peterson, revised by R. M. Ogilvie, E. H. Warmington, and M. Winterbottom (London: Heinemann, 1970).

Talon, Omer. *Rhetoricae Libri Duo* (Paris, 1545).

Tanner, J. R. (ed.). *Constitutional Documents of the Reign of James I A.D. 1603–1625, with an historical commentary* (Cambridge: Cambridge University Press, 1930).

    Tudor Constitutional Documents A.D. 1485–1603, second edition (Cambridge: Cambridge University Press, 1930).

Thornborough, John. *A Discourse Plainely Prouing the Euident Vtilitie and Vrgent Necessitie of the Desired Happie Vnion of the Two Famous Kingdomes of England and Scotland: by way of answer to certaine obiections against the same* (London, 1604).

Thucydides. *The Peloponnesian War*, trans. by Thomas Hobbes [1629] (Chicago: University of Chicago Press, 1989).

Ursinus, Zacharias. *The Summe of Christian Religion*, trans. by Henry Parrie (Oxford, 1587).

Vaughan, Rowland. *Most Approved, and Long Experienced Water-Workes* (London, 1610).

Virgil. *Aeneid*, trans. by H. R. Fairclough, 2 volumes (London: Heinemann, 1935).

Vives, Juan Luis, *On Education: A Translation of the De tradendis disciplinis*, trans. by Foster Watson (Cambridge: Cambridge University Press, 1913).

Vossius, G. J. *Oratorium institutionum* (1616).

Watson, Thomas. *English Poems*, ed. by Albert Chatterly (Norwich: Marion Hopkins, 2003).

Wilson, Thomas. *The Arte of Rhetorique* (London: Richard Grafton, 1553; facsimile Gainesville, FL: Scholars' Facsimiles and Reprints, 1962).

    The Arte of Rhetorique, ed. by G. H. Mair (Oxford: Clarendon Press, 1909).

Younge, Walter. *The Diary of Walter Younge, Esq.*, ed. by George Roberts (London: Camden Society, 1868).

SECONDARY WORKS

Adams, S. L. 'Captain Thomas Gainsford, the "Vox spiritus" and the "Vox populi"', *Bulletin of the Institute of Historical Research* 49 (1976): 141–44.

Armitage, C. M. 'Donne's Poems in Huntington Manuscript 198: New Light on "The Funerall"', *Studies in Philology* 63:5 (October 1966): 697–707.

    'Identification of New York Public Library Manuscript "Suckling Collection" and of Huntington Manuscript 198', *Studies in Bibliography* 19 (1966): 215–16.

Atherton, Ian. 'The Itch Grown a Disease: Manuscript Transmission of News in the Seventeenth Century', in *News, Newspapers and Society in Early Modern Britain*, ed. by Joad Raymond (London: Frank Cass, 1999), pp. 39–65.

Baker, J. H. 'Defamation', in *An Introduction to English Legal History*, third edition (London: Butterworths, 1990), pp. 495–508.

Bald, R. C. *John Donne. A Life* (Oxford: Clarendon Press, 1970).

Baldwin, T. W. *William Shakspere's Small Latine and Lesse Greeke*, 2 volumes (Urbana: University of Illinois, 1944).

Barthes, Roland. 'The Old Rhetoric: An Aide Mémoire', in *The Semiotic Challenge*, trans. by Richard Howard (Oxford: Basil Blackwell, 1988), pp. 11–94.

Beal, Peter. '"Notions in Garrison": The Seventeenth Century Commonplace Book', in *New Ways of Looking at Old Texts: Papers of the Renaissance English Text Society, 1985–1991*, Medieval and Renaissance Texts and Studies 107, ed. by W. Speed Hill (New York: Mediaeval and Renaissance Text Society, 1993), pp. 131–47.

Beaurline, L. A. 'An Editorial Experiment: Suckling's *A Sessions of the Poets*', *Studies in Bibliography* 16 (1963): 43–60.

Bellany, Alastair. 'Libels in Action: Ritual, Subversion, and the English Literary Underground, 1603–1642', in *The Politics of the Excluded, c. 1500–1850*, ed. by Tim Harris (Basingstoke: Palgrave, 2001), pp. 99–124.

'A Poem on the Archbishop's Hearse: Puritanism, Libel, and Sedition after the Hampton Court Conference', *Journal of British Studies* 34 (April 1995): 137–64.

The Politics of Court Scandal in Early Modern England: News Culture and the Overbury Affair, 1603–1660 (Cambridge: Cambridge University Press, 2002).

'"Raylinge Rymes and Vaunting Verse": Libellous Politics in Early Stuart England, 1603–1628', in *Culture and Politics in Early Stuart England*, ed. by Kevin Sharpe and Peter Lake (Basingstoke: Macmillan, 1994), pp. 285–310.

Bendall, Sarah, Christopher Brooke, and Patrick Collinson. *A History of Emmanuel College* (Woodbridge: The Boydell Press, 1999).

Bolgar, R. R. *The Classical Heritage and Its Beneficiaries* (Cambridge: Cambridge University Press, 1954).

Boutcher, Warren. 'Pilgrimage to Parnassus: Local Intellectual Traditions, Humanist Education and the Cultural Geography of Sixteenth-century England', in *Pedagogy and Power: Rhetorics of Classical Learning*, ed. by Niall Livingstone and Yun Lee Too (Cambridge: Cambridge University Press, 1998), pp. 110–47.

Brett, Annabel. *Liberty, Right, and Nature: Individual Rights in Later Scholastic Thought* (Cambridge: Cambridge University Press, 1997).

Brickhouse, T. C. and N. D. Smith. *Socrates on Trial* (Oxford, 1989).

Brigden, Susan. *New Worlds, Lost Worlds: The Reign of the Tudors 1485–1603* (Harmondsworth: Penguin, 2000).

Brioist, Pascal, 'Que de choses avons-nous vues et vécues à la Sirène', in *Culture et société dans l'Europe moderne et contemporaine*, ed. by Dominique Julia (Florence: European University Institute, 1992), pp. 89–132.

Brown, Peter. *Power and Persuasion in Late Antiquity: Towards a Christian Empire. The Curti Lectures 1988* (Madison: University of Wisconsin Press, 1992).

Bryant, Jerry H. 'John Reynolds of Exeter and his Canon', *The Library*, fifth series 15 (1960): 105–17.

'John Reynolds of Exeter and his Canon: A Footnote', *The Library*, fifth series 18 (1963): 299–303.

Burgess, Glenn. *Absolute Monarchy and the Stuart Constitution* (New Haven: Yale University Press, 1996).

'The Impact on Political Thought: Rhetorics for Troubled Times', in *The Impact of the English Civil War*, ed. by John Morrill (London: Collins & Brown, 1991), pp. 67–83.

Burke, Peter. *The Historical Anthropology of Early Modern Italy. Essays on Perception and Communication* (Cambridge: Cambridge University Press, 1987).

'Tacitism', in *Tacitus*, ed. by T. A. Dorey (London: Routledge and Kegan Paul, 1969), pp. 149–71.

'Tacitism, Scepticism, and Reason of State', in *The Cambridge History of Political Thought 1450–1700*, ed. by J. H. Burns with the assistance of Mark Goldie (Cambridge: Cambridge University Press, 1991), pp. 479–98.

Burns, J. H. (ed.), with the assistance of Mark Goldie. *The Cambridge History of Political Thought 1450-1700* (Cambridge: Cambridge University Press, 1991).

Butler, Judith. *Excitable Speech: A Politics of the Performative* (London: Routledge, 1997).

Carey, John. *John Donne: Life, Mind and Art*, new edition (London: Faber and Faber, 1900).

Carlson, Leland H. *Martin Marprelate, Gentleman: Master Job Throckmorton Laid Open in his Colours* (San Marino: Huntington Library, 1981).

Clegg, Cyndia Susan. *Press Censorship in Elizabethan England* (Cambridge: Cambridge University Press, 1997).

Press Censorship in Jacobean England (Cambridge: Cambridge University Press, 2001).

Clucas, Stephen and Rosalind Davies (eds.). *The Crisis of 1614 and the Addled Parliament: Literary and Historical Perspectives* (Aldershot: Ashgate, 2003).

Cogswell, Thomas. *The Blessed Revolution: English Politics and the Coming of War, 1621–1624* (Cambridge: Cambridge University Press, 1989).

'Underground Verse and the Transformation of Early Stuart Political Culture', in *Political Culture and Cultural Politics in Early Modern England*, ed. by Susan D. Amussen and Mark Kishlansky (Manchester: Manchester University Press, 1995), pp. 277–300.

Colclough, David. '"The Muses Recreation": John Hoskyns and the Manuscript Culture of the Seventeenth Century', *Huntington Library Quarterly* 61:3 and 4 (1998): 369–400.

'*Parrhesia*: The Rhetoric of Free Speech in Early Modern England', *Rhetorica* 17:2 (Spring 1999): 177–212.

'"Non canimus surdis, respondent omnia sylvae": Francis Bacon and the Transmission of Knowledge', in *Textures of Renaissance Knowledge*, ed. by Philippa Berry and Margaret Tudeau-Clayton (Manchester: Manchester University Press, 2003), pp. 81–97.

Collinson, Patrick, *Archbishop Grindal, 1519–1583: The Struggle for a Reformed Church* (London: Cape, 1979).

'*De Republica Anglorum*: Or, History with the Politics Put Back', in *Elizabethan Essays* (London: The Hambledon Press, 1994), pp. 1–29.

'Ecclesiastical Vitriol: Religious Satire in the 1590s and the Invention of Puritanism', in *The Reign of Elizabeth I*, ed. by John Guy (Cambridge: Cambridge University Press, 1995), pp. 150–70.

The Elizabethan Puritan Movement (Oxford: Clarendon Press, 1967).

'If Constantine, then also Theodosius: St Ambrose and the Integrity of the Elizabethan *Ecclesia Anglicana*', *Journal of Ecclesiastical History* 30:2 (April 1979): 205–29.

The Religion of Protestants: The Church in English Society 1559–1625 (Oxford: Clarendon Press, 1982).

Conrad, F. W. '"A Preservative Against Tyranny": Sir Thomas Elyot and the Rhetoric of Counsel', in *Reformation, Humanism, and 'Revolution'. Papers Presented at the Folger Institute Seminar 'Political Thought in the Henrician Age, 1500–1550'*, ed. by Gordon J. Schochet with Patricia E. Tatspaugh and Carol Brobeck (Washington: Folger Institute, 1990), pp. 191–206.

'The Problem of Counsel Reconsidered: The Case of Sir Thomas Elyot', in *Political Thought and the Tudor Commonwealth. Deep Structure, Discourse and Disguise*, ed. by Paul A. Fideler and T. F. Mayer (London: Routledge, 1992), pp. 75–107.

Cramer, Frederick H. 'Bookburning and Censorship in Ancient Rome. A Chapter from the History of Freedom of Speech', *Journal of the History of Ideas* 6:2 (April 1945): 157–96.

Crane, Mary Thomas. *Framing Authority: Sayings, Self, and Society in Sixteenth-Century England* (Princeton: Princeton University Press, 1993).

Croft, Pauline. 'Fresh Light on Bate's Case', *Historical Journal* 30 (1987): 523–39.

'The Reputation of Robert Cecil: Libels, Political Opinion and Popular Awareness in the Early Seventeenth Century', *Transactions of the Royal Historical Society* 6:1 (1991): 43–69.

Cust, Richard. *The Forced Loan and English Politics, 1626–1628* (Oxford: Clarendon Press, 1987).

'News and Politics in Early Seventeenth-Century England', *Past and Present* 112 (August 1986): 60–90.

'Politics and the Electorate in the 1620s', in *Conflict in Early Stuart England*, ed. by Cust and Hughes, pp. 134–67.

Cust, Richard and Ann Hughes (eds.). *Conflict in Early Stuart England: Studies in Religion and Politics, 1603–1642* (London: Longman, 1989).

Davidson, Peter. 'The Rainsford Family Notebook', *Notes and Queries* 31 (229) (June 1994): 2, 247–50.

Daybell, James (ed.). *Early Modern Women's Letter Writing, 1450–1700* (Basingstoke: Palgrave, 2001).

De Man, Paul. *Allegories of Reading. Figural Language in Rousseau, Nietzsche, Rilke, and Proust* (New Haven: Yale University Press, 1979).

Blindness and Insight. Essays in the Rhetoric of Contemporary Criticism (New York: Oxford University Press, 1971).

The Rhetoric of Romanticism (New York: Columbia University Press, 1984).

Dell'Arco, Mario. *Pasquino e le pasquinate* (Milan: A. Martello, 1957).

DeWitt, Norman W. 'Parresiastic Poems of Horace', *Classical Philology* 30 (October 1935): 312–19.

Dover, K. J. 'The Freedom of the Intellectual in Greek Society', in *The Greeks and their Legacy: Collected Papers*, volume II (Oxford: Basil Blackwell, 1988), pp. 135–58.

Dzelzainis, Martin. '*Parrhesia*, Print and Martyrdom in Restoration England', forthcoming in *Martyrs and Martyrdom: Early-Modern Perspectives*, ed. by P. S. Scott.

Eales, Jacqueline. *Puritans and Roundheads: The Harleys of Brampton Bryan and the Outbreak of the English Civil War* (Cambridge: Cambridge University Press, 1990).

Eisenstein, Elizabeth L. *The Printing Press as an Agent of Change*, 2 volumes (Cambridge: Cambridge University Press, 1979).

Elton, G. R. *The Parliament of England 1559–1581* (Cambridge: Cambridge University Press, 1986).

  Studies in Tudor and Stuart Politics and Government: Papers and Reviews 1946–1972, volume II: *Parliament and Political Thought* (Cambridge: Cambridge University Press, 1974).

Engberg-Pedersen, Troels. 'Plutarch to Prince Philopappus on How to Tell a Flatterer from a Friend', in *Friendship, Flattery, and Frankness of Speech. Studies on Friendship in the New Testament World*, ed. by John T. Fitzgerald (Leiden: E. J. Brill, 1996), pp. 61–79.

Faraday, Michael. *Ludlow 1085–1660. A Social, Economic and Political History* (Chichester: Phillimore, 1991).

Ferguson, Arthur B. *The Articulate Citizen and the English Renaissance* (Durham, NC: Duke University Press, 1965).

Ferrell, Lori Anne. *Government by Polemic: James I, the King's Preachers, and the Rhetorics of Conformity, 1603–1625* (Stanford: Stanford University Press, 1998).

Ferster, Judith. *Fictions of Advice: The Literature and Politics of Counsel in Late Medieval England* (Philadelphia: University of Pennsylvania Press, 1996).

Fincham, Kenneth and Peter Lake. 'The Ecclesiastical Policy of King James I', *Journal of British Studies* 24 (1985): 169–207.

  'The Ecclesiastical Policies of James I and Charles I', in *The Early Stuart Church*, ed. by Kenneth Fincham (Basingstoke: Macmillan, 1993), pp. 23–50.

Fish, Stanley. *There's No Such Thing as Free Speech and It's a Good Thing, Too* (Oxford: Oxford University Press, 1994).

  The Trouble with Principle (Cambridge, MA: Harvard University Press, 1999).

Fitzgerald, John T. (ed.). *Friendship, Flattery, and Frankness of Speech. Studies on Friendship in the New Testament World* (Leiden: E. J. Brill, 1996).

Foucault, Michel. *Fearless Speech*, ed. by Joseph Pearson (Los Angeles: Semiotext(e), 2001).

Fox, Adam. 'Ballads, Libels and Popular Ridicule in Jacobean England', *Past & Present* 145 (November 1994): 47–83.

  Oral and Literate Culture in England, 1500–1700 (Oxford: Oxford University Press, 2000).

Fredrickson, David E. 'Παρρησία in the Pauline Epistles', in *Friendship, Flattery, and Frankness of Speech. Studies on Friendship in the New Testament World*, ed. by John T. Fitzgerald (Leiden: E. J. Brill, 1996), pp. 163–83.

Gardiner, S. R. *History of England from the Accession of James I to the Outbreak of the Civil War*, 10 volumes (London: Longmans, Green, & Co., 1884).

Genette, Gérard. *Paratexts: Thresholds of Interpretation*, trans. by Jane E. Lewin (Cambridge: Cambridge University Press, 1997).

Gibson, Jonathan. 'Letters', in *A Companion to English Renaissance Literature and Culture*, ed. by Michael Hattaway (Oxford: Blackwell, 2000), pp. 615–19.

Ginzburg, Carlo. *No Island is an Island: Four Glances at English Literature in a World Perspective* (New York: Columbia University Press, 2000).

Glad, Clarence E. 'Frank Speech, Flattery, and Friendship in Philodemus', in *Friendship, Flattery, and Frankness of Speech. Studies on Friendship in the New Testament World*, ed. by John T. Fitzgerald (Leiden: E. J. Brill, 1996), pp. 21–59.

Gordon, Andrew. 'The Act of Libel: Conscripting Civic Space in Early Modern England', *Journal of Medieval and Early Modern Studies* 32:2 (Spring 2002): 375–97.

Guy, John. 'The Henrician Age', in *The Varieties of British Political Thought, 1500–1800*, ed. by J. G. A. Pocock, with the assistance of Gordon J. Schochet and Lois G. Schwoerer (Cambridge: Cambridge University Press, 1993), pp. 13–46.

The Public Career of Sir Thomas More (Brighton: Harvester Press, 1980).

'The Rhetoric of Counsel in Early Modern England', in *Tudor Political Culture*, ed. by Dale Hoak (Cambridge: Cambridge University Press, 1995), pp. 292–310.

Hadfield, Andrew. 'Censoring Ireland in Elizabethan England, 1580–1600', in *Literature and Censorship in Renaissance England*, ed. by Andrew Hadfield (Basingstoke: Palgrave, 2001), pp. 149–64.

Halliwell, Stephen. 'Between Public and Private: Tragedy and Athenian Experience of Rhetoric', in *Greek Tragedy and the Historian*, ed. by Christopher Pelling (Oxford : Clarendon Press, 1997), pp. 121–41.

'Comic Satire and Freedom of Speech in Classical Athens', *Journal of Hellenistic Studies* III (1991): 48–70.

Harland, Paul. 'Donne's Political Intervention in the Parliament of 1629', *John Donne Journal* 11:1 and 2 ('1992'; actually 1995): 21–37.

Heinemann, Margot. *Puritanism and Theatre: Thomas Middleton and Opposition Drama under the Early Stuarts* (Cambridge: Cambridge University Press, 1980).

Helgerson, Richard. *Forms of Nationhood: The Elizabethan Writing of England* (Chicago: University of Chicago Press, 1992).

Hexter, J. H. 'Introduction part I', to Thomas More, *Utopia*, ed. by Edward Surtz, SJ and J. H. Hexter, in *The Complete Works of St Thomas More*, 14 volumes (New Haven: Yale University Press, 1960–1997), volume IV, pp. xv–cxxiv.

Hexter, J. H. (ed.). 'Introduction', in *Parliament and Liberty from the Reign of Elizabeth to the English Civil War*, ed. by Hexter, pp. 1–19.

Parliament and Liberty from the Reign of Elizabeth to the English Civil War (Stanford: Stanford University Press, 1992).

Hirst, Derek M. 'Freedom, Revolution, and Beyond', in *Parliament and Liberty from the Reign of Elizabeth to the English Civil War*, ed. by Hexter, pp. 252–74.

Hobbs, Mary. 'Early Seventeenth-Century Verse Miscellanies and their Value for Textual Editors', *English Manuscript Studies* 1 (1989): 182–210.

Early Seventeenth-Century Verse Miscellany Manuscripts (Aldershot: Scolar Press, 1992).

Holdsworth, W. S. 'Defamation in the Sixteenth and Seventeenth Centuries', *Law Quarterly Review* 159 (July 1924): 302–15; *Law Quarterly Review* 160 (October 1924): 397–412; *Law Quarterly Review* 161 (January 1925): 13–31.

Hughes, Ann. *The Causes of the English Civil War* (Basingstoke: Macmillan, 1991).

Hulme, Harold. 'The Winning of Freedom of Speech by the House of Commons', *The American Historical Review* 61:4 (July 1956): 825–53.

Hunter, R. L. 'Horace on Friendship and Free Speech', *Hermes* 113 (1985): 480–90.

Hutson, Lorna and Erica Sheen. *Literature, Politics, and Law in Renaissance England* (Basingstoke: Palgrave, forthcoming).

Jaeger, H., SJ. 'Παρρησία et fiducia', *Studia Patristica* 1, Texte und Untersuchungen 63, ed. by K. Aland and F. L. Cross (Berlin: Akademie, 1957), pp. 221–39.

Jansson, Maija. 'Dues Paid', *Parliamentary History*, 15.2 (1996): 215–20.

Jardine, Lisa. *Francis Bacon: Discovery and the Art of Discourse* (Cambridge: Cambridge University Press, 1974).

Jardine, Lisa and Anthony Grafton. '"Studied for Action": How Gabriel Harvey Read his Livy', *Past and Present* 129 (November 1990): 30–78.

Jardine, Lisa and Alan Stewart. *Hostage to Fortune. The Troubled Life of Francis Bacon* (London: Victor Gollancz, 1998).

Jones, Norman. 'Parliament and the Political Society of Elizabethan England', in *Tudor Political Culture*, ed. by Dale Hoak (Cambridge: Cambridge University Press, 1995), pp. 226–42.

Jones, R. F. *The Triumph of the English Language: A Survey of Opinions Concerning the Vernacular from the Invention of Printing to the Restoration* (Stanford: Stanford University Press, 1953).

Kahn, Victoria. *Machiavellian Rhetoric from the Counter-Reformation to Milton* (Princeton: Princeton University Press, 1994).

Kaplan, M. Lindsay. *The Culture of Slander in Early Modern England* (Cambridge: Cambridge University Press, 1997).

Kennedy, George A. *The Art of Rhetoric in the Roman World 300 B.C.–A.D. 300* (Princeton: Princeton University Press, 1972).

Classical Rhetoric and Its Christian and Secular Traditions from Ancient to Modern Times (London: Croom Helm, 1980).

A New History of Classical Rhetoric (Princeton: Princeton University Press, 1994).

Kennedy, Mark E. 'Legislation, Foreign Policy, and the "Proper Business" of the Parliament of 1624', *Albion* 23:1 (Spring 1991): 41–60.

King, John N. *English Reformation Literature: The Tudor Origins of the Protestant Tradition* (Princeton: Princeton University Press, 1982).

'Spenser's *Shepheardes Calender* and Protestant Pastoral Satire', in *Renaissance Genres: Essays on Theory, History, and Interpretation*, ed. by Barbara Kiefer Lewalski (Cambridge, MA: Harvard University Press, 1986), pp. 369–98.

Klassen, William. 'Παρρησία in the Johannine Corpus', in *Friendship, Flattery, and Frankness of Speech. Studies on Friendship in the New Testament World*, ed. by John T. Fitzgerald (Leiden: E. J. Brill, 1996), pp. 227–54.

Knott, John R. *Discourses of Martyrdom in English Literature, 1563–1694* (Cambridge: Cambridge University Press, 1993).

Konstan, David. 'Friendship, Frankness and Flattery', in Fitzgerald (ed.), *Friendship, Flattery, and Frankness of Speech*, pp. 7–19.

— *Friendship in the Classical World* (Cambridge: Cambridge University Press, 1997).

Kyle, Chris R. (ed.). *Parliament, Politics and Elections 1604–1648*, Camden fifth series no. 17 (Cambridge: Cambridge University Press, 2001).

— 'Introduction' to *Parliament, Politics and Elections 1604–1648*, ed. by Kyle, pp. 1–12.

Lahan, Mary. *Pasquin et Marforio* (Paris, 1861).

Lake, Peter G. 'Anti-popery: The Structure of a Prejudice', in *Conflict in Early Stuart England*, ed. by Richard Cust and Ann Hughes (Harlow: Longman, 1989), pp. 72–106.

— 'Constitutional Consensus and Puritan Opposition in the 1620s: Thomas Scott and the Spanish Match', *The Historical Journal* 25:4 (1982): 805–25.

— 'Lancelot Andrewes, John Buckeridge, and Avant-Garde Conformity at the Court of James I', in *The Mental World of the Jacobean Court*, ed. by Linda Levy Peck (Cambridge: Cambridge University Press, 1991), pp. 111–33.

— 'The Moderate and Irenic Case for Religious War: Joseph Hall's *Via Media* in Context', in *Political Culture and Cultural Politics in Early Modern England* (Manchester: Manchester University Press, 1995), pp. 55–83.

Lambert, Sheila. 'Procedure in the House of Commons in the Early Stuart Period', *English Historical Review* 95 (1980): 753–81.

— 'State Control of the Press in Theory and Practice: The Role of the Stationers' Company before 1640', in *Censorship and the Control of Print in England and France 1600–1900*, ed. by Robin Myers and Michael Harris (Winchester: St Paul's Bibliographies, 1992), pp. 1–32.

Lampe, G. W. H. 'Martyrdom and Inspiration', in *Suffering and Martyrdom in the New Testament: Studies Presented to G. M. Styler by the Cambridge New Testament Seminar*, ed. by William Horbury and Brian McNeil (Cambridge: Cambridge University Press, 1981), pp. 118–35.

Lanham, Richard A. *A Handlist of Rhetorical Terms*, second edition (Berkeley and Los Angeles: University of California Press, 1991).

Levy, F. J. 'How Information Spread Among the Gentry, 1550–1640', *Journal of British Studies* 21 (1982): 1–24.

— 'Francis Bacon and the Style of Politics', *English Literary Renaissance* 16:1 (Winter 1986): 101–22.

Lewis, C. S. *English Literature in the Sixteenth Century excluding Drama* (Oxford: Clarendon Press, 1954).

Limon, Jerzy. *Dangerous Matter: English Drama and Politics 1623/4* (Cambridge: Cambridge University Press, 1986).

Loades, David. *Politics, Censorship, and the English Reformation* (London: Pinter, 1991).

Lockyer, Roger. *The Early Stuarts: A Political History of England 1603–1642* (Harlow: Longman, 1989).

Loraux, Nicole. *L'invention d'Athènes. Histoire de l'oration funèbre dans la «cité classique»* (Paris: Mouton, 1981).

Love, Harold. *The Culture and Commerce of Texts: Scribal Publication in Seventeenth-Century England* (Amherst: University of Massachusetts Press, 1998).

MacCaffrey, Wallace T. *Elizabeth I* (London: Edward Arnold, 1993).

   Queen Elizabeth and the Making of Policy, 1572–1588 (Princeton: Princeton University Press, 1981).

MacCulloch, Diarmaid. *Tudor Church Militant: Edward VI and the Protestant Reformation* (Harmondsworth: Penguin, 1999).

McCullough, Peter E. *Sermons at Court: Politics and Religion in Elizabethan and Jacobean Preaching* (Cambridge: Cambridge University Press, 1998).

McLaren, A. N. *Political Culture in the Reign of Elizabeth I: Queen and Commonwealth 1558–1585* (Cambridge: Cambridge University Press, 1999).

MacLure, Millar. *The Paul's Cross Sermons, 1534–1642* (Toronto: University of Toronto Press, 1958).

McRae, Andrew. 'The Literary Culture of Early Stuart Libelling', *Modern Philology* 97:3 (2000): 364–92.

   Literature, Satire, and the Early Stuart State (Cambridge: Cambridge University Press, 2004).

Mack, Peter. *Elizabethan Rhetoric: Theory and Practice* (Cambridge: Cambridge University Press, 2002).

Manning, Roger B. 'The Origins of the Doctrine of Sedition', *Albion* 12:2 (1980): 99–121.

Manzalaoui, M. A. '"Noght in the Registre of Venus": Gower's English Mirror for Princes', in *Medieval Studies for J. A. W. Bennett*, ed. by P. L. Heyworth (Oxford: Clarendon Press, 1981), pp. 159–83.

Marcuse, Herbert. 'Repressive Tolerance', in Robert Paul Wolff, Barrington Moore, Jr., and Herbert Marcuse, *A Critique of Pure Tolerance* (Boston: Beacon Press, 1965), pp. 81–117.

Marotti, Arthur F. *Manuscript, Print, and the English Renaissance Lyric* (Ithaca: Cornell University Press, 1995).

   'Folger MSS V.a.89 and V.a.345: Reading Lyric Poetry in Manuscript', in *The Reader Revealed*, ed. by Sabrina Alcorn Baron, with Elizabeth Walsh and Susan Scola (Washington, DC: Folger Shakespeare Library, 2001), pp. 45–57.

Marotti, Arthur F. (ed.). *Catholicism and Anti-Catholicism in Early Modern English Texts* (Basingstoke: Macmillan, 1999).

Marrow, Stanley B., SJ. '*Parrhesia* and the New Testament', *Catholic Biblical Quarterly* 44:3 (July 1982): 431–46.

May, Steven W. *The Elizabethan Courtier Poets: The Poems and their Contexts* (Asheville: Pegasus Press, 1999).

Mayer, T. F. *Thomas Starkey and the Commonweal: Humanist Politics and Religion in the Reign of Henry VIII* (Cambridge: Cambridge University Press, 1989).

Mermel, Jerry. 'Preparations for a Politic Life: Sir Thomas More's Entry into the King's Service', *The Journal of Medieval and Renaissance Studies* 7 (1977): 53–66.

Michels, Agnes Kirsopp. 'Παρρησία and the Satire of Horace', *Classical Philology* 39 (July 1944): 173–7.

Milton, Anthony. *Catholic and Reformed: The Roman and Protestant Churches in English Protestant Thought, 1600–1640* (Cambridge: Cambridge University Press, 1995).

Milward, Peter. *Religious Controversies of the Elizabethan Age: A Survey of Printed Sources* (Lincoln: University of Nebraska Press, 1977).

Mitchell, Alan C. 'Holding on to Confidence: Παρρησία in Hebrews', in *Friendship, Flattery, and Frankness of Speech. Studies on Friendship in the New Testament World*, ed. by John T. Fitzgerald (Leiden: E. J. Brill, 1996), pp. 203–26.

Moir, Thomas L. *The Addled Parliament of 1614* (Oxford: Clarendon Press, 1958).

Momigliano, Arnaldo. 'Freedom of Speech in Antiquity', in *Dictionary of the History of Ideas*, 6 volumes, ed. by Philip Wiener (New York: Charles Scribner's Sons, 1973), volume II, pp. 252–63.

Monfasani, John. 'Humanism and Rhetoric', in *Renaissance Humanism: Foundations, Forms, and Legacy*, ed. by Albert Rabil, Jr., 3 volumes (Philadelphia: University of Pennsylvania Press, 1988), volume III, *Humanism and the Disciplines*, pp. 171–235.

Monoson, S. Sara. 'Frank Speech, Democracy, and Philosophy: Plato's Debt to a Democratic Strategy of Civic Discourse', *Athenian Political Thought and the Reconstruction of American Democracy*, ed. by J. P. Euben, J. R. Wallach, and J. Ober (Ithaca: Cornell University Press, 1994), pp. 172–97.

Plato's Democratic Entanglements: Athenian Politics and the Practice of Philosophy (Princeton: Princeton University Press, 2000).

Morrill, John. 'Getting Over D'Ewes', *Parliamentary History* 15:2 (1996): 221–30.

'Paying One's D'Ewes', *Parliamentary History* 14:2 (1995): 179–86.

'Reconstructing the History of Early Stuart Parliaments', *Archives* 21:91 (1994): 67–72.

Revolt in the Provinces: The People of England and the Tragedies of War, second edition (Harlow: Longman, 1999).

'Taking Liberties with the Seventeenth Century', *Parliamentary History* 15:3 (1996): 379–91.

Morrill, John, Brian Manning, and David Underdown. 'What Was the English Revolution?', *History Today* 34 (March 1984): 11–25.

Morrissey, Mary. 'John Donne as a Conventional Paul's Cross Preacher', in *John Donne's Professional Lives*, ed. by David Colclough (Cambridge: D. S. Brewer, 2003), pp. 159–78.

Moss, Ann. *Printed Commonplace Books and the Structuring of Renaissance Thought* (Oxford: Clarendon Press, 1996).

Munden, R. C. 'James I and "The Growth of Mutual Distrust": King, Commons, and Reform, 1603–1604', in *Faction and Parliament: Essays on Early Stuart History*, ed. by Kevin Sharpe, pp. 43–72.

Murphy, James J. *Renaissance Rhetoric. A Short-Title Catalogue of Works on Rhetorical Theory from the Beginning of Printing to A.D. 1700* (New York: Garland, 1981).

Neale, J. E. 'Commons Journals of the Tudor Period', *Transactions of the Royal Historical Society* 4:3 (1920): 136–70.

'The Commons' Privilege of Free Speech in Parliament', in *Tudor Studies Presented . . . to Albert Frederick Pollard*, ed. by R. W. Seton-Watson (London: Longmans Green & Co., 1924), pp. 257–86.

Elizabeth I and her Parliaments, 2 volumes (London: Jonathan Cape, 1953–7).

Nelson, Eric. 'Greek Nonsense in More's *Utopia*', *Historical Journal* 44 (2001): 889–918.

The Greek Tradition in Republican Thought (Cambridge: Cambridge University Press, 2004).

Norbrook, David. '*Areopagitica*, Censorship, and the Early Modern Public Sphere', in *The Administration of Aesthetics: Censorship, Political Criticism, and the Public Sphere*, ed. by Richard Burt (Minneapolis: University of Minnesota Press, 1994), pp. 3–33.

Poetry and Politics in the English Renaissance, revised edition (Oxford: Oxford University Press, 2002).

'Rhetoric, Ideology and the Elizabethan World Picture', in *Renaissance Rhetoric*, ed. by Peter Mack (Basingstoke: Macmillan, 1994), pp. 140–64.

Writing the English Republic: Poetry, Rhetoric and Politics, 1627–1660 (Cambridge: Cambridge University Press, 1999).

Notestein, Wallace. *The House of Commons 1604–1610* (New Haven: Yale University Press, 1971).

'The Winning of the Initiative by the House of Commons', *Proceedings of the British Academy* 11 (1924–5): 125–75.

O'Callaghan, Michelle. *The 'Shepheards Nation': Jacobean Spenserians and Early Stuart Political Culture, 1612–1625* (Oxford: Clarendon Press, 2000).

Oliver, P. M. *Donne's Religious Writing: A Discourse of Feigned Devotion* (London: Longman, 1997).

Parker, Robert. *Athenian Religion: A History* (Oxford: Clarendon Press, 1996).

Parkin-Speer, Diane. 'Freedom of Speech in Sixteenth Century English Rhetorics', *Sixteenth Century Journal* 12:3 (1981): 65–72.

Patterson, Annabel. *Censorship and Interpretation: The Conditions of Writing and Reading in Early Modern England*, new edition (Madison: University of Wisconsin Press, 1990).

Pastoral and Ideology. Virgil to Valéry (Oxford: Clarendon Press, 1988).

Patterson, W. B. *King James VI and I and the Reunion of Christendom* (Cambridge: Cambridge University Press, 1997).

Peck, Linda Levy. 'Kingship, Counsel and Law in Early Stuart Britain', in *The Varieties of British Political Thought, 1500–1800*, ed. by J. G. A. Pocock, with the assistance of Gordon J. Schochet and Lois G. Schwoerer (Cambridge: Cambridge University Press, 1993), pp. 80–115.

Northampton: Patronage and Policy at the Court of James I (London: George Allen and Unwin, 1982).

Peltonen, Markku. 'Aristocratic and Democratic Citizenship in Elizabethan England', unpublished paper.

'Bacon's Political Philosophy', in *The Cambridge Companion to Bacon*, ed. by Peltonen, pp. 283–310.

Classical Humanism and Republicanism in English Political Thought, 1570–1640 (Cambridge: Cambridge University Press, 1995).

Peltonen, Markku (ed.). *The Cambridge Companion to Bacon* (Cambridge: Cambridge University Press, 1996).

Petti, Anthony G. 'Unknown Sonnets by Sir Toby Matthew', *Recusant History* 9:3 (October 1967): 123–58.

Pincombe, Michael. 'Some Sixteenth-Century Records of the Words *Humanist* and *Humanitian*', *RES* new series 44:173 (1993): 1–15.

Pocock, J. G. A. *The Machiavellian Moment. Florentine Political Thought and the Atlantic Republican Tradition* (Princeton: Princeton University Press, 1975).

Pocock, J. G. A. (ed.), with the assistance of Gordon J. Schochet and Lois G. Schwoerer. *The Varieties of British Political Thought, 1500–1800* (Cambridge: Cambridge University Press, 1993).

Pursell, Brennan. 'War or Peace? Jacobean Politics and the Parliament of 1621', in *Parliament, Politics and Elections*, ed. by Kyle, pp. 149–78.

Quintrell, B. W. 'The Royal Hunt and the Puritans, 1604–1605', *Journal of Ecclesiastical History* 31:1 (January 1980): 41–58.

Raab, Felix. *The English Face of Machiavelli. A Changing Interpretation 1500–1700* (London: Routledge and Kegan Paul, 1964).

Rabb, Theodore K. *Jacobean Gentleman: Sir Edwin Sandys, 1561–1629* (Princeton: Princeton University Press, 1998).

Raymond, Joad. *The Invention of the Newspaper: English Newsbooks, 1641–1649* (Oxford: Clarendon Press, 1996).

Pamphlets and Pamphleteering in Early Modern Britain (Cambridge: Cambridge University Press, 2003).

Rebhorn, Wayne A. *The Emperor of Men's Minds: Literature and the Renaissance Discourse of Rhetoric* (Ithaca: Cornell University Press, 1995).

Redworth, Glyn. *The Prince and the Infanta: The Cultural Politics of the Spanish Match* (New Haven: Yale University Press, 2003).

Reynolds, Anne. 'Cardinal Oliviero Carafa and the Early Cinquecento Tradition of the Feast of Pasquino', *Humanistica Lovaniensia* 34A (1985): 178–208.

'The Classical Continuum in Roman Humanism: The Festival of Pasquino, the *Robigalia*, and Satire', *Bibliothèque d'Humanisme et Renaissance* 49:2 (1987): 289–307.

Richards, Jennifer. *Rhetoric and Courtliness in Early Modern Literature* (Cambridge: Cambridge University Press, 2003).

Roskell, J. S. *The Commons and their Speakers in English Parliaments 1376–1523* (Manchester: Manchester University Press, 1965).

Ruigh, Robert E. *The Parliament of 1624: Politics and Foreign Policy* (Cambridge, MA: Harvard University Press, 1971).

Russell, Conrad. *The Addled Parliament of 1614: The Limits to Revision*, The Stenton Lecture 1991 (Reading: University of Reading, 1992).

The Causes of the English Civil War (Oxford: Clarendon Press, 1990).

'English Parliaments 1593–1606: One Epoch or Two?', in *The Parliaments of Elizabethan England*, ed. by D. M. Dean and N. L. Jones (Oxford: Blackwell, 1990), pp. 191–213.

'Parliamentary History in Perspective, 1604–1629', in Conrad Russell, *Unrevolutionary England, 1603–1642* (London: Hambledon Press, 1990), pp. 31–57.

Parliaments and English Politics 1621–1629 (Oxford: Clarendon Press, 1979).

Unrevolutionary England, 1603–1642 (London: Hambledon Press, 1990).

Russell, Conrad (ed.). *The Origins of the English Civil War* (Basingstoke: Macmillan, 1973).

Salmon, J. H. M. 'Seneca and Tacitus in Jacobean England', in *The Mental World of the Jacobean Court*, ed. by Linda Levy Peck (Cambridge: Cambridge University Press, 1991), pp. 169–88.

Saunders, J. W. 'The Stigma of Print: A Note on the Social Bases of Tudor Poetry', *Essays in Criticism* 1 (1951): 139–64.

Schmidt, Albert J. 'Thomas Wilson and the Tudor Commonwealth: An Essay in Civic Humanism', *Huntington Library Quarterly* 23 (1959–60): 49–60.

Scott, P. S. (ed.). *Martyrs and Martyrdom: Early-Modern Perspectives* (forthcoming).

Shami, Jeanne. 'Donne on Discretion', *English Literary History* 47:1 (1980): 48–66.

'Kings and Desperate Men: John Donne Preaches at Court', *John Donne Journal* 6:1 (1987): 9–23.

'Donne's Protestant Casuistry: Cases of Conscience in the *Sermons*', *Studies in Philology* 80 (1983): 53–66.

'"The Stars in their Order Fought Against Sisera": John Donne and the Pulpit Crisis of 1622', *John Donne Journal* 14 (1995): 1–58.

Shapiro, I. A. 'The "Mermaid Club"', *Modern Language Review* 45 (1950): 6–17.

Sharpe, J. A. *Defamation and Sexual Slander in Early Modern England: The Church Courts at York* (York: University of York, 1980).

Sharpe, Kevin. 'The Earl of Arundel, His Circle and the Opposition to the Duke of Buckingham, 1618–1628', in *Faction and Parliament: Essays on Early Stuart History*, ed. by Sharpe, pp. 209–44.

'Parliamentary History 1603–1629: In or Out of Perspective?', in *Faction and Parliament: Essays on Early Stuart History*, ed. by Kevin Sharpe (Oxford: Clarendon Press, 1978), pp. 1–42.

Reading Revolutions: The Politics of Reading in Early Modern England (New Haven: Yale University Press, 2000).

'Re-writing the History of Parliament in Seventeenth-century England', in Sharpe, *Remapping Early Modern England* (Cambridge: Cambridge University Press, 2000), pp. 269–93.

Shuger, Debora. 'Civility and Censorship in Early Modern England', in *Censorship and Silencing: Practices of Cultural Regulation*, ed. by Robert C. Post (Los Angeles: Getty Research Institute for the History of Art and the Humanities, 1998), pp. 89–110.

'Roman Catholicism, Roman Law, and the Regulation of Language in Early Modern England (*c.* 1558–1641)', unpublished paper.

Skinner, Quentin. *Liberty before Liberalism* (Cambridge: Cambridge University Press, 1998).

'Moral Ambiguity and the Renaissance Art of Eloquence' (F. W. Bateson Memorial Lecture), *Essays in Criticism* 44:4 (October 1994): 267–92.

Reason and Rhetoric in the Philosophy of Hobbes (Cambridge: Cambridge University Press, 1996).

'Sir Thomas More's *Utopia* and the Language of Renaissance Humanism', in *The Languages of Political Theory in Early-modern Europe*, ed. by Anthony Pagden (Cambridge: Cambridge University Press, 1987), pp. 123–57.

'Thomas Hobbes: Rhetoric and the Construction of Morality', *Proceedings of the British Academy* 76 (1991): 1–61.

Visions of Politics, 3 volumes (Cambridge: Cambridge University Press, 2002).

Slavin, Arthur J. 'Profitable Studies: Humanists and Government in Early Tudor England', *Viator* 1 (1970): 307–25.

Smith, David L. *The Stuart Parliaments 1603–1689* (London: Arnold, 1999).

Sommerville, J. P. 'John Donne the Controversialist: The Poet as Political Thinker', in *John Donne's Professional Lives*, ed. by David Colclough (Cambridge: D. S. Brewer, 2003), pp. 73–96.

'Parliament, Privilege, and the Liberty of the Subject', in *Parliament and Liberty from the Reign of Elizabeth to the English Civil War*, ed. by J. H. Hexter (Stanford: Stanford University Press, 1992), pp. 56–84.

Royalists and Patriots: Politics and Ideology in England 1603–1640 (London: Longman, 1999).

Spina, Luigi. *Il cittadino alla tribuna. Diritto e libertà di parola nell'Atene democratica* (Naples: Liguori, 1986).

Stephen, J. F. *A History of the Criminal Law of England*, 3 volumes (London: Macmillan, 1883).

Stone, I. F. *The Trial of Socrates* (London: Jonathan Cape, 1988).

Stone, Lawrence. *The Causes of the English Revolution* (London: Routledge & Kegan Paul, 1972).

Thompson, Christopher. *The Debate on Freedom of Speech in the House of Commons in February 1621* (Orsett: Orchard Press, 1985).

Tite, Colin G. C. *Impeachment and Parliamentary Judicature in Early Stuart England* (London: Athlone Press, 1974).

Tomlinson, Howard. 'The Causes of the War: A Historiographical Survey', in Howard Tomlinson (ed.), *Before the English Civil War: Essays on Early Stuart Politics and Government* (London: Macmillan, 1983).

Towers, S. Mutchow. *Control of Religious Printing in Early Stuart England* (Woodbridge: The Boydell Press, 2003).

Tuck, Richard. *Natural Rights Theories: Their Origin and Development* (Cambridge: Cambridge University Press, 1979).

Philosophy and Government, 1572–1651 (Cambridge: Cambridge University Press, 1993).

Vickers, Brian. *In Defence of Rhetoric* (Oxford: Clarendon Press, 1988; corrected edition, 1997).

'Rhetoric and Poetics', in *The Cambridge History of Renaissance Philosophy*, ed. by Charles B. Schmitt, Quentin Skinner, and Eckhard Kessler (Cambridge: Cambridge University Press, 1988), pp. 715–45.

'Rhetorical and Anti-rhetorical Tropes: On Writing the History of *Elocutio*', *Comparative Criticism* 3 (1981): 105–32.

Vlastos, Gregory. *Socrates: Ironist and Moral Philosopher* (Cambridge: Cambridge University Press, 1991).

Wallace, Robert W. 'Private Lives and Public Enemies: Freedom of Thought in Classical Athens', in *Athenian Identity and Civic Ideology*, ed. by Alan L. Boegehold and Adele C. Scafuro (Baltimore: Johns Hopkins University Press, 1994), pp. 127–55.

Wawn, Andrew N. 'Chaucer, *The Plowman's Tale* and Reformation Propaganda: The Testimonies of Thomas Godfray and *I Playne Piers*', *Bulletin of the John Rylands University Library* 56 (1973–4): 174–92.

'The Genesis of *The Plowman's Tale*', *Yearbook of English Studies* 2 (1972): 21–40.

Whitlock, Baird W. *John Hoskyns, Serjeant-at-Law* (Washington, DC: University Press of America, 1982).

Wildermuth, Mark E. 'The Rhetoric of Wilson's *Arte*: Reclaiming the Classical Heritage for English Protestants', *Philosophy and Rhetoric* 22:1 (1989): 43–58.

Winter, S. C. 'Παρρησία in Acts', in *Friendship, Flattery, and Frankness of Speech. Studies on Friendship in the New Testament World*, ed. by John T. Fitzgerald (Leiden: E. J. Brill, 1996), pp. 185–202.

Womersley, David. 'Sir Henry Savile's Translation of Tacitus and the Political Interpretation of Elizabethan Texts', *Review of English Studies* 42:167 (1991): 313–42.

Wootton, David. 'Francis Bacon: Your Flexible Friend', in *The World of the Favourite*, ed. by J. H. Elliott and L. W. B. Brockliss (New Haven: Yale University Press, 1999), pp. 184–204.

'Introduction' to Thomas More, *Utopia with Erasmus' The Sileni of Alcibiades*, ed. and trans. by David Wootton (Indianapolis: Hackett, 1999), pp. 1–34.

Woudhuysen, H. R. *Sir Philip Sidney and the Circulation of Manuscripts, 1558–1640* (Oxford: Clarendon Press, 1996).

Wright, Louis B. 'Propaganda against James I's "Appeasement" of Spain', *Huntington Library Quarterly* 6:2 (February 1943): 149–72.

Young, Michael B. 'Buckingham, War, and Parliament: Revisionism Gone Too Far', *Parliamentary History* 4 (1985): 45–69.

Zaller, Robert. *The Parliament of 1621: A Study in Constitutional Conflict* (Berkeley and Los Angeles: University of California Press, 1971).

UNPUBLISHED DISSERTATIONS

Adams, S. L. 'The Protestant Cause: Religious Alliance with the West European Calvinist Communities as a Political Issue in England, 1585–1630', University of Oxford, 1973.

Curtis, Catherine Mary. 'Richard Pace on Pedagogy, Counsel and Satire', University of Cambridge, 1996.

Morrissey, Mary. 'Rhetoric, Religion and Politics in the St Paul's Cross Sermons, 1603–1625', University of Cambridge, 1998.

Sanderson, James L. 'An Edition of an Early Seventeenth-Century Manuscript Collection of Poems (Rosenbach MS 186 [1083/15])', University of Pennsylvania, 1960.

Sommerville, Johann P. 'Jacobean Political Thought and the Controversy Over the Oath of Allegiance', University of Cambridge, 1981.

Index

IDEAS IN CONTEXT

Edited by QUENTIN SKINNER (*General Editor*),
LORRAINE DASTON, DOROTHY ROSS, and JAMES TULLY